A DIFFERENT PATH

A DIFFERENT PATH
An Emotional Autobiography

Neville Symington

KARNAC

First published in 2016 by
Karnac Books Ltd
118 Finchley Road
London NW3 5HT

British Library Cataloguing in Publication Data

A C.I.P. for this book is available from the British Library

ISBN-13: 978-1-78220-427-5

Typeset by Medlar Publishing Solutions Pvt Ltd, India

Printed in Great Britain by TJ International Ltd, Padstow, Cornwall

www.karnacbooks.com

For my Mother and Father

There are many ways of being a man ...

E. M. Forster*

*Forster, E. M. (1974). *A Passage to India* (p. 263). London: Penguin. The full sentence is: "There are many ways of being a man; mine is to express what is deepest in my heart." Quotation used by permission of Hodder & Stoughton Limited.

CONTENTS

ABOUT THE AUTHOR

Neville Symington is a member of the British and Australian Psycho-analytical Societies. His books include *Narcissism: A New Theory*, *The Making of a Psychotherapist*, *A Pattern of Madness* and *Becoming a Person Through Psychoanalysis* (all published by Karnac); *The Analytic Experience*, and *The Clinical Thinking of Wilfred Bion* (written with Joan Symington). He has a private psychoanalytic practice in New South Wales, Australia.

CHAPTER ONE

Father

The source of the Douro River is in the lakes of the Sierra Negra a little east of Soria in the northern centre of Spain and this dusty brown river winds its way past Vallodolid through the port wine vineyards of Portugal and ends by cutting the town of Oporto into two distinct parts—Porto to its north and Vila Nova de Gaia to its south, before pouring past a long sandbar and tumbling into the Atlantic Ocean. Three brothers lived north of the river but worked together on its southern bank. Those three brothers, who were English, between them fathered eight sons and four daughters. Seven of those eight sons live and work in Portugal in business. An eighth son lives in Australia and works as a psychoanalyst. This book is an inquiry into why that eighth son, the author, journeyed down a different path.

These three brothers, of whom my father was one, were the sons of Andrew James Symington, a Scotsman who was brought up in Paisley and who migrated to Oporto in 1880; there he married Beatrice Atkinson whose father was English and mother Portuguese. Andrew and Beatrice produced six children, five boys and a girl. So all those children which included my father were three quarters British and one quarter Portuguese. Two of the boys, the eldest and the youngest, died and the daughter married a soldier in the army and lived her adult life in England. My grandfather started as a humble clerical worker in a firm owned by a fellow Scotsman. He later moved into a port wine firm, was made a partner and when the owner, a bachelor, died he left the business to my grandfather. The firm flourished and his children were born into a prosperous inheritance.

* * *

I believe what led me along this unusual pathway was a mixture of two conflicting elements: a capacity for leadership in the field of psychological and philosophical understanding and an angry resentment towards an undigested authority that proclaimed and commanded how life on this earth should be lived. The understanding of this problem and its attempted resolution has been my life's emotional task. Someone who has in himself an inner aptitude may need to separate himself from his origins in order to develop it. To possess in one's heart a talent that is undeveloped can lead to extreme frustration. Arthur Bryant, the historian, clearly understood this when he said:

> Man is by nature, a producer or creator as well as a consumer, and unless the instinct to create and produce implanted in him by nature is satisfied, he will to a greater or lesser degree, be an unsatisfactory and discontented being.[1]

So I galloped away down a track where I was able to develop and exercise my potential. When I listened to my first lecture in philosophy I breathed a happy sigh of relief. At last I had come home and found my true love. So I could have become a philosopher and worked away happily in a university and seen out my days as a familiar figure on a campus: that was where my intellect would have taken me but my emotions could not let this happen; they had a different destiny for me. This is where turmoil lay and has found its lair within my soul and given me torment throughout life.

I have been torn between passionate love and violent hatred; the management of these emotions has been more than I could handle for

---

[1]Bryant, Arthur (1969). *The Lion and the Unicorn* (p. 268). London: Collins.

long stretches of my life but I had a potent yearning to control these tidal waves within me. I am a wild creature required to live within civilised society and smile and be polite. I learned both of these arts from my father and to a lesser extent from my mother. That wildness, those extremes of emotion came from my mother. My father was kind and polite to an almost absurd degree. He had an old-fashioned courtesy; he was a gentleman to his fingertips. Outsiders thought he was gentle but, although he could be, there was violence in him also. You only had to see him praying in church to see that. Passionate love of God is not possible without violent hatred of the devil. These storms were hidden away within my father; in my mother they were more apparent, and, for some reason, I became the repository of their concentrated essence. The great puzzle for outsiders, even intimate outsiders, has been that this essence of my being has been hidden. I have been constrained to don the mask of civilised society and the mask has been a very good one—so good that the disguise has been thought to be the genuine article. However, there have been individuals all my life who have seen through the mask and met my concentrated essence and with these I have forged deep friendships. Life would not have been bearable without these friendships. Friendship and wisdom are the most precious fruits of civilisation.

* * *

So, you will need to know what my father was like. He was an unsophisticated man. He loved nature and, what to many would seem a contradiction, he loved shooting. His greatest pleasure was to go shooting snipe on the marshes of northern Portugal. This was rough shooting—walking the birds up in the large Aveiro marshes to the south of Oporto. He would wear fisherman's waders, ploughing through watery rushes for mile after mile and would jump even quite wide canals to reach a bird that had fallen to his gun on the wrong side of a ditch. A boat punted by a Portuguese boatman would accompany him so that he could cross the wide canals from one part of the marsh to another. He would start from home early in the morning and arrive at the marsh as daylight was breaking. He would keep going all day and only finish as light was failing. Then, back at the car, he would pour himself a cup of tea from a thermos and put into it a measure of whisky which he believed relieved tiredness and eased the long drive home. The day was interrupted by

3

two important events: a *boucha*[2] at eleven o'clock and a full-scale lunch in the middle of the day. And the lunch really was a lunch. When I was with him we would have soup, *bolinhos de bacalhau*,[3] meat croquettes, and cheese and biscuits, and we would wash it down with strong red wine of which we would drink a bottle each and finish by demolishing a bottle of port between us. My father believed that he always shot better after this lunch. The art of shooting with a shotgun is to be spontaneous, and a little oiling with alcohol assisted the enterprise. I loved those shooting expeditions with him more than anything else. I started going with him when I was about eight and I would carry with me an air gun with which I would try to pot the odd lark or sparrow. When I was fifteen my father gave me a twenty-eight bore shotgun and I can still remember shooting my first snipe with it. I was walking up beside a ditch, my father on one side and Joaquim Manuel Calem on the other, and a snipe got up between me and our Portuguese friend. I raised the gun to my left shoulder, fired and the bird dived into the ground. Joaquim Manuel was delighted and so was my father. It was my initiation into adulthood. Now, surely I was a man.

On the long drive home every shot was discussed but especially the ones we had missed. When he shot a bird my father hardly mentioned it but it was the ones that he missed that were discussed from every angle. My father was a pessimist, even something of a defeatist. When the port trade was doing badly in the early 1950s he said the situation was hopeless. People were no longer interested in drinking port. There was nothing to be done about it. He was not motivated by the sense of challenge that this might present, how one might market port differently or adapt it to people's new eating habits. Port went with servants and large dinners and that era was over now. When criticised for this defeatist attitude he retreated into himself like a wounded animal. He was criticised particularly by my mother. I know now that he was very depressed and my guess is that he had been so all his life. His mother died when he was sixteen and, I believe, this was a tragedy for him from which he never recovered. My mother was also depressed. I don't know whether this depression of hers went back to her childhood. I have also been depressed all my life. It has always been an effort to summon the energy to fulfil the aspirations of my imagination. I also find it much

---

[2]Portuguese word for a snack.
[3]Round fishcakes made from dried cod.

4

easier to spend time in verbal conversation or in writing than doing practical tasks. Later in life, as a psychologist, when I did the IQ Test I learned that this was the classic sign of depression.

Concentrating on failure rather than success I later realised was not peculiar to my father. In spiritual devotion it was associated with "peccato-centrism". In psychiatric lingo the same quality is known as "negativism" which is one of the defining features of mental illness. When I first read this I thought it was so common that I could not reconcile it with the idea that someone imbued with it could be mentally ill. I later came to think that mental disease is extremely common and that people who are officially ill mentally are only caricatures of the normal run of ill health. Would it be fair to say that Dad was mentally ill? He was. I think he was quite severely ill. One sign of it was in his unhappy marriage.

In later life I read the *Journal of a Soul* which was the private record of the examination of conscience of that most benign of popes, Pope John XXIII. The early period of his life as a seminarian and then a young priest is full of attention to his sins, his faults, his failings, but in maturity he changed and wrote this:

> Above all, I am grateful to the Lord for the temperament he has given me, which preserves me from anxieties and tiresome perplexities. I feel I am under obedience in all things and I have noticed that this disposition, in great things and in small, gives me, unworthy though I am, a strength of daring simplicity, so wholly evangelical in its nature that it demands and obtains universal respect and edifies many.[4]

Surely this is a sign that he had soared out of illness into the fullness of health.

My father went to church not only on Sundays but every day and he suffered from religious scruples to an agonizing degree. He could not take criticism, had very fixed attitudes, and his religion was coloured by obsessional ideas. He believed in many superstitious devotions. For instance he believed that if he went to Mass on the first Friday of every month for nine consecutive months he would have a happy death. It was not a robust piety that sustained him through painful times. When

---

[4]Pope John XXIII (1964). *Journal of a Soul* (p. 299). London: Geoffey Chapman.

pain and torture came his way he backed away to his inner hiding place. He was not a happy man; he and my mother were not happy together. He became increasingly deaf as he grew older, developed Alzheimer's, and finally died in a home in England. He did not have a happy death.

He was the most unworldly man I have ever known. The world of sexual diversity, the Wolfenden Report, the welfare state, prison reform, drug abuse, birth control, or social science were unknown to him. Nature was his ruling passion. He loved the countryside and had a particular love of *bichos*.[5] He had one of the best butterfly collections in Portugal. He knew all the butterflies and moths that exist in Portugal. I would go with him in search of specimens that were missing in his collection. Once a butterfly or moth was caught in the net it was put into a killing-bottle. Back at home it would be "set" on a setting-board and I learned how to set butterflies and moths at the age of six. I loved going on butterfly expeditions with him—such as for white and yellow orange tips in springtime along the Tabuaço valley in the Douro. Loving nature is compatible with killing and collecting. A few specimens of each butterfly or moth were all we wanted. We reached a point when it was rare to choose to catch a butterfly or moth because we had examples of all of them in our collection.

I loved him dearly and some of my happiest memories are of being with him on the marshes of northern Portugal shooting snipe in the winter or catching butterflies in the spring and summertime and then setting them and carefully putting them into cabinets and tending them with care and devotion. His care and patience and his joy in teaching me the art of collecting butterflies gave me a fond love of him which still lives inside me. He was so kind, so courteous, so loving. It was a tragedy that inwardly he was so tortured and unhappy.

I remember once I was walking with him beside the Boavista fields near our home and he said to me that I would find happiness if I tried to put others first and not myself. It was obvious that this is what he always tried to do. He was loved dearly by his large community of friends in Oporto. He was loved by both the English and the Portuguese. We had many Portuguese cousins and they all loved *"Roninho"* and always spoke of him with great affection. Because his mother was half Portuguese we were, through her, all Catholics and we had numerous

---

[5]*Bicho* is the Portuguese for "creature" and can refer to a mammal or an insect.

Portuguese cousins. We were not intimate with them but at funerals and weddings we would enjoy a warm communion with them.

He told me several times a story which has recently been repeated by Paulo Coelho in the preface to *The Alchemist*:[6]

> The Virgin Mary, with the Infant Jesus in her arms, decided to come down to Earth and visit a monastery. Filled with pride the priests queued up and each one came before the Virgin to offer her his homage. One recited beautiful poems, another showed her his illuminated script for a Bible, and yet another one recited the names of all the saints. And so it went on with one monk after another giving his homage to the Virgin Mary and the Infant Jesus.
>
> At the very end of the queue was a priest, the most humble member of the community, who had never learned the wise sayings of the time. His parents were simple people who worked in an old circus and all that they had taught him was to throw balls in the air and juggle with them.
>
> When it was his turn to offer homage, the other priests wanted to end the devotions, because the old juggler did not have anything important to say and might sully the image of the monastery. Nevertheless, at the bottom of his heart, he felt a powerful urge to give something of himself to Jesus and the Virgin Mary.
>
> Ashamed and feeling the disapproving eyes of his brethren he took some oranges from his pocket and began to throw them up in the air and juggled with them, which was the only thing he knew how to do.
>
> It was only at that moment that the Infant Jesus smiled and began to beat the palms of his hands on the shoulders of Our Lady. And it was to this priest that the Virgin stretched out her hands and let him hold the Child for a little while.[7]

I remember how thrilled my father was when he saw this scene depicted in a stone sculpture on the outside of either Reims or Rouen Cathedral.[8] This story obviously meant a great deal to him and I think he must have thought of himself in this way, deep down inside himself.

---

[6]Coelho, Paulo (1988). *O Alquimista*. Cascais, Portugal: Editora Pergaminho.
[7]My own translation.
[8]I think it was one of these two rather than Chartres.

He was a simple man without any pretension. He had no cultured treasures to offer God. He just had his own unsophisticated abilities and it was these that he offered to God. It is very sad that my mother did not appreciate his unpretentious gift, and I regret greatly that I did not recognise it more adequately myself but rather took sides with my mother against him, not all the time but some of the time. I think later when I surged into the Church I took his side against her and then later still swung back to her side against him, and so I swung from one side to the other rather than appreciate the gift I had received from each one.

How does someone like my father deal with his simple innocence? One path, a rare one, is a deep acceptance out of which a new originality bursts forth, but this is neither the road that my father took nor that of the majority. He took the more common pathway: he reached out in obedient surrender to a belief system to camouflage this simplicity. That he liked the story so much indicates a knowledge of his own unpretentious simplicity, but I think then a psychological process kicked in whereby he adopted a system of thinking and belief to hide the simplicity of which he was ashamed. In his case he inserted himself into a system of thinking which, in one way, mirrored his inner simplicity, but in another it left him prey to the thinking of others and, as Steve Jobs said in his amazing talk at Stanford University in 2005, the attachment to the thinking of others results in a despotic dogmatism. What I am trying to get at here is that instead of the simplicity generating thoughts that are deep and true there gets installed a system that is in no way simple; a system that is full of superstitious practices that are far from the innocence of the simple monk of the tale retold by Paulo Coelho. An example of someone who had that strange innocent simplicity within the psychoanalytic world was Frances Tustin; with great courage, she built an understanding from it that has inspired psychotherapists and psychoanalysts ever since. Simplicity, not complexity, has been the great innovator in human affairs.

* * *

I once had an eerie experience when accompanying my father shooting. He would often go for a short shoot for a couple of hours near to home. One Sunday morning I went with him to Boa Nova, a district by the coast just north of Oporto, where there were sometimes golden plover; there was also a little marsh which, for some reason, my father called the *Pai e Mãe*.[9] I was walking behind him and up got a teal which he fired at and shot. I knew that this was a real event but it was dream-like to me. The whole incident had a very strong trance-like quality. I went out with him hundreds of times shooting snipe round about our home in Oporto. In fact there was a field just outside our back gate which sometimes had a snipe or two and my father would often slip out and see if he could get one or two in the early morning before going to work. Few weekends went by in the winter when my father would not go shooting and I went with him like a faithful dog following at his heels. Yet this occasion stands out in my mind incredibly strongly. It was its dreamy unearthly ethos that lights up my inner sky.

How to explain it? I think some message is contained in it—a message from the unexplored part of the mind. I have quite a long explanation for it which I will try to express. The fact that this little marsh was called *Pai e Mãe* is significant. This dream-like experience might have happened on one of the other hundred times I went out with my father but it occurred *this* time in the marsh called Dad and Mum.

I believe the first thing is that this single memory which is so internally vivid represents the whole of my child life at home in Oporto. This is often the case with a very vivid memory of a particular event which, viewed just as a fact, is insignificant. I was in a dream the whole time and this one memory represents the internal state of my mind during the whole of my childhood. In later life as a psychoanalyst patients have often told me in the initial consultation of some imagistic experience which may have only lasted for a few moments but it is remembered because it crystallises visually something which is an emotional undercurrent that is present all the time. Freud spoke of a *screen memory* that covers, like a palimpsest, an earlier event.[10] What I am talking of here is an event drawn in bright colours that represents an emotional current present throughout a period of someone's life.

I was living in a dream but the question is how was this dream constructed? What was operating inside me that turned the world I inhabited into a dream? There had to be a process inside me that turned what

---

9Portuguese for Dad and Mum.
10Freud, S. (1899a). Screen memories. The Standard Edition of the Complete Psychological Works of Sigmund Freud, Volume III. London: The Hogarth Press and The Institute of Psycho-Analysis.

was real into a dream. I come later to the suicidal thoughts that were operating in me. I think this early childhood dream was part of that suicidal pattern. In other words there was something in me that transformed the incoming sensations into something dream-like. In order to approach this I can best start by telling you of a patient. While I was speaking to him there was a voice speaking to him at the same time in this manner: he thinks you are absolutely useless; he is only saying this to be polite and so on. In other words an instantaneous translation was going on all the time. Therefore my words were not being heard as I was speaking them; they were being converted into a dark atmosphere within. It was not just the words that were being converted graphically into another set of words but rather a whole inner environment was being created. There was an inner darkness. I think something like this was going on inside me. But to compensate for this inner disarray I constructed a paradise that was unhitched to the real world in which I lived. Like all such constructions there was much truth in it. My childhood was something of a paradise. I had two parents who loved me, who gave to me an enormous amount of their time and attention, a brother and a sister that I got on well with, numerous uncles, aunts, and cousins who were warm and loving towards me. and the faithful Portuguese maids who lavished their affection upon me and attended to all my needs. And yet in every paradise there are dark spaces which are superficially hidden. In this atmosphere of love and affection I believed that my father and my mother were happy both in themselves and also between themselves. When I was shocked out of this then a Paradise Lost stormed the secure castle.

The question is, "What did this dream of mine construct?" How was the world around me made into something which was different from what it was? How was it different? I was so *in* the experience that I had no view of either the home situation or the cultural environment. One day I said to myself that at least I had God; that was one stable thing I could hold onto. I did not realise this at the time but it implied that things were in an abysmal chaos within. *"You are wicked, you will go to hell for all eternity."* An incident occurred that I shall come to shortly: that I believed I had committed a mortal sin followed by sacrilege and that I would, if I died, go to hell for all eternity. Just as the dreaminess of that occasion when my father shot the teal represented what was occurring the whole time, so also that day of committing a mortal sin for which I was damned as a wicked sinner was not just the situation

10

in that one instance but rather it was the occasion that manifested what was the inner state of affairs the whole time.

The belief that I was damned and deserved to be punished distorted my picture of the world I was in. It cut out the good fortune that was mine. I thought of my family as poor. There were of course some reasons for thinking this. The port trade was doing badly in the post-war years. We only had one car. My father took it off to work every day and my mother had to use the tram to get into town or anywhere else. From time to time it was mentioned that it would be a great advantage for my mother to have a car, but we could not afford it. My father was always complaining about the monthly rental which he had to pay to the landlord and the expense of things. When eating cereal one day at breakfast he told me that his brother John would not buy cereals for his family because he could not afford it. The family port firm owned three *quintas*[11] in the Douro but things were squeezed so they had to sell two of them: *Zimbro* and *Senhora da Ribeira*. My father's pessimism gave a tone to his outlook. My mother was captive to the same delusion. She spoke about how badly off we were. She told me one day that my father might have to leave the family firm and take a job as manager of one of the port firms whose owners lived in England but required a manager in Oporto. The two of them, *Pai e Mãe*, were in this pessimistic thrall together. There was, however, another side to the story to which I was entirely blind. I was totally "sucked into" this pessimistic gloom. It nourished my inner state of damned impoverishment. I had no Pope John to relieve me from it.

The other side to the story was this: we lived in a large house and had three maids. They lived at the top of the house in their own bedrooms. We had Maria, the cook, Carmen the parlourmaid, and Caterina who did all the washing. I never had to do any domestic work. My shoes were cleaned, clothes washed and ironed, and every meal was cooked and prepared and dishes washed up. My father had a lot of leisure time. He could take time off from the office when he wanted. We had our family firm's property in the Douro, the *Quinta do Bomfim*, to which we went several times a year, and there we lived with the same service and comfort as we did in Oporto. If we went by train to the Douro four men from the office would go to the train two hours before it was due to leave and sit in the seats we were to occupy. When we arrived

---

[11]*Quinta* is the Portuguese for a property.

11

they got up and left and we took the places they had vacated. There was no seat booking system at the time so men from Dad's office did this service for us. We often went on picnics and these were always prepared in style. There would be soup in a special thermos, *bolinhos de bacalhau*,[12] croquettes made of veal or beef, and then fruit and cheese and thermoses of tea and coffee and of course there was always dry port to drink beforehand, plenty of red wine, and a bottle of tawny port to finish with. At all our meals at home the faithful Carmen stood and served us. If one of us had finished a glass of wine or water or had eaten the vegetables on our plate she immediately came and offered us more. Uncle Maurice and Aunty Eileen also lived in similar style and so did Uncle John and his family. Uncle Maurice had a chauffeur, Uncle John had a butler, and Reg and Auriel also had a chauffeur. The car was always washed and cleaned at the office and, if it needed a service, one of the men from the office would take it to the garage and bring it back so it was ready for my father to drive home. Although I knew all this and it was part of life yet it was camouflaged by a big fog fashioned within by this inner gloom. Any outsider would have seen that we lived a prosperous, leisured life but this was something hidden from my eyes. We were poor. I was conditioned by this wretched inner state which structured my belief which blinded me to all good fortune. This was probably so of my sister, Jill, but not so of my brother, James. He always had the outsider's perspective and understood that there was a capital wealth behind things that made this lifestyle possible. The dream I constructed shut out both the good fortune and the bad. It was an imaginary world built up from the affection with which I was showered from all directions.

I have no doubt that my father, like me, also had this inner poverty. He was intensely scrupulous, very uncertain of himself, and in no way would you call him robust. There was an emotional frailty held together by a rigid determination. That he was inwardly persecuted in the way I am describing I am sure. It was there in my mother but not so obvious. She was often very dejected and I think she was afflicted by an inner desolation. I mention later how when I used to come home for lunch from the Oporto British School she used to be slumped in gloom over the luncheon table. It must have been significant that I was with my parents for five years from the age of six, when

---

[12]*Bolinhos de bacalhau* are little fried fish balls made of sun-cured cod.

we arrived back in Portugal from Canada, until eleven when I went to prep school in England. I imbibed this atmosphere that existed between them. I was exposed to it the whole time. Jill and James were boarding at St Julian's School at Carcavelos near Lisbon and they only came home in the holidays whereas I was with them all the time. I became "imprinted" with their inner melancholic state. I do not think that this is a total explanation because I must already have been susceptible to such imprinting. I believe this susceptibility arose through being wrenched apart from my mother at the time of my birth. I shall dwell on this in more detail later.

This nightmare quality that shut out the observer's view stayed with me into adult life and was a complementary part of that state where infernal pride and a savage God reigned supreme in the inner sanctum. When I was in the East End of London as a priest I was totally in it and unaware of its desolate quality. I remember going to Knightsbridge one day and seeing some of the elegant houses and realising how poverty-stricken and poor were the surroundings in which I was living. I had really anaesthetised myself to it. What I had really done was shut off an important part of myself. The inner demons of depletion had sat upon it and smothered it. The inner state governs our perception. I think in the East End experience, there was a twofold process. I shut out the wretchedness of the natural environment and endowed it with the "prosperous" or Knightsbridge part of me so I romanticised it. The other side of it was a gloomy perspective on life. When I was in the seminary at St Edmund's I adopted a positive perspective on redemption and religious life intellectually, but emotionally I remained a sullen pessimist. That we were all marked by the curse of original sin remained unchanged in the depths of my soul.

* * *

As an old man my father went with my mother to Argentina on a passenger liner. He found an interesting moth in his cabin so he took a female passenger to his cabin to show it to her. When he emerged from his cabin with her, another passenger asked him to introduce him to his wife. My father said that he would happily introduce her but that she was not his wife. The man said, "Oh, but I saw her coming out of your cabin with you." My father replied, "I took her to my cabin to show her

13

a moth," but my father said the man looked *disconfiado*.[13] I very much doubt whether my father ever had an affair. I argued vigorously many years later with my psychoanalyst, who could not believe that when he was separated from my mother for two and a half years during the war, he would not have visited prostitutes in the red light district of Oporto. I think it extremely unlikely that he would have done this.

He had a sharp eye for these *bichos*—butterflies, moths, lizards, newts, and birds of all kinds. From a young age he taught me how to recognise most birds from their flight. In the summer he also went fishing for trout or sea trout but it never held the same passion for him as shooting. I loved being with him in the countryside, whether it was the salt marshes of Aveiro, the *milho*[14] fields of the Minho, or in the rugged mountainside of the Douro. In the country he was tranquil and I could feel his loving nature. He was devoted to all his three children and I always knew that if I told him something in confidence he would never reveal it to a living soul. In this he was quite different from my mother who could not resist the temptation to spread it abroad.

He was born in Oporto, one of three brothers. There had been, as I have mentioned, two further brothers but they had died many years before my birth. His sister lived with her army husband at Littlestone-on-Sea in Kent. So, apart from my brother and sister, I lived in close harmony with nine first cousins. Christmas night was always spent with the uncles, their wives, and the cousins. I was soldered into a large loving family. There was a rhythmic ritual that governed the passage of the seasons. In the summer we went to the beach each day and all the cousins and other friends would be there. We went on picnics together. Once every year in the summer when the moon was full, a huge barge would be hired and punted out with about seventy people onto the Aveiro marshes to watch the sun set and the moon rise. On the open water the moon would surface above the horizon just as the sun disappeared from sight at the opposite horizon. Then there would be a large picnic, swimming, and fun for all.

My father's mother was half English and half Portuguese so we had many Portuguese cousins and, unlike most of the English community, we were Roman Catholics. To go inside a Protestant church except for a wedding was a sin, but apart from this we participated fully in all the

---

[13]*Disconfiado* is the Portuguese for "distrustful" or "suspicious".
[14]*Milho* is the Portuguese for "maize".

ritual life of the English community. Every Saturday afternoon in the summer there was a match at the cricket field. My father played regularly every week. He was not a good player and did not pretend to be but he was a perfect sportsman. He enjoyed the game and winning or losing did not matter a great deal to him. Eleven was the highest score I remember him making and I don't ever remember seeing him bowl but he taught me to bat at a young age. He would bowl to me on the lawn in the garden and he showed me how to defend my wicket. For two years there were eleven Symingtons so we had a match, "Symingtons versus the World", which took place two years running. Both times we won but each by a narrow margin. I learned at one of these matches that there was hostility towards the Symington tribe. Owen Underhill[15] was scoring and my cousin, Amyas, who was standing behind him, noticed that he did not record all the Symington runs. Amyas pointed this out to Owen's embarrassment.

There were also tennis courts and the club's full title was the Oporto Cricket and Lawn Tennis Club. It was not lawn tennis as such because they were hard courts and each year there was an annual match between the Lisbon Club and the Oporto Club. The cricket teams and tennis teams played at the same weekend. I am not sure what happened if someone played both cricket and tennis. I suppose he had to choose which game he would play. Some players took themselves very seriously and these I never liked. I remember one woman who used to get very bad-tempered if she lost at a game of tennis. From a young age I was sensitive to character traits of this sort. Both my mother and father were good sports in this regard and never sulked if they lost a game, and they taught me to behave in a similar manner and, unless I am deceiving myself, I think I am a good loser. So cricket and tennis took place every Saturday afternoon at the Campo Alegre. The wives of the players had a rota so that each Saturday one of them was responsible for preparing the tea. This was the kind of tea which was very appealing to children: ham and tomato sandwiches and then biscuits of which a good proportion were chocolate biscuits. We children were always under strict instructions to eat first some sandwiches and only then could we turn our attention to the biscuits.

On Sundays my parents frequently went to play golf at the Oporto British Golf Club at Espinho, south of Oporto. We would arrive in time

---

[15]This is a pseudonym.

to have a picnic lunch at the club and then my parents would walk out onto the verandah and pick a caddy. An assembly of caddies in tattered old clothes would eagerly hold up a number for identification and my parents would view them and then call out a number and the chosen man eagerly rushed forward. These caddies would often give advice and hints and would point out how my father or mother was playing wrongly.

Then there was the Factory House which was the very distinguished club house for those people who were partners in the English port wine firms. The Factory House was a solid eighteenth-century building made of grey granite. Here there was a lunch every Wednesday. When I was old enough my father would occasionally take me with him to lunch at this all-male institution. It was here that there was every year a New Year's Eve Ball and on certain occasions there would be dinners. At these dinners we all sat formally around a long forty-foot table. The entrée and first course were eaten at this table and then the sweet and vintage port were consumed at a parallel table which was laid with the same placing in an adjoining room. This was so the aroma of the vintage port would not be sullied by the smell of the soup and meat courses.

I now look back on these rituals with a faint amusement as they belong to a past era but at the time they were the world in which I lived just as the Portuguese maids waiting at table at breakfast, lunch, and dinner were also part of life. Everyone we knew had maids. I had never made a bed until I went to prep school in England and never washed up crockery after a meal until I shared a flat in London at the age of eighteen. I had never really cooked a decent meal until I taught myself after leaving the priesthood many years later.

The maids were of enormous importance to me emotionally. Maria do Carmo, our cook, had been with my father as his maid some nine years before he married and continued with us until I was in my teens when she went to be a maid in England. Then there was a second maid, also called Maria do Carmo but in order to differentiate them we called the cook Maria and the second maid Carmen. Carmen came to us when I was six and remained in service with my parents until she went into a home at the age of eighty-two. As a young boy I would sit for long hours in the kitchen talking with them. I have never known exactly the effect of this close emotional contact but, I suspect, one quality I have finds its origin there. In my life I have mixed widely with people of every social class, age, sex, race, and nationality. I have an inherent interest in people and there is a particular quality I look for in people but it is independent of their social class, sex, nationality, or professional identity. My parents, at least my father, would be categorised as upper middle class; the maids were working class and I mixed quite naturally with each.

Another member of this wider family was José the gardener. He was deeply suntanned; he rode to us on his bicycle two or three times a week and he tended our large garden with care and attention. There was a large vegetable garden separated from a flower garden by big, high box hedges. I would go out into the garden when José was there and spend long hours talking with him. He had a deep, hoarse voice which after speaking for a while he would drop down to a whisper. He would then tell me about the secret police and how unfairly the government treated the poor. My parents and the world I inhabited all thought extremely highly of Dr Salazar who was prime minister and dictator of Portugal and had been so since about 1928. He was widely revered and respected though he was not visible enough to be popular, but here was José whispering to me that things were not good below the surface. What he told me did not alter my high regard for Salazar but it must have sowed a seed of doubt. Later when I was at school in England I wrote a passionate letter to *The Observer* after it had published a disparaging article about Salazar. I had a considered letter in reply, advising that they did not want to discuss it further because they thought it would not change my opinion. They were right. There was something solid and reliable about José and like Maria he had been my father's employee from his bachelor days onwards. Servants, employees, beggars, and the many poor who lived near us all loved my father. His warm tenderness touched their hearts. When he heard that the cobbler down the road was having a bad time he would give him some money, and so with many others. He told me once that he did not say that the money was a gift but a loan, but then he winked at me and said, "But some loans one knows one will never get back," but he thought the recipient might feel patronized if it was offered as a gift. Later he would, in a casual way, say there was no need to pay back the loan as things were better for him financially.

I loved Carmen and when I last saw her in the *lar*, the old people's home in Oporto, she thanked me for coming to see her; I told her that she was my second mother—*segunda mãe*—and she kissed me with gratitude. Then she told me that she was old and said, *"Gosto de viver; tenho pena de morrer."*[16]

I was much moved when she said this and was tearful. There she was in a home—a *lar*—obviously caring for some of the others and loved by them, and she liked living. It was such a simple statement but profound. How many of us like living and are grateful for it? I also thought it was a generous statement to me. I went away knowing that she was happy. She had been with our family for fifty years and some of her joy in living must have been connected to her love for all of us. We must have contributed to her happiness and she wanted me to know it. It was the last time I saw her because five months later she died and I was so glad that I had been in Oporto and had that opportunity to speak with her before she died. That was in 1992.

I like being looked after by maids. To be relieved of the daily tasks of cleaning, cooking, washing clothes, and shopping is for me the ideal situation. I can then attend to what matters most to me: reading, writing, and thinking. However, I am not completely at ease with another human being doing these servile tasks for me. There is some inner disquiet about it. Why should this being who shares the emotional elements of my nature be serving me? Why should this manservant be polishing my shoes? Why should this woman be serving me at table with delicately prepared food while she eats inferior food in the kitchen? Trollope says:

> We, who have been born to the superior condition,—for in this matter I consider myself to be standing on a platform with Dukes and Princes and all others to whom plenty and education and liberty have been given,—cannot, I think, look upon the inane, unintellectual, and toil-bound life of those who cannot even feed themselves sufficiently by their sweat, without some feeling of injustice, some sting of pain.[17]

I have only ever found close friendship with those who are in emotional contact with life, with living. Socrates said that the unexamined life is not worth living by man. I would perhaps exchange the word "unnoticed" for "unexamined". The question, "What is life?" or "What

---

[16] I love living; I regret having to die.
[17] Trollope, Anthony (1996). *An Autobiography*. London: Penguin.

18

is life for?" makes the business of living a natural enquiry; that life *is* an enquiry. With others I am reasonably affable but my inner soul is closed off from them. The search for meaning has been at the centre of my life. "*Why? Why? Why?*" has lain at the centre of things. This was why I gave a sigh of relief at my first philosophy lecture. Philosophy searches for answers to the child who asks "Why, why, why?" Religion enshrines the mystery of it. In later years I became disenchanted with those philosophers who are preoccupied with "surface" questions and refuse to probe more deeply. Linguistic philosophy has always seemed to me to be superficial. The postmodern philosophy of Derrida seems to me to be an insult to those predecessors of people who have toiled to try to understand the deep meaning of life and the universe. Philosophy needs religion because the latter is concerned with how to live life, as Tolstoy said.

I am the only one of my family where this interest and orientation has been the governing principle of life. I have a feeling that contact with the Portuguese maids was partly responsible for it. I had a natural love for the maids. The fact that they were of a different social class did not cut me off from them. They were my friends. There is something deeper than the outer clothing. When I was a priest I frequently found a deeper resonance with a man who was an atheist than a fellow priest or Catholic. As a psychoanalyst I have similarly found deeper harmony with someone who is a behavioural psychologist than a fellow psychoanalyst. It is a quality of soul which I would call religious or philosophical, but I know that is not defined by any outer categorisation but by the person's inner orientation to life. It is a humble deference to something bigger, to an Absolute, to mystery. It is a spirit of enquiry. For convenience I will call it personal faith. To put it another way: I am drawn to those for whom a deep generosity of heart is the guiding principle of their lives. To this effect I have often quoted a passage about Herbert Read recorded in Graham Greene's autobiographical book called *Ways of Escape*:

> Certainly my meeting with Herbert Read was an important event in my life. He was the most gentle man I have ever known, but it was a gentleness which had been tested in the worst experiences of his generation. The young officer, who gained the Military Cross and a DSO in action on the Western Front, had carried with him to all that mud and death Robert Bridges's anthology *The Spirit of Man*, Plato's *Republic* and *Don Quixote*. Nothing had changed in

19

him. It was the same man twenty years later who could come into a room full of people and you wouldn't notice his coming—you noticed only that the whole atmosphere of a discussion had quietly altered, that even the relations of one guest with another had changed. No one any longer would be talking for effect, and when you looked round for an explanation there he was—complete honesty born of complete experience had entered the room and unobtrusively taken a chair.[18]

This inner generosity of heart which I think is being conveyed here in this passage about Herbert Read is something which Dostoyevsky knew and understood and which he epitomised in *The Idiot*.[19] Prince Myshkin never had any ulterior motives. When he went to visit General and Mrs. Yepanchin it was not to beg money from them but rather to meet them and come to know them as people. This is not quite the same as generosity of heart but it is close to it. Material ends are always secondary to a deep love for and interest in every person.

When this is not present there is a sign that tells me of its absence: I mean the missionary spirit. In essence the missionary spirit fails to respect this orientation of soul that I am talking of. The missionary is concerned with the outer. It is governed not by humble deference but by inner arrogance. Why is it so important to convert someone to Catholicism, psychoanalysis, transcendental meditation, Buddhism, or Communism? These outer clothes never guarantee the inner quality of soul that has been of central importance for me. I have, however, found it extremely difficult to convey this to those who are committed to the clothing.

* * *

The Symington family were all Catholics and devotion to the Catholic faith was as natural to us as eating and breathing. We always went to Mass on Sundays. Our family would usually go to the little baroque church in the *Frequesia de Nevogilde*—suburb of Oporto near the sea and close to the mouth of the Douro River. Sometimes we went to the

---

[18]Greene, G. (1980). *Ways of Escape* (p. 39). London: Bodley Head.
[19]Dostoyevsky, Fyodor (1977). *The Idiot*. London: Penguin.

Dominicanos,[20] and there we would often meet many of our cousins who went there too.

When I was aged eight I made my First Communion. For some months beforehand I used to go weekly to the Dorothean convent in Oporto to receive instruction from Mother Traynor. It was a convent of Portuguese nuns but she was Anglo-Irish. She went through the Ten Commandments and one day I asked her, "But what is adultery?" She told me that it was a sin that adults committed. I was very curious to know what this sin might be. My parents gave me no instruction in matters sexual. The words "penis" or "vagina" were never mentioned in our family. A young woman on the beach with us did not go swimming one day and I asked her why. My mother later tried to explain that women have periods and that they could not go swimming when they had one but she was so embarrassed that she did not manage to explain the matter with any clarity. I was a most innocent boy, like my father. The idea that there could be any sexual misdemeanour within the family ranks was quite unthinkable to me. We were all good Christians, devout Catholics. When I was confronted head-on with such a misdemeanour in the family in late adolescence it was a terrific shock.

We Catholics had the truth. Protestants were simply wrong and were to be pitied. We knew we were right. We must have been the most self-righteous family and some of the English of Oporto, I suspect, hated us for it. Owen Underhill, whom I have mentioned, was Protestant and I am sure that some of his hostility to us was because of our dogmatic conviction that we, and we alone, possessed the Truth. I was extremely self-righteous. As a Catholic I was in possession of the truth. I shared the superstitious piety of my father. One of the inner struggles of my life has been to take possession of personal faith and slough off the self-righteousness and superstition which are handmaidens of one another. Devotion to the Virgin Mary was extremely important to my father. In nearly all churches in Portugal there were statues to Our Lady of Fátima. In the year 1917 the Virgin Mary was believed to have appeared to three peasant children at the Cova da Iria near the village of Fátima in central Portugal. The thirteenth of May was the big pilgrimage date, being the day when the Virgin Mary was believed to have first appeared to the three children. My father often went to Fátima on this day and

---

[20] A church serviced by Dominican friars.

I went too when I reached my late teens. Miraculous cures occurred at Fátima, as at Lourdes. The Virgin had asked the three children to pray because unless people prayed terrible scourges would afflict mankind.

Two of these children, Francisco and Jacinta, were brother and sister and Lucia was their first cousin. The first two died in childhood but Lucia lived on and became a Dorothean nun and when I made my First Communion at the convent where I had been receiving instruction from Mother Traynor there was great excitement—while I had been receiving my First Communion, Lucia was at the back of the Church praying for me. She would have been saddened had she heard of my subsequent religious defection.

Tio Marto and Tia Olympia, the parents of Francisco and Jacinta, were still alive when I used to visit Fátima as a child. They lived, as they always had, in the little village of Aljustrel, near the Cova da Iria. I remember going and visiting them and hearing their account of what the children said when they came back from the first apparition. They described the children's excitement when they returned home and told their parents of the beautiful lady they had seen who appeared to them above an olive tree. I can remember Tio Marto with his floppy woollen hat with a bauble on the end of it. I liked the story of the American sceptic who said to Tio Marto, "This is all a superstitious folly," to which he replied instantly, "You go back to your home town and start a folly as big as this one."

When I was receiving instruction from Mother Traynor she explained that when the priest put the Host on my tongue I was to flip it back and swallow it and not allow it to touch my teeth. To let it touch my teeth would be making Jesus fall when he was carrying his Cross to Calvary. If the host touched my teeth it would be a mortal sin. I remember being in a paroxysm of terror at that First Communion lest this criminal event should occur. I believed implicitly all these superstitious injunctions. I was a frightened, paralysed child. I am sure that this was not obvious to those around me and it has made me realise how little members of the family know about the inner life of the individuals within its bosom. Even now it upsets me to understand what a frightened child I was and how I trembled before such a ferocious God. Little did Mother Traynor realise the terror she stirred within my soul. She was a kind and humane woman and I can still remember walking around the convent garden with her as she gave me my instructions. She was a gentle soul but imbued with absurd superstitions which she handed on, little appreciating what arsenic she was pouring into my innocent heart.

A very strict rule at that time for Catholics was that if you were going to Holy Communion in the morning you had to fast from midnight. You could not even have a drink of water. My First Communion went well and I remained in a state of grace and so also the second time I went to Holy Communion. Then my third communion was to be on Easter Sunday when the whole family was due to go together to receive the sacrament at the communion rail. As it was Easter Sunday some family member or friend had given me some chocolates the day before. When I woke I ate two of the chocolates. I had forgotten about the fast. My father came in smiling happily that we were all due to go to Holy Communion. Then I remembered the sinful chocolates but as I did not want to disappoint my father I did not tell him what I had done. So, lined up with my mother, father, brother, and sister at the communion rail, I received the sacred Host. I had committed a mortal sin. This deadly sin had cut me off from God and should I die now I would go straight to hell. But of course Catholics can wash away their sins by going to confession, what George Meredith called *the scarlet bath*.[21] So when I went to confession all would be well: I went a few days later but I was so terrified by what I had done that I did not dare tell the priest of my crime. If a Catholic goes to confession and does not tell of a mortal sin he has committed then that is a further mortal sin. Now I was deep in hell. It was a torture chamber within. For four years I went to confessions and communion, never daring to tell of my sacrilege. So mortal sin was piled upon mortal sin. I knew my soul was as black as pitch. I was terrified of death because I knew that if I died I would go to hell for all eternity, and the pictures of hell that had been painted for me in religious classes were appalling, but the worst aspect of it was that it was eternal—it would never come to an end. The constant thought of this was a torture.

Four years later, subsequent to numerous confessions and communions, I finally summoned the courage to tell a priest in confession of my awful sin. It was at the Junior House at Ampleforth College and Fr Kenneth was hearing confessions. He was a kind man and I think his gentle nature must have helped me. Anyway, I told him what had happened four years before and how I had been too frightened to tell ever

---

[21]Meredith, George (1914). *The Ordeal of Richard Feverel*. London: Constable.

since. He patted me on the shoulder, told me not to worry, gave me a small penance and then spoke the words of absolution over me. It was in the evening. I crept up to bed in the dormitory and the torture was at last over. I was once again in a state of grace and in favour with God above. I was so grateful to Fr Kenneth yet I don't know if he ever knew what a burden he had lifted off my soul. Years later I wrote this poem:

Father Kenneth

He was a quiet gentle man.
Looking kindly at the fair-haired boy.
Kneeling fearfully to shrive himself.
His knees cushioned beside the priest.

He had sinned a mortal sin.
A sacred sword cutting his bond to God.
His soul was devoured by devils
In the very depths of hell.

"I've sinned a very grievous sin,"
He whispered to the priest.
"Tell me what it is, dear boy,
Our loving Jesus will forgive."

The boy he sobbed and wet his cheek.
His throat was choking, he could not speak.
Fr Kenneth stretched out his hand
Touching his shoulder tenderly.

What had this fair child done?
To anger God so heinously?
He'd consumed the Sacred Host
After breaking the midnight fast.

It was on Easter morning.
Greeted by father's plaintive smile,
"We'll go all together to the sacrament
As a family gift to God."

The boy returned his smile
Seeing pleasure in his father's face.

Then memory of a fudgy chocolate
Swam before his inner eyes.

He struggled helpless 'twixt God and father,
Displease his earthly Dad or the eternal God?
Father's expectant smile he could not betray,
Better to hurt his distant God.

He'd go after to confess his sin.
It would soon be wiped away.
His father's fragile pleasure
Would remain intact today.

So to the altar rail he went
Beside his mother, sister and brother,
Father smiling happily at his
Newly god-born brood.

He put out his tongue
Like a nestling to its mother.
The priest placed upon it
The Body and Blood of Jesus Christ.

The devils cackled in obscene laughter.
He may look a fair-haired child of God
But now he belongs to us.
His soul is branded with our sign.

Outside the church was sunny light,
The family walking home in it.
The boy was holding mother's hand,
His soul was writhing hopelessly.

Next day he walked alone to Church.
It was a drizzling wettish day.
He saw the cassocked priest
Enter the wood confessional.

The boy he knelt in coffin darkness.
"What sins have you committed?"
He heard a savage angry God
Chiding him his fearful sin.

He hid in terror from the priest.
"I forgot my prayers and told a lie,"
Murmured the frightened boy.
A Latin pardon sentenced him.

He'd added now a further sin,
A sacrilege to keep it in,
And mock God's mercy
In the dark confessional.

So he went from sin to sin.
Every time he received communion
He was drinking of the devil's cup.
God's light was distant from his soul.

More deeply was he placed in hell.
Each month and year of Catholic practice
Placed him further into Satan's clutches.
Death would seal him into deepest hell.

Then gentle Fr Kenneth touched his head.
"No need to tell; you are forgiven."
The fair-haired boy looked at his face,
Confessing to him everything.

"Ego te absolvo in nomine patris et filii
et spiritus sancti—you are forgiven now.
God loves you, my child, go hither
In love and cheerfulness."

As I reflect upon it now, I realise that although I had been forgiven for
this package of sins yet the state of my soul whereby I believed I was
wicked and deserved to be punished was still present within me. This
I think demonstrates one of the limitations of confession: that the individual sin is forgiven but the state of the soul that has generated the
sin remains. Repentance is supposed to change this but I came to see
much later in life that there was no procedure within the Catholic
Church that was able to elucidate this problem. I much later had to
leave the Church because I was unable to find a solution within it so
I turned to psychoanalysis but later realised that there was only a partial solution within this system also. I had finally to construct my own

personal synthesis to transform the inner state from one of madness into one of sanity. My whole life has been dedicated to this project. "What interests you most?" people ask. I know the answer but it requires so long an explanation that I am unable to give it, so I smile and shrug my shoulders …

I think today I am gentle with patients whom I sense are persecuted in the way I was. I try to be like Fr Kenneth was with me. As I write I thank him in my heart for being how he was.

At a later time in my life I came to hate the Church which had made such an agony for me in my childhood. However, I now know that the fearsome God, although aided and abetted by superstitious injunctions, was a product of my own emotional state which I had projected onto and into the Church. I know that most of my fellow Catholics shrugged their shoulders at these superstitious mandates and did not take them with the seriousness which I did. Nevertheless I think the Church has much to answer for when it inculcates fears of this kind into its members. Later when I was a priest I met many working class Irish men and women who were tormented by the presence within them of sexual feelings which they believed, and had been encouraged to believe, were gravely sinful. I did what I could with the few I had contact with to relieve them from this internal torture. I tried to do for them what Fr Kenneth had done for me. A young Irish lad would say in confession that when dancing with his girlfriend: "I get feelings, Father." I told him it was a sign that his sexual organs were all working satisfactorily and as a penance asked him to say an Our Father and thank God that all his sexual body was working healthily. I did not only do this with this one man but with numerous young men and women.

All this torture had started because I did not want to disappoint my father. I am sure he would have been disappointed but why should that have had so powerful an effect upon me? I believe the explanation goes something like this. I think, in some way, I had an enormous disappointment during foetal life, infancy, or childhood. John Klauber, who psychoanalysed me, believed that I had gone into the Church to try to deal with some massive disappointment. He also believed that the Resurrection of Christ was "invented" by the apostles as an antidote to the huge disappointment of losing their leader when Jesus was crucified. Be that as it may, some big disappointment had probably happened to me. The big one happened when I was still in the womb but losing my loving father when I was three years old reinforced it. As I

27

was an extremely narcissistic little boy I magnified in my mind the disappointment that I would cause my father and this led to the tortuous path I have tried to describe. I know that in the narcissistic state you see the other through the lens of your own unseen pain. If I ask myself why I did not immediately tell the priest what I had done, it was also that I feared he would be enormously disappointed in me. Fear of disappointing the other person has been a crippling agent in my life. It is the inner emotional state that frames the colour of the outer world. In psychoanalytic terms I projected into my father my own disappointment but I do not think this is accurate. It is when a pain is unseen within that it magnifies the same pain in the other. I magnified what was already there. Such distortions only happen if there is some *harmony of the similar*[22] in the other person.

I do not know what this disappointment could have been but I think it must have been something which had shattered me and left me a mess of broken bits inside. This was not something that I knew or, more accurately, that I knew but was unaware of. There can be knowledge that lives in a dark place and remains unseen. I am sure that it is what is disowned and not embraced inwardly that becomes the lens through which emotional events in others are seen. It distorts the emotional event. I am sure that my father would have been disappointed on that Easter Sunday that I was unable to go to communion but he would have soon got over it. It would not have been a torture like it became for me. Was I trying to protect him from disappointment which I believed was so shattering? So what was this disappointment that I had suffered? One of my earliest memories is of my father coming and giving me a little string bag of farm animals before we were leaving by seaplane, the *Dixie Clipper*, for Canada in 1940.

I suspect that parting from him was an enormous disappointment for me. It could be that I had turned to him with particular love when my mother was so preoccupied with her damaged knee shortly after my birth, and that now to be parted from him was a big blow. I also know from observation of him with his young grandchildren, children of my sister and my brother, that he loved children and would read with fond love children's books to them and explain to them what the pictures meant and stood for. I certainly know that when we returned

---

[22]A phrase used by the Russian thinker, Vladimir Solovyov, in his book *The Justification of the Good* (1918, p. 68, London: Constable).

I loved him dearly and was his fond companion in pursuit of butterflies in summer and snipe and plover in the winter. I loved him so much that the thought of disappointing him was unbearable. So I do not think that it was only the disappointment that I conjectured I would cause him but also my love for him. But there is some distorted thinking here on my part because if he loved me he would have felt sorry for me and not only for himself that I had forgotten the fast and so would not be able to go to communion. It was his happy expectant face that disabled me. I would disappoint HIM. I was slave to this HIM and this was something greater than my father.

I was brought up to believe in a theory of redemption which paralleled my child's mind. When Adam sinned it was a crime against the infinite God hence only God himself could repair the damage, so he sent his only-begotten Son into manhood and through his sacrifice the debt was repaid. It is a shocking belief which does not require much reflection to realise its falsity but it was held very widely and must have been generated by something that paralleled my own state of heart. It is not possible for a creature to hurt God. The healthy story of redemption is that God, out of love for man, sent his Son to repair mankind's damaged condition. This HIM that I had offended was the same HIM that had generated my belief which I had projected onto my father. This idea of God was also fashioned on the lens of my own unseen condition. What do I mean? I was the one who would be offended if someone said something hurtful. I attributed this then to God but again greatly amplified. Was it some exposure of my child mind to a reality which it was impossible for my mind to encompass; that my mind was not developed enough to be able to do so and that when the mind is so presented with a truth for which it is not ready it becomes distorted into a fierce rape of the soul? The mind had to expand to contemplate the infinite; if it is not ready then the infinite is distorted from God into a devil.

But did my father suffer himself from disappointment? I think, despite what I have just suggested, that one cannot project a quality onto or into someone unless there is some receptivity to it in the individual at whom it is aimed. More accurately it can only be projected if it is a disowned disappointment in the individual. So did my father suffer from disappointment? And a disowned one? I think it likely on two counts. He was sixteen when his mother died while he was at public school in England. Two women came down to the school—the Oratory in Birmingham—to tell him and his twin brother that their mother had died. I have always felt a terrible sorrow for him when I think of him as a boy being told one day this appalling news by two friends of his mother's and then having to go back to his school duties as usual with all the cold atmosphere of a boy's boarding school. How on earth did he manage to cope with a tragedy like this in the unmothering atmosphere of an English public school? He was a very sensitive, kind, and loving man and it must have been a terrible blow. I think somehow I sensed this disappointment and tragedy within and was transfixed by it. It was as though a disappointment in me married up with one in him but the distortion was to think that this minor disappointment would somehow resurrect that much greater disappointment from his own past. Later I came to resent bitterly being so captive to his own emotional inner tragedies. The other unavowed disappointment was his own unhappy marriage.

There is another aspect to it. What completely captures me is the sense of disappointing a child. He was a grown man but he was a child in his emotions. He looked up to the priest, the doctor, the famous as a little child looks up to his parent. He was still a child. This is the captivating factor for me. The disappointed child is well and truly *in* me but hated and disowned. This enabled my mother and others to hypnotise me and I shall come to this later. Someone can only be hypnotised if there is an element in him which is unconnected to the rest of the self.

I had in me, in even more concentrated form, my father's religion of fear. How had this come to pass from him into me? Was it my love for him that led me to share his own attitudes? Or was it a lack of some essential inner quality that prevented me from throwing off the influence of this punishing God? My desire not to disappoint my father had been one of the reasons that prevented me from saying that I could not go to communion because I had broken the fast. I suspect that I had inner knowledge that he was a disappointed man and that I did not want to add to it. He was inwardly hurt and wounded by my mother's emotional rejection of him. The tragedy is that the later trajectory of my life gave him more and not less disappointment. I believe I was angry that I was hostage to him, an animal wounded by severe disappointment, hostage to such an extent that I suffered an inner agony partly on his account. Later I felt an enormous sympathy for him when I was confronted with the knowledge of his wife's infidelity.

In a deeper way, there was not a union between them but rather two life-attitudes which were antagonistic to each other and I was a go-between. I loved both my father and my mother and still do but I was angry that they had not emotionally consummated their marriage and fixed up the problem that existed between them and that we three children had to bear the fallout from their unresolved conflict. My sister was pulled into my mother's space, my brother into my father's, and myself torn between the two.

* * *

I was a sickly child at this time. I suffered from hay fever, asthma, bronchitis, and eczema. I am sure today that my physical state was closely connected to my emotional condition. There was something severely wrong with me but I always managed to laugh, joke, and entertain, and convey the impression that all was well with me. In this way I was like my mother, probably joined to my mother, who always laughed and joked on the outside but was in dire straits in her soul. It was the same with me: I joked and laughed and all appeared well but the eczema told a different story. I had cracked, dry skin between my nose and upper lip and below the lower lip. When I was shipped off to school in England I was mocked by the boys and called "Scaley". I brazened it out but was crying within. I am certain that the public school system is not suitable for children who are either out of the ordinary or handicapped in some way. I think this is probably so of boarding schools generally. I had no shoulder to cry upon and when I think of it now I don't know how I managed, especially as we would be away from home for seven months once we returned to school after Christmas. To this day when I pass King's Cross Station in London I shudder as I remember the school train that left from there on its sombre journey to Ampleforth, Yorkshire's concentration camp.

In the upbringing of children each culture has its pluses and minuses. Stiff upper lip is the hallmark of the English upper middle class and the aristocracy also. The English upper middle class display an outer "phlegm" and pragmatic ability to deal with the reverses of life but their ability to confront emotional challenges is extremely restricted. The problem with the stiff upper lip lies not in the determination that enables someone to get through appalling disasters and disappointments but rather in the obliteration of emotional timidity. The stiff upper lip hides fear, pretends that it is not there. The stiff upper lip is not courageous because in courage the person acts with full knowledge of his timidity.

I have got through a great deal in my life with the aid of the stiff upper lip. I have had courage also which has popped up on occasions.

It is rare to find someone who has passed through this English educational system that has emotional resilience. The indicator of emotional resilience is the ability to confront first one's own strengths and deficits and then to be able to manage emotional confrontation with another. Facing oneself or another needs to be scientific and not condemning. This is a quality which is extremely rare among those who have been educated through the English public school system but it is also rare in English culture generally. I am probably by implication giving this English education a lower rating than the education in other cultures. I imagined that within the psychoanalytic movement this would be much better developed but I have been bitterly disappointed in the ability of psychoanalysts to "grasp the nettle" when some awkward emotional issue has arisen in their midst. I know also from supervising and from treating patients who have had previous therapies that very few psychoanalysts or psychotherapists are able to confront emotional hot-points with any firmness or resolve.

A colleague used to refer with praise to this special English quality as ECG—"English Christian Gentleman". He meant by it the English reserve and failure to challenge emotional debility. However, there is something in the English character that admires the one who is emotionally pugnacious and challenging. Until recent times Churchill was a hero in England. From early on he challenged Hitler's tyranny and duplicity in lucid, unadulterated language. He was an English Christian Gentleman but he was not meek and mild. Also he was not inhumane and cruel, as he is often made out to be. He was defiant of tyranny but humane towards the afflicted. When his mother-in-law was dying he wrote this in a letter to his wife:

[22 March 1925–11 Downing Street]

My dearest darling,

I have just got your telegram. I feel for you so much—& poor Nellie too. Yr Mamma is a gt woman: & her life has been a noble life. When I think of all the courage & tenacity & self denial that she showed during the long hard years when she was fighting to bring

32

up you & Nellie & Bill, I feel what a true mother & grand woman she proved herself, & I am the more glad & proud to think her blood flows in the veins of our children.

My darling I grieve for you. An old and failing life going out on the tide, after the allotted space has been spent & after most joys have faded is not a case for human pity. It is only part of the immense tragedy of our existence here below against wh both hope & faith have rebelled—It is only what we all expect & await—unless cut off untimely. But the loss of a mother severs a chord in the heart and makes life seem lonely & its duration fleeting. I know the sense of amputation from my own experience three years ago. I deeply sorrow for yr pain.

I greatly admired & liked your Mother. She was an ideal mother-in-law. Never shall I allow that relationship to be spoken of with mockery—for her sake. I am pleased to think that perhaps she wd also have given me a good character. At any rate I am sure our marriage & life together were one of the gt satisfactions of her life. My darling sweet I kiss you.

I have been working all day (Sunday) at pensions & am vy tired. Please telegraph me how events develop & whether there is anything that I can do.

Good night my dearest,
Your devoted husband
W[23]

This shows that there was no stiff upper lip there in Churchill. Great courage and humane gentleness are partners.

In my life I have on various occasions acted in a way that gained my self-respect. Whenever I have chickened out and there have been occasions that stand before me with an accusing finger I know I am a lesser person for being an ostrich.

My own personal vocation in life has been to overcome the impulse to flee emotional challenge. The incident that I have just described where I was unable to face the challenge presented of refusing Holy

---

[23]Soames, Mary (Ed.) (1999). *Speaking for Themselves. The Personal Letters of Winston and Clementine Churchill*. London: Black Swan.

Communion and disappointing my father has stood for me as a sign writ large in the sky: this is the boxing ring that you have to enter, this is the enemy you have to overcome. When I have taken flight my conscience has reproached me. If I refuse the challenge I cannot live with myself. When I left the Church many years later my family, or some members of it, saw me as a Judas but actually I was being a better servant of the truth than I had been before, and today if I had to present myself before the eternal judgment seat I know I stand a better chance of reprieve than when I wore all the clothes of respectable decorum.

Ten years ago when I summarised the problems of the Australian Psychoanalytical Society as its newly elected president a colleague came up to me afterwards and said, "What you said is absolutely true but no one else but you would have dared to say them. I don't know how you do it." My answer to him would be that it has taken a lifetime of struggle to manage it.

I know that today I have achieved an emotional strength in this regard which is above the norm. I have been able to say things to patients, to colleagues, and to my wife and to myself which is unusual. It has been a case of the point of weakness standing in front of me and beckoning to me to overcome it. In this way a weakness has become a strength. It has been as St Paul said: "… it is when I am weak that I am strong."[24]

A question arises here. What is it in me that has challenged me to take cudgels up against this point of emotional weakness? I know from observation that the more usual path is for people to succumb to the weakness, not even to be aware of it. I have only known a few people who have seen this weakness and made it a point of personal honour to confront it in themselves. But where does this inner personal vocation come from? One of the people who definitely had this problem, faced it and achieved remarkable success in its achievement was Bob Gosling

---

[24] 2 Corinthians Ch. 12 v. 10. The full quote is as follows: "In view of the extraordinary nature of these revelations, to stop me from getting too proud I was given a thorn in the flesh, an angel of Satan to beat me and stop me from getting too proud! About this thing, I have pleaded with the Lord three times for it to leave me, but he has said, 'My grace is enough for you; my power is at its best in weakness. So I shall be happy to make my weaknesses my special boast so that the power of Christ may stay over me, and that is why I am quite content with my weaknesses, and with insults, hardships, persecutions, and the agonies I go through for Christ's sake. For it is when I am weak that I am strong.'"

who was chairman at the Tavistock Clinic when I first went there. He clearly believed that he had derived a special strength from his mother's love for him and his own identification with her generosity. This is what he wrote to me in one of his letters:

> In my view what gave me life, or at least saved me from death, is the amazing fact that my mother had inborn tendencies to minister to my infant helplessness and that they were sufficiently supported socially and culturally for her to work the miracle. From my point of view this was a totally unmerited gift—Grace, in fact. Ave Maria! So the choices we have to make every day now in so far as they are very derived or developed forms of this first relationship depend on how much we can acknowledge and honour this Gift (and become identified with it).

I suspect that my own determination in this regard also came from my mother. Yet I think it may have come also from a hidden strength in my father. I will come later to what he said to me in a moment of personal crisis.

I knew then as I still know today that in the hard furnace of emotional life my father and not my uncle was the stronger man. In practical life, however, my uncle was the more assertive and capable functionary. He was better off than my father, better at business, but in the underground mine from which emotions emanate I knew that my father had a streak of solid gold that my uncle did not possess.

This is the place to tell you about my father's twin brother. My father and his brother were identical twins and they looked so alike that people often mistook one for the other. Uncle John was much closer to us than a normal uncle. He lived in a beautiful house which he had bought when he married, called *Real*.[25] It was a large house sitting on a property of several acres on the northern side of Oporto. It had a tennis court and some woodland. Uncle John had six children. He had married six years earlier than my father. His wife, Aileen, whose brother was a Church of England clergyman, was a convert to Catholicism. John and Aileen were very much in love with each other. Sometimes when we drove

---

[25]It means "royal" in Portuguese and is pronounced "ree-ull".

35

past their home we would see them walking together arms linked in happy contentment. This love that existed between them I am sure has had a beneficial effect on the six children. The eldest, Elaine, became a nun and the other five, at least for some forty years subsequent to adulthood, were in settled married life. I put in this caution about "forty years subsequent to adulthood" because in later life some of the children and grandchildren of this marriage have experienced difficulties. But at least for a period the children of my uncle seemed less afflicted with torment than my father's three children. My sister had a disastrous first marriage which was full of distress. I have been a priest, left the Church, married twice, and been a "mixed-up kid". My brother's life and marriage have been more straightforward. I think the stability of John and Aileen's children is partly explained by their own parents' love for each other.

As children the *Reais*,[26] as we often called them, were closer to us than normal cousins. We spent so much enjoyable time in each other's company. We went on picnics together, went on shooting forays together in the winter and swimming expeditions in the summer. We were frequently in and out of each other's houses. John was kind and generous and very like my father though he was more assertive. I am certain that my father had suffered a great deal more than Uncle John; that he suffered from an inner tyrannical God and also from his unhappy marriage. My relations with Uncle John and Aunty Aileen had always been most warm-hearted and their love and generous-hearted attitude towards me and all of us seemed to be just part of the world into which I had been born. All this was shattered when I left the priesthood at the age of thirty. At Christmas I always sent cards to all members of the family and of course especially to Uncle John and Aunty Aileen. I could not believe it when they did not send one in reply after I had left the priesthood but my brother later told me that Aileen had told him that this had been quite deliberate. I was to be punished with a cold rejection. It was then that I saw the difference between my father and Uncle John. I hurt my father dreadfully by leaving the priesthood and the Church and he did not understand it but an inner love that went beyond all the outer ritual reached out of him towards me. His natural paternal love was not altered. I have often asked myself if this was because he was my father. Would he have been the same if one of Uncle John's boys had become

---

[26]The Portuguese for "the royals".

a priest and then left? And would Uncle John have been like my father towards me if I had been his son? These are absurd questions because they are based on fictitious "ifs" but they are aimed at trying to decide whether it was paternity alone which governed my father's attitude to me. I am fairly confident that it went deeper than paternity. If the situation were reversed and one of Uncle John's boys had become a priest and then left and sent my mother and father a Christmas card I am as certain as I can be that they would have sent a card back. This would have been partly dictated by an attitude of my mother's but I think it is something which my father would have shared. It was a shared attitude in their marriage which was generous towards the outcast, the sinner, or the alien. This was a dominant characteristic in my mother but, it has to be remembered, my father married such a woman.

This debacle was very much later but until the age of thirty I always enjoyed the love and interest of my father's twin brother and his wife. These two twins worked together at the office every day, they went shooting together and spent a great deal of time in each other's houses. Often when my father returned home from work he would say that he must ring John. My mother would reprimand him in exasperation, saying that he had been at the office all day with John and here he was now telephoning him. She was I am sure jealous of so intimate a relationship between these twins which I think she suspected was closer than the bond between her and him. I have several times treated twins as a psychoanalyst and am sure that the handicap of being a twin is greater than its benefits. To start with, the mother cannot give the attention which is possible in the case of a single child, but also the pairing of twins is a bond that hampers relations with others, and I have noticed that twins tend to set up twinning relations and it is more difficult for a twin to have a mental representation of another than it is for a singleton. You do not need to develop a mental representation when you have the physical presence always with you. For my father out of sight was, to some extent, out of mind and I think this is typical of twinhood.

How was it then that John made such a successful marriage but my father did not? There is one way of looking at it which is like this. The moralistic outlook which, as it emerged, was a strong character trait in Uncle John was also in my father but in him there was a counter-trait which, in his marriage, he was trying to give a place for, although it gave him much pain and it never reached the point of "triumphing" in his personality. He could not catch sight of his wife's mental attitude within himself but in his marriage to my mother I believe he was making the attempt; trying to assert a love and tolerance that went much deeper than any moralism. My father felt for *me* when I left the Church but Uncle John felt for the Church. I had a painful discussion with John two years after leaving the priesthood. There was a Dominican priest, Fr Bernardo, who was close to all our family. He knew my circumstances and thought my decision to leave the priesthood had been right. Protesting against Uncle John's dogmatic certainty that I had done the wrong thing I said to him: "Fr Bernardo thinks I have acted rightly so why do you think that is?" John answered honestly: "That is beyond my understanding … I just cannot understand how he could think that."

I felt a glimmer of hope that a chink was struggling here to get some other point of view established. My father married a woman who was a "friend of sinners"; my uncle married a woman who always held the high moral ground. The word "moral" is not right; "moralistic" is the correct word. My father's morality was tempered by a humanity towards the sinner. This was an important difference between them. I have always been moved by this passage from St John's Gospel:[27]

> The scribes and Pharisees brought a woman along who had been caught committing adultery; and making her stand there in full view of everybody, they said to Jesus, "Master, this woman was caught in the very act of committing adultery; and Moses has ordered us in the Law to condemn women like this to death by stoning. What have you to say?" They asked him this as a test, looking for something to use against him. But Jesus bent down and started writing on the ground with his finger. As they persisted with their question, he looked up and said, "If there is one of you who has not sinned, let him be the first to throw a stone at her." Then he bent down and wrote on the ground again. When they heard this they went away one by one, beginning with the eldest, until Jesus was left alone with the woman, who remained standing there. He looked up and said, "Woman, where are they? Has no one condemned you?" "No one, sir," she replied. "Neither do I condemn you," said Jesus. "Go away, and don't sin any more."[28]

---

[27]Biblical scholars say this passage was not written by St. John but this is the place where it is found in every Bible.
[28]Ch. 8. vv. 2–11 (Jerusalem Bible).

This would have been music to my mother's ears and I think, deep down, my father would have been in sympathy with her.

I have already stated that my mother and father were unhappily married but I want to reflect for a moment on what is meant by a happy marriage or an unhappy marriage. I think that my father did have some of that self-righteous attitude shared by Uncle John but he married a woman who challenged it whereas Uncle John married a woman who supported it. One could look at it this way—that my father was trying to solve this problem of self-righteousness and therefore married a woman who challenged it; that an element in his choice of marriage partner was an attempt to address a character fault in himself. This implies that there is knowledge (but not awareness) of this fault. This also means that there is some call within the self to repair a fault of this nature. This notion that we are called ultimately to be saints is enshrined deeply in the Christian faith and is I understand less present in Buddhism and Hinduism.

The so-called "happy marriage" may not be the one that is best for the human community in which it is an element. The two together may be happier but it may be a happiness based partly on unawareness of their shared character failing—in this case, self-righteousness. I have suggested that John and Aileen's children were more stable, yet, with a backwards view after an interval of several years, I am not sure that this is true. Many years later one child's marriage broke up and there were other signs of a discord that may have taken longer to mature than in my own family, in which the difficulties erupted straight away; in John's family they stole up to the surface a generation later.

Such a dark cloud descended when I left the Church that it distresses me even today when I think of how happy and how loved I was by John and Aileen and all their family until then. I am today grateful to them for this love which they showed to me as a child and young man but I still struggle with the violence of their rejection which came later.

Forty-five years have passed since I left the priesthood and my cousins today are kind and welcoming to me. When there is a shocking explosion it takes time for it to be digested and assimilated and for a new way of relating to the delinquent family member to emerge. I picture it today in this way. Imagine Uncle John and his wife are arranging a lovely picnic for all members of the family. Everyone is enjoying the warm and friendly atmosphere when suddenly a young adolescent starts shouting, throwing cups at people, breaking glasses, and screaming. Here now is the test for the patriarch. All other members he can tolerate but this delinquent is more than he can manage. I think I was that delinquent and it put my uncle to the sorest of tests. I was attacking his beloved family, the Church. I am today grateful to all my cousins for giving me a warm welcome though they cannot be in agreement with what I did.

I think one of the deepest human problems is an individual's capacity to thrust himself into something. Into what? A belief system. It may be Catholicism, Judaism, communism, or psychoanalysis. Often people will put themselves into one of their own creations—their own system of thinking. It is this capacity of human beings to put themselves into a way of being that is the cause of much sectarian violence in the world. It was not Catholicism that John and Aileen were defending but their wounded selves protected by an encircling armour called the Church.

Our human task is to be lived by Life. Life as a transcendent principle. It seems to me that a reliable test of whether we have lived worthwhile lives is this: is the world a better place for my having lived in it? Within the Christian dispensation we have the image of God separating the sheep from the goats at the Last Judgment. Buddhism and Hinduism also have such a Judgment built into their system of belief. This seems to lie at the heart of all the great religious traditions. I believe that this principle is not only true of the individual but also of a marriage or a partnership. It is better to think not of whether a marriage has been happy or unhappy but whether it has been a good marriage or a bad one. In other words, is the world better or worse for the event of that marriage having occurred within it?

* * *

My father had an elder brother, Maurice, who also lived in Oporto with his wife, Eileen, and his three children. Maurice also worked in the family firm. He was four years older than my father and John and lived in an imposing house on the Avenida da Boavista. Maurice loved children and knew how to entertain them. On my tenth birthday he came round to our house in the afternoon when my party was in progress and gave me a camera—a small Baby Brownie. I was so pleased with it and took some photographs on that very day of the children who were at my party. I still have these photographs on the first page of my first photograph album. What I particularly liked about this present was his realisation that, although I was a child of ten, yet I would be able to manage a camera. He respected the inner ability of a child. For him a child was never *just* a child. At the beginning of every holiday we would go to the Boavista and visit him and his wife. He would always take a keen interest in what we were doing. He never assumed that he knew. In this he was different from John and probably my father also.

In extended families the assumption that individual members are "known" is quite common. This probably breeds the feeling that to be loved requires individuality to be repressed. I am sure that the present of a camera from Uncle Maurice stands so strongly in mind because he saw beyond the "family assumption" into the mind of an individual child, an individuality that he wanted to foster. He must have thought quite carefully about that present and gone to the trouble to go and buy it, and I remember as I unwrapped it he showed me how to use it. To be thought about as a person in my own right was so important to me and, although as children we saw less of Maurice than John, yet I shall always be grateful to him for his love and interest. I remember him in the Douro telling me about a rock at the top of the *quinta*[29] where even on a hot day there were cool breezes. Later I wrote a poem about it which had a tragic twist at the end of it.

A woman came to me as a patient when I was a psychoanalyst many years later. She had also come from the extended kind of family although from a culture very different to mine, but what was most important to her was that I thought about her and she was very grateful to me for it. It may be that I passed on to her something of this quality that Uncle Maurice had given so generously to me. To be truly thought about is a great treasure.

* * *

So when I found myself unhappy at school, what is it that stopped me from just saying to my parents: "Please take me away; I am so unhappy here"? I am referring to being at school in Yorkshire. I think the simple answer would be "losing face", but more truly it was a terror of breaking down and I think this fear explains aspects of my behaviour on many subsequent occasions. I will mention later how, when I left the Church, I seriously considered asking to be admitted into a Richmond

---

[29]Portuguese word meaning "property".

Fellowship home but instead I put a brave face on it. Of course in fact the fear of breaking down represented breakdowns that were occurring all the time. There are many ways of going mad. Perhaps the healthiest is an open collapse when people rally round and put the patient in a convalescent home. I once nearly collapsed into this but bit my lip harder than ever and avoided it. The forms of breakdown that have afflicted me have been of the kind that have brought opprobrium on my head and particularly from those who have been close to me. What would have happened if I had tumbled into my housemaster's study at Ampleforth and burst into tears, saying that I was utterly miserable? And I *was* utterly miserable. With my face covered in eczema, my body subject to asthmatic attacks, and boys calling me "Scaley" I was crying, nay screaming within but, all the while, I put on a brave face. But to have gone to my housemaster and declared that I was miserable implies that I was aware of my distress, but this is a fictitious idea because it implies awareness which was not so. I had knowledge of my state but not awareness.

I was not aware that I was suicidal and I did not attempt suicide but I acted suicidally. I kept doing things, major life changes, that were suicidal in their character. In suicide someone kills himself physically but I killed who I was personally. My life is patterned with a catalogue of self-destructive acts. Then I have had a slow, hard uphill task of rescuing myself from what I have done. I was like someone who threw himself into a marshy bog, and I then had to use all the force of my being to struggle out of the mire. Did I throw myself or was I thrown in? I did it myself but under the power of a force throwing me. Only when I became aware of being suicidal did I begin to act in a more fulfilling way and to avoid such foolhardy behaviours.

To explain the difference between knowledge and awareness I adopt the distinction, pioneered by António Damásio, between *core consciousness* and *extended consciousness*.[30] In core consciousness there is knowledge of reality as a whole; in extended consciousness there is knowledge of particulars through the senses. If these are separated from one another there is knowledge but no awareness. When the knowledge in core consciousness becomes connected to a particular event existing in extended consciousness then at that moment awareness is born.

Although I had three years of psychoanalytic psychotherapy and eight years of full psychoanalysis I did not become aware of the suicidal

---

[30]Damasio, António (2000). *The Feeling of What Happens*. London: Random House.

in me, and the analyst never brought it to light yet I think he knew it also but was not aware of it. I must conclude that he had the same problem: that he had the suicidal in him but was not aware of it. He died of a heart attack, having taken on the two jobs of Freud Professor at University College in London and president of the British Psychoanalytical Society. That he died because he took on too much is probable—a suicidal act.

The suicidal is the core of madness. If I damage someone else I am bad; if I damage myself I am mad. If I set light to someone's house I am bad; if I set light to my own I am mad. If I slash someone's wrists with a razor I am bad; if I slash my own I am mad. To attack myself, to sabotage my own potential is madness; to prevent the development of my own creative capacities is mad. Looked at from this last viewpoint makes me think that our society is awash with madness.

Years later an event occurred which led me to feel suicidal. It was connected with "Disaster" which I describe in the last chapter of this book. I entered a state of extreme danger. I felt the strong impulse to kill myself. What had always been there confronted me in stark nakedness. For a frightening few months the threat of my killing myself pursued me night and day. I slowly assimilated this into my being and made a decision that I wanted to live. "I want to live." I think of Carmen's "*gosto de viver*"—this decision was a moment of health—the very root of mental health. It has left me with an understanding of suicide and I believe that I have been able to help some patients who have been similarly afflicted.

* * *

The three brothers who lived in Oporto were all in the port wine trade. In fact they owned, or came to own, two of the best known port wine brands. My father was taster for Dow's and his twin was taster for Warre's. I went from time to time to my father's sample room at the office in Vila Nova de Gaia and watched him blending and sampling. He had an old world love of what he was doing and it seemed to come naturally to him. He must have learned how to do it but that was not how it seemed to me. You do not think that someone once had to learn how to brush his teeth or do up his shoelaces but we know that he did. It was like this with my father. I would watch him putting his nose to the lip of the tapering tasting glass and smelling. Usually that was enough. Often he did not taste the wine and, if he did, he would swill it around in his mouth and then spit it out into a tray full of sawdust on the floor. He would taste all morning but none of the delicate liquid would he swallow.

So each weekday he would get up early and go to Mass, return and have breakfast, read the Portuguese newspaper, give my mother a peck on the cheek, and then drive to the office. Normally he would drive into town and then across the lower rung of the Ponte D. Luis Bridge and along the *cais*[31] of the Douro river on the Gaia side, and then up the stone-flagged street and into the large rambling acreage of the *armazem*[32] and offices. He would go to his sample room and spend the morning tasting, looking at the orders that had come in from England, blend the wine according to what was required, and then go into lunch with his two brothers. It was a leisurely lunch. He would return to work afterwards and usually get home by five or half past five.

When he arrived in the office his sample room assistant, Manuel Rocha, would have all the ports he was to taste poured out ready for him in the tasting glasses. He would not be satisfied with finalising a blend on the basis of a tasting of one day. He would taste the ports on every working day for a fortnight. He explained to me that you have on and off days with tasting, just as you have on and off days shooting or playing golf. He told me that sometimes he would detect a hint of acrid flavour in a port one day. Then he tasted it every day for the next eight tasting days and it seemed fine, and he said to himself that it must have been his imagination, but then on the tenth day he detected it again. I asked him that if the imperfection was so slight then did it really matter because surely the ordinary drinker in England would not notice it? He was a perfectionist and it was important to him to get it absolutely right. In recent times the port firms owned by the Symington family have prospered greatly and I believe this principle of my father's has been passed on to the younger generation and that the firms have profited thereby. In the London Tube there used to be an advertisement for some firm whose slogan was "… got big by bothering". I cannot remember the name of the firm but the reader can supply any name that seems to fit. I have in my own field inherited this principle. In a

---

[31]Quay.
[32]Warehouse.

lecture, talk, or paper it is very important for me to get it right. There is an obverse side to this: I am very critical of the work of others which seems to me to be defective in some particular regard. This has made me very unpopular with a few colleagues and, in some cases, even hated by them for a critique I have made of their work.

Port was part of family life. I always waited expectantly for father's return from the office. If it was summer I would go with him to the beach where we would have a swim on the Castelo do Queijo beach, changing before and after in a little *barraca*.[33] He did not like lying on the beach or sunbathing so we would change after our swim and then he would drive us home where he would change into quite formal clothes before dinner. He would mix a dry martini, shaking the cocktail shaker vigorously, then pour one for my mother and himself. I always drank dry port. We would sit in the sitting room, sipping and talking until Carmen opened the door and announced *"Está na mesa"*[34] and we went into the dining room to eat. We always started with soup; Carmen stood on watchful guard while we ate; after she cleared away the empty soup plates, we would move on to the fish or meat course and she would serve us with wine and water. The port was served with the sweet and cheese. It sat in a heavy hand-cut decanter. When the cheese was finished my mother and sister, if she was present, would leave the dining room and retire into the sitting room, and my brother and I would remain behind with my father when we would continue drinking the port and he usually smoked a cigar. We would usually drink and talk for half to three quarters of an hour. We always obeyed this ritual even if it was just myself with my father and mother. I am not sure what happened when my mother and father were on their own but I suspect the same ritual was maintained. My mother would go through into the sitting room where she would read the airmail edition of the *Daily Telegraph* which was four or five days after the day of issue.

I used to love sitting with my father drinking the port and he would confide to me some of his business worries, talk of plans for the weekend, or tell me of some conversation he had had with one of his brothers. Carmen would leave us and now we were on our own in this

---

[33]Tent.
[34]Dinner is served—literally "It is on the table."

male sanctuary. If friends had come to dinner and there were several men they would usually lapse into recounting dirty jokes.

We always drank port. It was part of daily life. My father would always encourage me to have another glass. This was partly out of natural courtesy and partly because he believed that it was healthy to eat and drink well. He liked to see people with some *corpo*[35] on them. The historian, Hugh Trevor-Roper said in a letter to the art connoisseur, Bernard Berenson that for Catholics good living was the eighth sacrament. My mother would get fed up if my father delayed more than three quarters of an hour before joining the ladies.

The port vines are grown on terraced slopes of the Alto Douro. The mountains of the Douro where the vineyards are carved out into the hillsides are the most beautiful on earth. I love the Douro and whenever I return there I feel like a baby returning to mummy's warm breast. We regularly went to the lovely Quinta do Bomfim at Easter, at the vintage and at the New Year. Sometimes I would go for a week in August with my father. My mother did not like going then as she found it too hot. I loved going to the Douro. We would either go by car or by train. If we went by train my father would drive us into the station by car and a "man from the office" would drive the car away and take it to the lodge in Gaia until we got back. The train journey would take four and a half hours. We would leave about nine in the morning and the exciting moment was when the train reached the Douro river somewhere near Caldas do Moledo and from there it tracked along the northern bank of the river all the way until we reached our patiently waiting quinta. When the train reached Regua it stopped for twenty minutes so people could get out and have lunch at the station restaurant. The waiters were ready with soups on the tables; as soon as that was eaten a *bacalhau*[36] dish was served and some cheese followed. The train would hoot and the station master would start hollering and we'd clamber back on the train. Three quarters of an hour later the engine chuffed into Pinhão and there Senhor Armindo would be waiting for us in the old Ford V8 at the station. Pinhão was and is a shabby cardboard box-like conglomerate of houses but the station which was pasted with *azuleijos* depicting vintage scenes was a joy to the heart. Senhor Armindo would

---

[35]Corpo is the Portuguese word for "body".
[36]Bacalhau is dried cod—a favourite Portuguese food which could be cooked in a hundred different ways.

drive us up to the quinta and on arrival would be welcomed by the warm, large bosomed Dona Mimi, his wife.

All the bedrooms had been perfectly prepared and the faithful maid, María, rushed out and carried in all our cases and bags and in the old fashioned stone-flagged kitchen the cook, Constancia, was already preparing a *bacalhau* dish for dinner. There was a refrigerator but no deep freeze and we lived off what was produced on the quinta. There were pigs, turkeys, chickens, ducks and geese, and plenty of vegetables. There was no running water in the bedrooms but washstands with big metal jugs, and the faithful María would constantly slip into the rooms and make sure that these were full, and in the morning, before breakfast, she would knock at the door and rush in with a smaller watering can-like jug filled with hot water for washing and shaving.

My father would sink into the atmosphere of the Douro hills. I would love walking with him up the mountain among the vines. He would inspect them and see how they were doing and try to make predictions about the vintage. The atmosphere was quite different "up the Douro" to the house in Oporto. It was more informal and the ritual of the men separating from the ladies at the time of the port did not occur in the Douro. We all loved the Douro. I have never met a Symington who does not love the Douro. The Douro river winding among the vine-clad mountains draws every member of the family to its charm with a strong nostalgic passion. It is our homeland where a nurturing mother nestles us all in her family bosom. The Douro hills are like burial mounds where the spirits of our father, grandfather, and ancestors still dwell and look down upon us with a caring embrace. I feel like the Prodigal Son who has been in a far country but is now drawn back to his father's estate.

My mother also enjoyed these trips to the Douro and there were always throngs of people at vintage time which she enjoyed. There is one memory though that stays with me. My father usually drove but my mother did sometimes. It happened several times that as we were driving through small mountain villages and the *garotos*[37] saw the car they would cry out "*Senhora aguiar*".[38] That would have been in the years between 1945 and 1955.

---

[37]Urchins.
[38]"Woman driving".

* * *

This was the real world of my childhood and yet it had a certain dream-like quality to it. I have only in recent years come to understand why it was dream-like. I believe I was beset within by the mad self-killer and I took flight from it. The emotional current of this flight became the template of my relation to what was happening around me. To see something *as it is* requires one to confront it emotionally in an active way. If instead of emotional confrontation you take flight emotionally from a horror within then this changes the way things are perceived; good things are not truly taken in and the ugly is either overemphasised or underemphasised. I was able to convince myself of things which were not true.

I think this is so important and relevant not only to myself but to others too that I want to make the effort to explain it more fully. The moment I am able to say to myself, "I am suicidal," "I am self-destructive," "I am greedy," "I am envious," "I am depressed," "I have a powerful imagination," or "I have a capacity to conceptualise and abstract," I am in a healthy state of mind. I am in emotional relation to something in myself. I grasp the nettle. When I shun something in myself and take flight from myself this structures the way I perceive not only my fellow human beings but also society and the human and non-human world around me. So, I am either engaged with the elements inside myself or in flight from them. If, in a state of terror, I am in flight from the elements inside myself this affects the way I am in relation to all the elements of my life. There is also a violent hatred in me for the state that I am in but the object of it is misperceived and attributed to something outside myself. The way this worked itself out in the direction of my life will unfold as this book proceeds.

CHAPTER TWO

Mother

My father was essentially a simple man but my mother was a complex creature. I think at heart she was lonely with a desperate longing to be understood. She attempted to satisfy this by sucking her children into the vortex of her inner world to alleviate a gaping agony.

She was born in Sydney, Australia, the second of three daughters. Her father, my grandfather, was an agricultural expert and adviser first to the government of New South Wales and then to the newly formed federal government of Australia. In 1912 he wrote the classic textbook *Dairying in Australasia*[1] which remained a basic text for agricultural students for many years. He was Irish, born in Tipperary in 1868, went to agricultural college in Copenhagen and, after qualifying, went to New South Wales. In September 1901 he married his wife, Alice, who was a New Zealander from Christchurch, born in 1877. In 1924 the Argentine government, wanting to develop their beef cattle, offered him the job of initiating this new project and proposed to pay him a salary which was three times what he was earning in Australia. He accepted this and moved his wife and family from Sydney to Buenos Aires, where

---

[1]O'Callaghan, M. A. (1912). *Dairying in Australasia*. Sydney: Angus & Robertson.

my mother lived for five years. She was eighteen at the time of this move. At the age of twenty-three she went to London and worked as a secretary for the actress, Mrs Nisbet, for two years. While in Buenos Aires she became a close friend of Audrey Bird whose father was the British consul there. In 1930 Mr Bird was posted as consul in Oporto and the next year my mother went to Oporto to stay with Audrey. There she met my father and married him the following year on 26th January, Australia Day, at St Mary's Church, Cadogan Street in Chelsea. She lived for the next fifty years in Oporto except for three years during the war when she and her three children went to Canada. She gave birth in the first five years of her marriage to three children: Jill, my sister, who was born in 1933, my brother, James, who was born at the end of the following year, and me in 1937.

There she was, my mother, in the midst of this large Symington tribe. She loved the food, the drink, and the party lifestyle that characterised Oporto in those days. When I think of my mother and the influence she had on my life I have to divide her life into two distinct phases. Before the menopause she lived in Oporto society as my father's companion and shared his friends and interests—at least externally. At the time of the menopause she rebelled, hated what she felt to be Oporto's provincial life, and sailed into a very different world of friendships and interests. She inhaled me and my sister into this world. My brother stood resolutely against this sudden volte-face in her emotional life.

One of her good friends before she began to disdain Oporto's parochial life was Auriel Cobb. Auriel's husband, Reg, was the owner of Cockburn's Port. Although they were rivals in business he and my father were the closest of friends. The Cobbs were so close to us that we used, as children, to call them Uncle and Aunt. When we first returned from Canada we rented a house with the Cobbs at Miramar, a small coastal town a little south of Oporto. Reg Cobb had a huge cup for his morning coffee at breakfast. He said that the second cup never tasted as good so he made sure that the first was capacious. I remember little of that holiday except the house which had a strange little glass gazebo crowning the top of it in which was my bedroom. There was a little nine hole golf course on which my parents and Reg and Auriel played; I think I may have tried my hand with a little club from time to time. What I do remember though was sitting at breakfast one morning, Reg drinking coffee from his large cup, with me asking him questions. I cannot remember what they were exactly but I think they were questions like,

"Uncle Reg, how are rocks formed?", and "Why do we get tides?", and "How is that trees are so tall?" After a while he said to me in irritation. "Oh, stop asking so many questions." Although I obeyed externally I remember saying to myself resolutely within that I would not stop asking questions. I have always asked questions in a never-ending trail. It was the greatest joy when many years later I arrived at St Edmund's and started studying philosophy, and realised that it was the discipline devoted to asking endless questions—"Why, why, why?" In later years still this eternal questioning, focussed upon the workings of the human mind, has never stopped. Neither Uncle Reg nor anyone since has ever been able to stop me. How this was present in me from such an early age I do not know. I must have been seven or eight when we spent that summer holiday in Miramar.

The Cobbs also had a house in the Minho north of Oporto, north of Viana do Castelo and about an hour from the Spanish frontier. It was a delightful house set in the trees and the property embraced a stretch of the crystal clear Ancora river. I caught my first trout from the bank there with a grasshopper. There was a meadow beside the river jumping with grasshoppers. I dangled one of them on the surface of the crystal clear water and I could see this trout circling round and looking at it and then going off again. Then another smaller trout came and looked as if it were going to take it and the larger one swooped in and took the bait. I was greatly excited as I reeled it in and Aunty Auriel had it grilled for me for breakfast the next day. Auriel adored children; she was full of jokes and tricks and there was never a dull moment when she was around. Every evening she would arrange games: charades, Nelson's Eye, and a whole variety of games where we made up stories in relay, which one person would start, then another continue, and so on, and it was all in the midst of great laughter. Reg and Auriel's son, Anthony, joined in all the fun. Nelson's Eye was a typical Auriel prank. It only worked with a visitor who did not know the game. Reg would be sat upon a chair with a bandage over one eye and Auriel would lead the visitor up and tell him that this was Nelson with only one eye and he now had to poke out the other eye but that he had to be blindfolded when he did it. She made the visitor look at the place of the good eye then blindfolded him and said, "Now, poke it out." The visitor's inhibitions would be overcome with loud words of encouragement from Auriel. Eventually he would poke his index finger forward confidently and it sank into a grapefruit which had been previously cut in two and placed in front of the good eye while the visitor was blindfolded. I can still remember when it was first done to me. All those standing around would roar with laughter. We used to go to Ancora for about two weeks of our summer holiday every year for several years, or until I was about twelve or thirteen when my mother turned in another direction socially.

After the menopause my mother cultivated a "salon" in Oporto. Artists, writers, and musicians all came to our house. My mother became a known hostess in that cultural milieu and whenever someone in the world of the arts was coming to Oporto they would be given an introduction to my mother. When I start to think of the people I met through her, names tumble out in all directions. Graham Greene came to dinner one night; Rosita Forbes, the travel writer, came and stayed with us at Quinta do Bomfim in the Douro with her husband, Arthur McGrath. Hector Bolitho, the historian of the Royal Family, after staying in the Douro, came and stayed in the Minho with my mother and father. Peter de Polnay frequently dined with us. Xan Fielding and his wife came to our home. My mother was friendly with the painter, Johnny Minton, who gave her two of his large canvases. She was very friendly with Bumble Dawson who designed clothes for theatre productions and through her she met many famous actors and actresses. When the Sadler's Wells Ballet Company came to Oporto she entertained many of them, including Margot Fonteyn. Somerset Maugham stayed in a quinta next to Bomfim but came over for dinner.

It was also at this time that my mother became very friendly with the Dean family who lived in a large house near Staines called Ankerwycke Priory. The patriarch of this household was Dick Dean who had been at school with my father. He was a bachelor but three of his sisters lived in the house and one of them, Clare Waters, was a very close friend of my mother. Clare had been married to Budge Waters who had also been at school with my father but he had died of tuberculosis at the end of the war. Budge had been my godfather and Clare was always very generous towards me. Every summer Clare and her daughter, Fleur, would come and spend the summer with us. My mother's friendship with Clare was very close. On one occasion they went on a holiday together to Tunisia to spend a few weeks with an American couple, the Hensons, who lived in Hammamet. They went in Clare's small car, crossing from Gibraltar to Tangier and driving across to Hammamet through Algeria. My mother and Clare developed a passion for bullfighting and often travelled together into Spain to see the Spanish bullfights. For one of my birthdays

Clare gave me Ernest Hemingway's *Death in the Afternoon*[2] and, under my mother's influence, I became very interested in bullfighting myself. Apart from going to bullfights, I read several books on it. The one I enjoyed most was Juan Belmonte's autobiography.[3] Clare was a sophisticated woman and "had been around". When the school holiday was over Fleur would return to England to school under the care of Cynth Waters, her aunt, and Clare would often stay on at home with my mother until November or early December. My mother was so caught up in this new friendship that she abandoned many of her old Oporto friends. My father felt excluded and alien in this world of sophomores. In my late teens I read Evelyn Waugh's novel *A Handful of Dust* and I thought my mother was very like Brenda Last, the protagonist of that tale.

My sister and I were very influenced by my mother and Clare. My mother first took up with Clare when I was about fourteen, just at the time when I went into the senior school at Ampleforth. I believe that I was hypnotised by my mother. I have for many years believed that hypnotism is a much wider psychological phenomenon than its restricted practice by certain psychiatrists and psychologists. One only has to think of the sway that people like Hitler, Billy Graham, the Ayatollah Khomeini, or Mao Tse-tung exercised over their slavish audiences. I was put into a hypnotic trance by my mother and I mean it quite literally. She would stare at me with a faraway penetrating look in her eyes and I was her victim. I am not sure whether she did this with my sister but I suspect she did. She failed to do it with my brother, James, but he had to develop a certain brusqueness of character to resist it. Consequently she paid him out by being very cruel to him. Someone who operates through this hypnotic function is extremely cruel to the one who manages to release him- or herself from its power. Whether my mother was conscious that she had this power I do not know though I suspect she did know. Knowledge and awareness, as I wrote in the last chapter, are two different states. So I believe my mother knew it but may not have been aware of it.

In Ronnie Laing's autobiographical book *Madness, Wisdom and Folly* he describes believing that Jeyes Fluid was sherry when he was under hypnosis and wonders at the power of a phenomenon which can even

[2]Hemingway, E. (1932). *Death in the Afternoon*. London: Jonathan Cape.
[3]Belmonte, J. (1937). *Juan Belmonte, Killer of Bulls: The Autobiography of a Matador*. Translated by Leslie Charteris. New York: Doubleday, Doran.

distort the sensory perception of taste. You would think, after all, that at least taste which is so immediate cannot be interfered with by any external intervention and yet it can. I believe I was hypnotised by my mother in just such a thoroughgoing way. My mother loved a Spanish brandy called Fundador and I loved it too, or so I believed, and drank it with relish. One day, when I was out of the hypnotic trance, I realised what a rough and unpleasant drink it was and I was amazed at the strength of my mother's mesmeric power. I have come under this power subsequently in life and as long as it is not mentioned or put into words the hypnotist remains equable towards her victim, but the moment that he speaks of it, revealing thereby knowledge of its power to the magician, he is hated with a supreme fury. Two opposites unmask this invisible phenomenon: one is an expansion of mind through a love which embraces not only the two people, the hypnotist and the hypnotised, but also the human communion in which both are participants. The hypnotic phenomenon can only work if the world encompassing the two participants is shut out. George Meredith clearly understood this, as can be seen in his novel *The Egoist*.[4] The second factor that disarms this occult power is a critical assessment of the other's philosophy, but these two both come from a perspective which is outside the precincts of the pair. So it is love, as an expansion of mind, which, at the same time, opens up a knowledge of mental realities which is responsible for torpedoing the sensual which is elemental to hypnotism. The hypnotist is able to anaesthetise something in the victim. So a woman, who introduced a lover into the domestic household, was able to anaesthetise her husband's sexual desire for her and therefore any hint of jealousy in him. He and his wife's lover would sit and talk in a friendly way many times a week. But the hypnotist also makes insensible any hatred, or derivative of hatred, in herself. My mother, I believe, was cruel to my brother, James, because he was resistant to her capacity to numb his determination. This magnetism that came from my mother was responsible for my sexual scruples which I shall mention later. This mesmerism in her came from an inner deep loneliness and to have me in her power relieved it. I say that it relieved it but did it do so really—in other words did it relieve it or just create a compensatory antidote as if it were a drug? I think the latter. The compensation was that she was now

---

[4]Meredith, George (1919). *The Egoist*. London: Constable.

no longer alone but had for ever a little infant who admired and loved her. I think Frances Tustin has put her finger upon this phenomenon:

> Sometimes the father had had to be away a great deal because of his work, or for some reason he was not emotionally available for the mother … Without being aware of it, the mother seems to have resorted to the baby inside her body for company and solace. Thus, the birth of this baby may have been difficult because, unconsciously, she did not want to lose the baby from inside her body. When the baby was born, this left a lonely, grief-stricken feeling inside her, which felt like a "black hole". Some mothers have told me that it felt like an amputation. It was as if they had lost a part of their body.[5]

Thus through hypnotism my mother reinstalled me within her womb. I became again her comforter. I think this partly explains the huge betrayal I felt when I discovered her infidelity—that she had taken me as her loyal comforter, her lover, and now she had betrayed me. I don't think the awful shock that permeated my whole being was fundamentally that she had betrayed my father. The scruples I have described concerning the taking of the sacrament of communion and later of sexual feelings received their power and force from this hypnotic power. She had enfolded me within her womb and being *in* the family was an extension of this. I don't think my problem was disappointing my father but ripping myself free from the enveloping strength of mother's hypnotic power. The dictates of the Church became wedded to my mother's hypnotic power and I became their slavish robot. It has been a long journey to free myself of this arcane dominion. After being my mother's vassal I later became vassal to the Church and later still to that fashionable new religion known as psychoanalysis. In recent times I again was sucked into this invisible power and on revealing it to the perpetrator I again suffered hatred. I think each time I have freed myself from this witchcraft it has finally strengthened my inner soul but always at the price of inner desolation and misery.

---

[5]Tustin, Frances (1990). *The Protective Shell in Children and Adults* (pp. 21–22). London: Karnac.

I wrote at the beginning that I thought my mother was in an agony of loneliness. I further think that the hypnotic act is a desperate attempt to anoint with solace this unfair scourge of the soul.

It is a fact, touched on by Jung, that when one function is very highly developed it does so to compensate for another function that is undeveloped. So in the individual in whom the hypnotic function is highly developed there is an opposite function that is only embryonic. In one woman it was the inability to decide anything for herself. She was not even sure whether she was thirsty or hungry. The inner compass that might have told her was dormant, was not living, so she was a slave to the dictates of others and so her hypnotised victim became her comforter.

To determine who is the real me and who is the hypnotised one, the false one, has been a central problem in my life and one that I have only recently begun to solve. I believe that I shall struggle with it right up to the time of my death. I became a priest; I wore the outer clothing but inside I was not truly a priest. There was a priest-like person but not the priest whom people outside thought I was. I was deeply hurt when people abandoned me when I left the priesthood because I realised that it meant they had never known me—the inner me. It was not a surprise to close friends but only to those who looked up to me as some holy icon. It took me a long time to realise that the inner me, the real me was not visible to people but only to close friends. I have had moments of close friendship where the inner me reaches across the barrier to the real person in another and such a meeting has sustained me for long periods. Today I am known as a psychoanalyst but I am also free of that enslavement.

* * *

My mother was a marvellous correspondent and kept up with her numerous friends. She could write quite a long letter extraordinarily quickly and she did not need to be at her writing desk. She would pull out a piece of paper, put it on a book, and start writing. She might be waiting for a train, sitting in a café or in a doctor's waiting room. When I was not with her she wrote to me at least weekly and each letter was packed with news of what her friends were doing and news of all family members. When I met a friend of hers, whether in London, Paris, Madrid, Auckland, or Rio de Janeiro, they would always

56

tell me that they had had a letter from my mother a week or so before. When one of her numerous friends mentioned that a friend or acquaintance was coming to Portugal she immediately offered to have the visitor stay.

This cultural world into which my mother introduced me has had a lasting influence. I need the company of creative people. Surround me with lawyers, accountants, business people, merchant bankers, computer experts, and my soul shrivels. When I hear that someone has written a novel, loves painting, reads philosophy, or enjoys poetry something leaps up in my soul to meet them. For me creative enquiry is the very heart of living. When I hear people repeating well-worn phrases, echoing clichés, I dry up inside. I know I should proclaim what I think, disagree with what they are saying, but sometimes I do not know where to begin. When I became a priest I found myself in a presbytery eating breakfast, lunch, and dinner with a man, the parish priest, whose outlook on life, religion, and people was a compendium of tranquilising pieties. I agreed with not a thing he said and his outlook was the opposite of mine in almost every department of life but especially in the religious domain. Living in daily contact with him for two and a half years suffocated me; a boa constrictor could not have done it better. I later wrote a novel, *A Priest's Affair*, which charted this life-strangling experience.

* * *

Shortly after I was born my mother developed a tubercular knee. I have a picture of her with her left leg in plaster. Later in Canada she had an operation which made her knee stiff and she remained with a stiff leg for the rest of her life. She had been told that she would not be able to drive a car or play golf any more. She defied all these medical fortune-tellers. She drove, played golf and even tennis for some years. In all the years I knew her, I never heard her complain of this disability. Only shortly before her death did I realise how much pain she kept to herself.

It is a great pity that she did not share more of her inner troubles. I believe that early on she gave up making the attempt with my father. She once said to me that she came to realise that my father was intensely self-centred and I believe that she hated him and he in turn hated her. People who knew them both would, I suspect, be shocked to hear me say this and wish to banish me from their presence yet I believe I am right. There is a particular kind of self-centredness which exists, or can exist, between a man and woman who are married or who are partners. My father had never made that leap away and out from his family of origin that is necessary for a man to build an intimate relationship with his sexual partner. A woman also needs to make this leap. I am not sure whether my mother made it. My conjecture is that she made the attempt but that when she discovered that my father was not responsive to her she relapsed back into the communal spirit which was her natural home.

Self-centredness is not easy for others to detect when it exists between a man and a woman who are married or are sexual partners. The self-centredness has to be surmounted if the marriage is to flourish and be anything more than an institutional arrangement. My mother hated my father for not being open to her so that she could share her inner troubles and aspirations. My father in turn hated her for hating him. There are several outcomes in a situation like this: divorce, extramarital affairs, and retreat into drink, drugs, religion, or the latest fashion in entertainment. I shall come in a moment to the avenues that were taken by my mother and father but I believe that all these are unsatisfactory solutions because the central problem, the self-centredness, remains undisturbed. There is only one way out of this impasse. The hatred has to be communicated between the partners in such a way that it can open the way to love. I am not saying that this will necessarily "work" but it is the only hope.

I hate the person who challenges my own self-centredness. It requires me to step out of myself and into an alien and frightening world. And yet this is the foundation stone for love. This is why the great religions of the Western world have put faith as the bedrock of devotion. Faith is the word that describes that emotional step where I take a risk, dare to make a venture, and dance into the unknown. Cardinal Newman said this in his sermon *The Ventures of Faith*:

> ... in this consists the excellence and nobleness of *faith*; this is the very reason why *faith* is singled out from other graces, and honoured as the especial means of our justification, because its presence implies that we have a heart to make a venture.[6]

---

[6]Newman, J. H. (1875). *Parochial and Plain Sermons, Vol IV* (p. 296). London: Rivingtons.

Rather than hold onto myself I step out and risk myself, expose myself to another. This is what I have to do and my partner will hate me if I do not do it. The hatred for not doing it needs to be openly expressed between the partners. Having an affair, turning to drink, retreating to God is hatred towards the partner but it is a hatred through turning my back upon the other. It is a violent act but it is cowardly. Rather than face the other with my hatred I take the coward's way out. If do not "dream" the hatred it becomes an explosion damaging myself and those around me. When I breathe it into a "dream" it becomes "hatred redeemed". Love which arises from hatred redeemed is a force much more powerful than love from which this hatred has been disconnected.

Someone who was struggling to take such a step into the void said to me that he thought it took as much courage as is needed to climb Mount Everest, and he was right. Someone can have great physical courage but be a coward emotionally. When I take the emotional step I risk being mocked, misunderstood, demeaned. Rather than base my self-esteem upon treasures which I store away like a miser, instead I take the risk and share them with my sexual partner. I risk doing it and then not having it returned and being left in loneliness. It takes courage to move from hoarding to sharing. But what exactly are those things that I hoard but need to share?

Is it not those things of which I am ashamed? That I am frightened of a woman who speaks harshly to me? That I am angry when my own pleasure is thwarted? That I put my own self-gratification in front of the care of another? That I neglect true care of myself in favour of gratifying surface pleasure? In other words: a suicide of the heart. There are two dimensions in which this shame operates: when I actively do something that is suicidal to myself, and when I fail to do something which could heal me. There is suicide through action and suicide through inaction. The suicidal in this way permeates the innermost sinews of our being.

The absolute in our being calls us to allow its own reality to be the supreme motivating principle in our lives and we are ashamed to the extent that we do not do this, to the extent that we prevent it, to the extent that we do not allow it. An act of courage allows what Plotinus called a "higher immediacy" to operate. The theologian, Karl Rahner, said, "Im letzte der Sünde der Will ist nicht Gott sein Gott zu lassen."[7]

---

[7]"In the final analysis sin is the desire not to allow God to be God."

Sharing the suicidal is the remedy and therefore to be unsharing is death to the self. In later years as a psychoanalyst I have known patients who tell me many details of their intimate personal lives. Sometimes it has seemed that what they were telling me was trivial and of no consequence but in that I am mistaken. The person is sharing with me his or her life's drama. It is a paradox that sharing that of which we are ashamed is the remedy that heals the suicidal. This kind of sharing which is the basis of friendship becomes the bedrock of health. It is a deep linking of ourselves in a togetherness and is the opposite of suicide and isolation.

Sharing pumps the medicine of healing through the arteries of our being. Hatred known and shared becomes love. Hatred unshared is manifest in alcholism, moaning to others, or inner withdrawal. All these escape mechanisms damage both me and those around me.

I am now talking of quite violent stuff. A lot of hatred of a lesser intensity is expressed through gently poking fun at the partner through humour. However, with my parents the hatred was intense and it was not shared, so they persecuted each other severely and their three children were pulled into the vortex of this unacknowledged hatred which found its expression in the most distorted ways. My sister was severely damaged by it from an early age, and my brother, although the most normal and probably the sanest of us three children, solved the problem by repudiating my mother's artistic contribution to the marriage. I was torn in two. I loved my father and valued enormously his love of nature, his simplicity, and innate courtesy, but I also loved my mother and her interest in artists, writers, historians, musicians, and the many others that make up our sophisticated cultural world. She also had a courage not shared by him. When she was dying I asked how she felt about it. She told me she was ready to face death. I told her that I knew she would face her coming death with courage and she replied firmly, "I will." To integrate these two perspectives that came from my father and mother and bring them into harmony within myself has been a hard task. When I am with people of my father's outlook I yearn for artists and writers and when I am with the latter and hear some of the alienated preciousness that seems so endemic to much of their discourse I long for my father's ingenuous simplicity and love of the earth. But in a deeper way I have always had enormous respect for courage. It is a rare gift. I have only the smallest grain of it myself but that grain is something I greatly treasure.

But of this I am sure: my mother and father hated each other and sabotaged each other to a horrifying degree. As a child when my mother attacked my father I felt terribly sorry for him, but also when he shut out my mother's pitying clamour I felt for her and I was torn between these powerful currents. The moralist and the "friend of sinners" clashed cruelly into one another. My mother suffered from severe depression and I regret that I was not more sympathetic towards her. She felt suicidal quite frequently. There was a pier jutting out into the sea near our house in Oporto and in later years she said to me quite frequently, "I feel like going out on the Molhe Pier and throwing myself into the sea." When a friend, Wulstan Weld-Forester, committed suicide by drinking a bottle of whisky and then swimming out to sea in north Africa my mother said, "What a wonderful way to go. I think I would like to do that."

There is another way of looking upon this matter. What is the basis upon which people attach themselves to one another? Crudely speaking, there are two: an outer clam-like clinging or inner faith-and-love. In the latter there is what Kierkegaard referred to as a "higher immediacy" that goes out from the inner to embrace the partner in the totality of being. This has never, I believe, been better expressed than by Viktor Frankl who describes his experience in the concentration camp under Hitler's tyranny in the following passage:

> That brought thoughts of my own wife to mind. And as we stumbled on for miles, slipping on icy spots, supporting each other time and again, dragging one another up and onward, nothing was said, but we both knew: each of us was thinking of his wife. Occasionally I looked at the sky, where the stars were fading and the pink light of the morning was beginning to spread behind a dark bank of clouds. But my mind clung to my wife's image, imagining it with an uncanny acuteness. I heard her answering me, saw her smile, her frank encouraging look. Real or not, her look was then more luminous than the sun which was beginning to rise.
>
> A thought transfixed me: for the first time in my life I saw the truth as it is set into song by so many poets, proclaimed as the final wisdom by so many thinkers. The truth—that love is the ultimate and the highest goal to which man can aspire. Then I grasped the meaning of the greatest secret that human poetry and human thought and belief have to impart: *The salvation of man is through*

love and in love. I understood how a man who has nothing left in this world still may know bliss, be it only for a brief moment, in the contemplation of his beloved. In a position of utter desolation, when man cannot express himself in positive action, when his only achievement may consist in enduring his sufferings in the right way—an honourable way—in such a position man can, through loving contemplation of the image he carries of his beloved, achieve fulfilment. For the first time in my life I was able to understand the meaning of the words, "The angels are lost in perpetual contemplation of an infinite glory."...

My mind still clung to the image of my wife. A thought crossed my mind: I didn't even know if she were still alive. I knew only one thing—which I have learned well by now: Love goes very far beyond the physical person of the beloved. It finds its deepest meaning in his spiritual being, his inner self. Whether or not he is actually present, whether or not he is still alive at all, ceases somehow to be of importance.

I did not know whether my wife was alive, and I had no means of finding out (during all my prison life there was no outgoing or incoming mail); but at that moment it ceased to matter. There was no need for me to know; nothing could touch the strength of my love, my thoughts, and the image of my beloved. Had I known then that my wife was dead, I think I would still have given myself, undisturbed by that knowledge, to the contemplation of her image, and that my mental conversation with her would have been just as vivid and just as satisfying. "Set me like a seal upon thy heart, love is as strong as death."[8]

So this is the inner "faith of the heart" through which one human being bonds inwardly to another. Then there is another which is through clam-like clinging.

In clam-like clinging there is attachment to the other but through an external sensuous clasping onto the other. In this kind of attachment there is no apprehension of the other as other. The personhood of the other is totally eliminated. When this kind of attachment is predominant a man can be married for fifty years but never know his wife

---

[8]Frankl, Viktor E. (1977). *Man's Search for Meaning* (pp. 36–38). London: Hodder and Stoughton.

62

(and vice versa). Bernard Shaw's wife, Charlotte, had a close friendship with Lawrence of Arabia and they corresponded and kept each other's letters. When Lawrence was killed on his motorbike in 1935 all Charlotte's letters were returned to her by his executors. She had then both his letters to her and hers to him in her possession. When she died the correspondence fell into the hands of Bernard Shaw who read the correspondence. He said that although he had been married to his wife for forty years he had never known her. He only came to know her when he read this correspondence after she had died. It is many years since I read first a biography of Charlotte and also of Bernard but I imagine that their mode of attachment was of this clinging sensuous kind. A friendship, even though it be a sexual affair, is I believe healthy if it articulates the inner union of souls. There is nothing to guarantee that it is in a marriage that this takes place. A moral philosophy that places this inner joining of hearts as the central value needs to replace a slavish devotion to the institutional supremacy accorded to the couple in wedlock.

I am certain that my father clung in a desperate way to my mother and she could not bear it. I think this kind of clinging is frequently stronger in twins. When clinging is of this kind then separations are a torment. It is, I am sure, significant that my father fell grievously ill within days of his wife and children leaving Portugal for Canada in 1940. My mother could not abide my father's clinging to her in this clam-like way. When she wanted to throw herself off the Molhe Pier into the foaming sea beneath I feel sure it was partly to get away from his addictive dependence which was so endorsed by the Catholicism, of which she was a part, that it smothered her like a a moth in a killing-bottle. But then a problem arises which I think goes something like this. My mother hates the clinging so leaves my father, goes to England, goes travelling with Clare Waters in North Africa, goes on bullfighting trips to Spain, goes to Lisbon to open a teashop in Cascais, and the more she does the more he hates her. It drives him ever more fixedly into superstitious religious rituals and he frustrates my mother by not letting her have enough money to spend … and the cycle goes round and round.

My mother hates this clinging and believes it is all in my father and that she is free of it, but this is not true because she clings to her children. My brother, James, resisted this clinging to him from my mother but my sister, Jill, and myself were caught in it. Probably my sister was caught in it more than myself but I would not be sure of this. So ultimately my mother hates this clinging because it suffocates her capacity for love. It would take a high level of psychological reflection to be able to realise that the hatred is not actually for the individuality of the other but rather for the mode of attachment which is so strangling. I say a "high level of psychological reflection" because I have been in the psychological world for forty years but have come across very few practitioners who view matters from this perspective. The majority "believe" the statements of the patient about the spouse, not realising that it is in this mode of attachment that the problem lies. So when my mother said to me that my father was self-centred it was accurate because this mode of attachment is of its nature centred on the self and not on the other, but what she did not realise was that she carried the same disease. The hatred of each other, then, is really a hatred of this clinging form of attachment which is common to both of them.

Of course life is never as simple as psychologists like to make it sound: Viktor Frankl was married from heart to heart whereas my parents clung to each other surface to surface. I suspect that when Frankl was in the concentration camp the clinging, as I am sure there is always some, diminished and the "faith of the heart" grew and so the latter was in a purer culture than is usually found. I do not think the "faith of the heart" was absent in my parents' marriage but it was suffocated under this appalling clam-like clinging so it never got a chance to breathe. My own emotional life has been aimed at trying to find this "faith of the heart" underneath all the clinging. When I later left the Church it was partly, I believe, an attempt to detach myself from this clinging (to the Church) and find the "faith of the heart" inside myself. Meister Eckhart was getting at this when he wrote in "On Detachment":

> The authorities also praise humility above many other virtues. But I praise detachment above all humility, and that is because, although there may be humility without detachment, there cannot be perfect detachment without humility, because perfect humility proceeds from annihilation of self. Now detachment approaches so closely to nothingness that there can be nothing between perfect detachment and nothingness. Therefore perfect detachment cannot exist without humility. Now two virtues are always better than one. The second reason why I praise detachment above humility is that perfect humility is always abasing itself below all created things, and in this abasement man goes out of himself toward created things,

but detachment remains within itself. Now there can never be any going out of self so excellent that remaining within self is not itself much more excellent. The prophet David said of this: "All the glory of the king's daughter is from her inwardness." Perfect detachment has no looking up to, no abasement, not beneath any created thing or above it; it wishes to be neither beneath nor above, it wants to exist by itself, not giving joy or sorrow to anyone, not wanting equality or inequality with any created thing, not wishing for this or that. All that it wants is to be. (pp. 286–287)[9]

* * *

One extremely important person came into the life of us three children: Joan Smith. She came to our home in Oporto when I was aged two and a half to be our governess. She was nineteen at the time and, as she had already been in Brazil, she could speak Portuguese as well as French, Danish, and English. She was a gentle and loving woman and she loved all of us three children. She travelled with us to Canada and when my mother went into hospital for a couple of months to have the operation on her knee Joan looked after us. I loved her dearly and howled and cried when parted from her at the end of our stay in Canada. It was just before my sixth birthday and she stayed behind in Montreal to complete her studies at McGill and we left by boat to return to Portugal. She was like a surrogate parent to all of us and right down the years until her death in 2004, we lived in her loving arms. I saw her six months before she died in a retirement home in St Louis. I stayed in the home for two days and saw her several times a day. She came twice to Australia and spent some weeks with us on each occasion. She loved our two boys and I think she had a special affection for me. On that last occasion when I saw her in St Louis I had long intimate conversations with her which I recorded thus:

Conversations with Joan Smith from 23rd–25th April 2003

I said to her that it might be the last time that I would see her. She did not say much at that moment when I said that so I was not sure whether she

[9]Eckhart, Meister. *The Essential Sermons, Commentaries, Treatises and Defense.* Mahwah, NJ: Paulist Press, 1981.

had taken it in. We went on and spoke about some other things and then about ten minutes later she said,

> "I feel sadness but also a great joy that you said it might be the last time we see each other."

I knew what she meant—that the parting was sad but that it was a joy to her that I had voiced it. This was confirmed when she went on to speak about how few people could talk about death. She remembered that when my wife drove her to the airport she had said she did not like long goodbyes but that Joan had said she liked to "spread it out". (There was a conference I had to go to.)

She spoke of the difficulty of being in a community—how she would be at a table of twelve people and the conversation was trivial. I said that what was needed was receptivity and she said it was the quality of receptivity which made community possible. (I realised that in terms of this definition there was not a community for her at Nazareth Living Centre.) She spoke of the lack of privacy.

She said how important freedom was but that she thought some more comprehensive term than freedom was necessary. She spoke of the struggle to integrate things—to make a oneness of her life. The struggle to understand and that freedom was a fruit of this struggle and not to be sought as a goal. (I was very impressed by this.)

She spoke of regrets. I asked her if she was happy about the Joan Smith Scholarship. She said she was but that it soon faded and that internal understanding was greater than any external reward. She spoke a lot about how she was trying to bring memories together. One surprising memory was a photograph of James with a fishing rod and this reminded her of my father taking her fishing and beckoning her and helping her across a stream. (I think in a way she was in love with my father and perhaps he with her—I remember he had a photograph of Joan Smith on his dressing table in his dressing room for many years. Also Joan was always somewhat antagonistic to my mother.)

She said she used to look people straight in the eye but she could not do this any more. Her eyes were weeping instead—somehow this got in the way of being able to look another in the eye. (It could be that her eyes, rather than looking at the other were weeping for not having been herself— her desire to integrate things seemed so paramount for her.)

She asked me if I had met any people I had not seen for a long time and that meeting them again had brought together memories for me and for the

66

other. I started to think and she mentioned Anthony Cobb and his skin.
I said that he had been treated unmercifully at school and that the group
had been very cruel to him. She said groups did not like to think that they,
members of the group, might be damaged. (I felt quite tearful when she
said this.)

She said she was under the impression that I had been able to speak
about some personal things to friends—that I had been able to share
personal things with them. I said that it was so. (I was impressed by her
intuitive knowledge of things.) This was confirmed shortly after when
I was telling her about my lecture in San Francisco on Healing the Mind
and how I had mentioned that I had been in a dark place and how this
personal bit was responsible, I thought, for the enthusiastic reception
which the paper had had. She said that as I was speaking she felt that
I was hovering on revealing something but then veered away. As this was
true I thought again how much she was directly in touch with my own
internal emotional movements.

She spoke a lot about coming to know an unknown third or unknown
part of one. (I wonder if it was this intuitive part?)

I refer again to Joan in the next chapter.

Another extremely important figure in my life was my grandfather, my mother's father. When my mother left the Argentine and came to Europe and married my father, "Old O'C" as we called him stayed in the Argentine tending his *mate* tea plantation in Missiones. In about 1949 when I was twelve he retired and returned to Europe where he and his wife rented a house at the end of our street and so I saw a lot of him. He took a particular interest in me. He taught me to play golf and I used to go with him to Espinho, south of Oporto, and play on the golf course there. He had been a scratch player as a young man in Australia. He was more masculine than my father and, unlike my father, had had to forge his way in the world. He had been an agricultural expert and he had specialist knowledge of irrigation but also had considerable knowledge of entomology and biochemistry. For instance, he asked my father for a chemical analysis of port which my father got for him from the Casa do Douro. He was very interested to discover that port had fluorine in it and did numerous tests to prove his hypothesis that it would be a good antidote to rheumatism. He believed that rheumatism derived from ailments in the gut and from bad teeth and that fluorine was medicinal for both of these. This was before fluorine was being put into water

67

and toothpaste for the sake of the teeth. The Symingtons gently mocked him, however, saying that it was well known that port caused gout. He challenged that traditional view saying he believed that it was not port that caused it but rather the rich foods and lifestyle that was associated with drinking port. I do not know whether he was right but it upset me that my father derided him and would not at least give serious attention to what he was saying. My grandfather said cynically once that if they were paying him a handsome fee for his advice they would then listen to him. It was the same with some of the recommendations he made for irrigating the quinta in the Douro more scientifically. He also examined the citrus trees on the quinta and pointed out various blights which he recommended be sprayed but he was ignored.

He used to tell me about his life in Australia and the Argentine. He was a man of integrity as my father was but he was more outgoing than my father. He had a great interest in the world of politics and he used to write little political plays. He also wrote some poetry. His own marriage had been unhappy but, unlike my mother and father, its failure was more out in the open. For about twenty-five years while he was in the Argentine, his wife lived in London. They only joined up and lived in the same house when he came to Portugal to retire but, after a few years, she returned again to London and he stayed in Oporto. She did not like living in a Latin country. I am not sure what went wrong between them or why they were incompatible but they both knew it and did not hide it from the world. When he died my grandmother said, "I am sad because it makes me think of our early days together," so I imagine the early years of marriage were happy and then things went bad, but grandpa was not an embittered man. He had a philosophical view of life. Also his attitude to the Church was quite different from my father's. He was a devout Catholic but scorned all the superstitions that were prized by my father. He said to me once that the devotion of the nine first Fridays was just the Church's way of encouraging people to come to Church—that in no way could it guarantee a happy death. This was an attitude so different from that of my father. I was extremely fond of him and was very sad when he died at the age of ninety during my first year at St Edmund's.

I think I have given some idea of the cradle in which I was born and reared. Now I must put the spotlight upon ME.

CHAPTER THREE

School and after school

I knew there was something wrong with me. I lived in an innocent world. I was walking along the beach one day and I said to myself: I'll put all my trust in God. Everything else had fallen away. It was a last resort. I was about fifteen at the time. From that time on I was haunted by this Hound of Heaven which was going to demand my life of me. I was terrified of it and it tortured me.

I was three when my mother, together with Jill, James, and Joan Smith, emigrated to Canada. My father was going to join up. In 1940, after the fall of France, it was thought that the Germans would invade Iberia and the British embassy in Lisbon advised English subjects to migrate to Canada or South Africa. I remember well my father coming and giving me a little string bag full of small model farm animals— his gift to me before a long parting. Parting has always been a trauma for me and even as I write this I am tearful. We flew to America from Lisbon in the *Dixie Clipper*[1] and I remember walking on the wide wooden gangway which took us from the shore of the Tagus into the wide open mouth of the seaplane. I remember a day we spent in the

---

[1]This was the same Boeing seaplane in which President Roosevelt flew to North Africa in 1943 for his historic meeting with Churchill in Casablanca.

Azores and picking up a piece of pumice stone on the beach and then landing at Bermuda. The landing at the Azores had been rough and bumpy but in Bermuda there was just a small spray of water on the windows and I remember my mother saying, "Oh, that was a gentle landing." A fair-haired girl called Alison Moreira was on the plane also and I can remember standing at one of the plane windows with her looking upon clouds that were down below us. Soon after arriving in Canada we had news that my father was seriously ill and could not go to England to join up.

* * *

On the mantelpiece in Canada was a photograph of my father sitting up in bed reading the newspaper. I have such a clear memory of this that his absence must have been emotionally very significant to me. He became my first love and I wonder also whether I did not come to love Joan Smith better at this time than my mother. I partly say this to try to make sense of a game that I used to play with a little girl of my age called Sally Wall. I am not sure quite what we called it but the end result was that she jumped and sat upon me; it was something which I invited and enjoyed and, even at that early age, had a sexual colouring. What to make of it? Was it a ritualized punishment for discarding my mother in favour of my father and Joan Smith? Joan was deeply fond of my father but was wary of my mother. As a sensitive child I might have sensed this, so that my fondness for Joan may also have been a vicarious link to my father and a desertion of my mother. Whatever that ritualised game symbolised, something of its inner character has remained with me all my life with a strong tendency to be "sat upon" by a woman, including Mother Church. Was it my own mother's vengeance against a filial betrayal? It is so deep and such a strong current in my life that I do not think I can account for it entirely through this turning to my father and Joan and forsaking of my mother. I suspect that there was a violent repudiation of her much earlier—that there was some abandonment of me as a newborn and that I reacted with a violent withdrawal from my mother and attachment to my father and Joan Smith in compensation. There is something submissive and passive about allowing, and even inviting, Sally to jump and sit on me and this aspect of it could represent the passive jelly-like state, like the condition of an army platoon all flattened by an enemy bomb. Also many years later I remember going

70

into that inert state of surrender on arrival at St Edmund's—an abdication of all responsibility and with happiness yielding myself to the authority of Mother Church.

As separation is so traumatic for me I believe that this parting from my father was, like a palimpsest, covering a hurt that might have occurred before birth. I believe that birth itself, being wrenched from my mother's womb, was a severe trauma. This would suggest to me that even as a foetus I was clinging. When my mother was pregnant with me she already had her tubercular knee; perhaps she did not want this new life in her womb. I certainly believe that a mother's emotional attitudes are transmitted to the foetus through the placental barrier. If this were so it would have led me to cling and perhaps interpret my discharge down the birth canal as a shocking rejection. In later life as a psychoanalyst I came to realise what a trauma the ending of a treatment relationship could be, and whether the pain of it was liberating or strangling depended upon whether the patient believed that I wanted to rid myself of her or wanted to launch her into a happier life. I am sure that the separation from my father was traumatic because I had already been wounded by an earlier experience.

I also think that if some particular area of emotional experience grips someone's attention it is often because it is of personal significance. When many years later I started to treat with psychotherapy the mentally handicapped I was very attracted to the view that the origins of such deficiency was due to some accident in the womb. This was the theory put forward by that very insightful and humane psychoanalyst Pierce Clark in his book *The Nature and Treatment of Amentia*.[2] I remember also becoming very upset when, at the time of our second son's birth, I read a book on the physiology of birth as if that wrenching from my mother's womb was an appalling calamity.

There is another element in my relations with my mother that, for me, confirm this belief that I had done something which constituted a betrayal for her. My mother was one of those people who had extreme sensitivity to the minutest change of emotional colouring in another. I suspect that in particular she noted the slightest rejection of her. She would sometimes look at me with the hooded darkened eyes of a judge.

---

[2]Pierce Clark, L. (1933). *The Nature and Treatment of Amentia*. Baltimore, MD: William Wood.

"I have not forgotten that deep betrayal, darling Neville ..." those eyes seemed to say.

I believe that some powerful maternal discharging force blanked out the person called Neville. But there was a little free remnant left, determined to fight for its place within my persona and to become its master.

* * *

After two and a half years we returned from Canada to Portugal on the *Serpa Pinto*, a boat which brought us safely back across the Atlantic to Lisbon in 1943. On its subsequent trip across the Atlantic the boat was stopped by a German submarine and the English and American passengers were taken off and sent to a prison in Germany. It was a dangerous journey to make across the Atlantic in the middle of the war. There was something reckless in my mother; she was fed up of being in Canada and wanted to return to Portugal and brushed aside all caution. In this respect I have been like her most of my life and am impatient with caution and self-protection. I have always tended to despise people who are protective of their reputation among their fellows.

There was the sad parting from Joan Smith, dear Muffety, as I called her. I howled on the train when she kissed me goodbye and I can still remember it. It was just before my sixth birthday. I next saw her briefly when I was fourteen but she was an enormously important figure for us three children and remained so all her long life. It was her sensitive lovingness that impressed into our souls a love of her. The drama of my entering the priesthood and then leaving it brought our two souls together. She helped me even in her last years and she would not let an incorrect statement pass. I spent a day with her in San Francisco in 1995 and I said, "Maybe it's arrogant of me ..." "Don't make those self-disparaging remarks, Neville. I love you and if you are being arrogant I will tell you." In this respect she was a true friend.

I had my sixth birthday on the boat in the middle of the Atlantic. Finally the ship docked in Lisbon. I can remember walking down the gangplank behind my mother and seeing my mother and father hugging each other as she reached the quay. That scene also still makes me tearful. Back in Oporto we stayed initially for some months with Uncle Maurice and Aunty Eileen in their well groomed house in the Boavista. I always had an affection for Uncle Maurice and I think its origin may have been in his kindness and warmth to us three children when we were staying in his home.

I was the baby of the family and whereas my brother and sister went to boarding school at Carcavelos outside Lisbon I went to the Oporto British School. From the age of seven I used to ride there on my bicycle. I was taught in a class of about twenty-five by the devoted and caring Mrs Cassells. I rode home for lunch and then back again after lunch. At lunch I used to sit with my mother at the little table in the nursery where we also used to have breakfast. Often her head was slumped into cupped hands. She must have been very depressed. I do not know the reason for it but I think, soon after our return from Canada, some disappointment must have set in. I believe it was because she was beginning to realise that her relationship with my father was empty. When we went to Canada she had been married to him for eight years and it was eleven years when we returned. She struggled all her life against depression. When she married my father in 1932 and came to live in Oporto it was a place of parties, wine, fun, and remarkable characters. The port trade was doing well and people were prosperous. Then came the war and after it the port trade slumped. The Oporto my mother returned to was a different place. My father had been severely ill and he was defeatist about the state of the trade. She had had a major operation on her knee which handicapped her for the rest of her life. They both needed more than wine and sparkle to carry them through these lean years. I suspect that my mother started to attack him for not facing difficulties with greater confidence and he withdrew hurt into himself, and she saw him as self-centred and without care for her. The colour had gone out of life for her and as an inner emptiness caught up with her she became depressed. I still can feel the atmosphere of gloom when I was a little boy sitting with her at the round green wooden luncheon table in the nursery. Carmen would come in and serve us but most of the time we were on our own. The maids would eat lunch next door at the kitchen table; the discussion at the servants' table was robust and animated that contrasted with my mother's gloom.

At a later time I cascaded into the most fearful depression and I wonder whether I did not ingest my mother's depression? A colleague from Israel, Yolanda Gampel, speaks of a radioactivity that passes into one person from another. I think it likely that I took into myself my mother's gloom. Yet this is shorthand for something more complex. A mother

73

has to be able to give to her baby from within. Love and spontaneous affection are required from within. If that is lacking there is within a great emptiness and futility. *This* depression (not all depression) was about this emptiness. Once there was not that inner spontaneous movement of the spirit then I was ruled instead by a tyrant God whose dictates I had to obey because I did not have any other. I think that we three children all lacked this inner substance. The disasters in the lives of my sister and myself I believe testify to it while my brother compensated in a different way, perhaps through acquiring great wealth.

I turned to my father during these years. I longed for his return from the office in the afternoon and Wednesday was a special day when he did not go back to the office after lunching at the Factory House. In summer I would go swimming with him but I did so many things with him. We would go out in search of tree frogs—those beautiful china green little frogs which sat on the leaves of a bramble bush by wetlands. My father was an acute observer and he taught me to look for them. We would catch two or three and put them into a big bowl covered with gauze. We put moss at the bottom of the bowl and then some bramble twigs so that the frogs could climb up and down. Then we would catch flies alive and put them into the bowl for the frogs to eat. It was great fun watching the tree frog looking pointedly at a fly and then leap, spurting out its tongue whereupon the luckless fly could be seen descending down its gullet. My father also taught me to catch flies alive and I can still do it to this day. Every day we would feed the tree frogs but when autumn came and flies became scarce we put the frogs back into the wild from where we had caught them. Each spring though my father and I would go out and catch a new clutch of tree frogs. But even when we had caught the tree frogs my father and I would always scan bramble bushes keenly to see if we could see any more. In a friendly way we competed with each other and would see who could spy most. To this day when I pass a bramble bush near to water in Portugal I scrutinizes it, hoping to see a tree frog, and I am disappointed when my search is unsuccessful.

Then we would go out in search of butterflies. We would either go armed with a butterfly net each and a killing-bottle or we would look for caterpillars. When we found a caterpillar we would bring it back together with leaves of the bush that it was eating and put it with its food into a special breeding box. We would have to put in fresh leaves every couple of days until it transformed itself into a chrysalis. Then we would watch the chrysalis carefully each day and if we were lucky would be present when the new creature broke out of its casing and crawled out with moist folded wings and then see its beautiful wings spread out to its full extent. I can still remember vividly a red admiral breaking out of its prison cell and slowly stretching its wet appendages and pumping air down them until a pair of beautiful wings shone in the light. I remember being so happy as I saw it leave the twig on which it sat and took flight in our garden. This one was allowed to go because we had a specimen in our collection, but if it was a butterfly we did not have we put it into the killing-bottle and when it was dead we would set it; when it was ready, after about three weeks, we put it proudly into our collection. Such a butterfly would, of course, be a perfect specimen.

We collected not only butterflies but also moths. Most of the moths arrived in our collection hatched from cocoons—that transforming super-egg that changed the caterpillar into the moth. Nearly all moths surround their chrysalis with a cocoon and usually it took much longer for the moth to come out. Most butterflies emerged from their pupae within three weeks but with moths it could be several months. We also used to catch moths by a light at night, but not all moths are attracted to light so we would also paint the trunks of trees in the garden with "hell's brew"—a mixture of beer and honey. Then we would at various times in the night come and examine the tree: we caught several moths through this method.

One consequence of having collected butterflies and moths lives permanently with me. I would never kill a butterfly or moth inconsequentially. Sometimes I see a moth flying around in someone's house and the owner tries to destroy it. This is a crime to me. My father and I both loved butterflies and moths and always treated them with love and respect. The few that we killed for the collection cemented into our minds for life a love of all their living kin. Even a clothes moth holds my respect and I would not dream of killing one.

My father, though, was interested in everything that crept, crawled, swam or flew and I inherited this from him. Lizards, snakes, bats, grasshoppers, fish, or birds always riveted our attention. Both my father and I had marvellous eyesight and we could detect a flock of birds, for instance, at a great distance and usually, from their flight, knew what they were. My father was not good, though, at recognising birdsong and this is the same for me. I am not sure why he was deficient in this regard but it may have been connected with the fact that he was not at all musical. There were many Symingtons in Oporto and none of them was musical. I am not sure why this was but it was also true of me. As I grew up I became passionately interested in philosophy, psychology, history, literature, and art, but music has always been a lacuna. I regret it as I know that I am deprived thereby of a great richness. Had I been educated in it as I was in knowing about the natural world I feel sure that today I would love music and be able to recognise its tonal differences. Although I had no education in art yet I have been able to understand it and appreciate it and I suspect this may originate from the keen development of my visual sense. My father's inability to identify birdsong probably lay in tone deafness. It may be that in each of the senses some awakening is needed and that in the field of musical sound that never happened. I think this awakening is probably stimulated through the passion of another. My father's passion for nature awakened a keen enthusiasm in me in which the visual was always central. Had I had, in my early years, a mentor with a similar passion for music I believe that I would love it today. This tone deafness had an emotional correlate. He was not sensitive to emotional atmosphere and would sometimes speak or say something that could shatter. At a funeral of a young man who was tragically killed in a car accident he approached some people and cheerily asked how they were. I think this was a source of great disharmony between him and my mother.

My mother was very much in the background when my father and I were engaged in our joint enthusiasm for the rich fauna around us. She did not interfere with us or discourage us but she was not interested in what we were doing. She was probably lonely and starved of her own natural interests and inclinations. My mother's field of interest was the human world; my father's was in the animate non-human world. The way things have worked out, my own professional career has taken me more into my mother's domain, yet something of my father's interest has contributed to my understanding of the human world. I am intrigued with the way humans have emerged from primates and have studied consistently but not deeply enough the researches into the first evidence of mankind as studied by Abbé Breuil, the Leakey family, Stephen Mithen, and others. I also studied with great interest the researches into the behaviour of chimpanzees and gorillas. I read with fascination Jane Goodall's two books on chimpanzees[3] and also the book on mountain gorillas by Dian Fossey.[4] The way human beings have evolved from the animal world and my intense preoccupation with this is, I am sure, an inheritance from my father. It is a link also between my mother and father—the missing link. My own emotional difficulties forced me to take an interest in the currents that drive human beings hither and thither over the vast canvas of the world's endeavours.

* * *

So there I was the baby of the family at the little school in Oporto while big brother and sister were now at school in England. I wanted to be treated like a big boy too. I did not like being the baby and apparently I said to my father one day: "I'll do no more study until you send me to school in England," so he decided that I should go to school in England too. My brother was already in the Junior House at Ampleforth in Yorkshire but I was too young for that so I was sent to St Martin's School at Nawton in Yorkshire. This was a little prep school founded a half-dozen years earlier by one of the masters from Ampleforth, Paul Blackden.

I started there after Easter at the age of eleven in 1948. I stood with doleful eyes as my parents departed down the drive and watched their car until it was out of sight. Then I turned back, a panic-stricken child, into the cold prison I had requested for myself.

That I was in a state of terror as a child and remained so into late adulthood was something I only came to realise when I started learning to fly forty years later. Then I was fully aware that I was in such a state. The flimsy plane being blown hither and thither like a piece of paper in the sky terrified me but I knew that this was the catalyst that blew the panic onto the surface of consciousness. The light plane I learned to fly in, a Tampico, was a robust little machine and the idea that it was flimsy was a projection of my own frail and turbulent centre onto this machine in which I was enclosed. Awareness dawned that I had been in a state of terror all my life. I was a very capable social performer on the outside while being in frozen panic within. There has always been something

---

[3]GOODALL, Jane (1971). *In the Shadow of Man*. London: Collins.
GOODALL, Jane (1990). *Through a Window*. London: Weidenfeld & Nicolson.
[4]FOSSEY, Dian (1983). *Gorillas in the Mist*. London: Hodder & Stoughton.

inviting me to struggle against it. Otherwise why would I have learned to do something which I found so frightening?

This panic led me into a state of obedient surrender to ... what? What was it that led me to go to communion when I had eaten chocolate so as not to disappoint my father? What paralysed my voice so that I was unable to confess it to the priest for four years? What was it that held the person I am inside a prisoner? A savage God who hypnotised me.

I think an angle on this terror is expressed lucidly by Teilhard de Chardin:

> For the first time in my life perhaps (although I am supposed to meditate every day), I took the lamp and, leaving the zone of every-day occupations and relationships where everything seems clear, I went down into my inmost self, to the deep abyss whence I feel dimly that my power of action emanates. But as I moved further and further away from the conventional certainties by which social life is superficially illuminated, I became aware that I was losing contact with myself. At each step of the descent a new person was disclosed within me of whose name I was no longer sure, and who no longer obeyed me. And when I had to stop my exploration because the path faded from beneath my steps, I found a bottom-less abyss at my feet, and out of it came—arising I know not from where—the current which I dare to call **my** life.[5]

I think part of the terror is of the name that no longer obeyed him. It is my life but it is not my own.

The moment of birth for the novice pilot is when he first goes solo. Then the fate of the plane is entirely in his hands. When my time came, the reality struck me .... There is no one I can turn to. I have to fly this machine with me in it myself. I cannot stop, as in a car, and look at a map and take a breather; I have to keep flying it. It is like death—something that I have to go into on my own, myself. It is the moment when I meet myself. Only when it is safely back on the ground can I turn to someone and ask advice. When solo I am on my own and responsible for my own life. I am responsible for looking after my life. Why is this so terrifying?

---

[5]Teilhard de Chardin, P. (1960). *Le Milieu Divin* (pp. 54–55). London: Collins.

To answer this question it is necessary to examine what my life is. I share life with all members of the human race, with the whole animal kingdom, and with the plant kingdom too, yet the life in me is differently organised to the life in anyone else. I think my life was a disorganised mess. A bomb has gone off and there the house is in bits and pieces all over the place. My job is to take all the bits and rebuild them into a coherent whole. Perhaps a better image is of myself as a doctor in the emergency ward of a hospital and someone is brought in with an eye hanging out, gut and blood oozing out of the stomach, and a bone from one of the legs poking through the flesh. I have to start to repair it yet my whole being revolts against this disgusting apparition. Then there is the resentment—why should *I* have to do this? I can see my colleague treating a healthy looking fellow who just has a touch of bronchitis. Why was I dealt *this* card? Yet this is me; this is the way life in me is. That moment when I decided "I want to live" I began not to be in revolt against myself, not to be disgusted by this monstrous apparition but let the doctor in me come to the fore. I love that sentence in *The Summing Up* by Somerset Maugham where he speaks of taking the utmost part he could in "this fantastic affair of being a man".[6] I might not have been but I am. A few rare authors have been gripped by this marvel. This is the marvel that surpasses all marvels. The other person who was entranced by this wonder in modern times was G. K. Chesterton: "At the back of our brains, so to speak, there was a forgotten blaze or burst of astonishment at our own existence."[7]

This I believe is the vision of the mystic. The mystic who wrote *The Epistle of Privy Counsel* puts it with succinct precision: "… think on the simplest manner, but by some man the wisest, not what thyself is, but that thyself is."[8]

So, partly out of my own stupidity, here I was in this strange new environment alienated by a long distance from my parents. My mother was a very faithful correspondent and wrote to me every week and

---

[6]Maugham, W. S. (1938). *The Summing Up* (p. 62). London: Pan, 1976.
[7]Chesterton, G. K. (1938). *Autobiography* (p. 94). London: Hutchinson.
[8]McCann, Justin (Ed.) (1952). *The Cloud of Unknowing and Other Treatises by a 14th Century English Mystic* (p. 105). London: Burns Oates.

I remember the joy with which I would grab hold of the envelope with the familiar sloping hand. I realised for the first time her love for me in those letters which were always packed with news of my father, Uncle John, all our numerous cousins, and the many friends who flowed in and out of our lives. Lonely and bereft on the Yorkshire moors in an alien manor house I treasured my mother's fidelity so manifest in these letters. She knew the state of her bereft child and her love for me stimulated my own love for her. I am sure this love for her stayed inside me all my life. Today when I conjure up her smiling face I know I am a loved human being. I think this love that developed between us led me to believe that in truth she was married to me. I think this was one reason why I was so unsettled when her infidelity was thrust before my face. My father loved me but in a different way. My mother, through some Celtic intuition, saw into the inner state of things. She knew her child was ill, was in panic. She did not know what to do about it but it was a comfort to me that she knew and I knew that she knew. She knew I was not happy. She knew I had not found the place where I needed to be. Shortly before her death she turned to me with a sad twinkle in her eye and asked, "Are you settled now?" I said "Yes" but I think she probably knew, as I did, that it was not true.

I think the unhealthy side of this was that she "joined" rather than ministered. As I came to know later she was also in a very messy state within and I think she gripped hold of this youngest child of hers and held him in an embrace with which to give herself some comfort and solace. I have already explained how I believe she hypnotised me to keep me in her womb. I will repeat again those words of Frances Tustin: "Without being aware of it, the mother seems to have resorted to the baby inside her body for company and solace."[9]

She could have done something but she, like so many mothers, was caught in a patriarchal system against which she protested but in the face of which she was powerless. I was, in this upper middle class borstal, a lost soul and in her letters to me she used to make suggestions. I remember one of them was that I should go to a school in Spain and train to become a bull manager. She had at this time become a bullfighting *aficionada* and was dragging me into this newfound craze of

---

[9]Tustin, Frances (1990). *The Protective Shell in Children and Adults* (pp. 21–22). London: Karnac.

80

hers, but there was a mixture here of some understanding of my plight together with a craziness of hers. The idea of me being in a school closer to home chimed with my inner yearning for the warmth and comfort of Portugal but it became hitched into this Spanish bullfighting passion of hers.

But what of these borstals into which are poured the youth of the English upper middle classes? What is wrong with them? I think they may be alright for well-adjusted boys but for someone who was disturbed and weird like me, they are a disaster. When I think now of what was wrong with them I centre my thoughts on personal space. How could I collect butterflies at St Martin's and later at Ampleforth? What cubbyhole did I have where I could have set them and what place did I have where I could put them? And had I engaged in such an activity I would have been laughed at, called a sissy, and mocked. There was no place for hobbies. These schools were really military establishments devoid of human warmth with a rigid discipline so that every hour of the day was organised and the place for individual and personal interests was obliterated from the programme. I was aware that I was being required to conform and inwardly I gritted my teeth. I would not conform and no one would make me. I must have known that I was peculiar, not one of the run-of-the-mill, and the attempt to make me fit a predetermined model stirred rebellion within. To this day when I see psychoanalysts trying to fit a patient into some heartless system I rebel instantly.

I was certainly unhappy at school. The headmaster of St Martin's was a sadist. He would shout at me when he saw my shirt hanging out. I was a tall, gangling, uncoordinated child and shouting at me only made the situation worse. A boy who was "naughty", who committed some mischievous act in class, was ordered to go *to the study*. This meant that in the half hour before lunch you had to queue up outside the headmaster's study to await punishment. On one occasion the art teacher sent me *to the study* for flicking a pellet at another boy in her class. I duly went and was given "twice-one" with the ferule on the palm of my hand. The worst sin was to be sent to the study and to fail to turn up for the appointment. The next day I was told, just before lunch, that Mr Blackden wanted to see me *in the study*. Trembling I entered the room. He stood there looking at me fiercely and said: "You *know* why I have summoned you here." He said it with a most menacing tone.

"No I don't," I said.

"Don't you try playing games with me," he threatened. I was terrified but managed to plead: "But I *don't* know why you have called me here."

"You know perfectly well and don't you pretend."

At this point I wondered whether it was anything to do with my having been sent *to the study* the day before, so I said, "Is it anything to do with Miss Johnson sending me to the study yesterday?"

"Ah, ha," he leered, "now you're remembering alright. And so why didn't you come, you little coward?"

"But I did come."

"Oh, no you didn't. Don't try any of your monkey tricks with me."

"But I did come," I insisted.

"Who was before you and after you in the queue?" he asked. Luckily I remembered and supplied the names, at which he looked up to the ceiling and my presence there the day before evidently trickled back into his memory. I must grant that he apologised but I was very frightened and unnerved by the incident and his menacing presence has remained in my memory ever since. On another occasion a few of us were having a pillow fight in the dormitory and he came and caned us all and when it was my turn he leered and said, "I suppose you've learned these sort of antics from Portuguese street urchins."

I was paralysed in fear of him. My father was a kind and loving man and I was ill-prepared for someone who seemed to relish cruelty. I suspect that I must have particularly annoyed him for some reason and that he disliked me but he was cruel to other boys as well. If ever something was stolen, usually some sweets, he would summon the whole school into a large classroom and we would not be allowed out until the culprit had publicly owned up. This frightening performance branded into my brain must have affected me greatly. I think that incidents of this kind can leave a trace that remains throughout life.

I became frightened of men and associated them with sadistic cruelty and I yearned for some female presence that would be kind towards me. This has been so throughout adulthood. I greatly enjoy women's company and some of my closest friends are women. In the absence of women at this cold-hearted prison I turned for comfort to the school chaplains. I was there for four terms and there was a different chaplain each term. One of them, an old Dominican, was very kind to me and used to let me come into his room and talk with him. He had been to

Oporto many years before and his presence was a reassuring link with my parents whom I knew loved me. There was something of the feminine in these priests. In their cassocks they dressed like women and the outer dress had also an inner correlate for me. It is possible that many years later I became a priest in order to inhabit a warm feminine presence. I have almost been undone when I have experienced cruelty from a woman.

When my mother came to collect me at the end of the fourth term she was appalled to find me looking ill and breathless. I had become asthmatic, which used to come on violently when I was playing rugger or taking part in athletic activities. My mother was very angry with the headmaster for not taking greater care of my health and she took me to see a specialist physician, Dr Evan Bedford, in Harley Street. Many years later I discovered that when Churchill was seriously ill, close to death in 1943 while at Casablanca, it was Evan Bedford who was summoned from England to attend to him. He examined me, put me into the Middlesex Hospital, and declared that I had a "pulmonary murmur". I was now "delicate": in danger of death from heart failure, and when I graduated to the Junior House at Ampleforth in September 1949 I arrived full of instructions. I was not to play games or athletics as these induced asthma and put the heart into danger. I also developed eczema very badly and all around my mouth I was covered with it. It was a visible blemish about which I was extremely sensitive. It was not long before I was called "Scaley" because all around my mouth the skin was dry and peeling like the dried zest of an orange. I was also deeply ashamed of not being able to play games and when everyone else was on a run or playing rugger I would mooch about not knowing what to do with myself. Sport is so much part of the life and ethos of an English public school that to be sent to such a school and forbidden to play games made me into a mummy's weakling.

But why was I ashamed? There was no doubt I had a pulmonary murmur and there was no doubt that I used to get fearful asthmatic attacks when I ran or played rugger. I also got hay fever very badly. So what was the shame about? I think there was some guilt too. I believed deep down that all this was self-generated; that there was something that I could have done which would have released me from all these conditions; that I was partly responsible for this cowardly withdrawal from the companion world of sport. I believe it was connected to an

83

attachment to my mother and my father's inability to rescue me from a needy grip which she had over me. Guilt suggests that I could have done something to release me from this condition or that I had done something that put me into it. Although my mother was a powerful influence and put considerable pressure upon me to relieve her neediness, yet life is a challenge and I had within me the wherewithal to do something about it. I think I had collapsed inside. Perhaps the guilt was associated with not speaking with anyone about my emotional distress within.

When I decided later to go into the Church it was certainly against my mother's wishes and it is remarkable that from the day I went into the Church I was free of all ill health, and from that day to this I have very rarely been ill physically. All the eczema cleared up and I have never had an asthmatic attack. This seems to prove that I was able to do something if I really wanted to. I flung myself out of Mum's tenacious grip and threw myself into the arms of Mother Church.

Shame I am sure was because of the messy state I was in. We are ashamed if our inner life is broken up and in a mess. Guilt is there to the extent to which we are responsible for it. The distinction between these two and also their connection are, I believe, very important to get clear if we want to have good psychological understanding of our states and also the states of others. Years later I learned about Freud's theory of repression and it was only years after that again before I realised that what he was wrapping up in a panoply of instinctual language was nothing other than familiar old shame. Later when I was at St Edmund's I came across the Russian philosopher and mystic, Vladimir Solovyov (sometimes spelt Soloviev or Solovyof) and a bright light lit up the darkness when I read his remarkable book *The Justification of the Good*.[10]

* * *

So I arrived at Ampleforth—that great gulag at the foot of the North Yorkshire Moors. We travelled up there on the school train from London which left from King's Cross and ended at Gilling station which was twenty miles down a branch line from York. To this day as I pass King's Cross station and see those two big arches that enclose a dozen

---

[10]Solovyov, Vladimir (1918). *The Justification of the Good*. London: Constable.

platforms my heart shivers within me and I quickly look the other way. I remember the stations that the train stopped at on its fateful journey—Peterborough, Grantham, Doncaster, York, and then finally Gilling station. We always arrived in the evening and the train was met by a flock of buses that took us on the two mile journey up to The College as it was known by the Yorkshire yokels.

I am sure the reader will understand that when I use terms like *gulag* and *concentration camp* I am relating my own experience and trying to convey the cold institutional atmosphere that living in a public school engendered in me. There were, of course, good things and I know this was not everyone's experience. I think what was best for me and what remained a treasure for the rest of my life were some of the monks who enshrined a wisdom that had been passed down through centuries of Benedictine life. I would like to emphasise, though, that this was only some. There were others who were narrow-minded and ill-informed and, quite simply, ignorant not only of the ways of the world but also of the ways of the spirit. However, it is the good ones, the wise ones that stand out in my mind like a light in the darkness. I have a nose for true wisdom and when I catch a whiff of it I go out of my way to imbibe some of it. The man who stands out in my mind above all others who had this quality was Fr Columba Cary-Elwes. Some flavour of the man can be caught in a book, *An Historian's Conscience*,[11] which enshrines the correspondence that passed between him and Arnold Toynbee. There were others however, such as Basil Hume who later became Abbot of Ampleforth and finally England's cardinal. Several of the monks came out to stay with us in Portugal at different times. One was Fr Maurus Green but he had a sectarian fundamentalism that was not helpful for me. Unfortunately I was too timid and withdrawn ever to truly make friends with one of the wise monks. I never reached a stage where I was able to open my heart in a reciprocal way. I recognised the wise ones and tried to drink in their philosophy of life but I was always a timid mite looking at them with admiration from afar. This, however, was not the impression I gave on the outside. To others I was entertaining, amusing, and always keeping my end up, like my mother—she was like that. Yet, even in those early days, I had some appalling problem that I was trying to solve. I was like some derelict sailor who had been cast off in his

---

[11]Peper, C. B. (1986). *An Historian's Conscience—The Correspondence of Arnold J. Toynbee and Columba Cary-Elwes, Monk of Ampleforth.* Oxford: Oxford University Press.

sleep upon an island and when he awoke he was confused and searched around the island trying to find out where on earth he was. The dissonance between the outer and the inner has been a problem all my life and it has been a cause of distress and an enigma to those close to me.

So, I arrived at the Junior House at Ampleforth in September 1949 when I was just twelve. At least I was away from that sadistic headmaster at St Martin's; also my brother and two or three others from Portugal were in the Upper School, and every Wednesday I met up with them. On Wednesdays school work came to an abrupt finish at midday. I would step out of the Junior House building and look across to the motley arrangement of buildings that made up the monastery and the Upper School and wait until I saw the familiar figures of my brother, James, and Hugh Kingsbury, Tony Starte, and Brian Mollet making their way over to where I was, always armed with a little suitcase. The suitcase housed some small bottles of port, a little cooker and tins of frankfurter sausages and Portuguese sardines. We would walk then a comfortable distance until we found a private place on the edge of the moors and there would eat, drink, and make merry, and enjoyed a gentle mockery of the school's restrictions and regulations. I think on these Wednesday afternoons we were for a few short hours transported back into our paradise in Portugal. Picnicking was so much part of family life in Portugal for all of us that we managed on those Wednesday afternoons to recreate something of that happy atmosphere.

I believe that rituals of this kind have the function of cradling an individual within the womb from which he was born. Through and in the ritual the individual lives out the uterine life and that life is always a struggle between clinging to the womb and moving out to be born. If there has been a good experience in the womb then he is happy to be pushed out into the world and the need to cling is not so powerful.

It is obvious that I was still clinging to the warm loving atmosphere of home life in Portugal. I never threw myself into the school life in which I found myself. I did well academically but even here when it came to choosing what subject area to specialise in for A Level I did modern languages which consisted of French and Spanish. As I knew and spoke Portuguese, Spanish came very easily and so I coasted through the curriculum of school life without much difficulty. Through Spanish I further maintained my emotional link with home. I very much regret that I did not step forth and do classics, history, or English as my special subjects for advanced study.

When I finally graduated from the Junior House I entered St Bede's House in the Upper School which had within its bosom my brother and the Portuguese contingent. Two brothers from Kenya, Christopher and Simon Fletcher, became adopted by the Portuguese platoon and were also companion members of the Wednesday afternoon escapades into the mountains. I had two attachments then in my school days: one was to the camaraderie of the Portuguese enclave at Ampleforth and the other was to the wisdom that I saw embodied in some of the monks.

I was always in great awe of Fr Paul Nevill who was Ampleforth's headmaster and had been for thirty years. He was an imposing man with a large head; he spoke in a slightly pedantic way. He would always say "Good morning to you" rather than just "Good morning". There were about 500 boys in the school and it was said that he knew every boy and also all the old boys who had passed through the school under his headmastership. When someone once said to him with wry cynicism: "Father Paul, you must know boys extremely well," he replied simply: "No, I don't. I know some individual boys." I remember he stopped me in the corridor once and asked after my mother and then added, "I always feel for her with that stiff leg of hers." I was amazed that he had first noted it and secondly retained it. Each morning all the boys of the school assembled in a wide passageway and Fr Paul would address us all and convey any information that was needed; he would then say a prayer to begin the day.

On one occasion the Portuguese contingent had, as usual on Wednesday, gone up onto the moors, lit a fire, cooked a meal, and were happily enjoying the post-prandial atmosphere when, to our horror, we saw a Land-Rover come across to us. It was strictly forbidden to light fires and this ranger was very angry with us. We apologised and helped him to put it out and made sure that no cinders remained. He must have rung the school to report the matter because the next day Fr Paul, in severe but majestic tones, said that a group of boys had lit a fire on the moors which was strictly forbidden. He said he was quite prepared to ask the ranger to come to the school to identify the culprits but because the ranger said we had all been extremely polite and courteous to him he would not do so. So our politeness saved us, no doubt, from a humiliating caning.

As headmaster of Ampleforth Fr Paul attended the annual meeting of the headmasters of England's public schools. On one occasion the person chairing the meeting asked each headmaster to say what he prepared his boys for. One headmaster said, "I prepare them for academic excellence." Another said, "I have as my aim to develop their characters." Others said, "I attempt to inculcate into them their duties as a citizen," and, "I put integrity as my highest aim." "And you, Fr Paul, what do you prepare your boys for?" Fr Paul answered with one word: "Death."

One day just before lunch I went into our housemaster's study to cash a cheque. The housemaster, Fr Paulinus, was just about to hand me the cash when the abbot appeared at the door and asked to speak to Fr Paulinus on his own for a moment. I went outside and after two minutes the abbot came out and I went back in. Fr Paulinus was standing quivering and overcome with emotion. He turned to me and said, "Fr Paul has just died." I was shocked to the core. I had seen him and spoken to him that very morning and could not believe that he was now dead. He had had a sudden heart attack and shortly after midday one of the monks went to his study and found him slumped over his desk, quite dead. He had been headmaster for thirty years. With an attitude to death which I have just mentioned one might assume that he was well prepared for the event which took him so suddenly from our midst. I had a photograph of him on my mantelpiece for a long time.

When self-esteem was so interlinked with being good at sport and so much of the ethos was imbued with it, and me asthmatic, bronchitic, and face covered in eczema, I found the surrounding atmosphere very difficult to deal with. When rugger or athletics was going on in the afternoon I would hide myself in the toilet. There was no other place to which I could go and remain undetected. The summer term was a relief because I was allowed to play cricket as it did not involve the running which brought on the asthma, and so I felt a normal member of the school community until on one dread occasion I was batting and hit a powerful off drive to the boundary but I twisted on my right knee as I played the shot and I collapsed in agony. Both cartilages had become dislodged. I was in the infirmary for a couple of weeks, laid up and unable to walk. Then I went to York twice a week to visit an osteopath but finally my mother came to the school, took advice, and carted me off to an orthopaedic surgeon in Harley Street; a few days later I was operated on at the Royal National Orthopaedic Hospital in central London. The operation was only partially successful as, apparently, because I had attempted to walk with the cartilages displaced a hole had been dented into the bone. I was on crutches for a month and used a walking stick for a year, so when I returned to school the following term I was a near-cripple. I hobbled along with a walking stick and it took me ages to get from one place to another in that hideous expanse of dormitories, church, library, classrooms, and so on.

It prevented me now even from playing cricket and from doing "corps". On two afternoons a week there was military corps, when monks discarded their habits and donned military uniforms. Once a year a general came to the school and made an inspection of the whole school regiment. On this occasion we would be treated to some form of military instruction. I remember on one occasion we were shown a film of "The Platoon in Attack". "What is the purpose of the attack?" the narrator asked and the answer was "To kill". I looked around and there were monks sitting placidly observing. These same monks would take us for religious instruction once a week and inculcated the Command-ments of which one is: Thou shalt not kill. How did these monks toler-ate such a contradiction? Later in life I learned all the Catholic rhetoric about a "just war" but the monks' placid acceptance of what was being drummed into us in that film amazed me. I would now understand it as a case of *splitting*, but at the time it was an enigma although I kept it within and never went and asked for advice about it. I was inwardly a troubled child.

When my knee was still defective I took up corps again. On one occa-sion I was a member of a platoon making an attack, while the military monk commander was on the top of a hill with a group of boys and using our tactic as a model from which to explain things. I limped along behind the others. One of the boys told me afterwards that this monk had pointed me out and said, "There's an example of a slacker bringing down the efficiency of the whole platoon." I was outraged. I waited that evening outside the monk's refectory and when the offending monk came out I said I wanted to speak to him. I told him that I had heard what he said and explained that I had a bad knee which had not fully recovered its function and that I thought it was most unkind to make an example of me in the way he had. He was not very generous in his reply but I think he did make in the end a somewhat limp apology.

My whole physical being was involved in this emotionally bro-ken-up condition. We had to do gym once a week which included vaulting the wooden horse. I would run up and leap but fail to get over it. I was the only boy who couldn't. The gym master, Mr Henry, used to look at me a bit quizzically. Then my housemaster, Fr Paulinus, suggested that I ask Fr Jerome if I might play golf, but I was too frightened to ask because only sixth formers were allowed to play golf and if I was made an exception I would stand out like a sore thumb. I tried to hide my condition. When games were on I would sit in one of the lavatories. I did not want to be seen. What in essence was this condition which I was so anxious to hide? Certainly I was frightened; I think I was inwardly clinging in terror to ...? my mother? I am not sure, but certainly to the Portuguese maids and to the ambience that embraced little Nevilinho with adoring warmth. But there was such terror and such fear of being seen it seems to me that there must have been something worse: that I was broken up inside. If someone looked in, all they would see would be a mess of decaying flesh strewn with maggots.

It was too expensive for my parents to let my brother and me come home to Portugal for the three holidays of the year, so at Easter we went down and stayed at Littlestone-on-Sea in Kent. My father's sister, Mabel, lived there with her retired soldier husband. We did not actually stay with them but round the corner with Cecily Yates who was another "Oporto connection". Several of us who could not return to Portugal at Easter would stay with her. We all had bicycles and used to cycle to Dungeness Lighthouse, play golf on the small nine-hole course or travel to Hythe on the famous miniature railway. Aunty Mabel was always very kind to us. She gave us lovely teas with oatcakes and chocolate cake. Her husband, Uncle Phil, was a wise and educated man. He read *The Times* from cover to cover every day. He yearned for social company but Mabel never wanted anyone in the house other than family. There was always a lingering sadness about these Easter holidays because we were not at home. It is difficult these days to realise that travelling to Oporto and back was much more of an endeavour than today. Either we went by boat which took three days each way and the boat schedules never fitted neatly into the allotted school holidays. Occasionally we travelled to Paris and then caught the Sud Express and our parents met us at Pampilhosa, but that also took two and a half days each way. In those days, flying was very expensive and there were no planes direct to Oporto so we would fly to Lisbon and then catch the train up to Oporto. The train took twelve hours. Today it takes two.

We had one very happy Easter holiday in 1949 when we three children flew to Bordeaux. Our parents met us there and we spent three weeks at St Jean-de-Luz at the Hotel de la Plage, facing the beach as the name suggests. St Jean-de-Luz is close to the Spanish border and nestles around a bay at the foot of the Pyrenees. I remember it as a very happy time. We used to go and watch the Basque game of *pelota*. There were two versions of the game: one where basket-type rackets were strapped to the right hand with which the player would hurl the ball at the wall, but there was a more primitive kind of *pelota* which we watched in small villages in the mountains. Here the ball of cricket ball hardness was hit violently against the wall with the closed fist of the bare hand and I was amazed that these tough men could endure the pain of it. Another time we went up the La Rhune mountain on the funicular railway. We travelled around in an old Vauxhall and took picnics to many different places and, on one occasion, we travelled to Lourdes which none of us liked as much as Fátima. Then came the sad ending to the holiday when we were driven back to the airport at Bordeaux and away again to the concentration camp. Evelyn Waugh makes one of his characters in prison say that he had had good training for it at his public school.[12] I knew exactly what Evelyn Waugh meant.

So, finally my six years at Ampleforth came to an end. I remember walking down the corridor at the end of the summer term in 1955 with Simon Fletcher who said goodbye to me. I next met him thirty-three years later at his farm in Australia. A lot of water had passed under the bridge by then.

* * *

So I left Ampleforth and for two years wandered aimlessly through a series of different jobs while sharing a flat with my brother and sister in Kensington. First I was offered a job in the wine trade by Clare Waters. She was the joint owner of a little wine firm called Coverdale's that had its offices in Rangoon Street just near Tower Hill. I used to go with the clerk whose job it was to release parcels of wine from bond. In the lunch hour I used to listen to the speakers on Tower Hill. The Catholic Evidence Guild had a stand there. On Fridays the speaker was Fr Vincent Rochford. I used to listen to him entranced; with his white hair, ruddy face, and sparkling eyes he always collected a sizeable crowd around him. On one occasion the man standing next to me

---

[12]In his novel *Decline and Fall*.

turned and said to me: "You may not believe his religion but he is a wonderful man."

He had a natural generosity combined with courage and humour. Later when I became a priest and was sent to Bow in the East End of London he was the parish priest in the Isle of Dogs and I came to know him well. In fact I used to go, as a priest, to confession to him. I have a joyful memory of him to this day.

That job only lasted three months. There was a conflict between Clare Waters and one of the other partners and, as I was Clare's protegé, the other partner asked me politely if I would leave; that it would make things easier. I obeyed like a lamb. That was Christmas 1955. So I was job hunting again. Through my mother and Clare Waters I went for an interview with a friend of theirs, Michael Chapman, who was one of the directors of Portland Cement. He received me kindly. As he told me the sort of career I could expect in Portland Cement I must have looked dispirited or made some remark that conveyed it to him. I have never forgotten the reply he gave me: "You know, Neville, once you get into the world of work you must accept that you will be ground down. You just have to accept that."

I am sure the timid mouse did not answer but inwardly I said to myself that I was not bloody well going to be *ground down*—those were his words: *ground down*. Can you think of any advice more dispiriting to a young man of eighteen on the brink of life? He said it with consummate kindness. I came to think that many young men accepted this destiny. Many school friends and other young men I met in the London swirl of parties had pledged themselves to a life sentence in Shell or Lloyds or the Stock Exchange or merchant banking or P&O or British European Airways or the civil service. I saw them as clerks, becoming even rich clerks as they climbed up the career ladder, but clerks nevertheless whose destiny was to be ground down into a powder which could be easily moulded into whichever form was most congenial to the company or institution.

It was during this time that I first tasted the excitement of contact with the opposite sex. While dancing with a girl at the Condor nightclub in Wardour Street she pressed herself against me and a flurry of excitement raced through my midriff. But then the spectre of mortal sin raised its head again. The same awful fears that ruled my manner of receiving the host now ruled the slightest sexual feelings. Just as I must not let the sacred host touch my teeth under pain of mortal sin so I must not allow a sexual thought, let alone an erection, occur if I were not to be cut off brutally from God's grace:

I say to you that every one who looks at a woman lustfully has already committed adultery with her in his heart.[13]

I believe this is one of the worst sayings of Jesus and one that has been grossly exploited by Christian moralists. The moral position of the Catholic Church in regard to sex was that there was no *parvity of matter*. This meant, for instance, that in the case of stealing, a minor theft was purely a venial sin whereas a major theft was a mortal sin but in the sexual arena a sexual thought, masturbation, or adultery were all mortal sins. In Catholic teaching venial sin marred the individual's relationship with God whereas mortal sin cut him off totally from God and should he die in that unregenerate state then he would go to hell for all eternity. Once again I was walking on the edge of a precipice. That first thrill of contact with the opposite sex brought along with it the most fearsome vengeance from God. As I felt the stirrings of an erection, instead of being pleased, I hurriedly said "Hail Marys" in a desperate attempt to subdue these sinful stirrings of the flesh. How such a fearsome God had become installed within me from such an early age was something I only began to understand when I was in my early fifties. Only my own self-analysis began slowly to bring the whole matter to the surface and I developed my own psychological schema to explain it. It was a problem at the centre of my emotional and spiritual life which has taken me decades to understand and resolve, linked as it is to a wide spectrum of spiritual and emotional issues. The impulse to suicide and spiritual arrogance were part of the spectrum.

The terror of suicide was constantly with me. When I went on the London Underground, which was daily when I was working in the City, catching it at Gloucester Road and exiting at Tower Hill, I had a strong impulse to throw myself onto the electric rail. So much so that when I arrived at the platform at Gloucester Road I would keep close to the wall of the tunnel and creep along by it so that when I entered the train I would do so at a point which would give me minimum distance to walk when I disembarked at Tower Hill. This terror which was with me daily was not in my sphere of awareness. When later I had psychoanalysis

---

[13]Matthew Ch. 5 v. 28.

with two different analysts, it was not something that I ever mentioned. It was not that I was trying to hide it but that it just was not on the landscape of my inner vision. This omission could be attributed to me, yet some responsibility for it must be laid at the door of the two psychoanalysts although I do not think that either of them was really the culprit. It was that both of them, in varying ways, were subject to a system of thinking which did not encompass a psychology that made sense of this. I shall come to this more deeply in Chapter Six.

As a psychoanalyst I have not come across many patients with a god condemning them for sexual intentions but I have had many who have within them a god who savages them in the most appalling way for even the mildest human desires. I have, I know, in recent years been able to help such patients in a way which was not possible for me in the past. The solution that I have begun to find to my own problem has had in some cases an enabling function for others. I was pleased to read the following in Maisie Ward's biography of Caryll Houselander:

> Of recent years we have learnt that there are fields in which none can help unless first they have needed help. Alcoholics Anonymous have more cures to their credit than all the rescuers who tried to rescue from the outside. Divorcees Anonymous have prevented divorces when the wisest marriage counsellors could not. The best swimmer cannot rescue the drowning man unless he is in the water with him.[14]

* * *

Often at weekends I would go to the Dean household at Ankerwycke Priory at the invitation of Clare Waters, my mother's friend. I would stay in "the bull room"—a bedroom plastered with posters and pictures of bullfighting. Ankerwycke was a strange institution. It was a huge Georgian mansion. Dick Dean lived in the west wing of it on the first floor. Clare had her own bedroom and sitting room just opposite the bull room. Another sister, Sylvia, had another set of rooms together with her husband, Carl Somerville, and Cynth Waters with Fleur, her charge, lived in the east wing of the house. All these different members of the family ate in the huge dining room downstairs. At dinner there might be five people or twenty-five. Dick would usually preside at the head of the table.

---

[14]Ward, Maisie (1962). *Caryll Houselander* (p. 265). New York: Sheed and Ward.

The house sat on a large acreage of which about a mile bordered the Thames, that part of the Thames near Runnymede. All the Dean household were Catholics and we would go to the little Catholic church at Datchet for Mass on Sundays. We often went for walks in Windsor Great Park which was close by, and frequently went to the repertory company productions at Windsor which I nearly always enjoyed. There was a certain seasonal ritual also. At Easter time we would always go to the Varsity Boat Race with friends who had a house at Barnes overlooking the river. My mother often came across from Portugal and would stay at Ankerwycke in Clare's apartment for quite long periods. Clare introduced my mother to night clubs and the seamier side of London life. Prostitutes, homosexuals, and people in show business would come to Ankerwycke. My father would sometimes come across and stay also but he was clearly so unhappy in this alien world. I felt dreadfully sorry for my father but also frequently irritated by him. It seemed to me at the time that the Dean family had a sense of fun and were full of energy, and I was ill at ease at my father's evident hostility to the goings-on. That these people were not him and that it was quite the wrong place for him to be in was obvious to anyone who knew my father. He was always polite to Clare and I believe liked her but he was happier back in Oporto with his old friends like Dick Yeatman, Reg Cobb, and his twin brother. We could all see that my father was unhappy in this cosmopolitan world. My mother tried to persuade herself otherwise.

Dick was a bachelor but cavorted with young girls. He would often bring for the weekend one of these girls who would spend the nights with him in his flat. It was always supposed by the family that he did not have genital sexual relations with these girls; that he fondled them and played with them but that it never reached intercourse. This was certainly how his sisters and other family members viewed the matter and I believed the same. Then he turned his attentions to my sister, Jill. She was at Bedford College, London University at the time, reading Italian. The boyfriend she took to the college dance was Dick. She was at the time twenty-one and he was fifty-four, thirty-three years older. We believed that he was playing around with her as he had with other girls. As the intensity of this developed more and more my mother became increasingly anxious. This saga ended with Dick marrying Jill and a baby being born six months after the wedding day. The family delusion that Dick's affairs stopped at sexual intercourse were once and for all exploded. The story of this whole drama could in itself fill a book and

I prefer to pass over it quickly. The marriage was extremely unhappy; two and a half years after the wedding Jill had a second child and she and Dick parted shortly after amid no lack of acrimony and bitterness.

One consequence of the marriage was that, as soon as it had happened, Clare, Dick's sister, turned upon my mother with vitriolic hatred. The love and erstwhile devotion turned to hatred. I did not and still do not fully understand the reasons for this volte-face though one aspect of it became clearer when I was in Lisbon a year later, as I shall describe. It was a very unhappy time for our family. I was eighteen or nineteen and it had a very powerful effect upon me. One was that I saw much distress and unhappiness result from an illicit sexual relationship, and I took some inner secret vow that I would not be the perpetrator of a similar distress. A celibate priesthood seemed the perfect solution to my problems.

So two years passed with me drifting in and out of different jobs, tasting something of London life and its parties and spending some weekends at Ankerwycke. In the second year I became a deb's delight. This happened through friendship with Sally Eaton who was presented to the queen at Buckingham Palace and had a coming-out ball at her family's lovely old home near Meopham in Kent. Then I went also to her sister's ball and I became one of the young men "on the list", and so found myself invited to dinners, dances, and cocktail parties by London hostesses whom I had never met. Some of these "dos" were black tie but a number of them were white tie so I equipped myself with the appropriate "gear" for these occasions.

The superficiality of this world began to hit me. All the young men seemed able to talk about were cars and I found them boring in the extreme and irritated by the debs who could be so entranced by them. But I loved Sally and was very fond of her father and could see something of my father in him. He put up with all this debutante nonsense and paid the bills but it was obvious that he scorned it inwardly. Sally though was fresh, fun, and lovely and she came to Portugal for a holiday. My own scruples in the sexual arena which I have already described prevented the consummation of *la grande passion*. But we have remained friends down the years and I believe remain fond of each other to this day.

In my relationship with her I caught the first glimpse of jealousy. I did not feel it but, as I came to know later, it is precisely when it is not felt that it is at its most intense. I have come to realise that this is not well understood even by experienced psychoanalysts. If something is not felt it does not exist—that is the common view. When you feel something it is conscious; when you don't feel it then it is unconscious. The error here though is in the supposition that it exists as a feeling in the unconscious, but as Freud said, with his genius for acute understanding, there are no feelings in the unconscious. This means that something is unconscious because the inner reality does not exist in the feeling mode. It is unconscious because it exists in a different mode. One of the wisest things that the psychoanalyst, Wilfred Bion, said was that there could be pain that was not felt, guilt that was not experienced, and shame that was hidden.

On one occasion Sally was dancing with a young man called David Penny at a party in Portugal. They were dancing in an intimate manner. I looked on from the perimeter of the dance floor. Afterwards when she came to talk to me I was as calm as a cool drink and she said to me: "Aren't you jealous, when you see me dancing with David?" and then went on, "There is something funny. You seem not to care in the slightest bit." When she said this, it did strike me and her words have stayed with me. This superior dissociation is today very familiar to me and I know it means that the jealousy was violently intense. I could now deduce that such a jealousy was manifest in another to whom I would feel indelibly attached. When I left the Church later this is exactly what happened to me. I became attached to a woman who was insanely jealous. I knew it but could not detach myself from it. The reason is, I believe, that I am hooked onto that element that belongs to me. If my hand is cut off I want to attach myself to it because it is mine. It is the same with psychological realities whether they be jealousy, envy, or greed. Looking kindly, as I do today, I say to myself that my emotional resources were not developed enough at the time to enable me to feel the jealousy. In the language of Wilfred Bion the *alpha function* within me was not well developed. By alpha function Bion meant a source in the personality that creates unprocessed elements into realities that we can subjectively experience. So there was a jealousy that had not been processed through this creative function and this meant that I was not aware of it. So what I am talking about here is a madness which was entirely obscured. The solution to all this was to go into the Church and, identified with a savage God, I would not see any of these dark forces of unreason within me.

But something was stirring in me because I yearned for something deeper. Life must have more to it than champagne parties, gossip, and sports cars. It was during this time that I met Christopher

Campbell-Johnston at a New Year's Eve cocktail party at the home of Sir Alexander Roger. Christopher was a Catholic and introduced me to a Jesuit-founded religious group called The Cell Movement. It was founded upon the principles of the Young Christian Workers which I shall describe later but this contact moved me away from the superficial world of debutante culture. Eventually, after two years of this drifting life in London, I went to Lisbon where I set myself up as an agent for various English products. I think also I was escaping from the sexual conflict. A stage was near approaching where I should have had to engage more deeply with Sally sexually and emotionally or part, and I took flight from this critical conflict.

An event of significance occurred to me in London one day. I was walking across Hyde Park from the north to the south; I had just reached the Serpentine and was on the bridge. As often was the case the traffic was banked up waiting for the lights to change at Kensington Road so the cars were stationary on the bridge that I was standing on. Just next to me was a large chauffeur-driven car and I looked in the back and there was Churchill, alone, asleep with a rug over his lap. It gave me a thrill of boyish excitement and he has remained a significant figure for me down the years. I went to his funeral when he died and shortly after read within the course of one week, by reading into the small hours of the morning, all six volumes of his *History of the Second World War*. I think his importance to me lay in the determination that was so central in his character but also a determination aimed at opposing, with all the energy of his being, tyrannies and the enemies of freedom. At two or three junctures in my life when I have felt absolutely without hope in the world I have repeated to myself his words: "We shall never NEVER surrender ..." and it has given me a little wellspring of confidence. I think he was also important for me for another reason. When the whole world was clapping and cheering at Neville Chamberlain's speech at the time of the Munich Agreement in 1938, Churchill, almost alone,[15] stood against the support of the masses. The way in which a whole movement can unquestioningly agree to something which is wrong whether in politics, in religion, or in philosophy or cultural attitudes has impressed

---

[15]I later came to admire Duff Cooper who resigned as First Lord of the Admiralty in 1938 in protest against the Munich Agreement but when he did so nearly every member of the Conservative Party cut him dead as he walked in and out of Parliament. Also the Duchess of Athlone commands my admiration for similar reasons.

itself upon my mind, and I sometimes have to bury my head in my lap and say to myself, "Don't be dissuaded from what you think because so many are crying in the opposite direction." It was one of the reasons why later I became so friendly with Vincent Rochford. He used to go each month to a conference in the deanery to which he belonged. At these conferences a paper would be given and he told me once that his own understanding was the complete opposite of all the other members of the conference, but he would return home to his presbytery and say to himself, "But I am a Catholic, I am a Catholic." In later life I have found the same thing myself within the world of psychoanalysis.

So I was tired of London. I would go to Lisbon and set up my own business. I wrote to several firms in London that did not have agencies for their goods in Portugal and offered myself as their agent. To my surprise I soon collected a bag of firms who wanted to employ me. I had about ten firms for whom I was their agent. With these goodies in my bag I set off for Lisbon.

CHAPTER FOUR

Nightmare in Lisbon

I arrived in Lisbon early in 1957 on the *Andes* which docked at the Alcantara Quay and I was met by my mother and Clay Wilson. After the violent rupture of my mother's friendship with Clare she became friendly with Clay and decided to set up a teashop with her in Cascais. Clay was the most unlikely person to be running a teashop. She was a fulsome figure of a woman who drank heavily, was somewhat insensitive, and very different from Clare. My mother and Clay were sharing a flat in Monte Estoril and had arranged for me to stay there too. I initially set up office with Count Gerald O'Kelly de Gallagh. He had been the Irish ambassador or minister in Lisbon and when he retired he started a small business selling French wine and brandy to a few gourmet customers. I worked for him and also started my own business. O'Kelly had a difficult task selling expensive French wines to the Portuguese who were well supplied with their own wine; his wines cost twenty times more than local varieties. His logo was: *The cheapest is never the best; the best is ever the cheapest.* The day after I arrived I went to visit him at the office which I was to share with him. He was a short, vigorous man with white hair and a goatee beard. He had hooded eyes that stimulated a distrust and reserve in me. At that first meeting he said he would like to ask me to dinner but his wife was a little ill that day, but as soon as she recovered he would invite me. The next day his wife died. I went to the funeral a day later. The coffin was brought to the graveside and he was standing there watching when, to my alarm, the coffin was opened with the body exposed and two men poured quicklime over the corpse. He stood there watching as all the diplomatic corps of Lisbon stood in a large circle gazing at this macabre scene. He seemed to me like a caged animal in a zoo being watched by voyeuristic tourists. I felt so sorry for him. A few days later he invited my mother and me to lunch. A little papillon dog came into the room and whined. He said, "He used to climb onto my wife's lap; he is whining because now there is no lap." When lunch was ended he asked if we would stay while he read aloud to us a story. I was too moved by his recent loss to hear the story but I remember he read with effective power. I came to know him quite well over the next few months but I was always somewhat timid in his presence.

I developed a close friendship in Lisbon with Patrick Thompson. He had a business in Lisbon importing bottling machines. He was and still is today a thinker about life. He sees beyond the external roles that people inhabit. He was twelve years my senior but we were boon companions and would sit up in Lisbon cafés drinking *brandy barato com soda*[1] until the early hours of the morning. We discussed every subject under the sun but there was a depth to these conversations which were extremely important to me and I believe to him also. It was such a contrast to the superficiality of the conversations I had with the idiotic "debs delights" in London. Patrick was a good Catholic and was close friends with several of the priests from the English College in Lisbon.[2] He was particularly friendly with its rector, Monsignor Sullivan.

Sullivan was a remarkable man of the widest culture. Although I did not see him often I always visited him when in Lisbon over all the years before I was a priest, when I was a priest, and after I had left the priesthood. He was undismayed by my changing roles. Although a devout Catholic he saw deeper into the human condition than the surface.

---

[1] "Cheap brandy and soda"—we discovered that cheap brandy was better with soda than the more expensive brands so we always ordered it in whichever café we happened to be.
[2] At the time of the Reformation when Catholic priests were banned and when therefore no training of priests could occur in England, seminaries for the training of English priests were set up in Lisbon, Valladolid, and Rome.

His understanding and acceptance of me when I left the Church were extremely important. He was a wise man. He taught moral theology to the students at the English College and he once confided to me his dilemma. He knew that much of the Catholic moral teaching was based on incorrect principles, particularly the Church's teaching on contraception. He said to me:

> It is very difficult to know what to do. If I teach them what I believe are the correct principles and the right teaching what will happen to them with their conservative bishops when they get back into parishes in the north of England?

I do not know how he solved this difficult dilemma. Patrick would go to a film with Monsignor Sullivan every week and after it they would discuss it in detail. They would discuss every subject from ladies' fashions to opera and baroque architecture. In a rather similar way Patrick and I would range over a wide spectrum of subjects as we sat drinking our *brandys baratos com soda*. This was the first of a series of friendships that have been of central importance in my life. There has been one thing in common with all these friends. We have had long conversations that cut through the superficial appearances to reach "the central fire",[3] to quote Bertrand Russell. Most of these friends have been men but some of them have been women. These friendships with women have been platonic. I have noticed that even in a sexual relationship the sexual aspect evaporates as soon as a deep theme begins to be discussed. It is as though the sexual is subsumed into something deeper and greater.

So when I was first in Lisbon I lived in Monte Estoril in Clay Wilson's flat. She was a close friend of my mother. It was a small flat and she had

---

[3]This phrase comes from Russell's account of his first meeting with Joseph Conrad. It is so striking that I will quote the essentials of it here: "My relation to Joseph Conrad was unlike any other that I have ever had. I saw him seldom, and not over a long period of years. In the out-works of our lives, we were almost strangers, but we shared a certain outlook on human life and human destiny, which, from the very first, made a bond of extreme strength ... At our very first meeting, we talked with continually increasing intimacy. We seemed to sink through layer after layer of what was superficial, till gradually both reached the central fire. We looked into each other's eyes, half appalled and half intoxicated to find ourselves in such a region. The emotion was as intense as passionate love, and at the same time all-embracing. I came away bewildered, and hardly able to find my way among ordinary affairs (1967, *The Autobiography of Bertrand Russell, vol. 1*, p. 209, London: Allen & Unwin).

offered to have me to stay when I came out to Lisbon. The sitting room in the flat was L-shaped and my room was created by getting a builder to erect a thin plywood divider that separated the tail of the L from the rest of the room. The significance of this was that I was able to hear all conversations going on in the sitting room. Visually I was not in the room but audibly I was.

Once I woke in the middle of the night and Clay was speaking in anguished terms with Katya d'Andrade, a friend who lived nearby. Clay was confessing to Katya her guilt at her sexual relationship with my mother. "I am committing the sin of sodom," she said, "with Norah and here I am pretending to be Neville's good friend." The conversation went on and on. I heard every word of it. I was shocked to the core. I was frightened, I was paralysed, I was angry and terribly distressed for my father, but what was I to do? Who could I speak with about it? I of course realised straight away that my mother's relationship with Clare Waters, Dick Dean's sister at Ankerwycke, had also been sexual and the latter's vitriolic volte-face had in it all the venom of a lover who felt betrayed. Clare I think was in a fury when Jill married her brother and blamed my mother for it.

But what was I to do with this knowledge? Hamlet's dilemma has ever since that day had a poignant significance for me. What was Hamlet to do with this knowledge revealed to him by his father's ghost? What was I to do with this knowledge of which I was the custodian? Why did I not speak to Patrick Thompson about it? I cannot think why I did not go and speak to Monsignor Sullivan. I so needed a confidant who would help me to sort out my anguish. I think somehow I had to pretend to be adult, to know how to deal with such things. Was that it? I am not sure. I doubt it somehow. I think it was also a deep shame within me. A child admires his parents: it is part of his own pride. The shame within me of what I now realised about my mother was unbearable. When I was at St Edmund's I did tell the priest to whom I used to go to confession, but he just slumped in his chair, looked very depressed and did not know what to say to me. Even much later when I went for psychoanalysis I was unable to convey the shock and trauma of this event. I had a sense that my psychoanalyst was a worldly sophomore for whom marital affairs were part of his daily menu, and therefore I did not convey to him my deep shame and distress about it.

I was torn violently in several directions. I went to confession to a very warm and friendly White Father called Victor Nijs but confession was of my own sins not my mother's. I did not know who to turn to for help with this emotional shock. I became very friendly at this time with Susan Marques. She was a niece of Hilaire Belloc and daughter of Marie Belloc Lowndes. She was a wonderful woman and I used to discuss the spiritual life with her. I never considered talking with her about what had shocked me so devastatingly. She was a friend of my mother but it was more than that. Susan was a very good person and it is very difficult to tell something shocking to a good person. It is quite possible however to do so to someone wise, someone who is a saint, someone who is unshockable though able to feel for another. Susan did not know the world and was probably not wise but Monsignor Sullivan was, so it did not explain why I could not speak to him.

Perhaps I did not want to betray my mother. I remember I thought of telling my mother that I knew of her secret affair. I travelled from Lisbon to Oporto on the train a few days after my unnerving discovery and I agonised on that long journey whether to speak to my mother when I arrived or whether to speak to my father. Violent emotions raged inside me. I was in the company of my mother and father and also of my uncles, aunts, and cousins with this fearful knowledge inside me. What would they have done had I told them? I believe that they would not have known what to do. I do not think that emotionally they would have been up to it and perhaps I sensed this and just had to bear it within. I am sure that people sense whether someone can bear a piece of information. "I can tell Mary but not Jane, I can tell Johnny but not Petrarch"—there is a knowledge of what can be handled emotionally by the other. I sensed that this would be too much for any member of my family. I may have sensed that it would be too much for Patrick, too much for Susan, but the reason why I could not speak to Monsignor Sullivan was different. What may have been true of Patrick, Susan, or my family I attributed to Monsignor Sullivan also. I was not able to bear it but I was not mature enough to say to myself, "I cannot bear it but Monsignor Sullivan may be able to bear it." I assumed that what was true of me was also true of him. In later years I formulated the principle that one attributes to others the undiscovered aspects of oneself. This is the narcissistic position.

As I write this I wonder why I did not think of killing myself. Perhaps that was, with my Catholic upbringing, also an unthinkable thought. I might not think it but I could act it unthinkingly and this I did. On the day that the infamous teashop opened in Cascais there was a party in the evening. At the end of it I drove one of the guests back to her home beyond Cascais at the Guincho. I was in a large American car. After leaving her I was driving fast back towards Cascais on the left hand side of the road. I saw the headlights of a car coming fast towards me. In a millisecond I realised that we were both on the same side of the road and that it was me who was on the wrong side, so I braked as hard as I could and, at the same time, pulled the driving wheel over to the right. The car spun around two and a half times in a tight circle and came to a stop facing the direction from which I had been coming. As the car came to rest I saw the other car also spinning a hundred yards further on, past my car and where I had been coming from. A young man in a white jacket got out of his sports car and came towards me. I got out and faced him. I said to him, "I am English. I have been driving in England—on the left hand side of the road and I forgot." He stared at me, said not a word, turned on his heels, and returned to his car. My experience was bad but not as bad as his. I think this was probably a suicide. It happened the night of a party when my mother was celebrating with Clay Wilson the opening of a teashop which was their joint venture. I have sometimes wondered what would have been my family's reaction had I been killed. There would have been considerable distress and in later years people would have said, "And, oh yes, there was a third child who was killed in a car accident when he was nineteen years old." The family would have been different without this member but how? This is one of the ifs of history.

Later, when I was at St Edmund's, I spoke about my mother's lesbian affair to Adrian Walker, another student I became friendly with. What I was not able to speak about either to him or later to a psychoanalyst was my own terrible shock. My conclusion is that emotional distress of an intense kind can only rarely be related to with sympathy by another. It is shattering for the hearer as it is for the confessor. The person listening has to be in touch with some parallel experience within in order to manage it. The professional role of the listener is no guarantee that the sympathiser can manage to be there with the person in his shock, in his terror. I did convey something of my shock when I spoke to the priest confessor but his inability to deal with it confirmed my intuition that people would not be able to help me with it. I am not sure that I have ever entirely processed it and one of my goals in writing this autobiography may be to try to do so fifty years later. I hinted at the subject with a cousin some dozen years ago but sensed it was too much for him

106

as it had been for me. He clearly brushed it away and did not want to hear more. This was some confirmation that I could not have spoken to any family members at the time.

How does someone process a shocking piece of knowledge like this? I am sure this was Hamlet's dilemma and Shakespeare must have realised what an appalling one it was. I presume Shakespeare must have had some cognate experience that enabled him to write so poignantly about it. Perhaps dramatising the problem through writing a play or a novel might be the way, the only way.

I ask myself whether such a revelation would be a shock to someone in the Bloomsbury set, for instance. I suspect even in a culture as liberal as that, where such affairs were the norm, revelations of this kind are a shock to a child. The issue must be the revelation to another of the state of shock. It must have been this that I was reluctant to do; I desperately needed help to sort out my own violent and contradictory emotions. Surely my emotions are my own? Surely I can manage my own emotions? They are mine after all. An invalid is ashamed of needing someone to help him to the lavatory. Was I ashamed that I could not manage the effect of this violent shock? I think the answer lies in this arena. As a psychoanalyst I have had patients who are ashamed that they are dependent upon another to be able to think. If you met an adult who was only able to add the sum of five and eight with the help of an abacus he would very likely be ashamed. I have come across many people who are only able to think in the helping presence of another and they are equally ashamed. It is the same with our emotions. My emotions are so intimately my own; I find it an insult if you come and tell me that I need some help in processing my own emotions. "Look," I say, "they are mine after all." They are more mine than my legs or arms. As a toddler I needed help to walk. "Are you telling me I am still a toddler? That I cannot process my own emotions?" I suspect this is another reason why I did not go and speak to anyone. I believe psychological events of this kind are always in their origin multifactorial. So, on the outside, I was smiling, being amusing and entertaining, while inside I was in a state of shock and confusion. And even with my mother I was outwardly the same and I doubt whether she noticed any difference in my demeanour.

But I do not think that what I have written above quite gets at the shock. An important part of it was that, on the outside, virtue was being paraded. I don't mean that my mother pretended to be saintly.

She joked and laughed and drank but she, with all the rest of the family, went to church every Sunday; she went to Holy Communion. There was something about this sexual infidelity that seemed like a sacrilegious insult in the midst of this pious community. My mother was the one who had told me that I would have the day off from school on the day of my First Communion. She had told me that it was a very important day and, although the event was early in the morning and left time for me to go to school, she had said she wanted me to have the day off so I would remember it and treasure its importance. Before I made my First Communion my mother used to read me stories from the Gospels and when I was at St Martin's School where I was confirmed by the Bishop of Middlesbrough my mother wrote and told me what an important day it was. And although I knew she drank, joked, and had fun I had never dreamt that she was being sexually unfaithful. It seemed so violently opposite to the family ethos. We were a good Catholic family. We prided ourselves on our piety and my mother was part of this. I somehow think that the shock was that here was a piece of knowledge that was so much the opposite of all this that I was unable to process it; that I did not have the cultural equipment with which to do so. All I knew was that it was an appalling sin. Also at this time I knew nothing about homosexuality. I knew it existed and that it existed between men and also between women but it was a dark enigmatic world to me and I think it frightened me.

This contrast between the outer display and the inner knowledge that I had acquired drove me mad. My phobic flight from the world and submission to God and the Church was a madness, but madness is generated by the disjunction between what is said and what is being done. What my mother, supported by the whole family structure, was "saying" was, "I am a good Catholic, faithful to Ron and faithful to the canons of the Church," and then here I was confronted with actions that belied it. This is what drove me mad. I believe that I was, in psychiatrists' language, "psychotic" but that this remained hidden even from the two psychoanalysts whose job it was to uncover just this. As I have explained, this was partly due to my own shame and difficulty in communicating it but I suspect also the emotional trauma was too great for either analyst. I do not mean by this that the event itself was traumatic to them but that they were unable to manage a patient who was in a severely traumatised state.

108

There was another reason why I did not speak about my mother's infidelity. In a deep way I felt that it was a betrayal of me. I loved my mother, adored her in fact, and she loved me deeply, and when I heard that she was having a sexual affair with Clay I felt not only that she had betrayed my father but that she had betrayed me. There was a secret love affair between me and her. This, I believe, went back to my earliest childhood so there was combined in me the child's love for his mother which had incorporated adult love into that intense childhood adoration. This was one reason why I felt guilty about sexual feelings for the girl at the Condor nightclub that I have described. I would "grass" on my father when, out with him, he did something which I knew would annoy my mother. I had been in a secret tryst with her. In my mind the relationship between me and her was sexual. I do not mean that that it was actually so but that, at a primitive level, there was a love-bond between us and it was this which was now shattered. The flight into the Church was partly a joining with my father against my mother. I say "partly" because I do not think that this was the whole story. Also the values that lie at the heart of all great religions was something that I loved and espoused and, after many years, they have become again central in my life, but my own understanding of it today is entirely different from what I believed as a Catholic. I would not today view my mother's act as sinful. People have to make choices and do the best they can with their own natural desires and sexual appetites. I have not the slightest doubt that the strength of sexual desire varies greatly and a sexual love relation can widen a human heart: that to give one's whole self to someone in love is one of the greatest human acts. I have not the slightest doubt that a sexual affair such as my mother's might be life enhancing. My understanding of religion lies in the direction of doing the best one can with what one has and not to try to be something which one is not. I am sympathetic to what Paul Tillich expresses thus:

> Be what you are—that is the only thing one can ask of any being. One cannot ask of a being to be something it was not before. It is as if life in all its forms desires to be asked, to receive demands. But no life can receive demands for something which it is not. It wants to be asked to become what it is and nothing else. This seems surprising but a little thought shows us that it is true.

We know that one cannot ask fruits from thorns, or grain from weeds, or water from a dry fountain, or love from a cold heart, or courage from a cowardly mind or strength from a weak life. If we ask such things from beings who do not have them, we are foolish; and either they will laugh at us or condemn us as unjust and hostile towards them. We can ask of anything or anyone only to bring forth what he has, to become what he is. Out of what is given to us we can act. Receiving precedes acting.[4]

I would judge with greater favour someone who, like Zorba in that moving film *Zorba the Greek,* sexually made passionate love with several women but who had a generosity of heart and an "in-touchness" with the pains and tragedies of life, than someone sexually more restrained but prudish, mean and "un-giving" towards the world. King Charles II had sexual relations with many different women and had children by several of them but I am sympathetic to what one of his biographers quotes him as saying:

Long ago he had told his sister that he was one of those bigots who regarded malice as a much greater sin than a poor frailty of nature. To design mischief, to be cruel and deny compassion, of these at least he had not been guilty; somehow, he trusted, he would climb up to Heaven's gate.[5]

I think King Charles was right. Malice and cruelty are far worse than "sins of the flesh" though it is always the latter that are reproached most strongly by religious people. This is also not only in the churches but also in psychoanalysis as well. A psychoanalyst who falls in love with a patient is condemned much more severely than one who acts maliciously towards someone. So, for me today, what I think of as religious is profoundly different from the way I understood it and had imbibed it through a puritanical Catholic lens. It could be that the shock that happened to me did, over a long period of time, shake me out of a self-righteous middle class pseudo-religious attitude and help towards a wider, more human understanding of life and the world. I would call

---

[4]Tillich, Paul (1973). *The Boundaries of our Being* (p. 118). London: Collins, Fontana Library of Theology and Philosophy.
[5]Bryant, Arthur (1955). *King Charles II* (p. 287). London: Collins.

myself religious today but it is the opposite of what would be described as religious by my father, my cousins, and most people practising religious devotions. Perhaps I am more attuned to the great mystics who did not think like churchgoing people.

There is another aspect to it. My mother had always treasured my sister, Jill. She had a privileged position in my mother's heart. James and I often felt in a rage about it; that we were being neglected in her favour. Yet I did not really believe this. I believed that I was loved as much as my sister was loved, but when I heard that my mother was having a sexual affair with a woman it drove home to me that Jill was her true lover; that she loved the woman more than the man; I now knew that I was not the loved one; Jill the woman was the precious one who was the receptacle for my mother's love and passion. I had also always had a deep sense that to earn my mother's love I needed to turn myself into a woman. This belief now had a striking confirmation.

At a later time when I had left the Church I went through a period of feeling hatred towards my mother. It was because I felt that she had been responsible for all these disasters which had enveloped my life. I believed that this unfaithfulness of hers had driven me into the Church.

I think one cannot talk about something distressing if one's own secret self-love has been wounded. It prevents one talking about it. Why? I think it is that there is a shame about self-love. There was I believe a shame in me that I demanded this loving tryst of my mother towards me and this silenced me.

* * *

I am sure today that I felt I was married to my mother so her infidelity was a betrayal of my marriage to her. I think my savage surge into the Church was motivated by a hatred of my mother's betrayal of me. Some evidence for this lay in the fact that I had all the superstitious devotion to the Virgin Mary that characterised much of folk Catholicism. When I started attending scripture lectures and reading theology there was much criticism of this sentimental devotion to Mary, the mother of Jesus, and I joined with this new theological outlook. I came to hate all the Marian devotions, saying the rosary, visiting Fátima or Lourdes. I came to hate Mother Church as well. I think the origin of this hatred lay in my mother's betrayal of me. Emotionally I was married to her.

111

So when I saw her going to communion and participating in all the Catholic devotions in which I also participated I believed that she and I were emotional lovers.

There was a hatred of my father too—his cowardly retreat into a thousand pious practices. Although it would have been upsetting I should have respected my parents more had they been able to recognise that they were not right for each other and that the best solution would have been to separate and divorce, but the pious Catholic pressure against this was overwhelmingly strong. To this day I am intolerant of a kind of weakness that sidesteps the truth and I have respect for the person who confronts a painful reality and acts accordingly.

* * *

I am here repeating the psychiatric dictum that it drives someone mad if what is said contradicts what is done. I believe this is so but why is it so? To have stuck to my observation that my mother was unfaithful to my father and to have followed through in the consequences of that would have required a revolution in my thinking about the world in which I had been reared. Another belief that was part and parcel of the family faith was that my father was the model Christian gentleman. Yet, on one occasion, my mother whispered to me that my father was a very self-centred man. Also when my brother was getting married my mother said to him to go to the trouble to get to know his wife. Her implication was that her own husband had not troubled to do this. She believed that he was wrapped up in himself. If I were really to take in the full implication of this revelation about my mother's infidelity it would have meant overthrowing the belief system in which I was reared. I perhaps sensed that Mgr Sullivan would not be able to help me. I may have been wrong in that but I was not wrong about the priest to whom I revealed it at St Edmund's. Let us say that my father was self-centred and that my mother was in violent rebellion against him and that the emotional fragility that is the necessary accompaniment of this prevented him from challenging his wife's own sadistic and, at times, bullying behaviour; that rather than take this path he retreated into a ritual of pious devotions. This would have required me to see his religious practice not as something to be admired but rather a coward's shelter. Yet his behaviour was admired and endorsed by the whole community not only of my large extended family but also of the whole Oporto society of which

112

I was a part. But what I knew would have required me to go further than this. The kind of piety that my father practised was something endorsed by the Church. Saints had been canonised whose piety was not dissimilar. I should have needed to question the Church's infallible authority. I should have needed to go further than this. If what I was witnessing was the manifestation of a self-centredness which seemed to be endorsed by the Church I would have needed to go further than this and question the idea that God had revealed himself to his chosen people and then through Christ to the whole Christian world and that we were in a position of special privilege. Was all this to be questioned? Was the whole value system that underpinned Western civilisation a self-centred, self-congratulatory ideology? In later years I have felt in great sympathy with the philosopher John Macmurray, who believed that the whole Western philosophical tradition was imbued with solipsism. Here was the antinomy between a thinking individual versus a vast weight of authority. I did not have the courage of a Copernicus, a Galileo, or a Kepler. I took the coward's route and fled into the Church and hid my head. I acted just like my father. My whole life, however, has been a slow process of thinking that has led me to challenge the basic assumptions of the Western value system. Further, it has not been replaced in my thinking by the Eastern one. My struggle with madness has been a battle between personal thought versus a vast crushing weight of authority. I think my problem was that I did not dare to question radically the whole structure of values in which I had been reared. My life has been a radical questioning, step by step. So, although it was true that I took the coward's path into the Church, yet there was a personal thinker trying to construct a different view of emotional life and the world—one that would ultimately make sense of my mother's infidelity. Later I quite forgave her but this took a long time. Before she died I had some intimate conversations with her and apologised to her for my cruel defection.

So I think a reason why I could not deal with my mother's infidelity is that it would have meant questioning the whole ideological structure in which I had been reared, in which all my family had been reared, and which in fact dominates thinking in the Western world. Someone reading this might say that Freud, with his newfound baby called psychoanalysis, was in contradiction to this but I do not think so. I said above that it would have meant overthrowing a whole spectrum of Western thought and embracing something from the East but I do not think this

113

is correct either. There are aspects of Buddhism, Hinduism, and Jainism which are also seriously faulted. I think the discovery of my mother's infidelity required me to build a personal philosophy of life that was not to be found in the Church, in psychoanalysis, in Eastern philosophy, in modern science, or entirely within the thinking of any of the greats in the philosophical tradition whether it be Plato, Aristotle, St Augustine, Thomas Aquinas, Descartes, Kant, Leibniz, Kierkegaard, or modern existentialism. I was required to overthrow the whole thing and start from a new foundation. As life has progressed I have moved closer and closer to this aim but, at the tender age of twenty and bred in an atmosphere of innocence, I did not have the resources to do it. It has taken me a further fifty-five years to try to erect a building which is adequate. My present problem is to explain my inner philosophy to another. My sense is that most people are servants to an ideological purpose whether it be Christianity, Buddhism, atheism, psychoanalysis, or anarchism. I live in a lonely place.

* * *

I suppose the world of psychotherapy does have a forum where I could have gone to someone and unburdened myself of my distress but the Catholic Church only had the confessional, which was for my own sins, but what about anguish caused by the sin of another? This was something that the Church had no forum for. If I were able to turn the clock back now I would have propelled myself into the confidence of Mgr Sullivan, but when I try to imagine myself doing this at the age of twenty I can only see myself collapsing—not in tears but in reckless behaviour. It was probably this that I was trying desperately to avoid. I believe, however, that, had I done so, my life would have been very different. My whole life has been an inner collapse and my task has been to erect a building out of the ruins.

I wrote earlier of the clinging attachment that so suffocated my parents' marriage. This sexual infidelity of my mother was part of her desperate flight from my father's clinging. My shock was to realise in a deeper way that love, a "faith of the heart" did not lie at the root of my parents' marriage. And what about the marriages of all the other Symingtons? And other Catholics? From then on when I saw people piously taking the sacrament at the communion rail I wondered whether it was outer ritual and that beneath it was an absence of "faith of the

114

heart". I think this was another element of the shock. I was shocked out of believing that the outer and the inner necessarily correspond in a tight way. Later, when I was a curate, I came into terrible conflict with my parish priest precisely over this issue. Even later as a psychoanalyst I have run into the same issue. There is no guarantee that the outer ritual enshrines an inner "faith of the heart" but I realise that many believe that it does. This shock was also an unnerving discovery that the outer may signify inner "faith of the heart" but that the latter may not be present.

* * *

This battle with my own personal arrogance became the central spiritual endeavour of my life and it was, I believe, a principle guiding my intentions in the Church. When I did finally go and ask for help many years later from a psychoanalyst it was only after I had tried all the recipes that the Church had to offer. Spiritual pride was looked upon as *the* major sin. St Aelred of Rievaulx said that if you are proud of your chastity it is then a sin because pride is a vice. While in the Church I searched for a solution to this problem but I could not find it. Spiritual pride requires emotional intimacy to shake it out but this is not easy to find as a celibate priest. So, in becoming a priest, I was trying to wrestle with this problem but I was taking a path which would make the battle, if not hopeless then extremely difficult. Marriage might be the answer and yet if the wife is autistic or psychologically isolated herself then the same problem arises. People who live together are not necessarily emotionally intimate. I remember a girlfriend saying to me, "You can be a thousand miles from the man you are in bed with."

* * *

After the shock of discovering my mother's infidelity and lesbian love life two things happened. One was minor and the other major. I decided forthwith to leave Clay Wilson's flat and I moved into the British Club in Lisbon. The major one was a masochistic addiction that ended in my determination to become a priest. I started to read the lives of saints and I read them by the dozen and also the New Testament in detail. I now believed I was a saint myself so I acted according to what I read. I put a stone in my shoe so that as I walked up and down Lisbon's hilly streets

I suffered the pain of it. I started going to Mass every day and saying the rosary six times a day. I fasted, went frequently on pilgrimages to Fátima and went to confession once a week. I had retreated into an awesome cave filled with the worst of superstitious practices. If I complain about my father's superstitious excesses they were no match for mine. In the midst of this mad frenzy I decided that I would become a priest. When in London I had once met Monsignor Butcher who was the president of St Edmund's College which was the seminary for priests of the Westminster diocese and so now I wrote to him declaring my intentions. He wrote, sent me an application form, and gave me a date for the next interviews.

I was in the grip of something which totally crushed my own individual creative self. In common language, I was mad. I had become possessed by a force that was stronger than me. There was no inner decision-making but a frantic determination. Somehow or other I was back in the dream that had crystallised when I watched my father shoot the teal in the *Pai e Mãe* marsh ten years before. To give oneself to something that is greater than oneself is ennobling, so there was something good being sought in what I was doing; so where was the flaw? I think it is the difference between taking possession of something rather than being possessed by it. This is the superficial difference. The real difference, which all great mystics knew, is being possessed by *being* itself rather than some particular sensual part of being. What I needed to do at that time was to assimilate something that was a shock to the system—my mother's infidelity. That was the psychic work that needed to be done. If I had mourned the loss of a treasured belief—that my mother was my father's faithful Catholic wife—which would have taken some time, perhaps a couple of years, then I may have been in a position to decide whether the priesthood was the right thing for me. What I did though was to fling myself into the Church in a state of shock so the whole edifice was built upon shaky ground. So one of the tasks of my emotional and intellectual life was to separate the "something good" from its corrupting foundation. In essence the something good has to be founded in a personal creative act, whereas I went into crushing submission to a force that was a substitute for creation. This was I believe to anaesthetise the shock of my mother's infidelity. To have faced it, with all its implications, would have been more than I could bear at the time: by implication I mean coming to accept the vacuum that existed between my mother and father and even further to wonder about why my mother had married my father; because, as I later realised, her lesbian propensities probably predated her marriage to my father.

In these worldly days many might think that I am making too much of this event but I was a loving and trusting boy, and sensitive, and this revelation about my mother was a terrific blow and I believe I was shattered by it. The dream that I was in the *Pai e Mãe* experience was to protect a loving child from a harsh and painful reality that was right in front of me in my own home.

So I set off for London, saint-like in a third class carriage in the train across Spain and France to London. I told no one in London of this trip except old Miss Fraser who was a Catholic academic; I stayed near her in a small hotel near King's Cross, and on a Saturday morning I went for my interviews at Archbishop's House adjoining Westminster Cathedral. I was interviewed by Monsignor Butcher, Monsignor Derek Worlock, Cardinal Godfrey, and a doctor. Monsignor Butcher, who had been so friendly when I had met him at Alfonso de Zulueta's presbytery in Chelsea, was now harsh and headmaster-like. He tested my Latin which apparently was good enough to allow me to enter direct into the seminary without having to go to a Latin crammer run by Jesuits at Osterley in West London. I have little memory of the interview with Cardinal Godfrey but my medical was more of a problem. My mother had filled in the section on my health as she was required to do and my heart trouble, my asthma, and general ill health were given all the emphasis she could muster. I decided to counter this as best I could and I told Derek Worlock that my mother was very against my becoming a priest and that her health report was overemphasised in the hope that I would be turned down. He smiled and I had the impression that I won him to my point of view. As soon as the interviews were over I returned, again by third class rail, back through France and Spain to Lisbon. I got back to Santa Apolonia station exactly a week after I had left. It was not long before I got a letter from Monsignor Butcher to say that I had been accepted and giving me the date for starting at St Edmund's.

So I packed up my little business in Lisbon, told all the family what I was planning to do, and in early September I set off for London again and on 22nd of that month I caught the train from Liverpool Street station to Ware in Hertfordshire. At the station I found five others and we all crammed into a taxi to make the five mile journey to St Edmund's College. We arrived in the evening just in time for supper.

CHAPTER FIVE

The seminary

A s I was walking along the corridor that led to my room—the room I was to inhabit for the next five and a half years—I saw at the end of the corridor a marble bust of the Sacred Heart of Jesus. Something happened as I looked at it. I gave myself over to this institution I had just entered. An act of submission occurred but one which I believe was injurious. In Tolstoy's novel *Resurrection* he writes,

> Military service always corrupts a man, placing him in conditions of complete idleness, that is, absence of all intelligent and useful work, and liberating him from the common obligations of humanity, for which it substitutes conventional considerations like the honour of the regiment, the uniform and the flag, and, on the one hand, investing him with unlimited power over other men, and, on the other, demanding slavish subjection to superior officers.[1]

An act of submission occurred at the moment when I looked at that marble bust, similar to the one that Tolstoy describes here. It was not a military institution but it did require obedience and devotion to

---

[1]Tolstoy, L. N. (1899). *Resurrection* (p. 76). London: Penguin, 1976.

the symbols that were endemic to the institution. Slavish obedience was demanded to the ceremonial duties of the institution. In that act was a renunciation of my own person, my own thinking, my own responsibility.

A few days later I was sitting in the Douai Hall Lecture Theatre along with about thirty others for my first lecture in philosophy. It was given by George Ekbery, a good solid northerner. The moment he spoke at the beginning of his first lecture I knew I had found what I had long been looking for. Here was someone going to the very foundations of existence, asking questions about the world, human life, and its purposes. We had four lectures a week from George Ekbery. In this first year they were on cosmology and psychology and in the second year they were on ontology. The lectures on psychology bore no relation to psychology as it has been studied since the time of Wundt. It was an inquiry into what constituted life—living things as opposed to what is inanimate.

It has always been extremely important to me to be taught by someone who knows the subject "from the inside", who has personally assimilated it, for whom the subject has come as an answer to questions which are of personal significance. Thirty-five years later when I learned to fly I knew straight away that my first instructor was handing on what he had been told, and I searched instead for someone for whom aeroplanes and flying were like his personal clothing. I was lucky enough to find just such a person. George Ekbery was a philosopher "from the inside". It was clear that all the philosophical questions which he addressed were of personal significance for him, that he had questioned all the traditional answers. He had a textbook which he would put on the desk and after looking at the first couple of sentences he would get up, move away from the podium, and spend the rest of the hour walking up and down and explaining the problem, the solutions which different philosophers had given, and the defects of each solution.

The second year of his lectures was entirely devoted to the subject of ontology. He made it absolutely clear that he was teaching this not to support some doctrine of the Catholic Church but in order to get some grasp of the mystery of existence. One day, early on in that second year, I suddenly grasped the nature of Being, of Reality, of *Ontos*. It was a groundbreaking experience that has stood as a foundation stone behind all learning that I have since imbibed. I only regret that when I was in the seminary I let various Christian dogmas shroud my life's infrastructure.

120

Later when I came to study psychology and psychoanalysis I let these doctrines also mask this ground of all being. Only after many years did I return to that foundation stone that George Ekbery had first opened my eyes to. I realised within psychoanalysis that in Wilfred Bion, who laid down O as the foundation stone, that I had met up with George's twin brother. Coming from different disciplines they each knew that *Ontos* was the foundation stone underlying all study of the human condition.

I was happier than I had ever been when attending George Ekbery's philosophy lectures. I loved this inquiry into the very basic foundation stones of life and the world. I knew from George's very first lecture that I had at last found what I had been looking for. This was the subject which gripped my heart and mind. If it had not been for my timidity I am sure that I would have pursued philosophy as a career; as it is it has always been a great interest. So I threw myself into the study of philosophy. The timetable at St Edmund's was such that the lectures were in the morning, leaving the afternoon and evening until supper at half-past seven for private study, so we had five to six hours every day for private study and I threw myself into it with vigour. I used to study either in my room or in one of the libraries.

From very early years in Portugal I had asked, "Why, why, why?", and now at last I had tumbled into the subject whose *raison d'etre* was to try to solve these questions. How had man come to be on the earth? How and when did he first evolve a language? When did he begin to bury the dead? Do human beings originate from one pair or from many? Do any stars, other than the sun, have planets which support life? Human life? Did capitalism really arise out of the Protestant ethic? Why did China not develop scientifically when it had sophisticated astronomical instruments earlier than the West? When did money as an exchange instrument start? What is consciousness? Are there mental processes that are not conscious? Why have religion and science been antithetical to each other? These and a thousand other questions were always troubling my mind. At last I had found a forum where it was encouraged to ask these questions and to try to answer them. It is such a tragedy that philosophy is looked upon as an esoteric subject rather than an inquiry into life, existence, and human purpose. I knew that these were not just academic abstractions—somewhere in them I would find solutions to problems that were of intimate concern for me and my life. This spirit of inquiry is part of my being and has sustained me through turbulence and crisis.

121

That first year of philosophy was extremely important in that it got my mind functioning and I addressed myself to all the cosmological and psychological questions and came to understand them, but it was the second year when we studied ontology and had four lectures a week on it for the whole academic year that a deep new world was opened to me. This became a foundation stone in my life. When I later lost my Catholic faith my ontological understanding remained. Through ontology I did not *believe* in God but knew the absolute nature of existence through intellectual and emotional conviction. Some may choose to call *the absolute nature of existence* god but I hasten to add that this was not the figure of that name usually associated with the Judaeo-Christian revelation but rather the god as elaborated by Spinoza. It has always stood as a rock against all forms of nihilism and relativism. I believe it is a better rock than the one provided by the Catholic Church on one side, or by realist philosophers on the other. It was only later that I realised this intellectual vision had first been grasped by the seers of the Upanishads.

There was a strange division that I knew but only became aware of about thirty years later. It was that truth, humility, and courage are founded on this ontological solidity and not upon the truths revealed by the Catholic Church, as popularly understood. I put in this cautionary phrase because I think the great Christian thinkers have all been grounded upon this ontological rock. Origen, St Augustine, St Thomas Aquinas, Meister Eckhart, Paul Tillich, or Martin Buber have all been rooted here. And I must add that Freud and Marx were not. In fact I came to accept that one reason why I had not been able to solve my problem of spiritual pride was that I was trying all along to use the instruments which the Catholic Church had to offer me but that none of these would do the job. Later I came to appreciate that psychoanalysis could not do the job either unless it were in partnership with ontological understanding. I realise that I am expressing myself here in a very condensed way but hope it will become more dilute and understandable as the further emotional story unfolds.

We had another philosophy lecturer who was a robot. He lectured (I would not say "taught") in the history of philosophy and in epistemology. He just read from notes and I doubt if he had written these notes himself. It was clear that he had no personal interest in the subject and very little understanding of it. I was sorry that epistemology was not one of George's subjects because he would have done it so well, but he did encompass it to some extent when discussing ontology. George introduced me to Maurice Blondel whose treatise *L'Action* has had a lasting influence upon my thinking. Another aspect to George's approach that was extremely important to me was that he distinguished very clearly between what was relevant and truly of significance to anyone trying to live what Socrates called "an examined life" and what was emotionally remote. He showed us, for instance, that Thomas Aquinas's proofs for the existence of God had little significance and that this was a crucial matter. George had been very influenced by Bergson and he told us the story of Jacques and Raissa Maritain who made a pact to kill themselves within a year unless they could find some meaning to life and that it was Bergson who was able to show them that life had a meaning. George was a priest and I believe a holy one but I think the meaningfulness of life for him lay in something that was more elemental than anything revealed through the religion of his faith. That which is truly relevant and what is not has and is of great importance to me. In more recent years I came across Meister Eckhart's statement that making what is secondary primary is the root of all error. I am certain that this was a very wise perception of his.[2] I have become impatient of many philosophers whose subject of inquiry does not warrant the time devoted to it, but I can say the same of a great deal of rhetoric within psychoanalysis and, for that matter, within sociology, psychology, and history.

I am very grateful to the Catholic Church for having given me this education. Although it was an education which ultimately led me out of membership of the Church it was and is spiritual in its nature and has given me an inner attitude to life and the world which is a treasure I value more than anything. It saddens me when I see Catholics today— and I mean devout "believing" Catholics—who have been seduced by relativistic forms of psychology and psychotherapy, believing thereby that they are being "up to date" but in truth spurning what is best about their faith. So many are victims to that modern epidemic known as postmodernism. Anyone who grasps the core of ontology can see how spurious the postmodern philosophy is.

The attempts to marry religion and psychology, in any of its forms, must fail unless the enquirer goes deeply into the roots of both. I have

---

[2]Kelley, C. F. (1977). *Meister Eckhart on Divine Knowledge* (p. 42). New Haven, CT: Yale University Press.

been to so many conferences that try to establish a marriage between religion and science, psychoanalysis and literature, psychology and philosophy, etc., but which are based on superficial connexions.

The first two years of study at St Edmund's was devoted to philosophy, the next four to theology but scripture was taught throughout the six years so we had Hubert Richards giving us lectures in scripture from the beginning of my time at St Edmund's. Those first two years of listening and understanding scripture exorcised much of the superstitious piety with which I was heavily laden when I arrived at St Edmund's. I soon came to understand that my scruples about whether the host touched my teeth or not were based upon an idea which was totally untrue and that the command of Jesus to "take and eat" was how it should be; that the presence of Christ in the Eucharist was in the form of bread and as such should be eaten just as bread is. The idea that one's teeth would be biting into Jesus and hurting him like when he fell, carrying his Cross on the way to Calvary, was based on a serious misconception. By the time I had finished my first year of scripture under Hubert Richards's tuition I had rid myself intellectually of all these superstitions that had been such a torture to me as a child. I use the adverb *intellectually* advisedly because I only began to be free of the emotional substrate of such scruples years later. The first emotional dawning of such liberation occurred when I arrived in the parish just after having been ordained a priest. Such scruples are a component of narcissism; they are essentially self-centred and self-preoccupied predicaments. This intellectual liberation created a great gulf between me and my father who remained attached, if not addicted, to many superstitious religious practices.

This gulf led to some estrangement between me and him when I returned for holidays. I realised that he clung to certain Catholic superstitions and that even when it was explained that a particular outlook was not in fact in line with Catholic thinking he remained adamant in his stance. It was, for instance, a piece of folklore that it was only Protestants who read the Old Testament and that Catholics neither did so nor indeed should do so. When my father repeated this piece of folklore I explained to him that although this was often said it was not true and told him how we were studying the Old Testament and that the Church was trying to alter the attitude of Catholics to this. He listened and then just said, "But Catholics should not read the Old Testament."

I was exasperated. I noticed that the same was true of some of my cousins but this unthinking attitude was strongest in my father.

124

As I learned more and more at St Edmund's my exasperation with my father became greater and greater. I realised that on any matters concerned with religion he was quite unable to think. He was stuck in a particular inner dogmatic mental frame and nothing would shift him from it. I began to understand my mother's frustration with him.

I was exasperated but loved him. We would go for long walks and I understood how unhappy he was in his marriage; I longed to stretch a helping hand towards him but was quite unable to do so. The question was, "What was I to do with this exasperation?" What I found was that this attitude of my father was shared by the majority of the clergy. This is the point at which to explain the historical moment of my time at St Edmund's which was pivotal both for the Church generally and for myself and other young priests at that time.

* * *

I arrived at St Edmund's on 22nd September 1958. A month later Pius XII died and Roncalli, the seventy-seven-year-old patriarch of Venice, was elected pope and took the name of John XXIII. Everyone thought that this was a "stopgap" pope who would do nothing until Montini, the Archbishop of Milan, was made a cardinal and so could be elected pope. This is what happened five years later but John XXIII initiated a radical reform in the Church. Within a short time of becoming pope he called a council which, when it met, was called the Second Vatican Council. This is what was happening on the world stage of the Church and it was mirrored in what was to become a significant thing that was happening at St Edmund's.

After the two years of philosophy I moved into the other lecture hall to start my four years of theology and here it was that I was taught by Charles Davis.

* * *

The six years at St Edmund's were very happy. Intellectually I threw myself first into philosophy and then theology. Charles Davis was an inspiring teacher. He was a more tortured man than George Ekbery and was not in touch with himself in the way that George was, but his passion for theology, which he communicated with a rare enthusiasm, inspired me and also a significant group of us. He lectured to us four times a week for about forty weeks a year. Each lecture was meticulously prepared and his thoroughness was remarkable. He covered the whole of Christian doctrine in those four years: *De Deo Uno, De Deo Trino, De Deo Creatore, The Incarnation and Redemption, Grace and the Church* and *the Sacraments. De Deo Uno et Trino* and *De Deo Creatore* took up a whole year of lectures and so did *The Incarnation and Redemption* as did *Grace and the Church,* and *the Sacraments* took a further year. It may be difficult for someone to imagine The Trinity could take six months of lectures to cover the subject. Charles, Charlie as we called him in those days, never presented these subjects as something abstract and external. Although he went in detail into all the early councils of the Church which had bit by bit formulated the Trinitarian doctrine, yet it was of central spiritual significance to us as Christians. We, through the redemptive acts of Christ, were drawn into the inner personal life of the triune God through saving grace. The whole of the four years of Christian doctrine in the hands of Charles Davis was the unfolding of the history of salvation, of God's amazing love for mankind. His teaching, coupled with that of Hubert Richards, revolutionised my whole understanding of the Catholic Church and Christianity. It was not just that I had learned more and knew more than the average Catholic layman but my whole understanding and orientation were entirely different from most of my fellow Catholics. It not only created a gulf between me and my father but between me and most of the Catholic clergy.

I was not of course the only one whose outlook changed under Charlie's teaching. There were several of us who were inspired by him. I am not sure of the percentage of students who were so radically changed in outlook but I should think it was about a quarter of the students. The other students, or *divines*, as we were called, tended to be hostile to Charles's disruptive teaching and the older clergy on the parishes were violently so. A group of us became fanatically attached to the "new doctrine". It was not new but rather a renewed understanding of the Christian message. Charlie's emphasis centred upon the presence of God's redemptive love present here and now through the Bible, the Church, and the Church's rituals.

At St Edmund's during these years I forged some of the closest friendships which have continued down the years: Richard Champion, John Perry, Bill McSweeney, and Patrick Carey were all students at St Edmund's. We were all enormously influenced by Charlie; we were all ordained and we all left the Church within a few years of ordination.

I often did not see them for some years but the bond of friendship remained as strong as ever. Two of them—Richard Champion and John Perry—have now died. We were all involved in this vital renewal in the Church and, when we were ordained, were all torn in two by the conflict we found ourselves in. A bond through being in the trenches together fashioned a friendship which was closer than normal. I don't think in subsequent years I have made any friends who are as close as these.

I studied with a passion through all these years. I read nearly the whole of Cardinal Newman: his *Grammar of Assent, The Development of Christian Doctrine, Apologia Pro Vita Sua*, and the eight volumes of his *Parochial and Plain Sermons*. From reading Newman I came to understand the Church in a new way. In particular his *Development of Christian Doctrine* reached through to a deep understanding of Christian life through its developmental history. I read the whole of Thomas Aquinas's *Summa Theologica* but also contemporary theologians like Karl Rahner, Schillebeecks, Louis Bouyer, Jungmann, Odo Casel, Pius Parsch, Hans Küng, Yves Congar, Jean Daniélou, and many others. I was particularly drawn to the works of Louis Bouyer who had the most penetrating psychological insight into the Bible, the liturgy, spirituality, monasticism, and Protestantism. He had been a Protestant and his book *The Spirit and Forms of Protestantism* is a profound and sympathetic insight into the inner soul of Protestantism.

* * *

This is as good a place as any to say something of the significance of books in my life. I believe it is possible to divide the world between those for whom reading is an inner necessity for the solution of life's problems and an essential ingredient for the business of life's journey, and those for whom reading is a leisure activity, something done to fill in time. I believe I have from early years had an emotional problem of a deep kind and that there has been something in me whose central preoccupation has been to solve it. In fact, my life's endeavour has been the solving of a problem and anyone who can give me some little piece of the jigsaw that will solve some aspect of it, however small, is thanked and treasured. Now, although my problem has been an emotional one, its solution has been through thought. Thinking is a creative act, whereby the inner components are rearranged into a

127

new synthesis. There is a creative centre whose activity becomes manifest in thinking. There is something I do not understand, cannot make sense of—and then suddenly I read something that makes sense of it. From early years I started reading with this serious intent. It started in an inchoate way at school where I remember being very engaged by Dostoevsky's *Crime and Punishment*. I must have read that when I was about sixteen. I read it again when I was about forty-two and again when I was aged seventy. Each time it made a deep impression upon me and I suspect that I may read it again before life's end. But the passion for reading started during the madness that overtook me when I was working in Lisbon. Partly under the guidance of Susan Marques I started to read seriously. It was during this time that I first read the New Testament carefully but it was also then that I read the lives of many of the saints, such as St Catherine of Siena. One of the authors who meant a lot to me at this time was G. K. Chesterton. I read his *Orthodoxy* but also *Heretics, St Francis of Assisi, St Thomas Aquinas, What's Wrong with the World, The Everlasting Man, The Victorian Age in Literature, Robert Browning*, and his *Autobiography*. I also read Maisie Ward's biography of him and then her subsequent book *Return to Chesterton*. His journey into Catholicism echoed the stepping stones of my journey into the Church. At St Edmund's I read him a little and then he disappeared out of my life for nearly forty years. More recently I read his *George Bernard Shaw* and loved it. I then reread his *St Francis of Assisi, St Thomas Aquinas, Heretics, Orthodoxy*, and his *Autobiography*, and again thought that he was a genius who has gone largely unrecognised. His simplicity, his love of England, his "in-touchness" with the common man, his love and understanding of fairy tales, his sense of life itself being a poem, and his magnanimous heart moved me into sympathetic understanding of him. He criticised certain mental attitudes with untrammelled determination but always with love. It is clear, for instance, that in his biography of Bernard Shaw he disagreed with him profoundly but loved him at the same time. His hatred of puritanism, his deep understanding of the Church's sacramentality, and his love of children gave me a sense that he had a deep understanding of life and he communicated something of this to me. Also in my recent rereading of him I have felt much joy when he emphasises that our talents, our insights, our genius even are the gifts of good fortune; also in his emphasis that we do not have a right to be loved, to be respected, but it is a great good fortune if it happens to us.

But this is just one example of an author who moved me and who was of great significance. I have already cited Louis Bouyer who was very significant for me and I have mentioned Cardinal Newman. I came across the Russian philosopher, Vladimir Solovyov, and I read everything I could of his that was available in any European language. I could not read Russian but I read all his books that had been translated into English. He wrote, while he was in exile in Paris, one or two books in French so I read these in the original. There was one book of his that made an enormous impact upon me. It was *The Justification of the Good*[3]; it still stands on my bookshelf and I turn its pages from time to time, but the reading of that book was a milestone in my ethical understanding. It moved me from an ethics based upon solipsistic principles to one based upon a relation to the other, a relation to persons. Pity, shame, and reverence were the three foundation stones upon which he built his ethical system. Pity became compassion, shame became conscience, and reverence shaded into the worship of God. I will explain what I mean by a solipsistic ethics. I had been taught that a lie occurred when the outer words did not correspond to the inner belief or thought, but Solovyov said that if I go out into an open field and there is no one in earshot and shout out, "The world is not round, it is flat," it is not a lie because it falls upon no human ear. The words do not correspond to what I know inside to be the truth but it is not a lie because no one hears them. A lie occurs when I tell the words *to* someone. This gave me a totally different orientation to morality and it was seriously at variance with ethics as it was being taught to me and according to the way I was brought up, but Solovyov's version of ethics held conviction for me.

There was a famous dilemma based upon what I would call the solipsistic definition of a lie. I think the dilemma had first been posed either by St Athanasius or St Cyprian in the fourth century. You are at home and a man beats on your door and asks you to give him shelter because a man is chasing him and intends to kill him. So you quickly take him in and hide him in your house. A few minutes later the murderer beats on your door and asks you if you have seen a man escaping in this direction. The traditional Catholic answer had to avoid "telling a lie". So, as the householder, you had, in your answer to the murderer, either to evade the question or equivocate. This was the answer given by Christian moral theologians for centuries. Solovyov said that if you

---

[3]Solovyov, Vladimir (1918). *The Justification of the Good*. London: Constable.

evaded the question or equivocated, the murderer would suspect that you knew where his victim was and would go in search of him. Solovyov said that as householder you had an *obligation* to tell the murderer that you had indeed seen the fleeing man and that he had gone in such-and-such a direction and point the direction out to the murderer with conviction. Your Christian duty here was to protect a man from being killed. Your words did not correspond to the actual truth but they represented a deeper truth—your duty to your neighbour. Before reading *The Justification of the Good* I had come across this dilemma when studying moral theology and Solovyov's dismissal of the traditional position and his reasoning had complete conviction for me. What I realise now with some surprise is that what I was responding to with enthusiasm was an ethical system based upon compassion rather than one which was solipsistic in nature. The surprise is that the solipsistic attitude was the one espoused by moral theologians throughout the Church and one that had a heritage going back to the fourth century. It is disturbing when you discover that maybe a whole tradition in thinking, and one endorsed by the greatest minds, could be wrong. There can be revolutions within thinking just as great as that of Copernicus within science. Solovyov was a Copernicus and I believe he suffered greatly for it with loneliness and isolation. It is a great comfort to the spirit to know that you are in the bosom of a tradition where what you think and believe is shared by numerous others down the centuries. Solovyov's dying words were, "The service of the Lord is hard." I knew that Cardinal Newman held firmly to the traditional ethical view. I think this had also been the view of St Augustine and St Thomas Aquinas. Later in life I came to address what I refer to as the "solipsistic attitude" as *narcissism* and this became a different formulation for a central problem for which I was seeking a solution. I was also convinced in Solovyov's book by his argument that capital punishment was the execution of revenge undertaken by the state and that because revenge is morally wrong then so is capital punishment. Thomas Aquinas, for instance, had argued that when a man had committed a crime he had lowered himself below the dignity of animals and, as we are entitled to kill animals, so now the state was entitled to kill the criminal. I was convinced by Solovyov's arguments against this position and, although I have occasionally wavered over it, I have held to that view.

Other works of Solovyov that I read were: *Lectures on Godmanhood, La Russie et l'Eglise Universelle, War Christianity and the End of History,* and some other works whose titles I have now forgotten. I also read a biography of him called *The Russian Newman*.[4] I had a higher opinion of him than of Newman. His mind had been forged in the powerful currents of contemporary thought. He had been a Marxist, an atheist; he understood the philosophical outlooks that underpinned most modern thinking and had forged his own position thereby. I obtained *The Justification of the Good* from the local Hertford library but it meant so much to me that I asked the Times Bookshop in Wigmore Street in London to search for it for me. They finally found it for me and I paid the sum of £4 10s which in 1960 was a lot of money for a book, but I was delighted to have it and even today nothing would make me part with it. He had more influence upon me than any other thinker and caused a revolution in my religious and philosophical outlook.

A small book which was introduced to me by Adrian Walker was *De Spirituali Amicitia* by Aelred of Rievaulx, translated as *Christian Friendship*.[5] This went against the attitude promulgated to all of us students at St Edmund's, especially by the president of the college, Monsignor Butcher: that the priesthood was a life without friendship, that this was something one had to sacrifice on behalf of God. Mgr Butcher used to give us a discourse in the chapel every Friday night and reiterated this on various occasions. I sensed in my bones that this was wrong. Aelred, who was a Cistercian monk of the twelfth century and Abbot of Rievaulx Abbey, which I knew well because it was close to Ampleforth, believed that friendship was at the heart of Christian living. At every point in St John's Gospel where Jesus uses the word "love" Aelred said he would be prepared to transpose the word "friendship".

Pierre Teilhard de Chardin was another important "find". His 1957 book *Le Milieu Divin*[6] which came out in English in 1960 was enormously influential upon several of us at St Edmund's. We had all been reared in the spiritual ethos of hatred of the world, of the opposition between God and the world, whereas Teilhard de Chardin dedicated that book "To Those Who Love the World". It was only very much later that I came to realise that an *ascesis of the heart* in the midst of the world was a far greater Christian sacrifice than that repudiation of the world,

[4]D'Herbigny, Michel (1918). *Vladimir Soloviev—A Russian Newman*. London: R. & T. Washbourne.
[5]Saint Aelred of Rievaulx (1942). *Christian Friendship*. London: The Catholic Book Club.
[6]Teilhard de Chardin, Pierre (1960). *Le Milieu Divin*. London: Collins.

the *fuga mundi*, which had been so central to Christian spirituality for centuries. Here was another case, like Solovyov, of someone rupturing what had been believed and preached for centuries in monasteries and theological colleges throughout the Western world. The knowledge of these false ideologies that have travelled down academic circles for centuries has convinced me also that within the human or social sciences we are all subject, or victim, to similar erroneous attitudes. Sometimes these attitudes are so endemic that we do not recognise them. These attitudes are not only within theology and philosophy but also within science.

Another enormously influential book was Caryll Houselander's *Guilt*.[7] She declared at the beginning of that book that she was an "ego-neurotic" and that she had managed to cure herself of it, and she offered this book to anyone else suffering from this condition. It was for me a mind-breaking book and, of course, she was addressing exactly the problem that I was struggling with. Some of the examples she gives in that book of her own ego-neurosis have stayed with me to this day and I believe that she understood the heart of spiritual health or what psychiatrists or psychoanalysts would call "sanity". She had absolutely no time for the sort of ascetic practices that took someone outside the pains of daily life. If you had to look for them, said Caryll Houselander, then you were taking flight from the ones that were under your nose. In another book she says that the greatest fallacy is that we all worship the same God. The God worshipped by one would be unrecognisable to the God worshipped by another. So I also read her books *The Reed of God*,[8] *This War Is the Passion*,[9] *The Risen Christ*,[10] and *The Flowering Tree*.[11] Her writings spoke to me in the most penetrating way and I still have her works on my bookshelf. Caryll Houselander had a psychological intuition of rare acuity unusual in Church circles. The Catholic psychiatrist, Eric Strauss, used to send patients to her although she had no formal training as a psychotherapist and it was said of her that she "loved them back to life". What I also appreciated in her was the total absence of sentimentality. This dovetailed well with the spiritual outlook that I was imbibing from Charles Davis and Hubert Richards but

[7]Houselander, Caryll (1952). *Guilt*. London: Sheed & Ward.
[8]Houselander, Caryll (1945). *The Reed of God*. London: The Catholic Book Club.
[9]Houselander, Caryll (1945). *This War Is the Passion*. London: Sheed & Ward.
[10]Houselander, Caryll (1959). *The Risen Christ*. London: Sheed & Ward.
[11]Houselander, Caryll (1946). *The Flowering Tree*. London: Sheed & Ward.

here, in Caryll Houselander, was an application into a deeper emotional realm than anything taught by Charlie or Bert.

The illumination that Caryll Houselander was able to give me into inner psychological processes separated me in my interests from both my teachers and my friends. I became deeply interested in the inner emotional structure of our lives. I read at this time most of the works of Carl Jung. The Catholic Church had given an unofficial *imprimatur* to the works of Jung so I read his works eagerly. I once tried to read one of Freud's works but at that time found him dry and uninteresting. I am not sure whether this was because the Church looked on Freud with disfavour and this influenced my reading of him or whether I was not ready to read him at that time. Later, when I was doing the psychoanalytic training I read nearly all his works and found them full of interest. However, his foundation stone is an arid determinism which still leaves me gasping for fresh air, imagination, and adventure. It was not that Freud himself did not have these but he tried to root them into the dogmatic framework of determinism. Of my friends who left the Church at the same time as me I was the only one who took up psychology as a professional career. Bill McSweeney read sociology and is now director of a college of international relations in Dublin, John Perry became a social worker, Patrick Carey a teacher, and Richard Champion a potter. When I was a priest on the parish I became involved with Alcoholics Anonymous and Gamblers Anonymous and continued reading psychological works. I remember the huge impact Piaget's *Moral Development of the Child* had upon me when I was in my first parish in Bow, in the East End of London.

Another important work that I read and studied with care was the *Summa Theologica* of St Thomas Aquinas. I read it *attente et devote* and when I had finished it I understood Catholicism in a new way. I realised then how Aquinas followed the loving theory of redemption right through into all the interstices of Catholic doctrine. Since reading this work of Aquinas and also those of Solovyov I have always treasured the value of reading and understanding the mind of a great thinker. It is I believe the foundation stone of any true education. The minds I had studied until this time were Newman, Aquinas, Solovyov, and Maurice Blondel. Together with attending, first and foremost, the lectures of George Ekbery and then those of Charles Davis and Bert Richards, these thinkers gave me an education. I had certainly not acquired an education at school. When I left the Church I did not think I was educated but when I was being analysed by John Klauber he one day said to me that he thought I was educated. Slowly I began to think that perhaps I was.

When I left the Church I followed this principle of studying the mind of a great thinker. I always regret that I did not study Karl Marx with the same care and attention that I had given to Solovyov, for instance. I did read *Das Kapital* but never followed through into a proper study of him. However, I read nearly all of Freud's works and also the works of Max Weber and Emile Durkheim. Studying Durkheim and Weber gave me an understanding of sociology and this perspective has always remained significant for me. I also read Darwin's *The Origin of Species* which I loved and, ever since reading it, I have had an evolutionary perspective on life. In more recent times I read all the works of the philosopher, John Macmurray, who has been enormously influential. The first book of his which I read was *Freedom in the Modern World*[12]; it was mind-blowing for me and I then read all his other books, the greatest of which was *The Self as Agent*.[13] I found him to be a prophetical thinker for our times. When later I came to study psychology I began to think that what the social sciences needed was a new Kant, but I then came to think that he had already arrived in the person of John Macmurray but had not yet been recognised as such.

I have followed, ever since my days at St Edmund's, two other principles which are closely connected. In Charles Davis's lectures which I attended, he used to hand out each week the most extensive reading list. I soon realised that it was impossible to keep up and to begin with I went into a minor panic. Then one day I was reading some theological work which I found illuminating, but it related to the topic of last week's lectures or those of the week before, so I was falling behind. I suddenly said to myself, "To hell with it. I am getting a lot out of this book: I will continue reading it even if I am falling behind." I stuck to that principle for the rest of my time at St Edmund's. When exam time came I did well so I did not seem to suffer on account of it. What I certainly know is that what I read I truly understood and it had a transformational effect on me. The second principle is closely connected with this first one. I only read works that are emotionally significant for me. The place where I am emotionally guides me in what I read. If people tell me, "You must read such-and-such," and I open the book and it does not grip me or engage me at

---

[12]Macmurray, John (1932). *Freedom in the Modern World*. London: Faber & Faber.
[13]Macmurray, John (1957). *The Self as Agent*. London: Faber & Faber.

the emotional level, I put it aside; but frequently the most obscure book, a dusty volume dug out of the top shelf of a second-hand bookshop, has been of enormous significance for me. I seem to smell out what will help me along on life's journey. Recently I read a passing remark of a journalist about *The Egoist* by George Meredith, about whom I knew nothing and whose works I had never read. I scoured second-hand bookshops for a copy and found it enormously illuminating and have read it three times and studied parts of it further. I am not a creature of fashion. I follow where my emotional instincts take me and often it is to the most obscure or little-known authors. Vladimir Solovyov and Caryll Houselander are not well known but their influence upon me has been enormous.[14] There are certain little-known novelists also, like R. C. Hutchinson, who have been hugely influential. I am quite sure that some of the greatest geniuses have gone almost unnoticed. There is a strange thing called fashion which alights on particular people who become "cult figures" but their glittering superficiality hypnotises the masses while the great thinkers and the wise go unnoticed. The sort of cult figures I mean are Hanna Arendt, Derrida, Levenson, but there are many others. More recently *The Human Situation* by Macneile Dixon has revolutionised my life.[15]

How is an emotional problem solved? It is through being changed by thought from hate to love. That is it at its simplest. Deep thinking has been for me the only solution. Superficial thinking is not thinking at all but rather the packaged thoughts of others wrapped in synthesised language. Deep thinking refers to the generation of new thoughts or rather the application of a thought from one arena into a totally different one. An example of this was when Darwin[16] was struck by a sentence in Malthus's *Essay on the Principle of Population* and realised its significance. The sentence was: "It may safely be pronounced, therefore, that population, when unchecked, goes on doubling itself every twenty-five years, or increases in geometrical ratio." This brought to Darwin the realisation that with such enormously fast multiplication it must mean there is a huge decay rate determined by environmental circumstances,

---

[14] I do not mean to give the impression that these two were equal in their status as thinkers. Caryll Houselander had sharp insights embedded in much that is superstitious and unprovable whereas Solovyov was I believe one of the greatest thinkers and probably the greatest religious thinker of the nineteenth century.
[15] Macneile Dixon, W. (1958). *The Human Situation*. London: Penguin.
[16] Quoted in: Clark, R. W. (1984). *Charles Darwin* (pp. 53–54). London: Weidenfeld & Nicolson.

and so, with this rapid rate of destruction, it must be the fittest to survive. This application of a thought in one realm to one in quite another is called by Koestler[17] the *bisociation of matrices*. This is why deep thinking cannot occur, or is very unlikely to occur, if someone's reading is confined to one discipline of thought. Deep thinking is the generation of thoughts to embrace disparate elements dispersed through hate and trauma. There is no doubt that a solution through deep thought can be clarifying for others as well. I know in later life some solutions to this fundamental problem that I was struggling with, which my whole life has been servant to, have been of significance to some other people. I think that this condition of mine and its partial solution has been an instance of what Ellenberger[18] has called a *creative illness*.

When I left the Church I plunged into literature. Within two weeks of leaving I read several of D. H. Lawrence's novels and then those of Thomas Hardy. Reading *Wuthering Heights* was a staggering inspiration and I read also the novels of Emily Brontë's two sisters, Charlotte and Anne and was amazed and still am that these three sisters living in a remote parsonage in Yorkshire could generate such marvels of psychological insight. The view that great thought and great literature is entirely conditioned by the historical circumstances that surrounded the given individual has always seemed to me to be blind to the sheer marvel of genius, and if ever proof were needed, not that it can be given, that genius is not purely the product of historical process or the spirit of the age or whatever then what better example could we have than the genius of those three sisters living with their mad father in a remote Yorkshire village? Then I read a lot of the Russian novels such as *The Brothers Karamazov, The Devils, The Idiot,* and once again *Crime and Punishment*. Then I read many of Turgenev's novels and finally I turned to Tolstoy and read *War and Peace* and *Anna Karenina. Anna Karenina* is I believe the greatest novel ever written. The whole drama of human life is there—birth, courtship, rejection, love, death, suicide, land reform. Whenever I am persuaded into reading a modern novel by an indifferent author I say to myself when I have finished—so much lost time which could have been spent rereading *Anna Karenina*.

This generation of thoughts as the cradle in which dispersed elements could be gathered into a new whole was the path of my solution. There

---

[17]Koestler, A. (1964). *The Act of Creation*. London: Picador/Pan, 1978.
[18]Ellenberger, H. F. (1970). *The Discovery of the Unconscious*. London: Penguin.

was no solution that someone else could give to me. It was something that I had to generate through my own inner processes. It had to be right for me and for this I had to range through a whole lot of experiences: going into the Church, studying at St Edmund's, working in a parish, undergoing psychoanalysis, becoming a psychoanalyst, teaching, marrying, migrating to Australia, and learning to fly. It has been a marriage of emotional experiences together with the process of thinking by which they become embraced in a new inner organisation.

* * *

The attitude towards Protestantism at St Edmund's was quite the opposite of what I had been brought up to in Oporto and at Ampleforth. At Ampleforth I had imbibed a narrow-minded self-righteous Catholicism. Now, here at St Edmund's, I was coming to realise that many of the protests of the reformers at the time of the Reformation were valid. One of the key issues turned out to be the attitude towards *Extra Ecclesia Nulla Salus*.[19] I now understood that the whole of mankind had been saved by Christ's redemption and that through inward love, which was God's hidden grace, salvation was within the reach of all mankind. So, therefore, if you did not need to be a member of the visible Church to be saved then what was the Church's purpose? This perspective radically altered my view of the Church's mission in the world. It had practical consequences when I was ordained and went as a curate into a parish. My parish priest took the view that only by being a member of the visible Church and through regular attendance at the sacraments could someone be saved. My view was totally different from this and it led to a terrible conflict between us at the practical work level.

The teaching which also radically altered my intellectual and emotional understanding was the changed theory of redemption. I had been taught that God was so offended by the sin of Adam that he sent his Son into the world because as He had been infinitely offended then only a being sharing his infinite nature could repay an infinite offence. The idea of God being offended I realised was a nonsense. It was turning God into a hypersensitive figure whom one might meet at a cocktail party. "Oh be careful if you speak to Mr Crookwell, he is

---

[19]"No salvation outside the Church".

frightfully sensitive and is very easily wounded." I had been taught that God was like this. I believe that all the superstition and false piety flowed from this image of God. As Catholics entered into sympathetic love for God they too were justified in their own hypersensitivity. And there were thousands of Catholics praying in churches, shrines, and before statues, pouring out their miseries towards a poor wounded God.

I now learned that God saw that Adam's sin had damaged mankind and God, out of love for man, sent his Son into the world to heal man. The centre of this was God's mysterious love for mankind. He had sent His Son into the world to rescue us and bring us from a state of alienation into the most intimate sharing of His own personal life. Here was a God of great grandeur whom we could revere and thank for His great gift to all of us. This view of redemption altered my way of seeing the Church's sacramental life and also all its rituals. Here was the Church, as God's agent, bestowing its love upon mankind in an ever-generous outpouring.

Just reading this on paper probably leaves no impression of what an enormous effect this changed outlook had on me. What were referred to as "conservative" priests or Catholics were those who believed in the "offended God" theory of redemption. It was also the outlook of my father and, I believe, of all my family. Although my mother knew nothing about theology and probably had imbibed the offended God theory, yet instinctively she knew that the emotional attitudes that went with it were wrong. So, although I did not realise it at the time, this changed understanding brought me closer to my mother again and I had more sympathy with her antagonism to my father's sentimental piety. When I was in the parish in the East End of London I came to think that the emotional attitudes that lay behind these two disparate theories of redemption divided people much more radically than any "outer" differences. So I felt more sympathy and friendship with an atheist whose emotional attitudes were more in line with the "healthy" theory of redemption than with an offended God Catholic.

What I did not know then but only came to understand years later was that, although I was totally dedicated to the healthy theory of redemption, I was myself an offended God adherent in my inner emotional nature. This turned me into a fanatic which I shall try to explain more fully when I describe my experiences in the parish at Bow but I shall try to describe what I mean about the inner situation now.

I was an emotionally fragile and hypersensitive god myself. I think though that my embracing of this new attitude to redemption represented a recognition that this was not the right way to be, but the idea that I was like that myself was far from my thoughts. What I came to hate in others was really what was true of myself. I got a lightning flash illumination of this when I went into psychoanalysis some years later. That revelation cast me into the deepest depression that it is possible to imagine.

However, it was not true that I had no grasp of this before I went into psychoanalysis because I did know that I was proud and arrogant but did not know how to overcome it. It was my central spiritual dilemma and I did not find any remedy for it within the Church.

I think it would be impossible to overestimate the influence that Charles Davis had upon a group of us at St Edmund's and, by historical chance, this influence coincided with the amazing changes which were occurring at the Vatican Council. The liturgy with the Mass at its centre had been celebrated in Latin in the West for seventeen hundred years and here now pope and council were overturning a practice that had been dear to Catholics all over the world, declaring that in future the Mass should be celebrated in the vernacular. What Charles Davis had been teaching us in the Douai Hall at St Edmund's was being mirrored almost exactly by the Church hierarchy. Our love and fondness for the new pope, John XXIII, was enormous and Charles Davis had now been vindicated by the highest authority in the Church. The old conservative priests were in the wrong; they had been outvoted and we, the enlightened ones, were in the right. We were all ready now, armed with our new understanding, to go out and convert the world.

I became passionately involved in these new currents in the Church. The renewal, though rooted in this different understanding of redemption, was channelled through three connected movements in the Church: the liturgy, the Bible, and Catechetics. I threw myself with passion into all three movements. I became a fervent evangelist of this new faith and thoroughly intolerant of the old superstitious piety. Of course this brought all of us with this orientation into the closest sympathy with Christians of other faiths and the conservative Catholics referred to us as Protestants. We, of course, were proud to see that the Catholic Church had at last "caught up" with the Protestant reform. The Protestants had emphasised the centrality of the Bible four hundred years before and had translated it into the vernacular. Now the Church was following suit four hundred years later.

Everything which had been held sacred within the Catholic Church was now open to question. It was an exciting time of enquiry and new revelations seemed to cascade down upon us week by week. By the time I was ordained I was ready to convert the world.

An emotional event of importance occurred in my second year of philosophy. A student arrived who was extremely cultured and what one might say "out of the top draw". He was also rather obviously homosexual. You would not describe him as camp but he had a distinctly feminine manner. The priest who taught moral theology made a couple of innuendoes aimed at this student in a public lecture. The student complained to the president of the college. The moral theology lecturer took revenge by sniffing out this student's previous history, declaimed him to the curia at Westminster, and had him dismissed from the seminary. I knew that this dismissal was being orchestrated before he actually went. Some very underhand and deceitful activities went on. I saw in the clearest light the cowardice and also malevolence of several priests. It shocked me but also made me realise that priestly robes did nothing to cleanse human nature of the inherent original sin in us all. That knowledge has stayed with me. Because someone is a cardinal, a pope, a psychoanalyst, a doctor, a professor, however much admired, this is no guarantee that he will not be devious, cowardly, or malevolent in the extreme. I have also come to realise that the majority do not see things this way. Most Catholics believe that the priest is holy by virtue of his office; even more believe that this is so of a bishop and a fortiori of cardinals and the pope. Since being a psychoanalyst I have come across colleagues who have written books, held high positions, and are admired by many, and yet they are clearly charlatans. I have never regretted realising that the outer role, however exalted, does not tell one about the character of the man or woman who occupies it, but it has led me on occasions to feel quite isolated. I think it likely in fact that in present day bureaucratic society the number of psychopaths in high positions is alarmingly great.

I was twenty-two at the time when this student was about to be dismissed. I felt sure that the manner in which he was being dismissed was quite wrong and I further thought that the dismissal itself was based on a very narrow-minded outlook. So I summoned all my courage and went and knocked one evening on the door of the president's office. A frightened shrimp entered his office. He showed me a seat next to his desk. I sat down and told him that I thought this student's dismissal was very narrow-minded, that it may be that he was not right for the ordinary parish, that there had been other cultured people at St Edmund's like Ronnie Knox (who was also homosexual though I did not say this) who had done a great service to the Church but never did ordinary parish work, and that I believed that this student was capable of scholarly work which would be of value to the Church. Monsignor Butcher was embarrassed and I think he was sympathetic to what I was saying, and told me in confidence that he had a very poor opinion of the professor of moral theology whom he told me was a very dangerous man. However, the student was dismissed, and I think Mgr Butcher was not courageous enough to withstand the machinations which had now reached up to the level of the cardinal himself.

I respected myself for acting in this way. I have on occasions done things which have taken some courage for me to do and I have respected myself for having done so. Also some instances stand out in my mind as everlasting reproaches for my cowardice.

It was recognised that I was one of the "bright boys" so further education was suggested. It was recommended that I go to Cambridge and take a degree in modern languages and then come back and teach in the school which adjoined the seminary. The other suggestion was that I go to Rome and study canon law. I passionately did not want to do either so I wrote to Cardinal Godfrey and begged him to excuse me from both these projects. I had trained to be a priest and did not want to end up being a teacher. If I had wanted to be a teacher then I would not have trained to become a priest, I thought. I also did not want to study canon law. I was bored by law and felt unsympathetic to the lawyer mentality. So I told Cardinal Godfrey in a long letter that I wanted to be a priest in a parish.

I think, however, I made a mistake. I should have loved to go and study philosophy in Rome but did not ask for this. I think the reason I did not do so lay deeper. Superficially it was that I thought it wrong somehow to "get what I wanted" or that I did not deserve the sort of happiness that would have come through an intellectual fulfilment of that kind. The emotional sense that I did not deserve happiness or fulfilment in life was a very deep issue. It was only years later that I came to recognise that it was part of a pathological pattern of which pride or arrogance was an aspect. It was also perhaps a knowledge that

141

I was here at St Edmund's under false pretences—in a cowardly retreat from the shock of my mother's infidelity. This inchoate knowledge told me that I did not deserve fulfilment: punishment was what I deserved and that is what I would get.

I went through a period where I thought I was not doing enough for God and that I should go into a Trappist monastery. However, something held me back from this. I wanted to be "in the world". Also, my friend, Adrian Walker, had been in such a monastery and told me some shocking stories of pride, deviousness, and spitefulness that he had encountered there. I had come to know that the idea that there was anywhere in the world a Utopia free of corruption, deviousness, and deceit was a mythological delusion. I am glad I did not take that step. A Christian monastery, a Buddhist sangha, a Judaic yeshiva, or a sufi brotherhood did not indicate that here was a loving and compassionate group. I learned this at the age of twenty-two and it has always stayed with me.

I also went through the kinds of doubts with which many religious people are assailed. I can remember it quite clearly. I was in the library and looking at the cover of a book and in the title of the book was the word "GOD". As I looked at it my belief in the existence of God suddenly crumbled from under me. I stood transfixed and I started to sweat and I was gripped by a panic. I suddenly realised that my vocation, career, and the whole direction of my life was anchored in this act of belief. And what if that belief vanished as it seemed to have done now? I cannot remember how I came out of this but I know the state of doubt and panic stayed with me for several days and it was a torment. The Catholic prescription for such a doubt is to pray to God, pray for faith, but how do you do that if you doubt the existence of the person from whom you are supposed to be getting the gift of faith? "It's a dark night of the soul," a spiritual director would say. I think now that the doubt was correct. I believe in God today but it is not the God that I was instructed to believe in at the time. It is the absolute reality reached by reflexion. It is godhead rather than God as Meister Eckhart had illustrated so clearly in his German Sermons. Because even the "new god" I had learned to believe in under the guidance of Charles Davis was ultimately a false god, an idol. If I had followed the direction of my doubt I would have been out of the Church, out of my vocation. This is what ultimately happened to me and this radical doubt was a premonitory prophetic flash. It terrified me and I am not surprised that it did because the path that has been my life has been difficult, lonely, and devoid of supportive comfort. I would not wish it upon another and yet I am deeply grateful for the gift of life. What a marvel! Think of all the accidental chances that coincided to bring me the gift of life. I hope I shall never lose sight of it. I treasure this statement by Macneile Dixon:

> The first and fundamental wonder is existence itself. That I should be alive, conscious, a person, a part of the whole, that I should have emerged out of nothingness, that the Void should have given birth not merely to things, but to me. Among the many millions who throughout the centuries have crossed the stage of time probably not more than a handful have looked about them with astonishment, or found their own presence within the visible scene in any way surprising.[20]

I share this outlook of Macneile Dixon. My own notion is almost the same as his except that for me the wonder is not my own existence but the fantastic fact that there is existence at all—not just mine. No scientist, no artist, no metaphysician can do anything but marvel at the sheer wonder of existence.

One day I was walking by a canal in Worcestershire and I saw a frog hop out in front of me and I was so pleased to think that I, as part of humanity, had evolved from this jumping amphibian. I thought of it as my cousin and remembered that lovely prayer of St Francis known as the Song of Brother Sun. Life that might not have been but is—what a mystery, what a marvel. I give thanks for it. I wrote this poem to try to give expression to this sentiment:

Hallucination at Hendon Aeronautical Museum

Staring at a flying machine,
Hanging from a high white ceiling
By threadlike nylon wires.
I was looking at his side
Planelike from a window wide.

He was walking solidly
Alone upon an open floor
Looking at these fragile flyers

---

[20]Macneile Dixon, W. (1958). *The Human Situation* (pp. 72–73). London: Penguin.

Resting quiet from turbulence.
In this morgue-like ambience.

It was man that caught my eye.
How had his being come to be?
Not only in this plane museum
But walking on the earth at all.
A thought that gut-like did appal.

Geological time was telescoped.
Yesterday he was a chimp,
The day before a vervet monkey,
A week before a crocodile,
A month ago a fish'n the Nile.

Focussed in this lonesome plodder,
Walking in casual concentration
Upon museum's spacious floor,
Embodying the human race
In unity of time and place.

Was this suited substance
What language called a man?
Or was I in some vast delusion?
How had his being come to be?
What was it that eluded me?

A fact taken all for granted
Became the huge-est question mark.
Burrowing into life's foundations,
With it all projects were suffused
And made my past all confused.

Beside a canal in Worcestershire
A frog jumped from beneath my feet
I looked at it with tenderness;
From its genes I am descended
In that sight something was mended.

The frame that silhouetted "man"
Dissolved and made me humble now,
Making cousinhood with fish and bird,

With amphibians and reptiles too,
All the denizens of the zoo.

The lens through which I viewed him now
Was latent in my mind before
But trained upon the world without:
The starry heavens and evolution
From which I looked without devotion.

My being was within him now.
I was not looking from without
For him and I were oned together.
This compound now has changed the lens,
Making what was past the present tense.

"A change of focus?"
Chimes the sophomore.
"You are outside as I once was;
No exegesis can enlighten you
For you live within a different hue."

"There are many ways of being a man"
Wrote our ancient E. M. Forster.
My own has at last been found.
My being has veered to its own direction
Which is to ask life's basic question.

I passed through the six years at St Edmund's without ever sinning
in a sexual way. People tend to think that sexual abstinence is not
possible for so long a period but my own experience repudiates
that. I neither had sexual contact with anyone nor ever masturbated.
I experienced sexual attraction and once powerfully so when on
holiday. I also experienced less powerful sexual feelings for my own
sex while in the seminary. This seems to be a common experience
for those who are in all-male institutions. I did not act on these feelings. When I left St Edmund's I experienced again, in a normal way,
sexual attraction for women. I think that sexual abstinence is possible
when devoted to a higher purpose and living in the company of good
friends. However, when closeted in a parish with one person, with
whom I had no emotional resonance, sexual abstinence became much
more difficult. I have noticed at other times in my life that when I

have been in the company of good friends sexual desire is less strong. This would support Freud's view that in friendship the sexual instinct is sublimated.

* * *

I was ordained a priest on 23rd May 1964 just shortly before my twenty-seventh birthday. Cardinal Godfrey had died some eighteen months before and his successor, Cardinal Heenan, ordained about ten of us in Westminster Cathedral. There was a full congregation and my mother and father were both there. It was a long service. When it was over all of us newly ordained priests went into a side chapel and we each gave the priest's new blessing to our families. I think I gave it first to my father who kneeled devoutly for it but my mother with her stiff leg could not kneel so I blessed her standing up. As I did so we looked into each other's eyes and there was a moment of timid embarrassment. I think in that look there was a knowledge in her and in me that this was some charade, that it was not from the heart. It was as if I had made a secret contract with her that although I was obeying all the externals my inner heart was wedded to her own love of life. I was embarrassed at being a priest. I had donned the robes of office but was an impostor and my mother knew it and no one else. Later in life I went through a period of terrible hatred towards my mother and I think it must have been that I believed that it was her infidelity that had driven me mad and scooped me into the Church.

When it was finished we went and had a late breakfast with the cardinal. He was bright, witty, amusing, and was an efficient prelate. At this time I had a wary admiration for him but it was not long before I hated him. He came to epitomise for me the efficient "businessman" prelate who had no knowledge of love although he preached sermons on it every week. I always liked the story told by a Trappist monk who came to give us a retreat when we were at St Edmund's. He told us that he once gave a retreat for bishops and one of the bishops confided in him how shocked he was that one of his priests had become involved with a woman. He told the monk that he could not understand how a priest could do this. So the monk said to him,

"You do not understand?"
"No, I just cannot understand," said the bishop.

"Then God will have to teach you," said the monk.

A year later the bishop came to the monk and said,

"God has taught me."

I liked that story but I am afraid Cardinal Heenan was not the bishop who had learned so salutary a lesson.

The day after I was ordained I said my first Mass at the convent chapel of the Sacred Heart in Brighton. My father served the Mass and Fr Peter de Rosa preached the sermon. About fifty friends and relatives were there. My father flew back to Portugal the next day and I and my mother set off by car overland to Oporto. We drove through France and Spain, taking nearly a week. I had not been on my own with my mother for such a long time ever and, after a few days, I realised I was bored in her company. On the surface she was bubbly, friendly, and very social but on that long drive I thought there was a terrible emptiness within her and it made me think of her, depressed and dejected, when I used to come home to lunch as a little boy. I felt sad for her and I knew she was very unhappy. I knew my father was too. I remember on that journey I could not bear the emptiness I found inside her but it was my discomfort rather than a sadness for her which filled my psychic space. There I was a priest in role but a self-centred man within.

We arrived back in Oporto where I celebrated a *Missa Nova* at the little baroque church of Nevogilde. It was a big occasion. The Symington family was out in force. I walked in a little procession with the parish priest and Fr Bernardo, a dear Dominican. Rockets were let off during that little journey and, as we arrived at the church, the wide porch in front of it had been turned into a design of a red chalice against a white background and the material used to produce it was entirely rose petals. It must have taken many people hours and hours to accomplish. After celebrating the Mass there was a reception back at home. All the Symington family, adults and children, were there and also many other English friends. Claire Bergqvist had come down from Quinta de la Rosa in the Douro. Reg and Auriel Cobb, John and Valerie Delaforce, Charles and Meriel Wall, and Dick and Beryl Yeatman were there. All these English friends were Protestants but they joined with the others in their congratulations and celebration.

It is significant that, although for instance I can remember my feelings when driving with my mother through France and Spain, I have no access to my feelings during the time of these celebrations. I was performing and I was the hero on the stage and I think I must have been cut off from my feelings. I do remember that I was embarrassed on that short walk from home to the church and did not like putting on the biretta which was insisted upon by the *abade*, the parish priest. I think the embarrassment was the feeling generated by the discrepancy between the outer appearance and the inner state of mind. Here was Neville, a dedicated priest, but the reality was a priest's robes and ritual while Neville the human person was utterly crushed by a savage God within. As a public figure I performed extremely well. For the three and a half years as a priest I functioned very well in the public role. In the celebration of the liturgy I always spoke extremely clearly and put myself, as an actor, fully into the performance. I also preached meaningfully to the congregation. In my last year as a priest, however, Neville the person began to emerge in the sermons. I spoke to the people from the heart. During those short years as a priest there was a transition from the robot public performer to a person engaging in communication with other persons. My audience shrank but became real. I am jumping ahead however.

The only other event I remember was celebrating a High Mass at the Cova da Iria at Fátima. I suspect that it must have been on 13th June which was a pilgrimage date because there were many people. My memory of meals, conversations, and so on is entirely blank. I think the public performer anaesthetised successfully the human person beneath the priestly garb.

I am sure the public performer generated great excitement within and that this drowned the person and the sign of it lies in the fact that I cannot today recall a memory of the many ordinary human interactions that must have taken place. There is a huge difference between joy and excitement. The former enhances the personality and makes love and creativity available; the latter crushes the person and leaves only red hot ashes radiating hatred in the personality.

* * *

CHAPTER SIX

The birth of subjectivity

I had been posted as curate to a parish in the East End of London: the Church of Our Lady and St Catherine of Siena at No. 181a Bow Road. I arrived there on the evening of 2nd July 1964, the day before my twenty-seventh birthday. My parish priest was a tall sandy-haired man called Tony Beagle. This is where my conscious journey of suffering began. Here I ran up against emotional intensities the like of which I had not before imagined.

Tony Beagle had been born and brought up in Barking which is further to the east of Bow. He had trained as a priest at the English College in Rome some twenty-three years before. He had spent his priestly life at Edmonton in north London and had been posted as parish priest to Bow some four months before I arrived. He was a man of extreme kindness and courtesy and totally dedicated to his life as a parish priest. He loved his Catholic flock and devoted himself to the work of bringing them first into the bosom of the Church and then, once firmly there, to the sacraments. In him I encountered a sentimental piety that had been unmodified by his theological training. I spent two and a half years in this parish with him. I had breakfast, lunch, and dinner with him every day. There were not two things I found myself in agreement with. His mentality and mine were totally opposite. I could not bear him but, at that novice time of my life, I was unable to manage this discord between us. He was equally disabled in this respect.

The difficulties crystallised in a practical way right at the beginning. The two of us lived in an old Victorian presbytery. We each had a bedroom on the top floor and studies on the first floor. The kitchen and dining room were on the ground floor. When I arrived, there was no housekeeper and the kitchen was an utter mess. On the table in the kitchen were cigarette butts, two or three saucers with rancid butter on them, bits of chewed meat on unwashed plates, and a putrid smell throughout the ground floor. Next door was a huge dining room with a vast oblong table with a typewriter at one end of it and dining chairs around the other end. The wallpaper was of deep red brocade and there were two pictures on the wall facing the windows: of the Sacred Heart of Jesus and the Immaculate Heart of Mary. These pictures had probably been bought in a Catholic souvenir shop in Ireland. They were the most unbeautiful pictures that it is possible to imagine. Tony Beagle was unaffected by these surroundings. He told me that he was expecting a housekeeper shortly.

I found these surroundings and the atmosphere depressing in the extreme. I was not clinically educated enough to realise that Tony Beagle was obviously a very depressed man although all the signs were there. Almost every evening after supper he would go into his office, slump in front of the television, and go to sleep before it; he would wake up at about one in the morning and then take himself to bed.

I arrived in the evening. I had a Mass to celebrate at eight in the morning. I went to bed early and I got up at five in the morning and cleaned up the kitchen. I washed all the plates and crockery and swept the place. When Tony Beagle came down later he smiled at me with delight. I duly celebrated Mass in the church which could hold about 400 people. On this ordinary weekday there were four women attending the Mass. Each of them was praying the rosary and two of them came to communion. This form of celebrating the liturgy was contrary to everything I had come to believe and understand from my six years of training at St Edmund's.

That afternoon I was in my study-cum-sitting room when I had two inner experiences which took me entirely by surprise. The first: I wanted to leave the priesthood there and then. I knew that this was not for me, that I had blindly stepped into this professional vocation like some misguided missile. I did not, at that time, connect this frenzied act to the shock of knowing my mother's infidelity. Stripped here, in this dismal presbytery, of all the philosophical and theological excitement and passionate discussion among close friends at St Edmund's, I faced what was the life of the priest in the parish and I knew that this was not for me. I had made a terrible mistake. This was absolutely clear but what was I to do?

When training to be a priest it is possible to leave at any point until being ordained a subdeacon, which is an order taken a year before the priesthood. Once a subdeacon and endorsed more solemnly still on being ordained a priest you could not leave. I had taken the most solemn vows to remain a priest for the rest of my life. Of course I knew that priests did leave the priesthood and in fact one of the brightest students at St Edmund's, Jim McDonnell, who had been ordained about three years before me, had gone to Cambridge and within a year had left, but it was a disgrace and a terrible sin in the eyes of God and, at that time, there was no dispensation from the vows which one had taken. Also while at St Edmund's we had two retreats each year and the priests invited to conduct them spoke with frightening emphasis that to leave the priesthood was to act like Judas Iscariot. So this lucid moment when I knew I had made a terrible mistake filled me with doom-like paralysis. I put it out of my mind and threw myself into my pastoral duties with a zealous fervour. But I was unable to avoid that glimpse of the truth and soon the chink of light became a new dawn that flooded the landscape.

The other experience is more difficult to describe but even more significant psychologically. Despite all the enlightened theological and scriptural study at St Edmund's, God was a dictator. He had changed under theological enlightenment from being a savage one into being a benign one yet he was a dictator whose ordinances I could not question, whose commandments I had to obey. I was his slave. Standing or sitting in my sitting room a ray from the sun penetrated into my soul. I was not God's slave but rather his free responsive partner. God was not a dictator but a Being who invited me to be his friend. I was not a slave but an honoured guest. I think that at this moment a subjective self was born inside my mortal frame. My whole life has been a slow journey where, by incremental steps, some large, some small, a robot has become transformed into a subjective person. But this was the very beginning of that transformation.

In Chapter Three I recounted how, when I was in London, between the ages of eighteen and twenty, I had a terror of committing suicide.

This was because the impulse to suicide pressed in upon me with great strength and fierceness and therefore I was in a panic that I might act on the impulse. Much later I came to realise that this strong inner pressure was connected to my being in Pinocchio mode. What do I mean by this? Pinocchio was a wooden doll until Jupetta breathed life into him and the wooden doll became a living person. I think that until this moment when subjectivity was born I had been a wooden toy. The impulse to suicide and this state of wooden immobility are partners. Why is this? It is because a man of flesh and blood is trapped within a mechanical frame. Suicide is an act of despair in the face of this imprisoned state. I think this had been in me before the discovery of my mother's infidelity but this brought it to the fore. I now had a suitable candidate to blame for my state. As I mentioned in Chapter Three I did not speak of this suicidal impulse in either of the two psychoanalyses which I underwent; this was partly down to my own unawareness but also due to a system of thinking which was not receptive to the emotional problem that lay behind it. It was only years later when I started to read the works of existentialists, like Paul Tillich, that things started to fall into place. At last I found a theoretical frame that fitted my own experience.

I have no doubt that these two events, which are clearly connected, were what led me out of the Church some three and a half years later. I was a free man. God the dictator and me the robot gave way to God the friend inviting me, the free person, to choose my own direction in life. A God who was better served by my freedom than by a panic-driven robot. I think the God whom I had sinned against as a child all those years ago when I had eaten chocolate before going to Holy Communion, a savage God who was going to consign me to hell for all eternity, had at last dissolved but, for some very odd reason, only after my having been ordained and having made my final vows. I had "gone into the Church" in a state of terror.

It was one of the most significant experiences of my life. It was entirely internal and no one around me would have noticed anything different but shortly afterwards, riding on my large police bicycle down Bow Road, I shuddered with fear at my new-found freedom. A few months later I was reading Piaget's *The Moral Judgment of the Child*[1] and this took my spirit by storm. A free spirit of inquiry was now possible for me and I was no longer hamstrung by the boundaries put to inquiry by

---

[1]Piaget, Jean (1932). *The Moral Judgment of the Child*. London: Kegan Paul.

the Church. It was enormously freeing but at the same time frightening. It was at some point during this time that I met Charles Davis at a local deanery conference and he recommended that I read Erich Fromm's *Fear of Freedom*.[2] I now knew that freedom, though longed for by human beings, is also a terror to all of us. A patient who visits me today has two conflicting desires: to be free to choose her own direction and, simultaneously, pleading with me to instruct her on which path to take.

After leaving the Church I believed that this Catholic mother (and the other traditional religions) imposed boundaries restricting free inquiry but that in Western secular democratic societies there were no such boundaries and that totally free inquiry was encouraged in all scientific pursuits; that academic freedom was the norm. It is only in recent years that I have come to recognise the fallacy of this belief. Western secular society is riddled with taboos just as fearsome as those of the Catholic Church. The difference between the two is that in secular society they are hidden whereas in the Catholic Church they are open and declared and, in the wisdom of hindsight, I have come to prefer the latter. There is for instance tyranny in many sectors of the postmodern culture and I have heard of cases of art historians, sociologists, philosophers, and historians being given the sack for not toeing the party line. Academic freedom is a very rare commodity. University education is rife with tyranny. The beliefs of one scientific school are derided by another. Examples of this are numerous. Macneile Dixon has given lucid expression to this:

> Pleasure, said Epictetus, is the chief good. It is the chiefest of evils, said Antisthenes. Men, declared Rousseau, are naturally good; they are naturally bad, said Machiavelli. It is on the same evidence that distinguished people contradict each other. Virtue, proclaimed the Stoics, is sufficient for happiness. Without external goods it is not sufficient, said Aristotle.[3]

* * *

The two and a half years in the parish of Bow in the East End of London were the most enlightening of my life. They were packed with a wealth

---

[2]Fromm, Erich (1942). *Fear of Freedom*. London: Routledge & Kegan Paul.
[3]Macneile Dixon, W. (1958). *The Human Situation* (pp. 53–54). London: Penguin.

of new experiences. I came from an English upper middle class family, brought up in Portugal, educated at an English public school and had been insulated against the cultural fabric of the modern world. Until I was ordained a priest I had never been to a public football match, I did not know what a probation officer was, had never met a psychiatric social worker, did not know that there was a discipline called sociology. Although I had close emotional ties with the Portuguese maids at home I had been educated within the culture of the English upper middle class. This had not been true of St Edmund's which was lower middle class in its cultural ethos but it was insulated from ordinary society rather in the way a prison is set apart from the world outside it. Now I was suddenly thrown into the midst of the vibrant East End culture.

There is, or was in my day, something special about London's East End. The cockneys were wedded lovingly to their dockland streets. These were their streets, it was their home, and no other area of London had the affection poured into it that the East End of London enjoyed. It was a great extended family network in which warmth, bodily violence, love, and hatred all swarmed together to make one of the most life-enhancing cultures in existence. The Catholic priest was not just respected in London's East End, but loved. I adored being among these people and responded with enthusiasm and missionary zeal to their frankly declared love. I was terribly sad when I came to leave that parish and it left in my being an "in-touchness" with the realities of working class life. In later years I came across many left wing socialists of the Fabian variety and, although they were full of Marxist theory whose slogans they chanted with monotonous regularity, I could see that they had not a clue about the motivating principles of working class culture. I loved the East End of London and, although I rarely go there today, it is a love which will never die.

The Catholic priest in a London parish had very few duties which he *had* to perform. I had Masses which I had to say each week and I had to hear confessions on a Saturday night. I had a few weddings and baptisms which I had to perform. In any one week my official duties could have been accomplished in about twelve to fifteen hours. It was up to me how I spent the rest of my time. This degree of freedom was a serious problem for many Catholic priests and it was I believe the reason why many turned to drink in middle and old age.

The most deepening human experience was being chaplain to St Andrews, the local general hospital. I went there every day, visited

154

all the wards, and tended the Catholic patients. I attended people who were dying, knew they were dying, and faced it with a quiet courage. I attended others who knew they were dying but were terrified of it, and yet others who cursed God for having let them down in their hour of need. I became more convinced than ever that the sort of superstitious piety which characterised so much of Catholic parish life did not sustain people in the face of the crisis of death. I remember being struck by the contrast between two Catholic women who died at about the same time. One had been a faithfully devout woman who came to Mass often, attended Benediction on Wednesday nights, and I had often seen her lighting a candle at the statue of Our Lady and would see her praying before it. She would be in the church three or four times a week. Then she got cancer and, in the terminal phase, was in hospital. She became bitter towards God who had delivered her such a blow after all she had done for Him. She had worshipped Him all her life, prayed every day, gone to Mass faithfully several times a week, and done much for the parish, and now here was God treating her with such treachery. I spoke with her and said that God had not abandoned her, that her prayers had not been ignored, that the pain and distress she was going through was what God often seemed to ask of his faithful ones. She remained adamant in her bitterness, would not allow me to hear her confession, would not receive Holy Communion or the Sacrament of the Anointing of the Sick, and she died cursing God. The other woman, also dying of cancer, had a deep gratitude to God for what he had done for her. She told me how she had been an alcoholic at one time in her life, how she had managed to recover from that condition, and she had a serenity in the face of her approaching death which evoked my love and admiration. Her idea of God was quite different from that of my other parishioner. For this one God was, in her inner belief, living in the very sinews of life. I gave her the sacraments but I believe she did more for me than I did for her. Her love and generous gratitude for the goodness in her life was an inspiration.

What I was witnessing here were two profoundly different conceptions of God apprehended at the emotional level. The significant thing, though, was that their outer piety was not very different; it was their inner attitude that was so different. Caryll Houselander was right; she said that the dictum, "We all worship the same god" is the supreme fallacy. So something inside was telling me that all my whizz-kid new liturgy could not of itself transform the heart but it was not a loud voice

155

inside me as I raced around the parish on my bicycle preaching the new gospel wherever I went.

I loved being chaplain to the hospital. Sometimes I would be called out in the middle of the night to attend to someone dying. There was something mystery-laden riding on my large old bicycle at two in the morning down to the hospital and giving the sacrament to someone who was shortly going to die. I remember once administering the sacrament of the Anointing of the Sick to a dear old lady. I spoke the prayers slowly and carefully in English and I could see her following them. When I had finished she smiled at me and said, "What beautiful prayers," then she lay back on her pillow and died peacefully. That was proof to me that the Church had been right to change the language of the liturgy from Latin into the vernacular. If that woman had died a year earlier then those prayers would have been mumbled in Latin and she would have been deprived of those words that moved her heart to God in her dying moments.

On another occasion there was a thirty-three-year-old woman in intensive care. She looked me right in the eye and asked me, "Father, am I dying? I want to know." I told her that I did not know but that I would ask the nurse or doctor and come back and let her know. I went into the ward sister's cubicle and asked what the situation was. She told me that the woman was due to die very soon but then said to me that on no account was I to tell her; that the doctor had given strict instructions that she should not be told. Here was a moral dilemma. I thought quickly but I had no doubt whatever that it was my duty to tell her the truth so I went back to her cubicle and I told her that she was dying. She sighed with relief and thanked me sincerely for telling her. To this day I am sure I did the right thing but the sister of the ward, whom I told what I had done, was furious. No doubt the doctor was too.

On another tragic occasion I arrived at the hospital just after a young woman had been brought in dead. I anointed her and then the charge nurse told me that she had lived just across the road and asked me to come with him and speak with the husband. He walked me across the road and showed me into the flat where a tall red-haired man was standing in the hallway. "What happened?" I asked. He took me into the kitchen which was full of the smell of gas; the oven door was open and a pillow was propped against it with a dent in the pillow where his wife's head had so recently been. She had committed suicide. The charge

156

nurse left and I sat for two hours with the man until some friends came to keep him company. In those two hours he gave me an account of his infidelity which his wife had found out about that day. She had left a suicide note. It was an agonising tale. Later I turned it into a short story which I called *The Cost of Maturity*.

I was summoned hastily to the hospital one day. A young West Indian woman had just died on the operating table. She had gone in for a D & C—a very minor procedure but something had gone wrong. I believe it was an error on the part of the anaesthetist. As I walked out of the hospital two young West Indian men were coming in and they asked me if I knew on which ward was ... the woman whom I knew had just died. I asked them whether they were related to her. One of them told me that she was his wife. I took the two men into a private room off the corridor and told them the awful news. The poor husband let out a primaeval yell that I shall remember till my dying day. He wept bitterly and then said, "I knew they should not cut her. I knew it, I knew it."

When someone was dying and the doctors were attending to the person I would often sit with husband, wife, or relatives. At so poignant a moment people would open their hearts and impart the guiding motives of their lives. One man, who was a stallholder at Poplar market, said to me that he had seen that when people were down on their luck other people often pushed them down further. He said, "In those circumstances I have always tried to give them a hand up." I was frequently deeply moved by the devotion and courage of straightforward and simple people who would at moments of crisis like this open their hearts. It was such a privilege to be entrusted with confidences of this sort and these people, although they did not know it, did more for me at these times than I did for them.

* * *

I started a youth club in an old London double-decker bus. Many people co-operated to bring this about. I had an introduction to a man who had some land next to his printing works and he allowed the bus to be stationed on this land. Another man donated the bus. A carpenter converted it into a coffee bar-cum-folk-singing environment and a wooden door was constructed at the entrance. Finally the bus was ready and on the opening night a well-known folk-singer came. From then on it was open every Tuesday night and young people

157

came from a wide area to attend. The club was open to Catholics and non-Catholics alike.

There was a vigorous movement called the Young Christian Workers which had been started originally by Joseph Cardijn in Belgium. He had found that as soon as young people started work after leaving school they lost their faith. He started small groups of young workers and brought to them the inspiration of the Gospel. The meetings were weekly and would be for a group of between five and eight people and were structured upon a simple but effective system. A short passage from the Gospel was read out and was treated to a three-pronged diagnosis under the headings "See, Judge, Act". Under the "See" there would be discussion as to what the passage actually meant in the Gospel. Here was no academic discourse but straightforward "hands-on" discussion of what the passage meant. These young factory workers had a better idea of the meaning of many a Gospel passage than scriptural scholars. There was a freshness and robustness of exposition which was inspiring. Gospel text came alive in a new and vital way and far from the pompous irrelevance of most pulpit oratory. Their interpretation of the Gospel passage, what it really meant, was always relevant.

Relevance of doctrine, any doctrine, to people's actual lives has always been a central concern. I believe that ninety-nine per cent of most teaching that purports to relate to people at the place where they are is at a distance from it. I believed this to be so in the Church and when I left the Church and started to study psychology and sociology I found the same; when I started studying psychoanalysis it was similar. People espouse theories or teachings which may have been relevant to someone else but bear no relation to either a single person's living or to a group's living. When studying sociology I had considerable contact with Marxist groups and when I heard the theorists chant the familiar slogans my eyes would glaze over. It was the same when I heard lengthy disquisitions on instinct theory, the death instinct, or the Oedipus complex within psychoanalysis, and the same when I listened to sermons from the pulpit. Here, however, in the Young Christian Workers was a new vitality. Gospel passages suddenly were bubbling with life.

When there was some consensus as to what a particular Gospel passage meant then the next piece of the diagnosis was addressed under the heading of "Judge". Having seen what the Gospel passage meant, now we would look at how it applied in the lives of the group present here in the East End of London in 1964. One would relate an incident,

158

usually from work, where he thought the principles of the passage applied to him; another would describe another incident from her experience, and so on. There would unfailingly unfurl a horrifying picture of inhuman behaviour in the workplace. How could the message of Jesus, just understood, be applied in these appalling circumstances? What could this small group of powerless workers do about it? This is the point at which the group considered things under the heading of "Act". A definite action would be decided upon. It turned out always to be something emotionally difficult and the courage of these young people amazed me. A couple would decide, for instance, to approach a foreman at work who was a bully and ask him not to use such disgusting language to those new recruits just arriving in the workplace. When the group met the following week the action would be reviewed to see what had happened, how it had been received. The individuals would get enormous moral support from the group. But every individual in the group would go away with a thing he or she had to do. There is so much waffle in many welfare projects because no effective action ever occurs. These young people acted with inspiring courage which I have never forgotten and from which I still draw inspiration.

The principles of the Young Christian Workers were similar to those of the Cell Movement which I have already mentioned but here I experienced the principles lived out with a down-to-earth vigour. I also started four groups of married couples whose meetings were structured upon similar principles. The problem then which Joseph Cardijn had already encountered was how to link up these vital movements with the dull bureaucratic piety enshrined in the devotional rituals of the parish. It was here at this crucial moment in 1964 with the liturgy being celebrated in English that the link became possible in a new way.

The vitality of the Gospel in these groups was, at that time, mirrored by the new liturgy: the Epistles, the Gospel, and the whole Mass was now celebrated in English and, further, the priest now celebrated at an altar that faced his congregation. It looked as if a new spirit was blowing through the Church. It is said that when Pope John XXIII was asked what he hoped to do for the Church he went across the room and opened a window so that the fresh breeze could blow in. I had at that time all the enthusiasm of youth and I believed that this pulsing Christian spirit which lived in so palpable a way in the meetings of the Young Christian Workers would now flow through into the desiccated traditional Church ritual. I put all my energies into trying to bring this about. Apart from the meetings of the Young Christian Workers and the married couples' meetings I also celebrated the liturgy on Sundays with love and clarity. I spoke the prayers as clearly as possible. Although the liturgy had gone into English I quickly became aware that, although the liturgy was also in English in the Church of England, yet a parsonical tone of voice and atmosphere could make the vernacular as distant from the people as Latin. I did all in my power to counteract this. In making this attempt I made an interesting discovery and it was so significant for me that I will give you the full history of it.

When I first arrived in Bow I was chaplain also to the Catholic High School in the next door parish of Poplar, and I went there once a week to give a class of religious instruction. It was a wild and delinquent environment and in my chosen class there were about forty children in their early teens. To hold their attention for more than a minute was a feat indeed and I almost despaired of being able to teach them anything. One day, in order to try to illustrate what was meant by "conversion" to true Christian life I decided to tell them the story of Leonard Cheshire VC. I thought this would fire the imaginations of young teenagers. So I told them about this bomber pilot and his bombing expeditions over Germany, then how he saw the atom bomb explode at Nagasaki from an observation plane, how that shocked him into changing his life direction from one of destruction to construction, and went on to tell them of the homes for the incurably sick which he had created. All through this account which I believe I related with some enthusiasm and verve the children in front of me whispered to each other, fired pellets at each other, made paper aeroplanes, and threw them over the heads of friends in the classroom. There was not a hint of interest in this priest droning away at the front of the classroom. Then, almost by chance, I mentioned that I had met Leonard Cheshire. The effect of this chance remark was electric. Every child turned and listened to me. "What, you have actually *met* him?" asked one of them. I was astounded and I realised in that moment that what engaged them was the personal element; that suddenly I was not talking about something outside experience but within it, something connected to my life, to their lives. It was real and not some irrelevant distant phantom. This experience was a stimulus to solving another problem which was vexing me at the time.

On Sundays there were five Masses: at eight o'clock, nine o'clock, ten o'clock, half-past eleven, and half-past six in the evening. Tony Beagle and I were on a fortnightly rota such that one Sunday he would celebrate the eight o'clock and nine o'clock Masses and I would do the other three and the next week we would do it the other way round. I had no difficulty in making contact in my sermon with the congregation when I was celebrating the three Masses at ten, half-past eleven, and half-past six in the evening. At all these Masses there was a healthy sample of the "common man and woman", made up of sinners and saints and all the grades of humanity in between. In my sermon which I had prepared carefully I spoke from the heart, delivered my message and it was received. I knew that the audience was "engaged". On one occasion an idiosyncratic parishioner dared to ask a question when I had finished the sermon. I was delighted and answered happily, and the congregation stared in amazement at this intrusion by a common man into a sacred rite. So I had no problem when I was preaching at those three Masses, but the situation was quite different when preaching at the eight o'clock and nine o'clock Mass in the morning.

At these two Masses on a Sunday there came a quiet pious group of people. They had not been up late on Saturday night. They had gone to bed early, risen early, said their morning prayers, and were seated punctually in time for the early morning Mass. I could see their glazed eyes as I preached, saying their rosaries as the liturgy proceeded; I realised that they were in some kind of self-enclosed world and that nothing I could say touched them personally in the slightest bit. Then I reflected on what I came to refer to as my "Cheshire experience". Could I do the same with this hypnotised congregation as I had done at the Cardinal Griffin School in Poplar? Then I thought of the parables which Jesus had used to teach his message. When he spoke about a man going down from Jerusalem to Jericho who fell among thieves he might have been talking of an actual person he had known or, if not, someone he had heard about; and his audience all knew the road down to Jericho. It was real, it was alive. I realised that if I started by saying that I thought today the parable of the Good Samaritan could be translated in the following way … the old eyes would glaze over. So I would do what Jesus had done: tell them of a personal experience. So I tried it out.

As it happened the Gospel passage for the next Sunday was the parable of the Good Samaritan. At the time there were race riots in Denver in America and the news was full of it. I started my sermon by saying that a friend of mine had just come back from Denver in the States. I noticed immediately that the congregation had abandoned their rosaries and were listening to me, looking at me intently. I went on to tell them how a young black boy fell wounded in a street inhabited mostly by whites. Two households, one a respected local magistrate and the other a good Catholic doctor stayed inside, but a rascal who had just come out of prison, lived in a little shack across the street with his wife and delinquent kids, ran out, risking bullets which were still flying, and carried the wounded black boy into his home. I described it very graphically and with some emotion as the man and his wife cleansed the boy's wounds and comforted him. The congregation was riveted. I ended as abruptly as I had begun. The message was obvious; it did not need any pious recommendations from me; it stood starkly for what it was. At the end of that Mass as people were hanging around the church door they were all talking not about "the sermon" but about this courageous man who had rescued the black boy in the city of Denver. I had cracked the shell of the comatose state. From then on I spoke in a similar vein every time that I had to preach to the congregation at the eight o'clock and nine o'clock Mass. After some weeks word began to get around that disturbing events were occurring at these Masses when I was preaching and slowly the congregations at these Masses swelled. I knew now what it was that touched people's hearts. On one occasion I told of the rivalry of two doctors which was so severe that a young boy died because of it. At the end of the Mass a very severe but devout old lady came up to me and said, "You know, I have been jealous in my life but it alarms me to think that it could have done harm to someone ..." I knew that I was touching a sensitive place in people, a place where God might be calling them to repentance, a place where conscience invited them to take a step.

The Midnight Mass on Christmas Day was a big event. On this particular Christmas, Tony Beagle was celebrating the Midnight Mass and I was supervising the flow of people entering the church. At midnight the Mass began and I saw a drunken fellow lurching towards the door of the church so I closed and bolted it. He hammered on the door and clamoured for me to let him in. I did not do so and then he shouted out loudly: "I have been shut out of God's church by a priest serving the devil ..."

I remained adamant and did not unbolt the door. He hammered on the door for all he was worth shouting abuses at me for at least another quarter of an hour. Eventually he went off yelling about my ill-treatment of him for all he was worth. Two days later I was walking down Bow Road and I saw him coming towards me in the opposite direction and I thought that I was now in for another quantum of abuse; I readied myself for it and said to him that I was sorry that I had had to prevent him from coming into the Church on Christmas night. He said to me: "Father, you shut the door against me. That was not enough—you should have punched me and hit me into the middle of Bow Road." That was an important lesson: the words, the abuse, and the vitriol were not what I needed to heed but rather my own inner instinct. That man's better nature coincided with my own sense that he was better kept out of the church. I also had great respect for him for saying what he did. No doubt he was a sinner but I felt he had found favour in the eyes of God much more than a sober, self-righteous parishioner. I do not know even if he is still alive but the image of his face and demeanour is still vivid before me.

* * *

I loved the East End of London. There is something magical about those "pocket boroughs" of Bethnal Green, Poplar, Bow, Mile End, and Stepney. The Catholic priest had a special place in people's affections. He was living there among his people. He was always invited to the family celebrations at a weekend. Social workers had all returned to their middle class homes in Hampstead or South Kensington but the Catholic priest remained in the midst of his people. A woman of Italian extraction had been "living in sin" with a man for about twenty years. Her husband had been married before in the Church of England in a parish in Surrey twenty-five years before. So she had married a divorcee and was banned from the sacraments. But, I realised, having studied canon law carefully at St Edmund's, that her husband's marriage in the Church of England church in Surrey was only valid if, in the eyes of the Catholic Church, the woman he had married was free to do so. If she were a divorcee herself and not free to marry, then according to Catholic legislation, her marriage to this man was not valid and if this marriage were not valid then he was unmarried and free to marry the Italian-cockney woman whom he had been living with for twenty years but as a sinner in the eyes of the Church. I told her I would investigate her case and she said: "It's no good, both the last two priests have tried to see if I can be right with the Church but it just is not possible, Father."

However, I was determined to see what could be done. I traced down her husband's first wife and unearthed her first marriage and got marriage and divorce certificates for all events. It became clear that the woman, because she had been married before, was not in fact free to marry the husband of my parishioner so her marriage to him was null and void, according to Catholic legal practice. I collected all the documentation. It took me some six months of investigation and finally I packaged all the documents plus a long and tedious letter from me indicating the significance of all of them and sent them off to the curia at Westminster. A long silence and then … a letter from Ralph Brown, who had been with me at St Edmund's, telling me that I was indeed correct and that my Italian parishioner was free to marry the man she was living with. I went around and told her. She threw her arms around me and gave me the most enthusiastic hug, and two days later I married them both in the church in a quiet little ceremony. The ceremony may have been quiet but the party that evening was the opposite and I was the hero.

The woman's brother was a docker and I got into deep conversation with him at that party. He told me that he was a devout Catholic but that he could not go to the sacraments. I asked him why and he told me his story. He was the father of four children who were all young. Three years before his wife had suddenly gone off with his sister's husband and left him in charge of the four children. In order to manage financially he worked, as well as a docker, also part-time as a chauffeur to the mayor of Tower Hamlets. He cooked the meals for the children, sewed their socks, and was mother and father to them all. Then he said,

> About once a month I get into a bad mood and I know what I have to do. I get a woman. I always make sure she is over twenty-four and not married and we sleep together. Then I am alright again and in a good mood and carry on looking after my children as I should. I can't come to the sacraments, Father, because I can't go to confession with a firm purpose of amendment because I know I shall do it again.

The significance of a woman over twenty-four was that she was someone experienced whose life he was not wrecking. When he told me this I thought here was a man making a mature moral judgment and I felt sure that what he did on those monthly occasions was not what constituted a mortal sin. The motive was good; it was in order to carry on his difficult task and be a good carer to his children and when he did take a woman he made sure that it was someone who knew what she was doing and neither an innocent young girl that he was deceiving nor someone whose marriage he might be breaking up. I came across case after case of this sort of thing and slowly began to get the sense that many of the people who were barred from the sacraments were people of greater maturity and holiness than many of those who were within the fold.

The moral dilemma in which I found myself grew ever greater— that the Church's definition of what constituted mortal sin and what didn't was based upon outer rather than inner markers and that the fostering of moral judgment through conscience was almost entirely absent and yet this was the basis of a moral life. My study of Newman's disquisitions on conscience had convinced me that conscience and not external laws lay at the foundation of moral life. I should have liked to encourage that man to make a judgment about the degree of sinfulness and, if he judged it not to be a heinous crime, then to go to the sacraments. If he once judged that it was not a mortal sin then he had no sin to confess. The way the Church operated, however, in people's minds was as an authoritarian judge who declared that this act was a sin and that one wasn't, but based on externals. Rather than be a guide to conscience the Church overrode conscience and in doing so deterred people from developing a conscience and the awesome task of making moral choices. In following conscience and making a moral choice you cannot *know* that you are right; you believe you are but as with faith you are always in the dark. The individual, by erecting the Church's directives in the place where conscience should be operating, was no longer under the burden of making moral choices. Under this system I can say to myself, "I *know* that I am right," and walk around in arrogant self-righteousness. I became more and more certain that the Church was fostering a flock of self-righteous pricks and leaving outside her gates the courageous and the holy.

As the truth of this began to dawn I realised that the new liturgy served some usefulness in that it opened an understanding of the Christian message to churchgoers, but left the real problem of the principles of a moral life untouched. I began to see more and more that my role was to bring people to God and that this was not the same as bringing people to the sacraments. I frequently came across people in situations similar to the one I described about the man whose wife had left him. There was a particular aspect to this in the East End of London where a sizeable proportion of the adult men at that time worked in the docks. I became chaplain to London's dockland. Once you passed through the gates into the docks you walked into a different culture. The language was rich indeed and there was an interlocking system of theft. Many homes in the area had in their larders goods that had been siphoned out of the docks through this system. The result was that no dockers—and many were Catholics—came to church. They were moral lepers. There was a difficult moral dilemma here. As a docker how sinful was I being by participating first in the coarse language of dockland and secondly in the organised system of theft? This needed to be put into historical context. At the time when I was in Bow dockers had a reasonable wage and working hours, but twenty-five years before that had not been so. The hours were extremely long, the pay very poor, and employment by the day uncertain, so how evil was this subterranean theft? The Church had totally opted out of this matter. Here was a place for the Church to try to learn the cultural dilemma and to move slowly towards working out a solution, but instead, like the ostrich, it had its head buried in the sand. It was dishing out sacraments to a pious group and turning its back on the cultural and moral dilemmas of the wider world.

I began to realise that there were two models operating in the minds of Catholic priests. One was of a group of faithful Catholics; the Church's job was to protect them from the wicked world outside so the children would be educated in a Catholic school, and the parish would have a Catholic youth club and create a Catholic social life by running dances and so on in the parish hall. An enormous amount of effort went into fund-raising in order to pay for the Catholic schools, build parish halls, and rent or buy premises for Catholic youth clubs—all this to hold and protect people within a Catholic environment.

The other model was based upon the words of Jesus: "You are the light of the world ..." and the job of the Church was to kindle an inner spirit of love and to carry this into the world around. It was the view that if this inner spirit were kindled then it was not necessary to have Catholic schools and Catholic youth clubs and these were a subversion of Christ's intent. Bit by bit I came more and more into conflict over this matter. What I found was a Church dedicated to the first model but a group of us young priests acted according to the principles of the second. Nearly all of us ultimately left the Church. It was two different religions masquerading under the nomenclature of one.

I came to realise that what separated these two approaches was the two different theories of redemption that I have already outlined and, behind these two, lay two very different conceptions of God. I recognised more and more the truth of Caryll Houselander's remark that the greatest fallacy was that we all worshipped the same God. Catholics with a wall around them derived from the image of a God who called them into exclusivity, who wanted this people for himself, that He, God, was a greedy fellow who demanded all this of his faithful ones. The other view was of a God overflowing with generosity towards mankind and as this life of God was in us then we let his own generous intent through us channel out into the world outside us. One view was introverted, the other extraverted; one self-oriented, the other world-oriented; one solipsistic, the other loving.

In later life I learned that these two dimensions ran right through not only religious attitudes but also psychological ones. Sacrificial acts that look marvellous are done to placate this greedy God, like the poor woman who had worshipped him so devotedly only now in her illness and death was deserted by him. Someone goes out of his way to help this person and that person, but the motivating principle is the same as the woman who had attended all the devotional rituals of the parish but died cursing God. In other words these acts are done to win approbation. If I light this candle then God will favour me; if I listen patiently to all Mrs Smith's complaints then God will favour me. In this view God is a very self-oriented fellow who is bribable. This does not only apply to those who have a declared religious faith. These two attitudes exist in all. Everyone acts in the belief of a God but it is either a bribable God, a God who will look with favour upon you if you offer Him some bribes, or a God who pours out His love and has no need for bribery. George Ekbery's lectures on ontology underpinned a fundamental dichotomy that not only existed in the Catholic Church but in all of life both practical and theoretical.

It was at this time that I met Chris Farmer. His father was the Methodist minister in Bow and Chris, his son, was a young doctor. I came to know Chris through Geoff Heath, another Methodist minister. Geoff and I decided to start an informal group where we would have a discussion once a month on matters psychological. Geoff and I each gathered a few people. One of the people I gathered was an Indian film-maker whom I met one day at St Andrew's Hospital. There he was in one of the wards surrounded by a group of fellow patients speaking passionately about the meaning of life. I was amazed and sat and listened as

167

he talked. He was a deep thinker. I asked him to join this newly formed group. One of the people that Geoff gathered in was Chris Farmer. I had already met his father and was pleased to meet Chris and it was obvious from the start that Chris was a ball of energy and fire and I detected in him also a rare quality: goodness. In a short story, *Salvatore*, Somerset Maugham describes this quality in an Italian peasant. I have met it rarely in life and it has nearly always been associated with a certain innocence. I will quote from the last paragraph of Somerset Maugham's story:

> I wanted to see whether I could hold your attention for a few pages while I drew for you the portrait of a man, just an ordinary fisherman who possessed nothing in the world except a quality which is the rarest, the most precious and the loveliest that anyone can have. Heaven only knows why he should so strangely and unexpectedly have possessed it. All I know is that it shone in him with a radiance that, if it had not been so unconscious and so humble, would have been to the common run of men hardly bearable. And in case you have not guessed what the quality was, I will tell you. Goodness, just goodness.[4]

Chris had this quality deep in his soul. He was and is one of those people whose sheer goodness is palpable. I would not call him wise, I would not call him simple, I would not call him exceptionally intelligent, I would not call him a deep thinker, but he had and has goodness to a remarkable degree. I mention him because, while I knew him in Bow, he decided to specialise and become a psychiatrist and later when disaster hit me he proved to be a wonderful friend and remains so.

* * *

I cannot avoid it any longer. I have to come to the great conflict that led me to leave the Church. What I have described above about the Church's failure to guide people's consciences and be a light in the world was a growing concern, but my own personal problem was living in daily contact with a man whose mental attitude was totally different

---

[4]Maugham, W. Somerset (1969). *Collected Short Stories—vol. 4. Salvatore* (p. 193). London: Penguin.

to mine. It was not only different but I found it deplorable. I will give two examples of his mentality but they are not adequate because a mentality is something that runs right through the whole structure of someone's life. It did not matter whether he was speaking about abortion, homosexuality, trade unions, seminaries, Charles Davis, the pope, contraception, lapsed Catholics, alcoholism, the working class, or the new liturgy. I was in disagreement but it was not just disagreement: I was deeply antipathetic to his point of view, to his emotional attitude to life. His view of things seemed a travesty of the truth to me. So I will relate the two incidents. The first was when he was preaching on the Gospel passage about the Good Samaritan. He said that sometimes it could even be possible that a convert to Catholicism could be closer to God than someone who had been born a Catholic. I shuddered in horror as I listened to this. There was not a hint of a thought that the Good Samaritan might be a non-Catholic, perhaps a Protestant, perhaps an atheist even. No, it had to be one of us righteous ones. It was past belief for me that he could not consider that the Good Samaritan might be a person with a generous heart and not a Catholic at all. The other incident seared itself onto my mind and is still there today.

Within the parish of Bow was a large rambling building which housed people in what was then known as "Part Four Accommodation". I had visited it on various occasions to try to sort out violent outbreaks between different people there. Into "Part Four Accommodation" were placed those families who had failed to pay their rent in their council flat accommodation. Whole families lived in one room and there was urine flowing down the corridors as unsupervised children relieved themselves in the corridors. The man in charge was a Salvationist who was humane and did as good a job as anyone could in such an environment. One morning the telephone rang and it was him. He asked if I could come down immediately because a five-year-old Catholic child had been killed. I got on my bicycle and cycled down and was there within quarter of an hour. The child had been playing around the back of a milk float which had come in to deliver milk. When the driver had delivered all the milk he got back into the truck and, not noticing the child, backed and the child who was clinging to one of the back wheels fell backwards and the wheel of the vehicle ran over his neck and he died instantly. He was one of five children. When I arrived the child's mother was crying inconsolably. I did all I could to comfort her. I must have been with her for an hour and a half.

In that time, in the best way I could but with all the inadequacy of destiny, I arranged for the funeral, said some prayers with the mother for the soul of her little boy, and waited with her until her husband, who worked on a building site, returned. Finally I took leave of her when he returned and I cycled back sadly to the presbytery. Tony Beagle, the parish priest, could see I was upset and asked me what had happened. I told him. He put his arm around my shoulder and said with all the protective kindness he could muster: "You know, Neville, it was just as well he was killed. If he had grown up he would never have come to Holy Communion ..."

I walked out and slammed the door and he looked dismayed after me. From that moment I hated Father Beagle. I wished he would die. I did not want to eat another meal with him. To this day I do not know how to live and keep company with someone with a mentality like that. I believe that it was forced conjunction with him that drove me from the Church. He was a much loved man, loved by his parishioners and considered a good and holy priest by the elders of the diocese. If that is holiness, then give me a sinner. Living for three years with this man destroyed a joy of the soul in me and I am not sure that I have ever fully recovered it.

I went once on a retreat with a Catholic organisation called The Better World Movement; it was orchestrated by a very humane Latin-American Irish priest and, strange to say, my dear old friend Monsignor Sullivan was there. The retreat was at Spode House in Staffordshire. Luís Dolan, the retreat giver, had the view that it is possible to make a relationship with anyone and this was his philosophy which he thought was the kernel of Christian life and spirituality. I sought him out and explained to him my difficulties with Tony Beagle. As he listened he looked more and more dejected and finally said to me in despair, "What you have told me makes me think that I may not be right."

I have never found the solution to this problem and I have run into it in a serious way on other occasions. What one is up against is not just a difference in viewpoint but an emotional orientation to life: the difference between one that is self-protective and one that is outgoing with a generosity of spirit. I do know that what is unmanageable must ultimately be something in oneself that is hated. This must be something that I shall have to struggle on with until my death. The only sign I have that there is something of this appalling self-protective attitude in

170

myself is that some fifteen years ago I wrote an autobiographical novel in which Tony Beagle featured largely. As I wrote it I felt more warmly towards him. I think that my apostolic fanaticism may have incited his self-protective mentality all the more; that he feared that this young curate would destroy all the devotions of the Church that he had loved since his youth and given his life to. I think now I can be more compassionate towards him but at the time his mentality so appalled me that I could not love him. I suppose that was my task but I did not manage it. Perhaps ... but ... the world I think requires a generosity towards it such as Teilhard de Chardin displayed.

However, I have to try to understand quite why daily conjunction with Tony Beagle was such an emotional problem to me. It must trench upon the old problem that first assaulted me all those years before when I broke the Holy Communion fast. A fierce savage God reigned in my world. When I went to St Edmund's I replaced the savage external God with a loving one but this was an intellectual exchange. The savage God was still there installed within and yet such a monstrous inner God is never just within but always installed without. His outer habitation was in Tony Beagle and in the "superstitious Church" more widely. But why was the personal confrontation with Tony Beagle so particularly difficult? What was it that churned up my soul into a state of inner hatred and torment? One way of looking at this is to say that all of what I refer to as "superstitious piety" is based on the assumption that God is bribable. You offer God prayers, sacrifices, devotions, and so on, and thus the savagery of God is bought off. This had been my piety. When I went to St Edmund's my idea of God changed as did all my external piety that went with it, but, unbeknown to myself, there remained within me the savage God who was bribable and I hated Him fiercely. What I met in Tony Beagle was an embodiment of that which I hated within with such venom. I could neither see it at that time nor get the slightest hint of it. Another reason why this interpretation of it is probably correct is that the only dim awareness I had once or twice was that my religious life was very external. When I read the mystics I sensed that I did not have that interior relation to God that they experienced and wrote about. When the focus is on the outside the reason is very often because the horror of what is within is so awful that it cannot be contemplated, so one flees to the outer for refuge which is prominent. The savage God is part of a self-protective, solipsistic manner of being. Tony Beagle was, in all his piety, devoted to a God who is bribable.

171

I hated this God and was fighting for all my worth against Him. I think there was a transformation on that first day in the parish. Something was beginning to shift but what I did not realise was that He had at that time only moved His location. He was now located in the Church. What I did not know in myself, what I disowned in myself was meeting me head-on in daily life in the person of Tony Beagle. In *A Midsummer Night's Dream* Shakespeare tells us: "The heresies men leave are hated most ..." I had I think *partly* left this behind but part of it was still in me, though unbeknown to myself and this was why I hated Him. The reason why the heresy which has been left is hated is because it is still in the person. I hated with violence this self-protective, savage God who inhabited part of me but I did not know it at the time. It was only when I went into psychoanalysis that I got some insight into it. Each step of the way in liberating myself from this savage God always brought with it a hatred of the previous state which I had left when I saw it in others. The only solution is to come to know that it is in me and then to accept it, understanding why it is there.

There are two further angles on the same problem. What I hated in Tony Beagle was his self-centredness, his sentimentality, his belief in his own goodness, and his subtle sneering at Denys Lucas in the next door parish, Charles Davis, and any of the avant-garde in the Church. I remember also when I became friendly with Rabbi Forscher from the synagogue at Aldgate that he was contemptuous of my friendship with him. I felt he was the greatest hypocrite, posing as the kindly holy priest while all the while deeply self-centred, ungenerous, and unloving. If a generous love lies at the heart of all the great religions then I did not have it. There was a striving for it and a certain generosity of spirit in me but I was smothered within with the very self-centredness that I found so intolerable in him.

I had sought out Rabbi Forscher because I had become involved in the Christian-Jewish dialogue. This had been partly stimulated by Hubert Richards when I was at St Edmunds. I became very friendly with a Jewish scholar who had attended some lectures I had given for the Catholic Evidence Guild so I had become not just engaged in the ecumenical dialogue with other Christian faiths but also with Judaism. I studied it closely and have, ever since, been interested and sympathetic to the core values of Judaism. As with Christianity, though, I have never been sympathetic to what Meister Eckhart referred to as the secondary matters. I was also interested in Buddhism and had read some of the sutras while at St Edmund's. I regret that I had not made more than a superficial study of Islam.

The other angle on my hatred of Tony Beagle was a frail emotional self-protectiveness which was prominent in him and which I despised. I felt that all his piety was geared to boosting a self-protective barrier around him, that the piety of the parishioners whom he treasured was similar, and that he was fashioning a church of such people— reproductions of himself. At the same time, hidden from view, this was present in me also. This was the reason why I had not been able to speak to Monsignor Sullivan in Lisbon about my mother's lesbian affairs. It would have required me to give of my inner self to him whereas this was something I wanted to protect.

But there is another question that needs answering. Why was it particularly the personal encounter between myself and him that I found such a torture? My hatred of the "savage God piety" in the Church generally had been of milder proportions but why was it particularly the person to person encounter that was my worst torture chamber? Why could I have not just said to Tony Beagle, "Look, Tony, I think you and I have very different outlooks and I think it would be better for you and for me if we parted and I go to another parish and you get a curate whom you would find more congenial to your way of doing things ..."

There are certain reasons why I did not want to do this. I loved being in the East End; I wanted to make a success of my first parish; I did not want to go complaining to my bishop that I could not get on with my parish priest so soon after ordination, and yet these reasons, though powerful, were not the core of the matter. To have been able to say something like the above would have required me to be separate from Tony Beagle, apart and certain of my own identity, whereas in fact I was enmeshed with him. He was in me and I was in him. There was a savage God institution in which we were both entangled. I was struggling to get out of it. Had I locked horns with him and had a row it would have been violent and there would have been the danger of my realising the presence within me of what I hated so much in him. It would have faced me with my own violence.

* * *

A pious nun who had been in the West Indies came to live in the parish. She had been sent by her order to do a training in nursing. So she lived in the nurses' home of St Andrew's Hospital to which I was chaplain. She came to Mass each day and one day she offered to do any parish work which might be needed. I had a list of all the Catholics in the parish as Tony Beagle and I had visited them. I gave her the name of some of them who were old, sick, or disabled and suggested she might visit them. She did this and was absolutely delighted. She had never done any work of this kind. She then offered to help keep all the vestments in the sacristy well ironed and cleaned. After a while I realised that she was very attached to me. On the other hand I did not feel in the least attached to her but I had become a god to her and she almost kissed the ground I walked upon. She asked my advice about all sorts of matters both spiritual and practical. At the general election she asked me for which party she should vote. I began to loathe this clinging attachment and would do anything to shake her off. I found it unbearable. When I moved parish to Tollington Park in the district of Finsbury Park she would come to Mass there, which was a journey of an hour or so by public transport. I once had a dream about her clinging desperately to me. By this time I was having psychoanalysis and the analyst said that it was unbearable because she represented a clinginess in me that I could not own. This was just a statement and I could make no emotional connection with it. It was very much later, years later, that I came to realise the truth of this.

After all I had clung to the Church desperately and before that I had clung to God. It was only very much later that I realised that this kind of clinging and hatred of a particular figure or institution were interrelated entities: that the figure to whom I clung was also hated because it was so entrapping. I also then realised that my mother and father clung to each other in this kind of way and that the hatred they had towards each other was a component of this emotional phenomenon. My father used, in his later years, to trail imploringly after my mother and she would rush away and signal him in fury to go away and leave her. Parents who cling to each other in this way also cling to their children in a similar way; there is an absence of separateness and no love for the person as he is. It is very difficult for children of clinging parents to develop a capacity to love; that capacity which is in everyone has to be "awakened" through the love coming from the parents, but if the parents relate through clinging rather than through separateness and love then they are unable to inspire such an awakening. I have struggled with this problem all my life. It is part of the same problem as the fear of the savage God. It is also part of the reason why I went through a long period of hatred towards my mother and also towards my father. It was not them that I hated but my mode of attachment to them.

* * *

One morning the doorbell rang and I opened the front door to an attractive young woman in her late twenties, dressed in black. Her husband had just died; he had committed suicide. She was staying with her sister who lived in the parish. Her husband had been at Downside School. She came for some spiritual comfort. I spoke to her for a little while and she went off. She lived in one of the Medway towns. She asked me for something but I cannot now remember what it was. On one occasion I visited her and had tea. By this time it was some four months since her husband had died. She asked me some advice about the education of her two children, Caroline and Richard, who were both very young at the time. I drove away and I heard no more of her. However, she was to re-enter my life some years later in a fateful way. Her name was Josephine Earth.

* * *

Two worlds were active. In the external world I was pedalling around the parish in a fever of activity. I was running the YCW groups, the married couple groups, the youth club in the London bus; I gave a series of talks on the Catholic faith. I visited the Catholics in the parish, visited the hospital, gave religious classes at the Cardinal Griffin School in Poplar, visited the parish primary school just near the church, said Mass every day, and heard confessions. I also engaged in some ecumenical activity and became friendly with the priests of an Anglican group ministry in Poplar, the Methodist minister who lived nearby, and was active in the Christian-Jewish dialogue. In the discussion group I had started with Geoff Heath, which consisted of about ten people, we discussed things like "What does personality mean?", "What do we mean when we call someone a person?", "Is God a person?", and so on. We met monthly and had the most lively discussions. We inquired into these questions untrammelled by any preconceived dogmatisms. So this was one world but then there was the tormented inner one.

175

I have already described the experience of realising I was in free response to God the day after I arrived in the parish. I have described my appalling conflict with Tony Beagle but it was also a conflict with the Church more generally. I think the act of disobedience to the Church, which I am about to describe, was the beginning of my leaving it. It was small when viewed from outside but was momentous from my own standpoint. From the time of being ordained a subdeacon I was obliged to "say the office". This was made up of the eight sets of "hours": matins, lauds, prime, terce, sext, none, vespers, and compline. Every priest was obliged under pain of mortal sin to say this office every day. It was a familiar sight to see priests armed with a breviary saying their office. These different hours were mostly made up of psalms which are very beautiful. In a monastery matins and lauds are sung in the morning and then prime, terce, sext, and none at intervals through the day, then vespers in the evening, and compline before nightfall. If spoken with thought and prayerfully the whole would take about an hour and a half to two hours. In addition we priests were all recommended very highly to meditate for half an hour in the morning, say Mass, offer a prayer of thanksgiving after Mass, pray the rosary, and do half an hour of spiritual reading each day. If done with care and devotion this would take about four hours a day. In reality very few priests spent this much time in prayer. Of these prayers the only one which was obligatory was the office and, in the face of other pressures upon the priest's time, the office was often "said" as quickly as possible. To omit it was a mortal sin—cut off from God, and should death intervene without repentance then the priest would be consigned to hell for all eternity. One day I had just finished saying the office when I started reading a piece of St Matthew's Gospel and came upon the passage in the Sermon on the Mount where Jesus says, "In your prayers do not babble as the pagans do, for they think that by using many words they will make themselves heard ..."[5] and I said to myself, "But what have I just been doing? Have I not been doing just that—babbling a whole lot of words like the pagans?" I sat and thought seriously. I wanted to pray with thought and care so I made my decision. I would no longer babble the divine office but instead put aside half an hour each day and pray to God quietly and carefully.

---

[5]Matthew Ch. 6. v. 7.

I would take a Gospel passage or one of the psalms from the office and say it carefully and think about it in a meditative way. I used to go to confession once a week to Denys Lucas who was the parish priest at Mile End, the neighbouring parish. I asked for his blessing upon it. He agreed that what I intended made perfect sense; he gave me his blessing but I could see he was worried by it.

It was a momentous decision because I had taken the law into my own hands. I had decided that what the Church decreed was wrong and put my faith in the words of Christ and his Gospel. I was in the shoes of Luther. I judged that it was not a mortal sin to fail to say the divine office. In future it was my conscience and not the Church's dictate that would be my guide. I was no longer the Church's slave but master of my own fate before God.

What I did not understand at the time was I was wrestling with an inner God, the same God that terrified me as a child when I had broken the fast before Holy Communion. Freeing myself of this inner tyrant was my life's work. There was a connection between this and my struggle with pride. I was twenty-eight when I made that decision to renounce saying the divine office in favour of half an hour of meditative prayer. I was aged about fifty-eight when I realised the connection between the inner tyrant and the grandiosity and also their intricate connection with some other elements in my personality. At this time, though, I thought the Church was the tyrant. I had not seen that I invested the Church with a tyrant that came from within my own personality. When I first got a glimpse of this I crashed into the most appalling depression that crippled me and almost put me into a mental hospital.

* * *

One night Tony Beagle became ill and I had to take him into the Hospital of St John and St Elizabeth in St John's Wood. He had a very bad bout of hepatitis and his heart had also been affected. He was away ill for six months and I was left in charge of the parish. Every weekend my friend John Perry came to help out with the Masses on Sunday. On Saturday night we sat up and discussed for hours the nature of the Church, what was the essential core of Christian life, what was the priest's central task. From week to week we drove our inquiry deeper and deeper until I believe we reached the central core.

177

There is something about making such an inquiry with a friend in whom there is a deep resonance that illuminates the core of living in a way which I believe no other inquiry does. Recently I came across this quote from Salley Vickers: "... the greatest wisdoms are not those which are written down but those which are passed between human beings who understand each other ..."[6]

There is some quality about an inquiry between true friends which reaches through to the core of things in a way that does not occur just through one's own thinking and reading, or at least in the formative period of one's life. I put in this last qualification because I have never since had such a deep investigative experience between myself and a friend in later life. I think the word "resonance" is what captures it most succinctly. The love that there is in friendship powers the inquiry but it is a different sort of love from that which existed between me and my parents. That is a love but without that special resonance. I long for that resonance above all else and I believe that I have been fruitlessly looking for it down the years. I have frequently been sexually attracted to different women over the years, though not acted to consummate that attraction, but I have thought that such attraction has been some kind of compensatory desire that replaces the real thing: that deep resonance in friendship that powers an inquiry. Bertrand Russell describes something of this sort in his account of his meeting with Joseph Conrad (as quoted earlier):

> At our very first meeting, we talked with continually increasing intimacy. We seemed to sink through layer after layer of what was superficial, till gradually we reached the central fire. It was an experience unlike any other that I have known. We looked into each other's eyes, half appalled and half intoxicated to find ourselves together in such a region. The emotion was as intense as passionate love, and at the same time all-embracing. I came away bewildered, and hardly able to find my way among ordinary affairs.[7]

I think this passage captures well something of what passed between John Perry and myself during this time. We certainly sank through

[6]Vickers, Salley (2000). *Miss Garnet's Angel* (pp. 232–233). London: Harper Collins.
[7]Russell, Bertrand (1971). *The Autobiography of Bertrand Russell, vol. 1* (p. 209). London: George Allen & Unwin.

layer after layer where all that was superficial was swept away and we reached "the central fire". "Fire" is the right word because it was a red hot flame that burnt away all the dross, but also that central flame lit up some realities and gave them a new prominence and placed others in a new context. It was an organising inner flame that reordered everything in a new perspective. I suspect that some great new movements of thought come from such deep encounters: Jesus and his apostles, Freud and his early circle, and many other significant movements.

I think that I have only ever had such deep friendships with men. Apart from John Perry my other two friends with whom I had deepening encounters were Bill McSweeney and Richard Champion. I think the sexual issue has prevented it in my encounters with women. I cannot imagine an inquiry of that deep friendship kind between myself and a woman occurring without it being consummated sexually. I think if I did throw myself into some friendships of that kind with a woman I would, like Bertrand Russell, also consummate the friendship sexually, but sexual fidelity has held me back from that.

It is very difficult adequately to describe what I mean by "resonance". It is something deeper than a harmony of intellectual understanding. It touches on belief and, for me, belief in the transcendent or infinite, but it is not that alone because it touches also upon the aesthetic and it may be a combination of these two. John Macmurray, the philosopher, in his excellent book *The Structure of Religious Experience*[8] says that there are three mental axes which form our orientation to the world: the scientific, the aesthetic, and the religious. When I refer to resonance I look for a conjunction of these three in some kind of a balance which is shared by my friend and myself. If there is a complete absence of any one of these three the resonance does not occur.

* * *

One of the great controversies at that time was whether or not birth control, as envisaged by the Catholic Church, was based upon sound moral principles or not. While I was at St Edmund's I was in doubt about it but generally believed that the Church's position was correct. However, even when I was at St Edmund's, I was certain that it was not

---

[8]Macmurray, John (1936). *The Structure of Religious Experience*. London: Faber and Faber.

a matter upon which the pope had pronounced infallibly. The teaching on contraception had first been enunciated by Pope Pius XI in *Casti Connubii* but this was not an infallible pronouncement. So when I left St Edmund's I knew that the Catholic position was a strong opinion but not an infallible doctrine. However, shortly after I was ordained, I read *Contraception and Holiness*,[9] which was a collection of papers arguing against the position which had been taken by Pius XI and adopted since by his successors and the Catholic hierarchy. I was entirely convinced upon reading this that the current Catholic position on this matter was wrong. One of the articles tackled the "natural law" argument which had been the basis for the Church's position. I was convinced that natural law had been misunderstood by the Church, that it had interpreted natural law according to an animal understanding rather than man as a decision-maker able to use or misuse technological means of limiting birth. This put me into a difficult position in the confessional especially at Easter time when Catholics poured into the confessional in great numbers. This was because the Church declared that to be a practising Catholic and not to be in mortal sin someone must go to Holy Communion at Easter time and this usually meant confession as well. A high percentage of these would confess to using contraception. Many of these were men and women living in two bedroom flats already with three or four children. People would make statements like, "I know the pope says it's wrong, Father, but you see we have three children already and we live in two rooms ..." and many variations on this theme. Here was I convinced that it was not wrong anyway, so what was I to do? I did not want to impose my view upon them any more than I thought the pope should impose his view upon them. I tried then to guide them according to their own consciences but these were people, often Irish men and women with little education, who had been brainwashed from the pulpit, so what chance had they of trusting their own judgment? After all, what trouble I had had giving up the recitation of the divine office after years of higher education? I tried my best nevertheless. I would ask these people what they thought themselves and they would say that they did not think they could have more children. So I would put a leading question,

---

[9] Roberts, T. D'E. (Ed.) (1965). *Contraception and Holiness: the Catholic predicament*. London: Collins—Fontana.

"So if it wasn't for the pope saying it was wrong you would feel it was alright?"

"Yes, for sure, Father ..."

and many variations of that. Sometimes I would ask the person to come and discuss it with me outside the confessional because then it was possible to go into it in much more detail and find out what he really thought. In such circumstances if people really thought they were right according to their conscience to practise birth control I would say then it was not a sin and that there was no need to confess it any more. It was very difficult though. I knew it was confusing for people. There was the pope declaring contraception to be sinful and it was being repeated by priests all over the world and here was this dissident priest telling them it was alright. I was not the only priest taking this line but nevertheless we were the few.

The majority of confessions were ritualistic with a set series of sins pattered out with monotonous constancy. Nowhere was this more true than with children's confessions. They had been taught to regurgitate a template of sins which, if they bore any relation to what the individual child had actually done, it was a lucky chance. On one occasion about fifty children were queuing up outside my confessional and one after the other they obediently poured out the ritual, "I've told lies, I've been uncharitable to my neighbour, I've forgotten to say my prayers ..." About thirty children had been in and out each with the same litany of sins. Then one child came in and started the litany and then suddenly stopped and looked up at me and said, "I broke a chair."[10] I could have hugged her. This is clearly something that had actually happened but how was it that this one child broke free of the mantra and made contact with something she had actually done? The dissociation between what is being said and what is actually done was the norm in most Catholic practice. However, it would be unfair to lay this behaviour at the door of the Catholic Church alone. In the practice of psychotherapy I have come across something not quite so stark but nevertheless similar. But what was it about that little child that enabled her to break through the hypnotic trance? I wish I knew. I think, though, the fact she looked up and stared me in the face had something to do with it. Here she was

---

[10]This was not actually what the child had done but a kind of equivalent. I do this to prevent any chance of identification.

in relation to a person, not under the direction of a hypnotising God, and in that moment of being in relation she made contact with her own true acting self. I would love to know whether this moment was just a moment or whether she went on to lead a personal life in a rather unique way. I shall never know but even these fifty years later my heart goes out to her and I wish her well on life's journey.

I never knew a case where the secrecy of the confessional was broken by a priest. It was the most heinous crime for a priest to reveal the name and identity of someone and then relate the sin that he had been told. It was so strict a rule that even if someone who had been to confession to a priest then later saw the priest outside the confessional and referred to something he had said inside the confessional the priest had to say that he did not know what the person was talking about. When I asked someone to come and speak to me about a matter outside the confessional I had to explain in the confessional that they would have to start from scratch as though I knew nothing about the matter. Catholics absolutely trusted their priests not to reveal their identity or the sin they had committed.

When I later became a psychoanalyst I soon realised that the confidentiality was far looser than what I had known as a priest. I have often heard psychoanalysts and psychotherapists talking quite freely about particular patients and what they have said or done. In my years as a Catholic priest I never heard one instance of such a betrayal of trust.

I had enormous energy at this time of my life. The number of activities I had on the go at the same time was enormous. Apart from being chaplain to St Andrew's Hospital and going there every day and sometimes at night, I taught in the local primary school, I went once a week to the comprehensive school in Poplar, I said Mass every day, I heard confessions, I ran the youth club in the converted double-decker bus, I gave talks on the Catholic faith, I continued to read a lot, I ran the YCW group, I ran four marital groups. I was chaplain also to St Clement's which was a psychiatric hospital. I also became involved in ecumenical work and participated in the religious study programme at Queen Mary College which was part of London University and just down the road from the church at Bow. I also used to lecture occasionally for a Catholic academic organisation under the direction of Cecily Hastings at Westminster Cathedral and I became involved in a sociological study of cultural groupings in East London that was headed by a team in Bethnal Green. I began also to take a particular interest in West Indians. I read books about them, their arrival in London in the fifties, and I visited the homes of all of them in the parish; I tried to come to understand why nearly all the Catholic West Indians lapsed from the practice of their Catholic faith whereas a much higher proportion of the Irish continued their practice. I gave scripture lessons and talks on the new liturgy. I did not have a car but cycled around the parish. I rarely went to bed before one in the morning and was up by six o'clock. I co-operated with the local probation service and social work teams over various parishioners who were clients of one of these two services and I became friendly with both the social workers in the hospital and also the probation officers. I became involved both with Alcoholics Anonymous and Gamblers Anonymous and helped parishioners who had difficulties with these addictions to affiliate themselves to these organisations.

When trying to help alcoholics I came across a woman called Stella Mines who had been severely afflicted with alcoholism for many years. She was so well known in East London that no shelter or accommodation would have her. On one occasion after she was discharged from hospital she was in the medical social worker's car plus myself and we knew not where to take her. Eventually we took her to St Giles's crypt in Camberwell where they took her in and also found accommodation for her nearby. Through this I met Heather Campbell who was one of the two workers running the crypt. She had had psychoanalysis. I came to know her quite well and she first introduced me to the language of it, though at that time it was utterly mysterious to me what she meant. On one occasion she told me, "In my analysis I had to face Mum." I had not a clue what she was talking about though I sensed it was a significant arena from which I was excluded. I sensed that she was talking about a level of inner experience that I was not in touch with but that I needed to be. The fact that I had many conversations with her was indicative that I was searching for someone to help me reach into myself in an area from which I was utterly shut off.

I threw myself into the life of the East End of London with enormous energy and enthusiasm. I had such an enormous range of new experiences, relationships, and contacts that it took me years to assimilate it all, and it continues to influence me considerably. I had lived protected in this respectable upper middle class Catholic world and here now I plunged into the working class culture of East London with all its structural fibres. I came to realise how cut off are the English upper middle class from the more basic throbbing emotions of ordinary life. It is not an experience I would have missed for the world. I loved it. It was a new baptism and I emerged from it a different person.

At this time I came to know Vincent Rochford, a priest whom I loved. He had been parish priest on the Isle of Dogs for seventeen years and ahead of his time had come to understand the inner soul of the liturgical, catechetical, and biblical movement. He was the man who twelve years earlier I had heard talking for the Catholic Evidence Guild in the City outside the Tower of London in the lunch hour. He knew that religion was a matter of the heart—of the heart's connection with God. Cultivating this in the souls of his parishioners was what mattered. He prided himself on having reduced rather than increased the size of his congregation. Those that belonged to it were pledged to God in their hearts. He knew that the rosary, benediction, and indulgences were peripheral devotions but he also knew that because someone was with-it and knew all the renewal spirit which was blowing through the Church it did not mean that their heart was in the right place. He was outspoken, said what he thought, and cared not a shred what pope, bishop, or priest thought of him. He was highly intelligent, a man of courage but he was in no way "an intellectual". He thought on his feet. He applied his intelligence to the practical job of being a priest in the parish and bringing God to the people. He had an enormous sense of fun and good wit and was always totally fair in conversation even about the most diehard conservative priests.

I came to know him quite well and when Denys Lucas from Mile End went off on the missions to Uganda I started going to confession to Vincent Rochford; afterwards I used to have long conversations with him. What impressed me most was the degree to which he was in contact with himself, his own passions. It is so common for religious people to come to believe that, treading the path of Christ, they have achieved it: that they are not arrogant, not angry, not envious, and so on, and to be totally unaware of what they do to others emotionally. My experience of Vincent was that he enlarged my spirit, brought home to me that love was at the centre of the business; my experience of Tony Beagle was that he crippled my spirit. I am sure that the difference lay in the fact that Vincent's own heart was robust and that it had become so through loving. I believe that the whole of Tony Beagle's piety was self-protective in nature.

I have always had great difficulty with those who are emotionally frail but particularly when they stand in some position of authority towards me. I can work happily as second in command to someone who is robust emotionally but with someone emotionally frail I find it impossible. This has not changed down the years.

After two and a half years matters reached a climax with Tony Beagle and finally the bishop, Cardinal Heenan, moved me to a parish near Finsbury Park, but by that time I was nearly broken inwardly. Vincent Rochford also moved and became parish priest at Duncan Terrace in Islington and I used to go down and see him about once a week. His presence was a tonic but by this time I knew I needed help, help of a deeper kind than was possible from anyone I knew. I knew I needed to be reached somewhere inside me where I never had been reached. Just as I had not spoken to Monsignor Sullivan when I had the shock of discovering my mother's lesbian affairs in Lisbon ten years before, so also I did not speak about my difficulties with Tony Beagle when with Vincent Rochford. I thought they would not understand or connect with what my problem was. I suspect that I may have been correct with Vincent though I am not sure that I was in the case of Mgr Sullivan. However, both these men had values and a "nobility of soul" which was much greater than most psychoanalysts I have come across and certainly the one to whom I first went for help.

I had been two years in the parish at Bow when my sister, Jill, had a breakdown. Her marriage had broken up some eight years before but now she broke down and went into Halliwick Hospital in north London. I spoke to the psychiatrists who were in charge of her, but as I spoke to them of what I thought were her difficulties and explained to them something of my family background, I was aware that I spoke as if I were myself insulated from these family influences.

I arrived at the new parish disheartened. The area itself had none of the unique personality of the East End of London. It was a drab, soulless area with no pride in its traditions. I knew when I arrived that I would have to seek help for myself. I needed someone who could "reach me". I have described how when I arrived in Bow I had that experience of a subjective personal relationship with God. It was this person in me that needed to be reached. I knew I needed more than a bit of counselling. I was fearful, though, of going to a psychoanalyst who was not a Catholic. So, through a recommendation from a doctor, I went to Dr Ronald St Blaize-Molony at the Langham Clinic in central London. I remember going to the waiting room of this clinic and being overcome with an uneasy feeling of a "soft comfort", of furnishings arranged by people who did not know the cut and thrust of life, who had not sat with dying people in hospitals, whose assumptions of what mattered in life were very different from mine. This deep feeling that struck me as I was sitting in that waiting room for the first time has stayed with me in my lengthy journey down the corridors of the psychoanalytic world: that this world also is subject to an insulated culture whose values are bureaucratic and whose highest aspiration is mediocrity.

So the doctor arrived, called me out and, after an interview, it was arranged that I would come and see him twice a week. I felt a thrill of excitement and, at the same time, of fear. This was something *I* had decided to do. It was a personal decision like the decision to abandon saying the divine office; something that came from what was really me. It seems an odd statement from someone who had decided to become a priest yet I believe it was so. It took more inner courage to decide to go and have myself psychoanalysed than it had been to go into the Church to become a priest. In the decision to become a priest I was being carried along by an outer hurricane. It was as if someone had thrown me into the surging current of a river whose violent eddies carried me downstream. When I had been at St Edmund's for some years I used to feel that the fuel that fired this passion was running out. In a moment of violent passion I had generated the steam to push me along but now I sensed that it was ebbing away. This sense of an ebbing tide started two years before I was ordained. The prospect of ordination carried me forth to the end of my time at the seminary. This passion that ferried me along this surging waterway was one that was profoundly pleasing to my father, my uncle, and my aunt, and there must have been a component in it of hatred of my mother. But it is love and not hatred that holds permanence in the personality. The choice of starting psychoanalysis was a decision. It came in answer to a deep place in me. Somewhere I knew it was going to be difficult, that it would not win the approval of my father or even my mother. I began to understand what Heather Campbell meant about "facing Mum". It was fear that directed me to a psychoanalyst who was a Catholic so there was in it something of the need for approval but there was a bit of the pure gold as well. On reflexion I think there was something of the pure gold also in my decision to become a priest but it was masked by this auto-generated passion to please a hungry God.

It must have been in either the first session or the second that I was cast into the abyss of the most appalling depression. I lay on the couch

186

and there the priest of passion disappeared and was replaced by a panic-stricken child. "Where I shall I start?" I asked after I had lain down and the psychoanalyst sat behind me. "I will not direct you; you are on your own now," he said. I was now in a lonesome, cold, empty place. I was on my own in a friendless universe. I do not remember where I started but either in that first session or the second I was speaking with venom about the controlling nature of the Church when the psychoanalyst showed me clearly that what I complained of in the Church was so much of me and that I was the controlling one. He did it in such a way that I saw it absolutely clearly and could not evade it. I plunged there and then into the darkest depression imaginable. For a year it took all my energy to drag myself from bed in the morning. Whereas until then I had got up in sprightly manner at six in the morning I would now sleep until nine in the morning if I had no duty to perform. If I did have an early Mass to say I dragged myself up with the greatest difficulty. I would be sitting in a chair and, just out of reach, would be a book I wanted to read. I could not summon the energy to get up and fetch it but would sit moribund for half an hour or more. I was giving a series of talks at the Islington Evening Institute on Christian Spirituality and I could not summon the energy to prepare them. I would sit at my desk in front of a blank sheet of paper for an hour with no mark made upon it. As the months went by the situation deteriorated more and more. I do not think it was visible to those outside. I just managed to plough myself through what had to be done so I suppose the inner inertia was not noticed. At one time I was on holiday back in Portugal and at night I could not sleep and was tormented with fearful fantasies and imaginings and felt a huge gulf between myself and my family. The torment and distress of the soul in the year before I left the priesthood was the worst of my life or at least my life until the time of writing this.

When I refer to needing to be reached, there was a person in me yearning for recognition like a foetus pushing to break through into the light outside the womb. That experience when I first arrived in the parish of Bow of suddenly realising that I was in free response to God was the first dawning of my own subjectivity. I think that from the time of learning of my mother's infidelity I had, in a great ecstasy of passion, fashioned a god-made barricade that smothered utterly my own selfhood. I had become dislocated from myself so that my perceptions were distorted and stripped of the capacity for comparative judgment. For instance, I had loved the parish of Bow and embraced with enthusiasm the life and culture of the East End of London and convinced myself of its beauty. One day I went to Knightsbridge and when walking in one of those early Victorian squares I realised that the East End was almost devoid of architectural beauty. In my enthusiastic embrace I had shut out the rest of London so that I did not have within me any other part with which to compare it. I had done the same with my embrace of the renewal movement within the Church when I was at St Edmund's. It was, I now recognise, another version of that very first ecstatic clasping of the Church when I learned of my mother's infidelity.

Whereas I had been slim I now put on weight. There was an old woman to whom I used to take Holy Communion once a week and I twice forgot to take it to her. Such an oversight had never occurred before. She came to Mass and reproached me and I felt ashamed. It was a large church with crowds of people thronging into all the Masses on a Sunday. Despite the depression or perhaps because of it I preached better than I had ever done. I spoke in a simple way about the essentials of Christian life: faith, trust, hope, love, patience, courage, and gentleness. I spoke in a very direct way and illustrated these fundamentals of Christian life with examples that were always interpersonal in nature and, as I had done in Bow, I created dramas out of ordinary daily life to demonstrate the topic of the sermon. I also spoke *to* the people in a very direct way and looked members of the audience in the eye as I did so. I would prepare the sermon carefully and read through it several times but then would deliver it from memory. I have frequently used this method with lecturing in later years. The disadvantage is that I would always forget some item I had intended to include but I think that is more than compensated for by the direct personal nature of the communication. I was sitting in the confessional one day and a man came in and made his confession and I gave him absolution. Before he left he said, "Father, when you are up there giving your sermons on Sunday you probably think no one is listening. Well, I'd like to tell you that they mean a great deal to me—thank you, Father."

I felt so encouraged by that comment. The thing I warmed to most was that he bothered to come and tell me but it was also a great joy to know that some of the things I had been saying had touched his heart in an important way. I have since come to believe that in any sermon or, later in life, in any lecture if one person derives significant benefit from it then it has been worthwhile. Cardinal Manning said in his book *The Eternal Priesthood* that one soul makes a diocese. I have stuck to that principle all my life. I have also always tried to act like that man did and commend someone for something that he has done which has been important to me, but I have carried it further than that. I have always spoken to people or written to them when I have heard that something distressing has happened to them or that they have done something that deserves congratulation. I have come to realise that I am not in a majority in this practice. Many people fear to intrude but I do not think that this inhibitory voice is to be heeded. When a death occurs, a marriage breaks up, or a member of someone's family goes to gaol a communication from a friend is always a great help. I learned this for myself when I left the priesthood.

I want to reflect a bit more on why these sermons were so good and how that was possible when I was in such a depressed state. In depression I have always been thrown back on what is most essential. All the peripheral activities of life fall away and I attend to what is most essential and it is the communication of this to another or others that makes its mark. Depression is an intense feeling and it is always there on account of something. Let us suppose that I was depressed because much of my energy was being spent in exercising my own controlling behaviour; further, that what I believed was altruism was in fact an expression of my own solipsism; that my external clinging to the Church was my way of dealing with the shock of my mother's infidelity; that really I was an impostor in disguise. These would be more than sufficient to make me depressed. I think that what the analyst demonstrated was just the tip of the iceberg. I don't think it is what he revealed that made me depressed but rather the knowledge of what he had not revealed which I was beginning to bring to the surface. If these general lines are true then my sermons would have begun to have in them something of the detective revealing the impostor but in a personal way. What Albert Schweitzer called "elemental thought" would have been taking the place of "unelemental thought".[11] This person to person contact always makes an impact. That is why that man who came into my confessional that day was affected by what I was saying in those sermons. I do not remember

---

[11]Schweitzer, Albert (1958). *My Life and Thought* (pp. 260ff). London: George Allen & Unwin.

189

their content except that they concentrated on what was internal as opposed to what was external. Numbers, Sunday observance at Mass, and so on were placed where they belong: in second place—that they were a means to an end. I specifically said that missing Mass on Sunday might not be a mortal sin whereas a hateful act towards a neighbour might be. I do not think that this is what touched that young man, but that I managed to give expression to matters that were internal in a personal way.

* * *

I was in my sitting room one afternoon in early December in the year 1966 when the telephone rang. It was Malcolm Stewart who had been at St Edmund's with me. About a year earlier he had left the Church and was now working for Granada Television. I picked up the receiver:

> "Hello."
> "Is that you, Neville?"
> "Yes."
> "I've got some news that is going to shock you ..."
> "What?"
> "Charles Davis has left the Church."

I could not believe it. I asked him to explain. He told me that Charles had decided to leave the Church, had resigned as editor of the *Clergy Review* and was going to get married. He was going to marry Florence Henderson who was a prominent Catholic laywoman who had been working in Edinburgh. He further told me that news of it would be in all the newspapers the following morning.

This news was a thunderbolt that shook me to the core. Although Charles had been a radical in the Church he had always been absolutely faithful and loyal to it. The conservative priests hated him and he was the guarantor for all of us avant-garde priests. He had gone to Rome as a *peritus*[12] invited by Cardinal Heenan. The hierarchy looked with disfavour upon Hans Küng but felt that though Charles Davis was avant-garde, he was safe. All of us radical priests on the parishes had always

---

[12]That is, an expert. Most bishops who went to the Vatican Council in Rome took with them an "expert"—a theologian who was a scholar in the subject under discussion.

been able to say, "But Charles Davis says ..." and that was accepted just as if it had been spoken by the pope. My understanding of the Church had been inspired by Charles. It was impossible to believe that he had left the Church. I rang Bill McSweeney and told him. A little while later Bill rang me back to ask me if I was absolutely sure that what I said was correct, wondering if I had been misinformed or gone slightly crackers.

I did not know how to assimilate this piece of shocking news. The next day it was in all the newspapers. I had lunch with three other priests at a restaurant in north London. Two of them were Hilary Crewe and Sav Reynolds but I do not remember who the third one was. It was the gloomiest meal I have ever had. We sat much of the time in glum silence. We knew also that our shield against the conservative priests was gone. They were now in triumph. I found their taunts and cynical remarks unbearable. I went and visited my friend John Perry and also Bert Richards. We were all engaged in the same process: how to assimilate and make sense of this news which was such a shock to all of us. I went and visited Vincent Rochford. He said he thought this would affect my generation of priests very severely. He said, "No one will leave now but in a year's time they will." His prediction was acutely accurate. I left just over a year later and Bill McSweeney, John Perry, Richard Champion, Ted Matthews, and Patrick Carey all did as well.

As Malcolm Stewart had predicted, Charles's defection was front page news in all the daily newspapers and that evening Charles himself was a guest on the David Frost show on television. I read all the accounts in the newspapers and watched the David Frost programme. Charles looked very grim on that programme. In it he accused the pope of lying. Paul VI had recently said that on the issue of contraception there was no state of doubt in the Church. As on the pope's own commission on the subject there was a minority section who had submitted a report recommending that the Church's teaching be changed because they believed it to be wrong, there was no way in which it was possible to say that there was no state of doubt on the matter in the Church. Charles said that the pope was simply lying. I cannot remember the rest of the interview. About two or three weeks later *The Observer* ran a huge two page lift-out on why Charles Davis left the Church and it was written by himself.

I think that when Charles left I inwardly must have given up. It was as great a shock as the news of my mother's infidelity. I was left reeling. It was different from my mother's infidelity in that Charles's leaving was a public event and I discussed it at length with all my priest friends. It was an earthquake to all of us and we tried to master it and work out what the implications of it would be.

I discussed it with my psychoanalyst but in this arena I met with incomprehension. He was a traditional Catholic but also was not involved in the Church with his heart so he did not understand the passions which surged in my soul. I do not know how long it took me to integrate this event and make some sense of it but to the extent that I did it was through talking to priest friends. All these friends had also been "converts" to the new faith within the Church. For us Charlie had been the guarantor of our orthodoxy. In doubt and uncertainty we turned to him. He was our intellectual leader. His sheer knowledge of the Church, its development, and doctrinal position was staggering. He always spoke to us from within the Church. That was his undoubted position; we took it for granted and now he had left and suddenly. One day he was in the Church and the next he had left it.

What was the process by which I slowly made sense of it? So that from a shocking event which left me staggering it slowly became part of the landscape of my mind? What did I do for that to occur? Talking to my priest friends must have been a crucial factor. Leaving the priesthood fifteen months later must have been another. How did talking achieve something? It must have been instrumental in bringing knowledge, which had always been there, from the periphery to the centre. Charles's own motivational processes came to the fore in my mind and this was through talking. When I was still at St Edmund's and Charlie had just returned from being in Rome for a term at the Vatican Council he gave us a talk on the ethos of the chatter and intrigue in the corridors of power. In that talk he mentioned Paul Blanshard, an American journalist who criticised Catholicism unmercifully, and Charlie said with a certain fascination in his voice: "He hates the Church ..." and when he said it something reverberated from him that left an impression upon me. I think he hated it himself, perhaps not wholly but in some part of him. That had been an emotional impression. When he left the Church this emotional impression moved from the wings to centre stage but I think it needed me to express it for that to happen. The very act of talking, of communicating, moved it from the periphery to the centre.

The process of communication must be instrumental in locating an event differently in the mind. The mind is made up of parts which have been joined together in a certain configuration. It becomes the governing

192

principle ordering the direction of one's thinking and behaviour. When I communicate with another there must be a passing-between. I am sure that I would have told John Perry or Richard Champion my memories of that incident when Charlie spoke about Paul Blanshard, and they will have said things to me. I remember that John read out to me an editorial that Charles had written in the *Clergy Review* some months before where he wrote about fearing and hating the Church. So when I tell him the Paul Blanshard incident and he reads that to me there is a passing between us of the same emotional content. It gives it a new emphasis in the constellation. It becomes an organising centre of the different parts within. In order for that to happen I need outer confirmation, like the sealing of a document. It seems that on its own in me it has no substance but when it receives an echoing confirmation from another then it "stands" and takes a new place. In the communication there must be a touching of the similar elements one with the other and this is necessary for its establishment.

This must mean that there is a connection between the outer and the inner—that the meeting of the inner emotional experience with something similar in another from outside endows my inner one with certainty. It seems that the joining of two emotional elements that echo one another occurs through a bond of sympathy which is articulated through language. The language is the vehicle which carries the one emotional element across to the other. These two find each other drawn together through a joint recognition like two people falling in love with each other. When this happens there is a wedding ceremony that affirms and establishes what until then had only been half-formed. Wilfred Bion called it a preconception becoming a conception.[13] However, he believed that this is a state of expectation mating with a sense impression. I think it is one emotional state which could be called a state of expectation or an inchoate or half-formed emotional state which mates *not* with a sense impression but with another half-formed emotional state and the two coming together form what we might call emotional certainty.

The question then is how this new-found certainty, this new establishment functions in the personality. It becomes a new organising centre and that is then me: I become it or it becomes me. That is the person then who I am. That the personhood comes about as the result of this joint intercourse between the two emotional states and that *is* me.

---

[13]Bion, W. R. (1962). *Learning from Experience* (p. 91). London: Karnac (1991).

That then is the act of becoming. This must be what Bion meant by "becoming O"[14]—his angle on it was from a different perspective. It was the idea that infinite being emerged and this then *became* me. This would mean that the coming together of my emotional element with that of another, the "wedding ceremony"—forming a new reality which is *me*, that the becoming the Absolute or Infinite or O is through this process of the joining of inchoate emotional elements into fully formed ones. The meeting place of the Absolute and the Contingent is through this meeting of elements across the divide between persons. But, even without this perspective of Bion's, it seems that this way of understanding the coming to birth of an emotional reality between two people is what lies at the core of psychoanalysis. The new positioning of an inchoate emotional element from periphery to centre is the core of the psychoanalytic process and that very happening is a becoming.

If one thinks of a belief as the manifestation of the inner reality then a new inner reality has become established and therefore with it a new belief, and this became at variance with the belief of the organisational grouping of which I was a part. I believe that the new reality that became established in me was different from that of Charles. My belief put me in opposition to revealed religion but with Charles it did not. I think that what came into the centre for me was that rational contemplative vision of the absolute character of being that occurred for me when being taught ontology by George Ekbery at St Edmund's. That was what was central but it took a long time, my life until now in fact, for me to take possession of that fact. In the way I am trying to characterise it here it would be that it took time for that to move into the centre and for all the other elements of my personality to orientate themselves and centre themselves into this one reality.

I think the emotional element that formed together in me into what I now realise was a newborn reality through conjunction with others was connected to the solution within me of my problem of pride. Being or becoming this new element was the source of an inspiration but from within the human creative coupling and not through being chosen from on high. It was not the result of a call from without but rather from a human joining, something springing from within and between. There is something so frightening about this, so alone-making that an escape into submissive devotion to an established community of belief is a route to

[14]Bion, W. R. (1965). *Transformations* (pp. 147–149). London: Karnac (1991).

avoid madness. So it is not just one coupling but several that come together as a new centre. This particular element I found through a "wedding ceremony" with John Macmurray whose books I have already mentioned.

"I have been chosen" or "I am special" seems to be an important component of pride or what psychoanalysts call "omnipotence". If these two senses are generated from a relation within, between one's individual self and selfhood, or the contingent and the absolute—through an act of inner insightful inspiration, then the human individual bears the burden of his own insight with all the self-doubt and uncertainty that must accompany it. The moment I disown my own intuitive insight into "God" then pride or omnipotence have taken over. While I hold it earthbound within the confines of intrapsychic and interpersonal life then what has been generated is "natural religion". As soon as I disown it into God I have submitted to revealed religion. It is possible to go through the Old Testament and separate what is natural religion from revealed religion, and now I come to think of it I should amend the capitalisation of the first letters thus: Natural Religion and revealed religion and Being to god. Revealed religion, as it has historically developed through Judaism, Christianity, and Islam, are three different streams of this group egotism. They are of course, all three, permeated with natural religion and I believe that this is encountered in its purest form in the wisdom of the mystics of all three faiths.

The solution of my own personal problem required me to renounce revealed religion and embrace natural religion. This was both an intellectual and moral solution to a deep problem that I was wrestling with. I returned to it again when I entered into the arena of psychoanalysis. In other words the disowning of personal insight into the analyst is the same process by which revealed religion was created.

It seems that when something shocking happens it is necessary to find antecedents; that there is a belief that it cannot have arisen from nowhere; that signs of pregnancy must have been present. That if such signs can be found, it can be assimilated. The sense is that a huge sudden onrush of disparate information cannot be assimilated; that the mind can only take on one small bit at a time.

* * *

The demon I was wrestling with was a harsh punishing God which had become embodied in the Catholic Church for me. At that time I could

195

not disentangle it from the Church. It seems that it had grasped hold of me at the time when I learned of my mother's infidelity, but that I think only established what had already been there. When I was in London and before going to Lisbon I had felt bad, or that something was wrong, or something happening which should not be happening when I got an erection when dancing, and this was already present in early childhood at the time when I made my First Communion which was when I was aged about eight. That panic lest the sacred host touch my teeth and then my conviction that I was the worst sinner on earth when I broke the fast on the occasion of my third communion. I think really that my mother's infidelity was just the occasion when this savage God, now embodied in me, was directed against my mother.

So the question is, "How and why was this savage tormenting God inhabiting me from this early age?" I do not know the answer but want to try to investigate its architecture. The only way I can get at this is by resorting to my own constructed theory because I do not know why I had this savage God within me. I am sure that my brother was not tortured with it, though I suspect that my sister was and probably still is. So something must have happened for me to develop it. My theory is that the presence of such a savage God within is the living presence of a trauma—that some traumatic event occurred whose living form is partly constituted by the savage God within. The question is what trauma had I undergone? That is the 64,000 dollar question that I am not able to answer. In a consultation psychoanalysts sometimes ask a patient for his or her earliest memory. It is the idea that in this memory is a crystallisation of the individual's trauma. My earliest memory is of seeing in the garden a large white plaster cast from my mother's leg and closely associated with this is a memory of her sitting with her injured leg bound in plaster and bandages and up upon a footstool of some sort. It conjures up for me a "mother at a distance"—it is not a picture of warm affectionate closeness. My sister, Jill, has had severe mental difficulties and was, at one time, in a psychiatric unit. I think it possible that my mother's way of relating to Jill was through taking her into herself to repair something which she felt to be damaged within. When I was born she was actually physically damaged as well as emotionally.

I do not know the source of my mother's sexual difficulties but I think it likely that they represented an emotional lacuna. There was something masculine about her. You would neither describe her as "butch" nor as truly feminine. Her closest friends were nearly all women. An exception was Johnny Cobb but he was homosexual. I have thought that she scooped Jill into the role of compensating for some emotional deficiency and that it was something about her being a girl that enabled her to do this. Then two years later James came along. James has always been very masculine in the presentation of himself. My mother was antipathetic towards him and certainly as a boy and adolescent she was very cruel to him and treated him extremely unfairly. Then two years later I came along. I was fair-haired, unlike James who was dark-haired. When she saw this little fair-haired child I believe that she tried to turn me into a girl and then use me in a way similar to how she had used Jill: to compensate for an emotional abyss within her. I certainly had the feeling in adolescence and early adulthood that she wanted me to be homosexual. I am certain that she was deeply unhappy in herself and that she tried to use Jill and me as sticking plasters to make good the unhappiness.

That there was something severely wrong with me I am certain and that it started at a very young age is also certain. The above explanation may not be right but I think elements of it probably are. What my own theory tells me is that the presence of a savage tyrant God within is the result of a violent trauma. Also one of the central battles in my emotional life has been the resisting of pressure from the social environment surrounding me and from the Establishment, and following what is truly me as opposed to what has been imposed on me. This is the reason why I felt so inspired by George Ekbery within the orbit of the Church and later by Wilfred Bion within the perimeter of psychoanalysis.

* * *

At this time, however, I had no clue about any of this. The savage God was firmly implanted in the Church and her moral directives. This was still so despite my depression and realisation that I was myself controlling and authoritarian just as the Church was. I set about trying to free myself from the jaws of this savage Church that had me in her claws. I became strongly drawn to a very attractive young woman. I did not have sexual intercourse with her but I did have sexual contact with her. I did not confess it as I convinced myself that this was not a mortal sin so I took communion. According to the Church's book I had certainly committed a mortal sin. I took it on myself to make the judgment that it was not. Was it or wasn't it? Was it wrong of me? Had I done something very wrong or not?

I have done things of which I am ashamed but I do not think that this was one of them. I was, I believe, on a journey towards the establishment of love and conscience in my heart; from an outer guide to an inner one. I was trying to free myself of a savage God. Of course I was going about it in the wrong way. I believed that I had freed myself from a savage God when I came to believe in a loving God at St Edmund's. I had not freed myself of this savage God but only relocated him from the throne of Yahweh to the Church.

So if this was the wrong way then what was the right way? I do not believe that I could have solved it in the Church. I knew already that I was proud and that the Church had provided no solution to it. The Church's solution was to pray to God for humility. I do not think that this was fatuous because what this advice encouraged was desire and without the desire there could be no change and I do believe that if there is a strong desire of this sort it will point the way. So the Church encouraged the desire and I am grateful to the Church for having done so. My reading of G. K. Chesterton had also fostered this desire and it is not a desire that is much encouraged in secular society today. Perhaps I had to go into the Church to have that desire fostered.

What the Church was unable to do was provide the means by which that desire might be attained. It is this that I sought in psychoanalysis and it did provide the means to some degree, but only to a limited degree for reasons that I will come to later.

So I was on a journey and I was blundering along in a blindfold manner, and I damaged myself and others on the way, but I think the sexual contact I had was a minor misdemeanour. The major ones arose from self-centredness or what I have referred to as pride. I did something when I was in that north London parish that still shames me when I think of it. A parishioner had arranged to organise a special social *do* to try to bring about a relationship between the Irish and English parishioners and those from the West Indies. I had encouraged him in this venture and it took place in the church hall which was nearby. He obviously relied on my support and involvement in the event itself but at the due time there were some visitors from an ecumenical centre and I was engaged in a passionate discussion with them at the presbytery and I could not drag myself away. At one point the parishioner came and begged me to come to the social event. I said I would come and went for a few minutes but then hurried back to the intellectual debate. To this day I hang my head in shame when I think of it and I believe this was a worse sin than the sexual one. I let that man down terribly and I have not the slightest excuse for it.

* * *

I was attending analytic sessions twice a week, lying on the couch. One day I had the emotional feeling of having acquired in my analyst a "strong father" and I clung to him. I think I was wrong about this. I do not think he was an emotionally strong man but I made him into such. It was therefore a delusion that I fashioned. His words were strong but his character was emotionally frail. Out of what components did I fashion this delusion? And why did I need to? And why did I cling to words rather than my intuitive perception of his character? Why is it that if there are two contradictory signals—one coming from the words spoken and the other from the emotional centre—that I believe the former? It must be that I had a strong wish to believe him to be a strong father, but that I cannot believe it without something to support it so I cling to the words. It is even more than that—that I want it so much that I promote the sort of answers and declarations from him that will confirm the wish. I will speak with uncertainty and hesitation and this provokes him into a more decided manner of speech so I have then fashioned the firm father I was looking for. What this suggests, however, is that the signal to trust is the one coming from the emotional centre. At this time when I was tottering within the Church and full of uncertainty I endowed him with a rock-like quality. I have done similarly at other points in my life.

It is often said that discordance between words and emotional reality drives someone mad but what truly drives someone mad is a wish so powerful that it clings to even the most unreliable signal. From earliest days I must have felt that I was slipping around in quicksand and therefore clinging desperately to anything that seemed stable and secure. That early experience in my teens when I said to myself that the one thing I could totally rely upon was God was an instance of this because the God I put my faith in was a false God, a savage one that persecuted me. I suppose the savagery must come from the fact that the figure clung to despises the clinger. The figure clung to hates being clung to and vents fury on the clinging one. What about when the clung-to

199

figure is God—an invisible mythological creation? It is that the savage aspects are selected and the benign ones brushed aside. If this is so, it can only be that this means that there is a knowledge of the clinging and, at the same time, a hatred of it. This would make sense of my early experience where, as a clinging child, I was desperate not to disappoint my father because then I might lose the rock I was clinging to. It would explain why my father favoured financially my brother, James, who did not cling in the way that I did. When at St Edmund's I turned God intellectually into a loving figure then the Church became the savage one. When I left the Church I found myself savage figures in the characters of women.

* * *

I used from time to time to go and speak to Peter de Rosa who was at that time at Corpus Christi College at Notting Hill Gate. On one occasion I was driving away and it became crystal clear that I would leave the priesthood. I felt myself on a pinnacle of light on top of a mountain in the midst of darkness, unsupported by any outer suggestion. This realisation came entirely from within. I felt myself in utter loneliness, a point of light surrounded by darkness. It was so clear that there was no doubting it or escaping from it. I did not know quite how I was going to execute the decision but the decision had been made. It was a moment of becoming. The first such moment was when I realised on that first day in the parish that I was in free responsiveness to God. The second was when I was riding down Bow Road on my bicycle when I shrunk with fear at seeing the path where my inquiry was taking me. The third was when I decided to abandon the duty of divine office and pray meditatively for half an hour each day instead. The fourth was when I decided to go into psychoanalysis, and the fifth was this moment when I knew I would leave the priesthood but this last was the culminating one. The year that preceded that moment was the worst of my life. After leaving the priesthood I went through all sorts of traumas but they were not as bad as this year. It is that the torture of a period prior to clarification and decision was worse than storms on the outside.

* * *

CHAPTER SEVEN

In exile

So at the end of February 1968 I left the parish in north London. A few days before I had visited a men's outfitting shop and bought myself some layman's clothes. I tried on a herringbone grey suit. I felt awkward in it. A few days earlier I had had an interview with Cardinal Heenan. He was an unsympathetic man with little feeling for the difficulties of people like myself. He looked at me through his bifocal lenses and made a few castigating remarks. He had tried to be "modern" and in tune with the changes taking place at the Vatican Council but it was mostly an outer show. He was a grim conservative within. There was, however, one attitude which I appreciated. His view was, "Either stay in and be a good priest or get out". He had no patience with those who moaned but stayed in the Church, all the while making a nuisance of themselves.

On my visit to see him I caught the bus to Victoria station and walked along to Archbishop's House. Inside I felt an empty shell with no substance in me. I was a loose shabby suit walking along with no body inside. In that mode I am sure I was aggressive towards him. I hated him at the time but over the years have become more conciliatory towards him. He was very opposed to my having had psychoanalysis and thought I should have gone and had a long retreat at some religious house. At one moment he was dismissive of me as a priest. I protested that my work in the East End had been recognised to be good. He agreed and apologised. I don't think he really knew what to say. Many priests were leaving and he did not know what the trouble was in the Church. He gave me a letter granting me "leave of absence". So for six months or so I was in limbo. I was neither in nor out. I had to decide whether to leave or to stay. To make the final step was an unnerving decision.

Where was I to go? My father had written to say that he thought it would be awkward for me to come to Oporto so I had to try to sort out my life in England, and I was lucky in having some wonderful friends who made life possible for me.

So I said Mass one morning then stepped out of my clerical clothes and into the layman's ones I had so recently bought; when I had said my Mass, I had breakfast, then got into my Mini Traveller, left the presbytery for the last time, and headed up the motorway towards Nottingham. Colin Allen who had been at St Edmund's with me but had left before taking final vows was an assistant prison governor at Lowdham Grange near Nottingham. He was married to Geraldine and at that time had no children. I stayed for a fortnight. He was very troubled at my leaving and put a lot of arguments against my doing so. That was not what I needed at the time. I was so shattered inside that I wanted sympathetic company and nothing more. Being in the homeland of D. H. Lawrence I read some of his novels: *The White Peacock*, *Sons and Lovers*, *Lady Chatterley's Lover*, and *Women in Love*. It was the start of trying to make good a big lacuna in my education. I had since first going to St Edmund's ten years earlier read and studied ardently theology, philosophy, and Church history, but had hardly read a decent English novel. To this day this has only been partly remedied, but I have derived enormous enjoyment from reading some of the classics of English literature. I have never been a fan of D. H. Lawrence and the novel of his which I enjoyed most was *Women in Love*, though some of the passages where he describes the life of a miner in *Sons and Lovers* are superb. I have always felt that he is an overrated novelist. I don't think of him as a writer of first rank but rather someone who is high up within the second rank. So I read those four novels of his when staying at Lowdham Grange. It was being in Nottingham, which was Lawrence's homeland, that led me at that time to read his novels. It was

202

not an easy two weeks. It was very disturbing to Colin that I had left and he argued fiercely against what I had done.

So a fortnight later I returned to London and arrived on the doorstep of the Carey family in Lee, near Lewisham, in south London. I rang the doorbell and Frances, with a gentle smile, showed me in; that was the start of a long love affair with the Carey family which has lasted to this day. Their son, Patrick, had been with me at St Edmund's and was ordained on the same day as me, and, after going to Cambridge to read modern languages, he had been sent as a curate to a parish in the town of Hertford. I had been in conversation with him prior to leaving and he had been one of us who had been deeply shocked by Charles Davis's departure from the Church. He had suggested to me that when I returned to London I might go and stay with his family in south London. His father, Charlie, was a GP and his surgery was tacked onto the side of their large eight bedroom house at 179 Burnt Ash Hill. Charlie was one of the warmest and kindest men I have ever met. He was solid and imperturbable and loved by all his patients and his family. Clare, his wife, was amusing, fun, and slightly histrionic. She promoted the furtherance of education and on a bookshelf in the dining room were dictionaries, encyclopaedias, and books of reference. In any discussion at table if some topic came up and the question was raised "What year did Mao Tse-tung take power in China?", or "What is the French for avocado pear?", or "Which star, after the sun, is nearest to the Earth?", then immediately one member of the family would take down the appropriate reference book and search for the answer. Clare, ever since her children had been young, had foreign au pair girls from France, Spain, or Italy. This had been a deliberate policy on her part to encourage the family to learn to speak these languages. Consequently all family members were fluent in several languages.

The house was large and the front door was always open with no lock upon it day or night. Meals were usually large casseroles containing meat and vegetables so two or three extra guests could easily be accommodated. Frequently friends would drop in for either lunch or dinner and often stay the night as well. I believe the Carey household at Lee was the most welcoming home in London. The eldest son, Charles, was a barrister and he lived at home. The two eldest daughters, Mary and Ann, both lived with their husbands and children nearby. Frances, the youngest of the family, also lived at home. Patrick was a priest of the parish and Peter lived at home also but was not around much when

I was there. So I was thrown into the bosom of this welcoming family and I believe that staying there for nearly six months I began to slowly get better and recover my equilibrium.

There was one short break in my stay. The plan had been for me to remain two weeks and then go to share a flat in Wimbledon with Malcolm Stewart and a friend of his who was the editor of *The Tablet*. Malcolm had also been at St Edmund's with me, was ordained a priest two years before me, and had left the priesthood about two years before I did, and was about to marry Ruth. It was Malcolm who had rung me on that fateful afternoon to tell me that Charles Davis had left the Church. So, after two weeks I left the Carey family, and went to take up my place at this flat in Wimbledon. Malcolm and the editor, John Wilkins, were out most of the time. There was no common room. It was a flat of three small bedrooms and a small kitchen and bathroom. I had no job, knew no one in Wimbledon, and was absolutely miserable. I went out and ate in pubs in the area and walked from time to time on Wimbledon Common. After two weeks I rang Clare Carey and asked if I could come back. "Come back this afternoon," she said spontaneously and so I did.

In the bosom of the Carey family I felt well. Those two weeks at Wimbledon should have warned me, however, that I was far from well. The kindness and warmth of the Carey family protected me from a shocking depression and inner lassitude. So I was back with the Carey family and I stayed there for five months. They became my adopted family. Although they were all devout Catholics they showed no disfavour towards me and never questioned me about my motives for leaving the priesthood. They simply embraced me as a new member of the family. I would go to bed at ten or eleven at night and I used to sleep without waking until midday or ten in the morning at the earliest. It felt like the most curative sleep I have ever experienced. I believe that, although in the outer works of my life, I was doing practically nothing, yet I was engaged in a very arduous emotional work within. I think I was sleeping so much because of the enormous emotional toil that was going on within. When subjectivity is being born it takes a huge amount of energy. What looked so energetic before when I was pedalling around the parish on my bicycle was not an energy from within but from an outer pressure.

I have explained how just after I had arrived at my first parish I had that illuminating experience of my own subjective responsiveness to God. I am sure that it was the development of this that led me out of the

204

Church; that later I decided not to say all the hours of the divine office but rather to pray for half an hour peacefully upon one of the passages from the psalms. There was a struggle between a savage impersonal God on the one hand and the development of an embryonic person on the other. As the battle became fiercer I then attacked back with an equal savagery at this God. When I had a sexual contact with a woman and then decided within myself that this was not a mortal sin and celebrated Mass I was doing violence to something in myself and my received world. As I was, like a chick, breaking free of the brittle eggshell that had imprisoned me, so I flailed my arms in a demonic fury at my erstwhile gaoler. Now I had at last broken free of the external fabric of the Church. The external act had been performed but now the internal emotional work had to be done and this was what I was now doing within the enfolding arms of the accepting Carey family. The outer pressure I have just mentioned was coupled with a huge grandiosity. When I had rushed furiously around the parish of Bow, visiting the sick, running YCW groups, taking scripture classes, and doing a hundred and one other activities, it was fuelled with the energy deriving from this grandiose source. It was this same source that drove me helter-skelter into the Church. It was an auto-generated energy that powered things on the surface but there was a huge emotional work now to be done. I think when I was in that marvellous Carey asylum I was engaged in the emotional work of developing that embryo within, but this was work issuing forth from the heart of me and therefore a demand on the system which was far greater than this surface, external activity. I was therefore working very hard and at the end of each day I was exhausted and needed hours of sleep.

* * *

The concept of inner emotional work is not well understood. To the extent to which I had been driven by an inner savage God, exactly to that extent had there been no inner work. The lack of inner emotional work is compensated for by outer God-driven work. The latter is dependent upon the passing stimulating imagery of the moment and is a way of dealing with some massive traumatic happening. I have to go back to that infidelity of my mother's. It was a tremendous shock. The question is: "What are the emotions that go to make up that shock?" Perhaps the way to get hold of that is to ask what it is that paralyses? The answer must be hatred. A savage God is a hating God of great violence. I think at the moment when I discovered my mother's infidelity I was overtaken by a hatred so violent that all my rational processes were brought to a halt. Now, to understand this properly one must suppose that before that fateful night when I actually heard in Clay Wilson's unequivocal language that my mother was committing "the sin of sodom", as she explicitly put it, there had been a precursor: that this was the *dénouement* of a long process in which I had been involved. My own involvement was obviously a crucial part of the process but what I want to do first is to trace the precursors. It cannot be that my mother suddenly fell into bed with Clay and that there had been no previous history of this. There was in it I think a hatred of men. It is particularly this that needs examination.

It was not that my mother hated men in the ordinary social sense of her life. Her flirtatious, jokey attitude to my father's male friends was part and parcel of her character. What I am talking of only came into play with the man with whom she was called upon to share a destiny of emotional intimacy. Let us say that what she hated was the erect penis penetrating her. Yet this is a physical act. The question is: "What does it represent?" To answer this question I think of it under two modes. The first is that it represents a force that penetrates and brutalises the other. This leads me to think of my mother's hypnotic power that over-whelmed my own personal sensibility. This was certainly something that I came to hate but what I am positing here is that it was hated by my mother herself. In other words, the erect penetrating penis is hated because it represents power—this persuasive hypnotic power. But why would my mother hate this herself? The answer to this question lies in the assumption that what human beings most want is a free loving rela-tionship with another person—that it is this that is longed for more than any other human good, that if this is achieved then all other goods take on a position that is subservient to it. Therefore a force that violently obstructs, makes impossible, such a relation is then hated; but rather than the inner force being the object that is hated, instead it is the erect penis that represents it. But why is this? Why isn't the obstructing force itself hated? The answer is that in a primitive way it is. The hatred is the expulsion of the force into the outer object—in this case the erect penis. The erect phallus is a symbol of power but under these circumstances it is of a destructive power because this hypnotising force is something that blanks out what is personally creative.

The question then is, "Why does my mother hate the erect penis rather than the hypnotising force that the penis represents?" And yet this is not the right way to formulate the question. The expulsion of the hypnotic force *is* the hatred. To be consistent semantically then the verb for my mother's "hatred" of the erect penis needs to be something different. The word I would choose is "detest". This has more the sense of the loathing of a static object whereas hatred has a more active sense to it. So let us formulate it this way: that my mother *detests* the erect penis because it represents the hypnotic force which she *hates*. She sweeps the hypnotic force out into an object that swells up with this new content. What better object to symbolise this than the penis inflating with erectile fluid?

There is, however, another question which is more fundamental. Why is it easier for my mother to turn her attention to the outer object which she *detests* rather than the hypnotic force within that she *hates*? Why is it that self-knowledge of this sort is eschewed? Rather than apply this to my mother I can ask a similar question of myself. Why do I prefer to see bullying behaviour in another rather than in myself? We so take it for granted that this is so but why is it so? Why do I hate to see such behaviour in myself? What is gratified by sanctifying myself and denigrating the other? Why this erotic investment of my own self? Is it because it is so frightening a thing to be lived by the Infinite within? If I don't inflate my own self but live the truth of my own nature then I am involved in mankind; I am part and parcel of the world. If there is always the invitation of conscience to *become* then the demand of this inner call to change is only heard when I know the truth about myself. A hatred of change would then be what makes me puff up and make myself into a delusional figure that does not require change. I am a good person, a saintly person so do not need to change. I am already what I am required to become.

The other mode of approaching this question leads to the same answer ultimately. It is that the erect penis represents the instrument of interpenetration, of lovemaking, of fruition. This requires a flow of life from the self; a something has to come out of the self. Love is also a demand to become and the erect penis symbolises this and it is therefore hated. I feel this is not quite right but the best I can manage at the moment.

The more obvious approach is that the hypnotic power is, like all emotional activities, not known directly. It can only be known indirectly through a sensible object that represents it. The erect penis represents this power. Why? Because the penis penetrates as hypnosis does.

* * *

So I stayed with the Careys. We often played bridge in the evenings and during the day I would take Clare Carey shopping. She could not drive and so I drove her around. She chatted freely about all her six children and I came to know her well. She was highly expressive and she felt everything that happened to her with a high intensity.

I was still having psychoanalytic psychotherapy twice a week and was slowly trying to find my way to some new form of life. One day I saw an advertisement in the personal column of *The Times* for under-graduates to work as guides for American tourists. I answered the adver-tisement and went for interview and was accepted after my knowledge of London and England had been examined. It was a system where I would be rung up and asked to go to a London hotel and pick up in my car one, two, or three American tourists and either take them on a whole day or half-day tour of London, or a tour to places within strik-ing distance of London such as Windsor, Hampton Court, Canterbury, Cambridge, Oxford, or Warwick. Because I could speak Spanish and Portuguese I would also be asked quite frequently to take tourists from South America. As a rehabilitative job this was quite satisfactory. I was not required to enter into a deep relationship with the tourists and I quite enjoyed getting to know many of the historic buildings which, until then, I had only known superficially. Driving through Reading one day on the way to somewhere a woman turned to me and said, "Now tell us about Reading." There were only three pieces of informa-tion that came to mind. I told her and her friends that it was here that Oscar Wilde had been imprisoned, that Dominic Barberi who was a Pas-sionist priest who had received John Henry Newman into the Catholic Church in 1845 had collapsed and died in the Station Hotel, and that Bishop Butler who was the auxiliary bishop at Westminster Cathedral was born in Reading. The woman was satisfied with my disquisition on Reading and seemed to have no idea that the last two pieces of informa-tion, though true, were somewhat idiosyncratic.

But this job was of its nature temporary. I had to find a new path. I had been at the Carey family for three or four months and felt I must find my own accommodation, which I did. I rented a very pleasant

208

unfurnished flat in Holland Park Avenue while still doing my job as a tour guide. The depression had not gone but was at times so severe that I thought I could not manage outside some hospital situation. I considered applying to be taken into a Richmond Fellowship home. This organisation set up by Elly Jansen was composed of a series of homes for the rehabilitation of people who had had breakdowns. In each home there were between a dozen and a score of residents. At times I could hardly drag myself up in the morning and to make my way to the car was a tremendous effort. I felt the need to collapse into the arms of a caring organisation. Would it have been better had I done so? When I started a second analysis with John Klauber he was strongly of the opinion that it was much better to manage out of hospital or some equivalent setting. I think he believed that it was such a blow to the individual's self-esteem that it was then difficult to get over it. However, I have often wondered whether it would not have been better. There would then have been a full acknowledgment on my part that I was ill and in a state of mental breakdown, and then all psychic energies could have been mobilised towards regaining my health. I think it would also have brought more sympathetic support from Uncle John, Aunty Aileen, and an array of cousins which may have made a great difference. As it was they saw me as a sacrilegious rebel who had desecrated what was most dear to them. Had I instead generated their sympathy I may have relaxed and allowed myself to regress into illness and slowly get better. But I don't know because I did in the end recover but not before another massive disaster.

* * *

That I was severely ill I have no doubt but, although I knew it, I also managed to hide it from myself and made a supreme effort to put a brave face to the world. The charade was not new to me. I had felt exactly the same when I was at Ampleforth—knowing that I was ill, that something was wrong with me, that I was in a pitiable state yet putting all this energy into putting on a brave face. This problem has bedevilled my life and also caused confusion in others. I believe that if I had gone into a Richmond Fellowship home then the outer and inner would have coincided and been in sympathetic relation to each other. Then if I had solved that problem of personal dissonance my life might have taken a very different course.

There is, however, an argument that goes against this point of view. It is that recovery meant finding a different philosophical and religious solution: one that "fitted" my soul; recovery was not possible without this being achieved and, I believe, this course would always have set up opposition, if not antagonism, from some sectors of my family and of devout people in the Catholic world. It was the solution suggested to me by Cardinal Heenan but there must have been an embryonic voice in me crying out for a religious philosophy that would "fit" the yearnings of my soul. It is probably significant that when I decided to become a priest I wanted to become a *secular* priest. Having been at Ampleforth the natural niche for my vocational ambitions might have been to enter the monastery there but I had a strong desire to be "in the world". The idea of a spirituality in the world had a deep appeal and I warmed to Teilhard de Chardin who dedicated his treatise *Le Milieu Divin* "For Those Who Love the World". I think my illness had within it a nugget of what Henri Ellenberger called *creative illness*.

I want to describe as accurately as I can, from my own personal point of view, what is meant by this term *creative illness*. When I first came across this idea in Ellenberger's book *The Discovery of the Unconscious*[1] it spoke to my soul and I knew that it had a special significance for me.

One of the ways of being ill is if the internal and external are not in synchrony with each other. I was certainly ill in this sense so I was looking for an external system of belief that corresponded with the stirrings of my soul. Catholicism did not fit the world within. It was not that it was entirely wrong. So I had to find something that externally represented what was within and, as it was not readily available on a plate, I had to construct it for myself. I had an architectural plan within and now I had to make sure that the building that I was constructing outside was a faithful representation of the architect's drawing. Until I had achieved this I would be ill.

Now how did I go about this? Through faith in "statements embodying emotional significance": these were the lines making up the architect's drawing. There was a huge turbulence going on outside and a process embracing statements of emotional significance inside. I was looking for voices that spoke to *me*. When this happened things made sense, they came together, I felt an inner thrill, and peace came over me.

[1]Ellenberger, Henri F. (1970). *The Discovery of the Unconscious* (pp. 447–448). London: Penguin.

A plane had been battling in a storm cloud and suddenly it broke through into the clear open air. A great sense of relief came over me and, for a short while, I bathed in glorious sunlight. It was always a discovery. It was utterly new, or maybe a series of disparate jigsaw bits came together and there in front of me was a startling new pattern. What were the spoken things? It would often be something I was reading. I would come across a new author and to my joy I found that what he was saying spoke to *me*. So what does this really mean? It found an echo in my soul. It stirred a response in my true being. It would seem to mean that the emotions were in some unformed state and were waiting for something from outside to pattern them. Yet that cannot be quite right because there has to be something that "recognises" the outer voice—like a dog that recognises the call of its master. And it has to be something that is not truly in existence until the "call" occurs. The outer voice waters the dry seed into life. What I am struggling for here is a model that will fit what I am looking for. Earlier I proposed the idea of bits on the periphery that are moved into the centre. Later I was very attracted by Wilfred Bion's idea of a preconception waiting to mate with a realisation. So here is the emotional stuff waiting for an outer voice. It seems that the reality only comes into being through the connection of the two. The inner is looking for the right words. The words and the emotions "marry". It reminds me of Vygotsky who said that the debate about thought without words is not right because the word and the thought make up a unity;[2] that the emotions and the voice form into a unity. At the moment of the "marriage" a new reality comes into being but one that was there waiting. I suppose the sperm and the ovum must be the best model. It is only when the sperm and ovum join that the new reality comes into being but the ovum is "waiting" for the sperm.

Yet it is as if the sperms have been collected. I have said, "Oh yes, that is a valuable sperm. I must keep it because I shall need it one day"—as if there is knowledge of the ovum that is waiting. I understand that all the ova of a woman's fertile lifetime are there. I know they are there so I gather up the sperm for the time when the ovum will be released. I can think of "sperms" that I have gathered which have only joined up with the ovum as much as forty years later. These so-called sperms can seem quite different yet there is some connecting thread between them. One sperm was the realisation of the absoluteness of reality which I stored

---

[2]Vygotsky, L. S. (1975). *Thought and Language*. Cambridge, MA: MIT Press.

away when I was twenty-two but only married up to an ovum thirty-eight years later. Another was George Eliot's insight into Lydgate's torture in Middlemarch which I stored when I was thirty-five but only realised it when I was sixty-three. The ovum inside tingled when the "Lydgate voice" was heard so I stored it away. And I believe that this process of the gathering of the sperms and the effecting of their union is the process that through my life is responsible for making me whole, endowing me with health, restoring me to life. This has been the benign process in my life for which I am enormously grateful. I cannot know why it is in me or how it came to be but only that I am so thankful for it.

Then there was this other mad, disintegrating process going on. My flight into the Church was of this nature. Great wild passions have suddenly gripped hold of me and no restraining force has been able to tame them. To be able to distinguish between what is wild and mad from what is adventurous and sane has only begun to come to me at the beginnings of old age. I think these great passions have been triggered by a huge upset. I am sure that my flight into the Church and my disappointment and rage with my mother are linked. There was something solipsistic about it. It did not result from a sifting of the problem. I did not discuss it with anyone. I "solved" the disaster by taking flight, making a unilateral decision. The madness is in the solipsism. Then I ask myself about being in psychoanalysis which should be a remedy for solipsism but in fact it was not. When I reflect upon it, I realise that I never conveyed my sense of shock and distress to either analyst. I certainly told each about my mother's lesbian affairs but I had the idea that the analyst was a "man of the world" and that such a matter was to be expected, was not something so very untoward, so I told him, I am sure, in an offhand or "I am a man of the world" sort of manner. Therefore I never spoke about the shock it had been to me, so the trauma remained enclosed in a solipsistic cocoon. To understand more fully the flights into madness or what exactly the madness consisted in will come up for more reflection when I examine the next mad passion that seized my soul.

* * *

So I was installed in my flat in Holland Park Avenue and still doing my tour guiding and still seeing my analyst. I was certainly in a shocking state and I think my analyst could not really have appreciated it. I draw two conclusions from this: 1) that I had a capacity to hide the disturbed state, and 2) that the analyst himself was closed to the deeper storms of the soul; so we were together: the blind leading the blind. At the moment the first of these two is the more important because I obviously "impress" people with a good sane front and that all is well. I hide the inner torment and misery. Because my analyst believed me to be well he recommended that I go to Brunel to read psychology, and gave me an introduction to Elliott Jaques who was the professor of social science at this new university. So, off I went for interviews and was accepted as a mature student. "Mature" referred in my case purely to age and not to the emotional level of development of my character. So I started my degree in psychology at Brunel University in September 1968. I was in a miserable depressed state and I loathed it there. Frequently when I was in the library studying I fell asleep over the book I was trying to read.

* * *

It was at the time I went to Brunel that I finally wrote to my parents to tell them that I had definitely decided to leave the priesthood. When I left the parish at the end of February Cardinal Heenan had given me "leave of absence"—a period of asylum, so during these seven months I had been in a state of indecision. Should I leave the priesthood or not? I was torn in two. I could not make that final irrevocable step. The Church had meant so much to me. I had put my whole life and energy into it and I loved the Church, its history, its traditions, and its philosophy, yet when I left I was hating it. To cut the bond that bound me seemed a terrible disaster. I agonised over it but finally, just before starting at Brunel, I decided and wrote to my father the following letter:

155 Holland Park Avenue,
London W.11.
Thursday, 19th September.

Dear Paisâo,

Here at last is the English text of the Canon of the Mass. This is the Canon which is regularly said at Mass in England. There has come out recently the text of three newly formulated Canons which will be used from the beginning of Advent. I am sending you just the present one which I hope is what your friend wants. I have the other in my possession so if he wants it let me know and I shall send it direct to you.

I know you must be rather worried about me and you must be wondering what I intend to do in the future. The first thing I would like to assure you is that I am at the moment happier than I have been for about four years. I was ordained in order to bring a knowledge of God among the people to whom I was sent and to try to promote Christian love—in short to try to do what the apostles did who were sent by Christ into the world after his death. In fact in both parishes where I worked this was impossible. In each place any worthwhile work was impeded. I was also frequently put into a position where I was expected to support behaviour which was quite unchristian. I think if you spoke to Fr. Bernardo he would elaborate what I mean. It is rather as if you were being driven in a car by a reckless driver who had a crash who then tried to persuade you that he was driving carefully. In all honesty you could not. Twice I asked for other sort of work which I felt would suit me better and which would allow me out of the parish but on each occasion I was refused.

I was faced therefore with a decision. Either I had to lie down and accept living in a situation where I was unable to practise the priesthood or put into effect all that I had learnt to believe in over a period of six year training or ask for a period when I could live as a layman and during that time to try and work out a future for myself. To do the former would have been moral suicide. To have gone on living in a completely frustrating atmosphere would have been wrong. I decided therefore on the latter—to live as a layman for a period. One of the considerations which made me decide this was this: I could have allowed the previous situation to drift on saying to myself, "Oh, well, things might get better" or "We may have another bishop in five years' time." In other words to wait vaguely that things might happen. I decided not to wait for this reason: I am aged 31: at 31 it is still possible to become qualified and re-mould one's life but at 36 or 37 it is much more difficult. On the last day of this month I start the degree course in Social Psychology. This degree qualifies the graduate to take a post in Social Work, to become an industrial psychologist, a clinical psychologist in hospital work or in the prison service. My own greatest interest lies along two possible spheres: that of social deprivation in a city like London or work in a social institute in a part of the world like South America.

When in February I asked for this release from active duty it was on the understanding that I would probably return after two years. Several general things make this now unlikely e.g. the unlikelihood of being placed in any better situation than before, the inability on my part to be keen about many trivialities etc but in particular two recent factors make it extremely unlikely. One is the birth-control issue. I have for the last two and a half years taught clearly and plainly that artificial means of birth control are good and right if used judiciously and within a Christian view of marriage. I could not therefore preach or teach the Pope's recent directives on the matter. If I had been on the parish I should have already been suspended. What saddens me more is that authority should have been exercised in this way. If this is the legal side of how the Church is going to be run and if its laws are going to be enforced, particularly on priests, then I will have no part in it. It also indicates a whole approach to moral matters which I think is destructive to the human personality. There are important matters to be tackled by Christians in the Church: coloured-white problem, in developing countries the problem of hunger, social injustice in South America, juvenile delinquency, modern methods of education. A Christian layman can go ahead and tackle these problems: a priest, especially now, had to spend all his time discussing the Pope and contraception. The second factor is that Cardinal Heenan gave me his word that he would allow me to live as a layman 'for at least two years'. He seems now to have gone back on his word. I intend now to go on this course in Social Psychology with or without his approval. I am living as a layman at the moment but very probably shall remain a layman for life.

I know you will be saddened by this but I think there are several considerations it would be good to bear in mind. The first is the training I underwent and the four years of active priesthood are not wasted. In the first place the experience it has given me of people and social institutions has been invaluable but more important it has given me a grasp of the Catholic faith which I should never otherwise have had. The Christian faith is more important to me than anything else and my education through the seminary and priesthood are largely though not entirely responsible for this. The sad conclusion is that I left the active priesthood in order to be able to live a better Christian life rather as in days gone by the early Christians fled from the city of Rome as they found amidst so much paganism it was impossible to practise the Christian faith. I have taken no decisive step at present but wished to let you know what was in my mind first but I actually do. I do not think you understood the whole position partly because Oporto is rather a long way from the hub of things.

You may wonder what the legal position is regarding priests who decide to return to lay life? They ask for a dispensation and their bishop requests it in Rome. To-day priests are dispensed from celibacy as well as other obligations.

215

There is another consideration you should bear in mind, I think. Catholic life has changed immensely in the last eight years. Who would have thought eight years ago that the Mass would all be in English? Many would have thought the idea a blasphemy. Who would have thought that the Pope would be flying to Bogotá and Fátima? In Portugal the Church is still more traditional but in England now it is common for priests to express their vocation in a different way. It will become more and more common.

I would suggest that you show this letter to Mum and to James. I also suggest that you take it along to Fr. Bernardo and discuss it with him.

Much love,
from,
I hope you have your gun all ready and I don't mean for snipe!

When I read this letter now, forty-five years later, what strikes me most forcibly is the lack of any self-awareness. I put all the blame on the Church and Cardinal Heenan. There is no hint that I was in a disturbed state. It was always me who was in the right. It seems now, on reading it, a polemic of self-justification. I must have been terribly guilty. The question is though: what was the guilt really about? Was it that the action I was taking was the wrong one? Or was I guilty precisely because I was not being honest about the real situation: that I was in a very disturbed state, that perhaps I should have been in some hospital setting? That the guilt was because I was covering this up. It would, I am sure, have been so much better for me if I had admitted to myself and intimates that I was in an emotionally disturbed state because then I might have found a remedy for my soul. To deny myself the remedy I needed would be sufficient to make me guilty.

I received the following reply from my father:

Warre & Ca., Lda,
Travessa Barão de Forrester
Vila Nova de Gaia,
Portugal.
Wednesday Oct 2nd

My dear Nevelão,

I'm afraid I have been rather long in answering your letter of 18th September.

I know Mumão has written. I waited however till I'd seen Fr. Bernardo, whom I only saw yesterday as he has been away. He is himself now being transferred to Fátima which does not please him. This does not mean that he will not come up on an occasional visit to Oporto. Still I'm sorry he is going as I've always appreciated him, and as you probably know he has an affection for you.

I do not want to write by the mile re your letter. It has indeed made me feel very sad as I'd always had such happiness and pleasure out of your becoming a priest. I do however appreciate the great difficulties you have been through and I feel very much for you.

I feel very sorry that there is no way of your being able to find work under another bishop which might make the work you like more possible?

Fr. Bernardo was very sympathetic about the difficult times you have been through and he said he would write to you.

As I have already said I don't want to write to you by the mile, but as you may know if there is any way in which you can continue with the Priesthood it would give me <u>great</u> happiness. I do however feel very sympathetic about the hardships you have gone through, which I know has hit so many priests especially the younger ones. The Church is no doubt going through a crisis and it is a pity some of the young priests can't get together to overcome this difficult crisis?

I will say no more except that my prayers will be very much with you and they have been already as your leaving the Priesthood if you do does sadden me a lot.

Mum is going to England as you will know leaving here 19th (I think) from Vigo. We are going for the week-end to Afife on Friday. Clay Wilson is going direct there on Friday too. Jameão is in the Douro. Jameão's family is coming to Afife but there is a possibility that Penny may go up the Douro just for the night on Friday as the Jennings have an enormous party for their daughter Carol's 21st birthday at Val de Mendiz in their Douro house. We were asked too but we are not going. Of course if anything happens to Salazar before then (if he died) I imagine everything would have to be put off.

The weather has warmed up and is much better weather for the vintage but the previous cold and wet weather had already done some damage especially to quintas more in the altos.

Mum will speak to you re your finances and she will let me know so as that I can see how I can help.

217

I will end up and I repeat that I shall pray very hard that you may come to the right decision and that everything should also be for your happiness. You know that anything you do can never alter my affection for you.

Lots of love from
Dad P.T.O.

I forgot to say that they have at last struck water in the well at Afife. They have made a big extension to the well (rather expensive) but I think it will make all the difference and I hope when we go up on Friday to find the swimming pool full for us to bathe. It was such a disappointment not to be able to use all the time Jill and small Margaret were here. The cottage is also well advanced.

I so loved my father and when I read those final words, "*You know that anything you do can never alter my affection for you*" I burst out crying. I felt so grateful to him. In those words I found a compassion that went beyond all externals and it touched my heart. To this day I am filled with bitter sadness and regret when I think of how much I hurt and disappointed him in his failing years.

My mother wrote me a sensible and supportive letter back:

Quinta do Bomfim
Pinhâo,
Alto Douro
27th Sept

Dearest Neville,

Your very clear and explanatory letter was at home when got back from Afife on Monday. I thought it was an excellent letter and made your situation very understandable. Dad was very sad of course but has been more or less expecting this news. However I want him to go to see Bernardo, who is leaving Oporto now alas—going to Fátima. He's been away but will be back in Oporto for 3 days this next week so Dad will see him. Dad has also suggested to John he goes and sees Bernardo too. James took your letter to show Michael and the Reais—it seemed the best idea as it speaks for itself. John told Dad he was writing to you but Dad doesn't really know his reactions or what he's writing about. I hope he doesn't write and say anything that may upset you. John & Aileen go to India to-day week.

218

Ian is up here. He & Michael have both been very impressed by your letter & have spoken to Dad about it.

As soon as you have decided or have made the move towards obtaining a dispensation etc we will then tell other people—so just say the word. It is natural that a lot of people may have already heard rumours as I don't suppose Michael and Elizabeth etc. have kept what they heard in England entirely to themselves.

This has been a very sad and difficult year for you I know and I am so sorry you should have had all this sadness, & to make the decision you have is not done lightly but requires great courage to face up to it. So many in your situation drift on & must lead very unsatisfactory and unfulfilled lives.

Jill wrote a long and descriptive account of the "Teach-In" & said she would send some papers about it—so I hope she does. I've not seen the English paper yet with the account of the Bishops' findings—but read a short account in the local paper & it would appear that they have done nothing—but until I read it fully—can't be sure.

Jill also wrote & told us about your flat which sounds very nice indeed and when you can fit it up hope will be something of a home for you.

I have decided to go to England on 20th Oct on the Aragon from Vigo—due England on 22nd I imagine. Could you possibly let me know as soon as possible what I can bring for you? Bairro stuff etc etc as coming by sea I can take a fair amount so do let me know as soon as possible. I have quite a lot of spare china and glasses at home—stone Persian china—you may remember some of them—& various things like that which could be of use to you.

We came up here yesterday p.m. rather unexpectedly really. The Ambassador & wife were coming at the invitation of Michael but of course may have not been able to leave Lisbon at present. Michael flew to Ireland yesterday for a few days—so Ian is here, & a young man in Kinloch's—David Lake. When we arrived last evening we found Norman Fraser here—he'd come on chance to see if we were here—it was 15 years since he was here with his sister. He stayed the night and he & Dad & I are going over to lunch with Claire as she is a friend of Norman's too. Claire only has Adam Hogg staying. He's grown into a nice young man & is now in Courages.

Maurice & Eileen come up this p.m. so for the moment it's quite a small peaceful party. We go down on Monday.

Clay is coming up on 4th for ten days. She'll go direct to Afife where we'll spend this week-end. Her job with Phyllis de la Faie goes on but her salary there has been cut in half. It was a question of her accepting that or leaving as money is tight. The most important part of the job for Clay is having a free house, light etc.

It was a beautiful day yesterday but now it is raining—lightly but still no good for vintaging. All is cubas here now so not at all attractive. One has to go a long way off the beaten track to find any lagars.

I am not sure whether to come direct to London when I arrive—or go to Jill's first for a few days. I shall write to Morton Court to see if I can get a room there. I wrote to Joyce some time ago & suggested driving around with her for a week & seeing friends here & there etc. so shall see how she feels about this.

I'll write to Jill in a day or two but if you see her when you get this, tell her my plans please.

I will go and see my doctor for a check up I expect. I feel I need to get away on my own for 3 or 4 weeks to see my friends etc. as it is good for me mentally.

You will be starting your studies on Monday & I shall be thinking of you & will pray that your future now will be a happy one & that you will find the kind of life & work to satisfy you. I know the financial side is a worry for you, but perhaps Dad will be able to help you some more. As soon as the Afife obras—mainly the cottage now—are finished, he should have some more cash available. Don't try to do too much part time work as well as studying as you will find this a strain I am sure—it's no good undermining your health.

Must send this to the post but I'll write again soon, & please realize how much I sympathise with you in this very difficult time you are going through.

> *Much love from*
> *Mum*

I could not have had two kinder letters from my mother and father. Their love and care for me was so definite and unqualified. Both were wanting the best for me and wanting me to find fulfilment but I was so full of anger and feeling victimised that I did not appreciate their love and kindness towards me. I was in a self-centred capsule and could only think of myself and the injuries that I was receiving. When I read these letters now—forty-four years later—I am ashamed at my lack of love and gratitude towards them. I could not have had parents who were more loving and caring but all I could do was point out their shortcomings. However, that is not 100 per cent true because I sent this reply to my father:

155 Holland Park Avenue,
London W.11.
Friday, 4th October 1968.

Dear Paisâo,

Thank you so much for your letter. I think you must know that I do realize what your feelings must be. I also know that you have been through great suffering through Jill's affairs and that, on the whole, the last few years of your life have been unhappy. I know what it cost you also to retire from the firm. I know what very great distress you must have had over all this. To be very truthful I think I might have left the priesthood some time ago but desisted, knowing what great distress it would cause you. Finally I came to the conclusion that my happiness would mean more to you than whether I remained within the priesthood or not.

When I was in Bow nearly all observers thought I was happy but in fact immensely unhappy. I do not think you were aware of this, nor was Mum, Jill or anyone else. In fact I was extremely unhappy. I do not think there is much point in indicating the reasons except to say that some of my close priest friends wondered how I managed to stay so long. Some time after leaving Bow and going to Tollington Park where I again encountered a most unpleasant situation (which Bernardo can verify. Bernardo immediately told me I should ask to be moved from there. After thinking some time I did this but it was an unsympathetic hearing) I really wanted to leave and return just to a simple layman's life. It was not the priesthood I disliked but the way in which I had to live it. The distress I knew this would cause you, in large measure, stopped me doing this but, deep down, I do not believe you would have wished me to remain and be miserable.

Please be assured that I will do anything I can to make things easier for you. I would not have wished any unhappiness on you—or anyone else. I also have known all along that your affection for me would remain unchanged.

Lots of Love from,
Neville

* * *

This last letter of mine makes me want to understand more thoroughly the power that my father's hurt had upon me. It is strange that in both my father's letter and my mother's Clay Wilson is mentioned. It was the revelation of my mother's sexual affair with her in Lisbon, exactly ten years before, that had set off such a turmoil within me, and yet when her name is mentioned in both these letters ten years later I do not think I was very affected by it. I think that I "played out" the conflict I had between my father and mother in the realm of the Church and culture. Whether the affair with Clay was still active I do not know but it did not seem to worry me at this time. I think the whole drama had been transposed into the territory of the Church.

When I was knocked down by my mother's infidelity I went into a sympathetic alignment with my father. By becoming a priest I would heal his hurt. When I first arrived at St Edmund's I was entombed within my father's piety. I was stuffed with superstitious devotions. I was very resentful towards Bert Richards when he started to establish us in a biblical piety that thrust to the periphery devotion to Our Lady of Fátima or to St James of Compostela. I was in my father; I was my father, and when these devotions were attacked his resentment in me—my resentment—rose up against these sacrilegious assaults upon what I most treasured. I had fallen in love with a precious treasury of devotions and here was an obscene rapist scattering them with scorn upon the highway. Charles Davis and Bert Richards felt like vile atheists taking heavy axes to statues which I loved and adored. Quite soon, however, I was converted to their point of view and then all the violence of my hatred was turned upon my father's superstitions. I began to loathe devotion to Our Lady of Fátima, the nine first Fridays, belief that St James was really buried at Compostela.

What was really happening here? Why was I so *in* my father? I was certainly now having to expel him with violence. I had been sucked into the quagmire of his hurt and disappointment. I was now beginning to hate his disappointment and self-pity that had such a powerful control upon me. But why was it able to have such an engulfing effect upon me? There must have been something similar in myself that went into sympathetic union with him—was it this? Why was my whole being so much *in* him? When I saw him attacked by my mother's infidelity my whole being plunged into him. I don't think this would have happened unless I was myself intensely sensitive to being attacked. It was like two victims hugging each other in a sympathetic embrace. So it was not really sympathy for him but for myself. There was this hurt, wounded me and at that moment the rest of me became engulfed in that hurt and wounded enclave of my personality. At the moment of discovering my mother's infidelity a bad marriage took place between the hurt wounded enclave in my father and its twin in me.

When I began to hate devotion to Our Lady of Fátima I think then I was beginning to plunge into my mother's hatred of my father's wounded and controlling self. And my intense conflict with Tony Beagle in Bow was that I met again this hurt wounded self in the persona of my parish priest. I then poured my whole self into my critical, cruel attacking mother.

I hated my father's wounded and hurt self and, at the time of leaving the priesthood, found support in my mother. It was support against this remote self-protecting attitude that I saw represented in Tony Beagle and Cardinal Heenan. I hated it because I found no sympathy for anyone outside the charmed circle. I plunged then into my mother who was on good terms with the atheist, the outcast, and the sinner. I was now that myself. I was outside the charmed circle of the family, the Church, and all that I knew and loved. Was it that my hatred for Tony Beagle when he had no love or interest for those outside the Church meant this was me? Was it that deep inside me I was the atheist? It is probably so because my sympathies today are for those outside these belief systems. I am neither sympathetic to atheism nor to theism. I think this meant that there was always a me, hidden away, that was an outsider, that was not part of the Church, not part of my own family culture. And I suspect that it must have been something quite central in me. When, at the age of fifteen, I clamoured within and said that God was the only bit of solid ground I must have experienced myself as other. I was clinging to God in a panic, a fear based on the knowledge that there was something else in me; that I had some inner belief system that was quite different from that of the family culture. Perhaps this was epitomised, from a religious point of view, in the intellectual and emotional illumination that occurred when studying ontology under George Ekbery's tutelage. This was the vision of reality grasped through an act of understanding. It was this that was to stand; this was the rock on which I built my personal faith. At the same time as I was building this faith I was fully involved in the sacramental life of the Church. I was extremely dutiful in all my observances. In all these I was within the family culture and smiled upon by everyone, but there was in me this other person, and this was the true me, which was outside this belief system. So I hated Tony

223

Beagle because I knew (but was not aware) that he rejected what was most essentially me. But this was also why my father's statement that anything I did would not alter his affection for me was so important. That deep down his fatherly love accepted this real me and that this was a deeper matter than all the external claptrap and that, in a moment of testing crisis, he reached through to what was deeper: a union between himself and me which was not occasioned by the superficial togetherness of a *Gemeinschaft* culture, but a bond between human beings based upon a shared nature. His love for me as father for son was deeper in him than what was on the surface. His personality was entrenched in superstition and self-referential piety but there was in him, at a deeper level, a true faith; this is what I found in him at this moment of great crisis and I am today still deeply grateful to him for it.

At a later time I turned with violence against my mother and, although this came a lot later, this seems the place to try to understand it. My problem was that I was too much *in* the two of them. The key to this may lie in the tearfulness I always feel when I remember that scene of my mother and father hugging each other at the bottom of the gangplank of the *Serpa Pinto* on our return from Canada when I was aged six. This scene represents a deep longing within me: a longing to bring two very disparate parts together. Maybe to bring together the superstition inherent in revealed religion and in the family culture together with that reality in which we all participate, which is the source of all life and energy in the universe. That I was torn between my mother and father alienated them from each other, yet there was one thing they shared in common: their undoubted love for their three children.

I had always seen the superstitious religiosity and the true religion in a fatal antagonism to each other but I think now the former is a perverted manifestation of the latter. That what I found in my father is nearly always there though much distorted in its outer form, just as within Hinduism there is a faith in Brahman behind all the superstitious devotions to Ganesh and a hundred other idols.

Actions, whose motivation is to please an awesome God, whatever they be, are based on superstition. Superstition is based on the false belief that God is bribable. I will visit this shrine at Fátima or Santiago de Compostela and God will agree not to punish me. Its motive is self-protection but based upon a belief that I do not need to do anything instrumental myself. I am the pilot of a plane and I offer a prayer for my protection rather than learn how to fly the plane properly. Rather than give myself to the other emotionally, which requires effort, I remain inwardly passive while in an attitude of "sympathy". I do not give of myself. I remain in a self-enclosed capsule while putting a demand on the other to entertain me. God is bribable. If I do this I shall be thought well of; God will smile upon me; society will not punish me. I do not go forth into a strange land of darkness; I take no risk; I make a payment to God and this absolves me from stepping forth into frightening new territory. This "payment to God" is an action based on fear. I have used the images of visiting shrines but in contact with others I can either engage with the other, give of myself to him or her, or visit the shrine, make payment to God, and remain where I am. The two interactions may look the same but they are profoundly different. It is like those two women who were dying when I was working as a priest in Bow. Both said the rosary devoutly but for one woman it was an expression of self-giving and with the other it was to solicit God's protection of her.

A relationship is something that has to be made, just as a plane has to be flown. I can, though, put down a bribe instead of making a relationship. "God accept this please and do not demand of me that I make a relationship." There are signs that can give some indication as to which of these two is in operation. So, for instance, with those two women the one who was giving of herself told me that she had been an alcoholic for many years and had "done bad things", whereas the one who was bribing God did not. The former gave of herself whereas the latter did not. The former I knew, the latter I did not. When my father wrote that whatever I did it would not alter his affection for me he was giving of himself; I presented myself in crisis and, at that moment, he gave of himself. When I am bribing God so the other will think well of me I am not in contact with the other at all. I have hallucinated the other out of my own "stuff". What is this stuff? I have rejected what is deepest and most fundamental; what I have referred to as Brahman above or what Solovyov refers to as the *unity of nature*[3] in this way:

> The feeling of pity or compassion which is the basis of man's right relation to his fellow-beings expresses not merely the mental condition of a given person, but also a certain universal objective truth, namely, the unity of nature of the real solidarity of all beings. If they were alien and external to one another, one being could not put

[3]Solovyov, V. (1918). *The Justification of the Good* (p. 161). London: Constable.

himself into the place of another, could not transfer the sufferings of others to himself or feel together with others; for compassion is an actual state and not an imagined state, not an abstract idea.

Hallucination comes out of a fractured reality where the *unity of nature* or *Brahman* has been violently repudiated and the surface, the phenomenon, clung to and used as the clay out of which I fashion my world, but it has to be an illusory world because the reality of it has been repudiated. If this repudiation has occurred then compassion is pseudo-compassion; what has been drummed up has come from a fractured reality where the individuality of one's own self has been the source out of which the image of the other is constructed. This is the hallucinated other rather than the real other.

Here was I, caught between these two rivals but I don't think I would have been so caught in it had I not repudiated violently the reality of existence. So when I transferred my hatred from Bert Richards's iconoclasm to my father's superstitious piety I must, at the same time, have shifted to my mother's side of the equation. There was a split within a split. What Charles Davis was against, and violently against, was my father's superstition, but the very hatred indicated that there was no transformation here but only an expulsion of part of the personality out onto "folk Catholicism". There is no transformation. Ganesh has not been embraced within Brahman. Saying the rosary was the ex-alcoholic woman's expression of giving herself to Brahman just as devotion to Ganesh could be an expression of the same for a pious Hindu. Charles Davis and reformers in the Church were right to try to find forms that gave better expression, but the hatred must ultimately mean that this phenomenal self has not been embraced as part of the *unity of nature*, Brahman, or just That.

But here was I, on the surface, pulled first onto my father's side against my mother and going into the Church in the saddle of a violent monster, and then swapping sides and being violently against my father and on my mother's side, but I was only on my mother's side because she now supported me against my father. I was caught in her drama, her hallucination. I was still *in* this phenomenal world in which the ultimate, the *unity of nature* had been repudiated. At a later stage I began to hate my mother with a violence which lasted at least a dozen years. I was laying all my disasters at her door. It was only near to her death that I forgave her but this belongs in a second book.

* * *

Then I received a letter from Uncle John:

Quinta de Real, Matosinhos, Portugal.
25/9/68

Dear Neville,

As your father's twin brother, with whom I have lived all my life in such close and affectionate understanding, I feel that I cannot in conscience just go off next week to India and leave your Dad in such terrible and dire misery as the result of the letter you have just written to him and all that has led up to it. I repeat I would be failing in my love and friendship with your Dad if I did not frankly tell you what I feel about what you have done.

I do <u>sincerely</u> hope before it is too late that you will in humility and true love and charity go back on what you have done and so reap that happiness you so keenly desire but are striving to get in quite the wrong way. Don't <u>mislead yourself</u> by all the support you may get now by the very difficult times we are passing through as a result of the Pope's encyclical for in your case your trouble was long before that. I hate having to write to you in this way but unless I write what I <u>truly feel</u> my appeal to you would be fruitless. I know you have been through very difficult times and that there was much you wished and <u>rightly</u> wished to improve. But if you weighed up (all the frustration from not being able to carry out what you sincerely thought was so necessary) against the <u>terrible harm</u> you are causing by abandoning your priesthood and the terrible sorrow you are giving your parents and your friends would seem to me to have no comparison.

One sees the old story in history repeating itself. The church needing reform but not by a "reformation" and abandoning ship but by humility and sacrifice <u>within</u> the church <u>not</u> a breaking it up.

This is doubtless a badly expressed letter but I do appeal to you to go back and put things right.

When you became a priest your vocation caused wonders here and in England and did real good by your action and now you are doing the very opposite.

I can only pray that you will put things right and I will pray that you will do so.

With love from
John

P.S. Aileen sends her love to you. Aileen and I offered up our Mass and Holy Communion for you this morning.

We leave on the 4th for India to see Elaine and will be staying at "The West End Hotel" Bangalore as usual.

I wrote him a severe letter back:

155 Holland Park Avenue,
London W.11.
Monday, 30th September '68.

Dear Uncle John,

Thank you very much for your letter. I respect you for two things: one that you have written honestly to me what you think rather than talk harmfully behind someone's back and two because clearly you have written with sincerity and have acted according to what you see to be your duty.

I could not without seeing you give a full explanation for my present position but instead I would just ask you to reflect a little more and think about some of the things which you say in your letter to me. A little experience in dealing with people quickly taught me one thing: never to make a judgment (especially a condemnation) too quickly. Often at first sight a step which seems to be disastrous for someone turns out on further acquaintance to be for the best. How often I have heard people saying, 'How terrible that Mr. Smith does not go to Mass', 'How awful that Mrs. Jones sends her child so young to a boarding school' etc. but when one is in the position to have a person's confidence (as a priest has) one quickly learns that what may at first appear to be a disaster may be in fact the best thing. I say this because those people who have listened carefully to me have finally judged that I have acted for the best. I am talking of wise people: Michael Campbell-Johnstone, Fr. Peter de Rosa who preached at my first Mass, Fr. de Zulueta who attended my ordination and not least dear Fr. Bernardo to whom I explained everything. I think you would do well to listen, reflect and pray gently before judging too quickly that I have acted wrongly. I quote to you from a letter from my dear friend Fr. Vincent Rochford who sadly died earlier this year. He was a great priest and a great Christian and he wrote in a letter two weeks before he died, "... I know that men like Ted Matthews and yourself do not make such a decision without fully adequate reasons. In any case this is a frightful period for priests, so uncertain of their role, so sure that much of their time is occupied with irrelevant materialist preoccupations, and hardly knowing where to start to re-form their people to some concept of what it is all about." There are many good men, holy men, men who pray who have decided that they can be more faithful to Christ and the Church by leaving the priesthood than remaining in it. I do not say they are right but there are many good people who have sincerely made this decision.

I do of course know how you feel. I know you think that someone who leaves the priesthood has abandoned God and given up his Christian vocation. You show clearly that this is what you feel by the expressions you use in your letter. You feel that just by being a priest it is to be more virtuous than not being so—that it would be better to be a drunken priest, a dishonest priest, a proud priest, an unloving priest than to cease to be a priest. You see in your letter you just say in effect, **"Stay in the priesthood whatever happens"**—you do not ask me to try and be more honest in my way of life, to try to be more loving, to act according to my conscience, to dedicate myself more closely to Christ but you just say, **"Stay in the priesthood"**. For me **"to stay in the priesthood"** would have been to be willing to be dishonest, to go against my conscience (i.e. to sin). The priesthood is a particular status within the Church just as to be a director is a particular status in a firm. Would you praise or condemn a director of a company who resigned because he was being forced to act dishonestly by the firm he represented? Actually I had no desire to be in my present position but was not prepared to continue in an unChristian situation in which I was in.

In your letter you clearly think that I am leaving the Church. You talk of "breaking up" the Church. I have been striving to do some useful work for the Church for the past four years and have reached the sad conclusion that one can work better for the Church in the lay state than within the priesthood. This is of course not always so. A person like Michael Campbell-Johnstone is doing most valuable work and could I have done some work of that nature I would have remained a priest but in fact much of my time was taken up with irrelevant work: appeals for money, counting money, running bingo etc. I am a person who must put his heart into what he is doing. I could not put my heart into the sort of things listed above. I have more faith and love for the Church than before. I hope I shall serve her better in the future than in the past.

You never speak of God in your letter. In all this matter I have first and foremost considered my fidelity to God in conscience. At the time of ordination I made a vow that I would give myself to spread God's love and

229

the message of Christ in a world that is in dire need of it. I made this vow to God. God has called each one of us to grow in love, in the understanding of His Son and then he sends us out into the world to spread this message. It was this call from God which I tried, often failing, to answer. It was in duty to this call that I am in my present position. In the parish situation in which I was I could not be faithful to this call. We only do good in this life to the extent to which we answer this call from God. He calls us to grow in love, to deepen our understanding of His love, to mature in wisdom and acceptance of our fellows. The Gospel message is that to be faithful to Christ we must not be controlled by the feelings of others. I hope that I did not become a priest "to cause wonders" or for the admiration of the crowd. If people did admire and were pleased it made me happy but was incidental. Each man and woman must do what he feels is right. Jesus himself went up to Jerusalem to his passion to the grave disappointment of his followers.

I am sorry to sound harsh in some of the things I say but I would like you to realize that I have struggled and sweated blood over this problem. I have stayed much longer than I otherwise would in order not to cause hurt to Dad and others. I also waited to make sure that things could not improve.

I was a chaplain to four hospitals, one of which was a maternity hospital. A woman was having her fourth child and nearly died. If she became pregnant again death was certain. The gynaecologist said she should be sterilized to prevent this. She is a Catholic so she asks me whether she can have the sterilization. Sterilization is strictly forbidden by the Church. What did I say to her? I allowed her to be sterilized. Cases such as these happened every week. What would you have said to such a woman? If you could in good conscience say to her that she must not be sterilized and death would be the better thing then you could in good conscience remain a priest. If, like I, went against the teaching of the Church (though not infallible teaching) it is difficult to remain a priest. It had already caused me immense difficulties (I could write a book on the terrible sufferings people go through and the particular cases I have had to deal with) and was one of the factors that made me ask for release from parish life. If the Pope's recent declaration on birth-control had been more liberal then the position would be different but it is now quite certain that I can not continue against the Pope's and bishops' express ruling on the matter. I said at the beginning that I would not go into the actual reasons which made me leave the active priesthood but would just refer to some points in your letter so I shall not go into the reasons but I assure you there were good reasons. The above is just an indication of the sort of thing I mean.

The only thing that saddens me about your letter is that you ask me 'in humility and true love and charity' to go back on what I have done. Clearly you must think I have acted in a very unhumble way and an unloving way. I leave God to judge this but I am sorry that you make this judgement because it is a very unkind one. You talk of 'going back and putting things right' as though I had committed a sin. It also saddens me to think that you feel this way. I do go frequently to Holy Communion and I hope not sacrilegiously. I think you wrote the letter quickly and I hope that you did not really mean what you said as I am sure you did not. I quite understand you being upset and writing and expressing your sadness.

Now there is a thing you can do to help me. As you say you are very close to Dad and I would ask you as a friend to try and help him. Mum I know has tried to do this and I would ask you to do the same.

It is a difficult time. The world has changed a great deal in the last few decades. I pray that the world will become a better place for the efforts of us all. I pray that God may welcome us into His Kingdom at the end of our journey.

God bless you.
My fondest love to you and Aileen,
from,
Neville

When he received my letter he was just off to India but he sent a short note before he went:

Tel: Oporto 950053   Quinta de Real, Matosinhos, Portugal
4/10/68

Dear Neville,

Thank you very much for your letter. I appreciated you writing to me so fully.

We are off to India this evening. I just want to assure you that our friendship which I greatly value is not at all impaired from my point of view and I feel confident that you feel the same and it is for this reason that I am writing this hurried line.

I will not discuss _any_ of the many points in my or your letter because if one discusses some points and not others or even _one_ point it throws the

231

whole subject "out of ballance".[4] *There are obviously points of disagree-*
ment between us but I am very anxious before leaving to assure you that
my affection for you is <u>*not*</u> *impaired and I have already prayed a lot for you*
and will continue to do so in order that Our Lord's "will be done".

Always your sincere "amigo".
<u>*John*</u>

Aileen sends her love to you

Looking at these letters forty-four years later certain things are clear. In his first letter where he says 'for in your case your trouble was long before that' he was pointing to my own personal difficulties, and also, at a later point, in a discussion he implied that I was sheltering my own personal difficulties under the disguise of the Church's time of crisis. I think this was correct. What I was not facing and would not face was my own personal disturbance. The more I think of it now the more certain I am that it would have been better had I gone into a Richmond Fellowship hostel or some such place. My own personal acknowledgment that I was ill would have been more truthful. I would then have been living outwardly what was true inwardly. My mother knew that her child was ill.

His second letter was softer and kinder but, at the time, I was quite unable to appreciate that.

My own letter was a mixture. It obviously had some softening effect upon John because his second letter was so much more compassionate than the first. I am appalled at my own complacent and patronising manner, though I was right to point out firmly what the difficulties were for a priest trying to dispense Christian teaching in the face of papal directives on birth control, sterilisation, and so on. I was also right to ask him to reflect a bit upon himself and wonder why some priests thought I was acting rightly. In a discussion with him later he could not understand Fr Bernardo's point of view. He said frankly that he just could not understand it. He was rigid and definite in his views. There was no space for another point of view. There was a self-righteousness in him that found support in his wife. My father had this in him as well but it was not supported by his wife, my mother. She was, like Jesus, always a friend of sinners.

Was I being hypocritical when I was talking about my devotion to Christ and so on? I think the answer was "Yes" and "No". I was in

---

[4]Misspelt in the original.

232

transition at the time. Later I definitely lost faith in the central doctrines of the Catholic Church. I could not believe in transubstantiation. At the time of the letter I did not realise that I had lost faith. I remember that time of terrible doubts about transubstantiation when I was at St Edmund's. I can still feel now the inner relief at not having to persuade myself that it was true. I remember a year after being ordained being in the Douro in Portugal and celebrating Mass at a little chapel that belonged to Quinta da Rueda next to Bomfim, and looking at the consecrated host and having the thought that it was just bread and no more but then thrusting away the thought in a kind of panic. Once I ceased to believe, it was like coming out of a hypnotic trance and becoming myself. I think I truly had been in a hypnotic trance. I believed that what was to all evidence bread and wine had become the body and blood of Christ; that this occurred when the priest spoke specified words over the bread and wine and that, at this moment, a magical transformation took place. It was such a great relief not to believe this any more; to be free of the hypnotic trance in which I persuaded myself that this was true. At the time when I wrote that letter to Uncle John I was on the way towards relinquishment of that belief. I cannot remember when I finally faced it and realised that I no longer had faith. This letter to Uncle John was written at the end of September 1968. Certainly by about 1971 I no longer believed because I remember being at Afife in Portugal. By this time I had ceased going to church; I did not have faith and I tried to explain this to my father but it was incomprehensible to him. I remember pointing to my breast and saying to him that the problem was "in there"—that I did not have belief. So, was I being hypocritical in my pious statements in my letter to Uncle John? I think I partly was. I think I was right to ask him to reflect a bit more and not to be dogmatically certain that he was right.

What was the difference between the perspective of Uncle John and Fr Bernardo? Fr Bernardo had come and visited me once when I was in the presbytery at Tollington Park in north London. He was appalled at the atmosphere there and believed that I should get out of it. I think he must also have realised that something was gravely wrong and he wrote me a letter in which he advised, "Your first duty is to be a human man; the second to be a Christian, and the third to be a priest—in that order."[5]

What was the philosophy here? And how was it different from Uncle John's? It must somehow be that for Bernardo the priesthood was the

---

[5]Quoted from memory as I have lost the letter.

outer clothing, even a Christian believer was outer clothing, that there was something more fundamental than this. What was it? I think conscience must come into it. I don't think that he was recommending that I live the life of an immoral reprobate. He was saying that to live the life of a decent human being was more important than all else. He knew that to be a good Muhammadan was better than being a shabby priest; better to be a good living atheist than a dissolute Christian. He would have had some theological knowledge that would have supported this view. The theology of the *anonymous Christian* was current and respected at that time. This was the idea that those who had lived before the time of Christ or those who lived outside the missionary arms of the Churches nevertheless belonged to Christ through their own inner moral acts. However, I do not think that the difference between Bernardo and Uncle John rested upon the fact that one was better versed in theology than the other. The difference lies in the emotional attitude of their inner being: that John's was one of clinging whereas Bernardo's was being rooted in a "godhood" that comprised his own being and that of all others and its "voice" was in conscience. Bernardo was a great help to me at this time and I shall always be grateful to him. He was a great help to my father too.

I do think that my mode of expression to Uncle John was patronising—I had knowledge and understanding of people and affairs that he did not. In some ways that was true. For him the priesthood was a jewel to be admired rather than a life of struggle and conflict to be lived. However, I then used this to claim that I had more knowledge of people's inner lives than he. It was clear that I was angrily defending my position. I was going to be right and he wrong. Even so, some of the things I say in my letter to him are right. He would have been a better example of Christian faith had he said he was sad but refrained from making the condemning judgment. Again the difference between him and my father showed up in their response to this crisis in their midst.

There is another angle to the question of faith. What I have been saying about the belief that the bread and wine is changed into the body and blood of Christ can be looked at in a different way. From my perspective it is a false belief. I had been hypnotised into believing it but I was not alone in this. Some five hundred million Catholics in the world believe in this. It is a permitted craziness within society; that society has certain allotted circumscribed pigeonholes for the containment of madness. I was detaching myself from this collective madness but I was being left with my own, the nature of which I shall try to define shortly.

I must have hated this doctrine of transubstantiation. I had been through hell as a child because of it. Then as a priest I had reversed this when I celebrated Mass subsequent to a sexual contact which the Church defined as mortally sinful without having gone to confession. I judged that this was not a mortal sin. At the age of eight I had been crushed under the Church's dictum that it was a mortal sin to break the midnight fast and go to communion. Then at the age of thirty I was having a sexual contact and judging that this was not a mortal sin. I had not reached the different conclusion that the bread and wine in front of me was purely bread and wine, yet what I did was a kind of "belief in action". The time of this correspondence with my mother, father, and Uncle John was September 1968. Certainly by 1971 I no longer believed in transubstantiation but cannot pinpoint the day when that realisation became clear. It is strange that so important a moment has disappeared from my memory. It was also part of that slow transformation from a robot state to one in which I was becoming a person.

The beginning of this journey away from belief in Catholicism began on that first day in the parish at Bow when I had the realisation that God is not a dictator but a being who invited me into a free responsive relation with Him. What I hated was the dictator that condemned me. I was silly enough to believe that by repudiating the Church I would rid myself of this tyrant. I have come across many people who believe that by repudiating religion and becoming atheists they thereby rid themselves of this despotic torture. This, of course, is sheer magical nonsense.

Belief in transubstantiation lies at the heart of Catholic faith and so when I say that I ceased to believe that, it means that the whole edifice collapsed. But it was just one link in the chain. I did not believe that Jesus was God, the second person of the Trinity, but the matter stretched further than this and it has taken years for me to realise the ramifications of it all because it goes out beyond the boundaries of Catholicism. It is that I believe revealed religion to be false and natural religion to be true. It is why George Ekbery who led me to understand the absolute character of reality set a foundation stone upon which all my subsequent understandings rest. So it is not only transubstantiation that I don't believe in but I do not believe that Christ was God; I do not believe that God chose the Jews for his special revelation; I do not believe that God revealed his special law to Muhammad. These are different versions of the dictator God and ultimately they crush conscience and divert attention from the place where guilt really lies. When I was so guilty as an eight-year-old child about eating chocolates before going to Holy Communion there was a guilt in me that had become attached to this, but what was the true origin of the guilt? Where did the guilt really belong?

It was part of a pattern which I have only come to discover now. Within the Catholic system the guilt was located in my breaking the Holy Communion fast and then not confessing it. But, one might ask, what was it that an eight year old was so guilty about? What deep problem was I trying to solve by going into the Church with such passion? What guilt was I trying to expiate? Then I say at the age of eight, but there was that business of Sally sitting on me when I was aged five in Canada and the masochistic orgy when I was in Lisbon just prior to going into the Church—a masochism which has been a violent current in my life ever since. Masochism is one of those words used to fill in a gap in our knowledge, as Christopher Burney says. It is a violent self-flagellation. In what consisted my wickedness? Can a young child be wicked? Emily Brontë certainly thought so for she portrayed Heathcliff as such in *Wuthering Heights*. I do not have answers to this question, but I want to look further into it when I come to examine this madness which burst out again in fury a little later; but I want to follow up something else from my correspondence and later dialogue with Uncle John that might give a clue. If I am an object, a Pinocchio, then it is right to treat myself as a worthless piece of rubbish. This was with me from a very young age, perhaps even from before birth when I was yet a foetus.

* * *

I have in recent years had what I believe is a more mature reflection on the doctrine of transubstantiation. When someone utters a truth that has a resonance for me then there is a relation between that person and me. Whether that person is alive or dead physically makes no difference to this. When Socrates said that one cannot know that something is evil and yet do it, this statement of his "spoke" to me. The fact that he has been dead for 2,400 years makes no difference. There is a living relation between myself and him. The same is true when I read Tolstoy's statement in *Anna Karenin*: "… it was not until he saw his dying wife that he knew his own heart."[6] It too spoke to me.

---

[6]Tolstoy, L. N. (1986). *Anna Karenin* (translated by Rosemary Edmonds) (p. 444). London: Penguin.

Tolstoy is physically dead but the relation between me and him is alive. The same is so for many statements that Jesus made. In this sense, although Jesus is physically dead, yet there is a living relation between me and him when things he said speak to me. So when Jesus said, "Do this in memory of me"—he meant, I believe, to encourage a living relation between himself and the truths he was enunciating and future generations of people. What has happened is that what he meant has been made physically concrete, which deprives it of its aliveness. So I now go to communion if I am attending a Mass. I usually do so now when attending the Easter ceremonies. For some six years I have been doing so at the Monastery of New Norcia in Western Australia. I was encouraged in this by the abbot, Placid Spearritt. I said to him that I could not with certainty assert that Jesus was God or that the bread had turned into the actual physical body of Christ. He replied that the kind of certainty I was talking of always meant that one was putting one's own self-assertion, covering insecurity, into the doctrine. Placid had a deep wisdom rarely met.

* * *

There was one subject which was ducked both in Uncle John's letter to me, my letter to him, and in a later conversation that we had: one which was hinted at in my own disturbed state. I did not tell him that I was having psychoanalytic psychotherapy. I avoided speaking about this; I avoided knowing it myself. The other thing which I knew and resented when I received his letter was his implication that this was causing great sadness to both my parents, yet this was not truly so and he knew that because the main thrust of his letter was what a misery this was causing my father, and only once does he refer to the terrible sadness I was caus-ing my parents. He knew that it did not cause the same sadness to my mother as it did to my father. What was not discussed was the unhappy state of the relation between my mother and father.

Three years before this, in 1965, when I was still a priest, my father was forced to retire from the firm. This was not something he wanted. On one occasion Uncle John told me emphatically that it was the best thing for my father, giving as his reason that the firm had developed and changed; it was now the time for the new generation to play its role in it and he and my father were too "out of it" to be able to participate effectively. When he was informing me of this in his persuasive manner

237

it went through my mind that this was alright for him because he was happily married but it was not alright for my father because he was not. So now also, when I was leaving the priesthood, his letter ducked this issue. He knew rightly that my leaving the priesthood caused my father dire misery, but did it cause my mother great unhappiness? He knew that there was a difference here between my mother and father. I also funked it when I had a conversation with him a couple of years later.

There are two questions here. Why did he avoid this issue? And why did I go along with it? It may be that what was being transferred into the realm of Catholic practice in the case of my guilt was also being done here—that a severe sickness in the relationship between my mother and father was being violently annihilated from awareness and that the whole drama was being transferred into a discussion of my abandoning the priesthood. Here was something sick and terrible which Uncle John was locating in my leaving the Church, but what could not be alluded to by him was that my mother was not distressed by it in the way my father was. Uncle John knew this but why did he not refer to it? However, it is alluded to by omission with his emphasis upon Dad's distress and his silence concerning my mother's. He knew that my mother was not distressed in the way my father was. What was it that made touching on this subject so terrible? Why did it all have to be elevated into the sacramental life of the Catholic Church? I want to address this question head on but I want to orientate my mind first by taking a more abstract angle upon it. It is the angle that John Macmurray discusses in his book *The Structure of Religious Experience*.[7]

Macmurray distinguishes between science, aesthetics, and religion by noting first that each of them is an attitude of mind: the scientific being the essentially utilitarian judgment that is made about a thing according to its usefulness to human beings; the aesthetic is the pleasure that something gives to human beings, and the religious attitude is a judgment concerning the value of what an individual—in this case me—gives to others. This giving is not judged according to external actions. St Paul made this clear in his "hymn to love" in his first letter to the Corinthians:

> If I have all the eloquence of men or of angels, but speak with-
> out love, I am simply a gong booming or a cymbal clashing. If I

---

[7]Macmurray, John (1936). *The Structure of Religious Experience*. London: Faber & Faber.

have the gift of prophecy, understanding all the mysteries there are, and knowing everything, and if I have faith in all its fullness, to move mountains, but without love, then I am nothing at all. If I give away all I possess, piece by piece, and if I even let them take my body to burn it, but am without love, it will do me no good whatever.[8]

Two things are clear: that this giving, this love that St Paul is talking about refers to an attitude of the heart. He is talking of whether or not I *give* emotionally to the other. The second thing is that I must be able to *see* the other in order to give emotionally to him or her but paradoxically it is the giving to the other that enables me to *see* the other so the two are interrelated factors. It means that an emotional openness to the other generates a seeing of the subjective self of the other. And that this relatedness to the other is the core of religion and paradoxically this relatedness to the other goes in concert with a relatedness to myself and a seeing of myself.

Somehow cultic religion is a displacement from this core to a place of grandiose fantasy. There was a religious illumination in the ancient Israelites that placed conscience as the central guide of action. This is typified in the beautiful story of the encounter of King David with the prophet Nathan:

Yahweh sent Nathan the prophet to David. He came to him and said:

> In the same town were two men, one rich, the other poor. The rich man had flocks and herds in great abundance; the poor man had nothing but an ewe lamb, one only, a small one he had bought. This he fed, and it grew up with him and his children, eating his bread, drinking from his cup, sleeping on his breast; it was like a daughter to him. When there came a traveller to stay, the rich man refused to take one of his own flock or herd to provide for the wayfarer who had come to him. Instead he took the poor man's lamb and prepared it for his guest.
>
> David's anger flared up against the man. "As Yahweh lives," he said to Nathan, "the man who did this deserves to die! He must make fourfold restitution for the lamb, for doing such a thing and showing no compassion."

[8] 1 Corinthians Ch. 13 vv. 1–3. Jerusalem Bible.

Then Nathan said to David, "You are the man ..." David said to Nathan, "I have sinned against Yahweh."[9]

It was a religious enlightenment that put conscience as the guiding principle of action and this was voiced and safeguarded by the prophets; it was a new consciousness among men, a human construction. Just as we might say that there arose among Italians at the time of the Renaissance an artistic genius so also in ancient Israel there arose a religious genius. It was a fateful day, however, when this was attributed to a god outside of man, an almighty figure who rose proudly over the world and out of all the nations of the earth chose the Israelites as his favoured race. It was a fateful transition from a human achievement arrived at through thought, work, and emotional suffering to a belief in a people's own superiority. They had been chosen. From that moment they could lie back passively as inheritors of that divine favour.

I heard a story which is a modern analogy. When Mike Brearley was captain of the Middlesex cricket team they had a period of unbroken success, winning eleven matches on the run; then they began to do very badly and Mike investigated the reason. The team had truly done well through players' own efforts but, flushed with success, they were then overtaken with a belief that they no longer needed to practise in the nets before a game—they were invincible. This was the reason for the team's deterioration. They had been overtaken by *hubris*.

This is what occurred in ancient Israel and the Christian Church has inherited that same cultic superiority, so that the core of religion which lies in the emotional relation between one and another has decayed and been supplanted by a grandiosity in the liturgical and cultic life of the Church. Is it a truth that the greater the devotion to the cultic life of the Church the more poverty-stricken are the emotional relations between people? I do not think it need necessarily be so; the instance of those two dying women in the parish in Bow exemplify how in one case it was so and in another it was not. I also think that when I left the Church the different attitude towards me of Uncle John on one side and Fr Bernardo and Mgr Sullivan on the other illustrate the fact that one cannot make the blanket statement that cultic devotion equals absence of emotional love in human relations. However, I think a blind attachment to cultic

---

[9] 2 Samuel Ch. 12 vv. 1–15. Jerusalem Bible.

240

life, come what may, such as Uncle John demonstrated in his letter, is a sure sign that there is a severe deficiency in the relationship sphere.

So the question is why did he avoid the fact that my mother supported my leaving the priesthood? I will try to answer this first and then come to the question of why I went along with it. The matter that was being ducked was the disastrous nature of the relationship between my mother and father; that my mother and father were very unhappy. When Uncle John referred to my father's "dire misery", that was surely true, and that I was causing him enormous disappointment was certainly true, but my father's misery was also a function of his unhappy marriage. Why was this a subject which could not be faced by Uncle John, or at least not broached in a confidential conversation? What was so threatening about it? Why did a pretence have to be kept up that the marriage was happy and that the relation between my mother and father was a loving and contented one? Certainly seeing my mother and father going to church and taking communion was a sign of love and unity between them. If John had recognised and spoken about my parents' unhappy relation with each other then some solution would have to be found, something would have to be done. I think John's appeal to me not to "break it up" must give some clue to it. If it were openly admitted that my parents' marriage was unhappy then something would break. What is it that would break? Certainly the illusion that they were happily married. Why was it so important to John to maintain that illusion? I am quite sure that he was wary of my mother, distrusted her, and probably did not like her.

Is there another pathway towards getting at this question? I am certain that my father never spoke to anyone about how unhappy he was in his marriage. But why? Why could he not speak to a priest about it, for instance? I am sure of one thing: that once one starts to speak about such a thing the very act of speaking alters the situation. Things begin to change. Something is revealed. Something is revealed about oneself. I suspect that thing which would have become revealed to my father, or threatened to become revealed, would be the same thing that would become revealed to Uncle John. But what is that thing? Is it that in the relation between my mother and father, that relationship of such supreme importance, there was an absence of love—an absence of the very foundation upon which the whole edifice of religion and purpose in life is based?

Whatever it is that could not be faced in my parents' marriage by Uncle John must have been present to some degree in Uncle John's own life. I believe that Uncle John was happily married but this does not mean that there was no "disease" in him; that there was no factor in him of which he was ashamed or which he did not want to know about. I believe that one needs to posit that there was some "false coinage": something that looked like love that was not. I do not mean that this was the whole of him but that some parcel of false coinage existed in him and which he did not want to know about.

There is one thing which may bear upon it. My mother once told me that my father had been in love with Aileen and that he had wanted to marry her but that she had married John instead. John married six years before my father—in 1926. John was the more forceful twin. If it is so that there was competition between the two twins for the one woman and John, rather than my father, won, then it would make sense if John were guilty and did not want to see that my father's marriage was unhappy. The persuasive trait in John's character is a sign of guilt: he had to persuade himself that my father was happy, that all his unhappiness was due to my action of leaving the priesthood.

I go back to that conversation with John about my father's retirement. He was persuading me that it was the best thing for my father to retire. This was against a background where he knew that my father did not want to retire; and he did not want to retire because his marriage was so unhappy that to be able to go to the office and be away from my mother was a relief for him. What I was unable to say to John when we had that conversation, which was in 1965 when I was a priest, was that my father was unhappy in his marriage and that this was the reason for my father wanting to continue at the office. Now I am not able to verify this thing that my mother told me but in more recent years I have had some confirmation from another member of the family. A cousin of mine told me that Elaine, John's eldest daughter who was a nun, always maintained that my father had been in love with Aileen, her mother, and had wanted to marry her. However, when my mother told me I had never heard it from any other source, and I remember it was a surprise to me when she told me, but the question is why was it a surprise? It was this utopian notion that all in the family was happy and serene, hence my mother's statement was a shock. It was that the external roles harmonised with the internal and yet this is patently untrue. Part of the shock of my mother's infidelity was realising that the external appearance did not accord with the internal truth. Suddenly, underneath a surface of calmness and loving affection was rivalry and violent feeling. Because if what my mother

242

said *was* true, and what Elaine had said was true, then there must have been a rivalrous violence both in my father and in John.

The central theme in Macmurray's book is that relations between people are incredibly difficult and that we do everything to take flight from them. There was this belief that all in the garden was lovely. Then I left the priesthood and suddenly a bomb exploded in this idyllic garden. What was wrong with this child who had suddenly violated all the canons of family values? Was everything rotten in the state of Denmark? Or if something was rotten, what was? Something so awful that it could not be spoken about.

I was very much in this culture of not being able to speak about something that was too awful. In 1967, which was the year before I left the priesthood and the year after Charles Davis had left the Church, I was in Portugal. Uncle John said to me one day when I was over at his home at Real that wasn't it a strange thing that that priest Charles Davis should have left the Church. He had no idea that Charles had been my professor at St Edmund's and that he was a very significant figure for me, and I did not enlighten him. I just agreed and said that it was strange, but why did I not say to him how upsetting it had been for me? Why did I hide my feelings? It was the same way in which I had hidden my shock when I heard of my mother's lesbian affair with Clay Wilson. If I had said to John that Charles's leaving had been a terrible shock to me and was upsetting me grievously, it's as if some terrible thing would have begun to have been unearthed—that the calm surface of this family piously bowing their heads at the communion rail on Sunday covered some fearful emotions that must not be voiced.

I had lived as a child in this utopian world which was suddenly shattered by the pain of my mother's infidelity, and then there were other traumas. Certainly Charles Davis's departure from the Church was another shock but not as great as the one when I learned of my mother's infidelity. I think all these traumas were locked inside me, and my violent entry into the Church and then the equally violent departure from it were the actions of a man enacting the traumata. Much later when I came to read that Wilfred Bion said—that there are pains which are not felt but acted—it made complete sense to me. I enacted in a huge way these traumas that reverberated through my being. I would like to emphasise, though, that I think these later traumas were built upon those very early ones from my childhood and probably from the time when I was in the womb.

243

I was a frightened child pretending to be an adult; a child clinging to Mummy in fear and trembling; a child pretending that he was a robust adult and going off to school in England because he was a healthy adult, but there when he arrived his eczema broke out worse than ever, he was mocked by the boys, and collapsed with asthma and hayfever. This child terrified of God, hell, and eternal punishment left the Church in strident tones but was quivering within. I dared not go to Oporto and face the accusation and recriminations especially from John and Aileen. Here was this quivering child pretending to be an adult. Was what was focussed in me like an image of the family as a whole in a magnifying glass? Was what was being witnessed a family of frightened children bowing their heads before a fearsome, adult God? I could not return to Oporto because this God was embodied in Uncle John, Aunty Aileen, and the family, and their reproach of me was terrifying, just like the picture that Jesus draws of the final judgment in chapter twenty-four of St Matthew's Gospel.

Certainly my father was a very frightened infant. Something in his relation to my mother could not be faced. My mother was also shockingly deferential to authority, to the "expert". Everything that was true of what existed between human members of the family was experienced also in relation to God. The terror of a just and punishing God was tempered by interceding with Mary who would quieten His fury at her behest and lighten His punishment.

What would have happened had I said to Uncle John:

> You know it is not true that my mother is upset at my leaving the priesthood. She supports it. You know that she and my father are unhappily married; that my father has lived in disappointment ever since you robbed Aileen from him; that he married my mother still under the wound of disappointment and this is the true cause of his "dire misery" and this leaving of the Church by me is only an additional spike in a crown of thorns which you fashioned for him.

This particular issue may not be correct even if the emotional lines of the story are right, but the question I have to answer for myself is, "Why was the whole matter focussed in me?" Like the sunlight in a magnifying glass focussed into a point where everything burnt up and I was that point.

I think the matter may go back further—to my grandmother's death. My father's mother, Beatrice, died when the twins were sixteen and still at school in England. Recently my cousin, Amyas, sent me a copy of the letter she wrote just before she died:

Saturday May 13, 1916.

Dearest Mabel and twins,

After all it is decided that my operation is to be to-morrow, Sunday, morning, so I won't be able to write to you again for sometime. I hope by the time you get this you will have heard by telegram that it is all safely over as I much hope it will be. In any case my darlings shd God wish it otherwise I want you to know how much I will have been thinking of you all and pray that you may be always good children and do yr duty even if it is not easy and especially don't drift out of the way of frequent confession and Communion—There are many things I'd like to say but are difficult to write. Anyhow do yr best and look after father the best way you can and don't ever do anything that you wd not like me to know you had done. I got Mabel's letter from school and also John's and Ron's from Eastbourne enclosed in Mabel's last from there. I am so sorry abt his cough and hope it will get quite alright, a neglected cough may turn out very badly. Keep on going to the doctor and if it really gets no better write to Mrs. Baker & ask her if he had better go to her and take him to a good doctor. Say I said you were to do so she said but I much hope it will not be needed. M's last letter of May 2nd but one that was missing of 29th has just come. He has been having the worse time ever since he went out of bad gas attacks, poison gas, not shells. He sounds upset poor boy having been just collecting the gassed people. Good bye dears it tires me to sit and write in bed. I can't tell you half I feel only kiss you all three and send you so much love that I have always had for you—

Yr loving Mother
B. Symington

Send this to twins to read. I am going to try to send them a p.c. and if Ron shd still be away see that he gets all news of home.

My father told me once that when she died he and John were at the Oratory School in Birmingham and two women came down to the school to tell them that their mother had died. I always had the sense that his mother's death was a terrible blow to him; something which he never got over. Was his disappointment what I was trying to assuage on that Easter Sunday when I went to communion? That his mother would have so loved to see him with all his children at the communion rail? Did I become a priest to try to comfort him when I learned of my mother's lesbian affair? What a joy it would have been to my grandmother had she known that Ron's son had become a priest. How proudly my father would have shown this priest-son to his mother. If all this is true then why was I the one designated to assuage my father's awful disappointment? I think I buried my own self-pity in his disappointment. Somehow I related straight through to his inner emotional distress.

His disappointment, his wounded self was a very powerful emotional factor in the family. I believe that severe shocks, such as my father received when his mother died, remained untransformed all his life. It probably lay behind my mother's statement that my father was self-centred; that he was in some way turned in on himself and having to devote his attention to licking his wounds. It was a policy to try to protect him from bad news—a sense that nothing must be added to the burden. A severe shock which is unassimilated lives on as a self-centredness. When we see self-centredness then we are witnessing a trauma that is still living in the personality.

If it is true that I went into this prison of the priesthood to comfort and give solace to my father then it does explain a gathering hatred of him. It was a hatred of being imprisoned, of my freedom being circumscribed. The hatred was not consciously of him but rather of the kind of piety which typified his "woundedness". I began to hate the sort of piety that centred upon the poor suffering Jesus. Think of the poor Jesus falling under the weight of the Cross, think of the poor Jesus being crowned with thorns. For this kind of piety I substituted the glorious Christ who had triumphed over suffering and death in his marvellous Resurrection. It was the Risen Christ in all his majesty and glory who was our Saviour. I did not realise at the time that it was the woundedness in my father that I hated. I hated it because I had allowed it to be my gaoler. When my father wrote in that letter that nothing I did would alter his affection for me I think I must have made a distinction between a noble loving outgoing father that was in him and this wounded self-pitying father that had imprisoned me. To this day I loathe any hint of sentimentality. The most important thing here is that although I was espousing this robust Risen Christ piety yet a wounded, self-pitying Jesus-like person within remained untransformed. This has a relevance to the robust Kleinian form of psychoanalysis that I became attracted to many years later. This was like a Risen Christ spirituality and although it looked as if people were robust who followed it yet the self-pity remained untransformed. The important question, though, is: how does such self-pity become transformed into a healthy component within the personality? I shall try to address that later when I come to discuss the different schools of psychoanalysis.

If my father was crying within for his lost mother and also for Aileen whom he had lost to John it would have been a very potent source of jealousy and envy in my mother. Her lesbian affairs which I believe started or restarted when she was in her mid-forties were a violent turning away from my father—a hatred in action. And of course when I left the Church and she was supportive of me I was "joined with her" against the wounded entrapping emotional power in my father. But none of this answers why, from an early age, I and not James was caught in this inner emotional maelstrom.

I have already mentioned in the first chapter that when I sent Christmas cards to my uncles and aunts in Oporto and the cousins in Portugal, I got no reply. Although it happened and stared me in the face I could not believe it. I could not believe that these uncles and aunts who had been so warm and loving towards me had now turned cruelly against me. This triggered a fateful disease: self-pity. This cancerous condition stayed with me for a quarter of a century and it only dissolved when I became aware of it during a leisure period in France.

I was the wounded one, I was the suffering Jesus who had now fallen under the weight of the Cross. I was sorry for myself. This terrible disease took hold of my soul and remained a faithful companion within for many years. I reproach psychoanalysis for the fact that it was a disease that remained untouched by this form of mental healing. So this tendency towards self-pity was obviously already in me before the drama of leaving the Church. When my cousins in Oporto snubbed me it was the trigger that released the self-pity that then flooded my personality.

It seems a paradox but self-pity protects from pain. It is a painful event to have been a loved child within the bosom of a family and then to be hurled out, but self-pity protects the individual from the pain of it. But why and how? It is that when the focus is on *my* hurt that which produces the hurt is shut out. There is the hurting agent and the sufferer. To experience the pain both need to be encompassed because the pain is not experienced if one of these two poles is excluded from the field of vision. Probably this account here tends to give the impression that Uncle John and Aunty Aileen were well within my field of vision but I don't think this is so. They were throwing the javelin at me so I saw the thrower of the javelin but what was shut out of my vision was the person who launched it. Uncle John had been a warm kind uncle. His daughter, Mary, was my own age and frequently I had been to his house and, for instance, on one occasion he and his wife, Aileen, took Mary and me on a trip to Santiago de Compostela. He paid for my hotel bill in Santiago but especially made the point that he was doing so because he so appreciated the good friendship that had been forged between Mary and myself. This was just one of numerous occasions. Under self-pity all this was utterly shut out. Had I let it in it would have been much more painful.

Forty-five years later I had stayed in the home a friend and her three daughters and I had been warmly welcomed and came to know both the mother and daughters. The mother had said things to me like, "Neville, you are a member of the family" and other remarks of that sort indicating that I was truly welcome. Then, on another occasion when I was staying in her home, she cast me out saying it was awkward for her. On this occasion there was no self-pity, the pain was severe, and a picture of mother and her three daughters was strongly present in the visual field. It was repetition of what had happened to me nearly half a century earlier. I then experienced not only the pain of the present event but also of the former one. I think it possible that the repetition of an experience can occur in order that the original of which the later one is a copy if the pain of the first one has not been experienced.

I think though that this self-pity must have been in me from an early age and this led me to merge into my father's wounded disappointment. I disappeared *into* him. But what was I licking my wounds about at that early age? Why was I steeped in self-pity and self-centredness? Why did I, years later on being ordained a priest, need the admiration of the crowd, the fawning love of all the family, with a consequent rage at being entrapped in such a bond of fealty? Why was my brother, James, comparatively free of such bondage?

To answer such a question I can only rely on speculation. I am sure that there must have been something wrong with me from an early age. There is one thing I do know: that I am torn in two by partings. I am distraught beyond words by death. When I part from my wife or boys I am enormously upset. When our dog died thirteen years ago I was beside myself with grief. I think in recent times I have been in touch with this distress but earlier on it led me down a different path. I was intensely sorry for myself. It is clearly a crisis with which I cannot deal. I have noticed that an intense pain is sometimes converted into a persecution or punishment because either of these is more bearable. When we parted from Joan Smith when we left Canada I howled with pain. In Lisbon when we were leaving for Canada on the *Dixie Clipper* my father came and gave me a string bag with toy animals in it—it was a parting gift. Today when I think of it tears come to my eyes. Back in Portugal after our return from Canada we had a cook called Mecalina. I became very attached to her and when she left I again howled in pain. In more recent times when I went to see Carmen at her home in Oporto and, on leaving, knew I would not see her again, I was distraught and as I write this I burst into tears. I surmise that I had some early parting from my mother that was unbearable. When I went to St Martin's I found solace in the priest chaplain because it attached me back to home where my mother and father and family lived in happy unity with the Church. But what was this early parting from my mother? Yet I also think that for a parting to be so disastrous I must also have been very closely attached. Becoming a priest attached me very closely and found me loved by all the family. There was some need to attach myself in that way and then to find such an attachment suffocating. I certainly attached myself in a very fond loving way to people, but especially to women. There was something unmanly about me, and when I think of myself at school estranged from the crowd, my face covered with eczema, pouring out catarrh in fits of asthma and hayfever, I was anything but the healthy boy striving towards manhood. I was a frightened child. But in some ways I think I was a female boy. And when in adolescence I would get an erection when dancing I would go to the loo, say Hail Marys in an attempt to detumesce my penis. Was it that my mother would only love me without a penis? That when I was born she looked at me and fell in love with a female child; some fateful sort of love that was full of neediness? That I not only had to assuage my father's disappointment but also be the female child for my mother, and thus split in two was the school weakling?

Was I torn in two with one half clinging to mother and the other clinging to father? A priest in a flowing cassock is a kind of female man. When I talk of being attached in the wrong way it means a kind of clinging but is such a clinging, such an attachment due to a broken up state inside? That my father needed love, needed to be loved, needed people

249

around him to love, I am certain. I also surmise that he needed it to assuage an appallingly harsh punishing God inside him. Fr Bernardo once told me that my father had an appalling superego inside him and that he was persecuted with scruples. This was obvious to anyone observing him in his religious devotions. That he needed this last child of his to love him and give him solace I feel sure. Also that my mother needed this too although it was more hidden in her than in him, yet it was a centrally powerful factor inside her. So to offer solace to my father meant being on his side against my mother; to offer solace to my mother meant being on her side against my father. I was therefore torn in two. When someone is torn into two like that his emotional foundation is precarious. This is why when I was about fifteen I had that moment when I said to myself that God was the one being upon whom I could put my trust. The shifting broken marshy ground under my feet unnerved me and I clutched out and put all my faith in God, but this God was not God but an idol. It was only later that I came to realise that it was the God of the Upanishads, the God of George Ekbery, who was the solid rock and not the cultic God. It articulated that difference which mystics have known: the difference between godhead and God. But back to this precarious state—an addictive kind of clinging is correlated always with a broken emotional state. Our emotional life is broken into bits and it is the work of early parenthood to breathe a love that binds the bits into one. This did not happen: I had two parents each needing me for themselves and against each other.

It seems quite a good model: the baby is born in bits and it requires an act of love from mother to bind those bits into a knitted-together oneness. When that love is suffused with neediness the bits are not bound together. This neediness then is also partly a function of the state between the two parents. A psychoanalyst in Australia, Shahid Najeeb, works on the principle that everyone needs love. If the pair are not getting it from each other and are unhappy and yearning for it they turn to their baby to find it. There is some evidence for this in that when I was six on our return from Canada my brother and sister went to boarding school at Carcavelos, near Lisbon, and I stayed at home. Then when I was eleven, or perhaps ten, Jill and James were sent off to school in England and I was still at home with my parents in Oporto until one day I said defiantly to my father that I would not do another stroke of work if I was going to be left any longer at school in Oporto. I demanded to be sent to school in England. I was protesting that I did not want to be this baby. I don't think I would have said this if I had been a happy baby but if I were a baby torn in two, nurturing to the neediness of my mother and father then it would make sense. When I got to school in England I collapsed. I got asthma, hayfever, and the eczema broke out worse than ever, and then at the end of four terms when this ill health had become a severe worry to my mother I was taken to see Dr Evan Bedford in Harley Street. He declared that I had a "pulmonary murmur" and put me into the Middlesex Hospital where I was investigated for a week.[10]

I surmise that I was in a collapsed state emotionally: that this baby standing up defiantly saying "I will be a baby no more" was desperately wanting to get away from this neediness of my parents but that my inner state was one of collapse. Throughout my school years I was in a physically debilitated state. This was a clamour for help. Something similar happened when I went into the Church. When I left the priesthood a clamour was yelling to the heavens but it was not recognised as such by others or by me.

* * *

There is another way of looking at the drama of my leaving the Church. Clearly from my earliest youth I was overshadowed by a tyrant God of the fiercest kind. I located this God somewhere in the heavens. When I got to St Edmund's my teachers, Charlie and Bert, taught me that this God was a God of Love; a God who, out of infinite love for mankind, entered the human scene to rescue us from a terrible plight which we had fashioned for ourselves. So now I believed that the tyrant God was in existence no longer; that by a magical sleight of hand he had been exorcised, like a devil, out of my existence; but in fact he had not been banished but only relocated, given a new residence, and the place where he now resided was in the Church; this relocation was finalised in that experience of free responsiveness to God on my very first day in the parish at Bow. The oppressiveness of this tyrant God embodied in the Church became so overpowering that I would exorcise it by leaving the Church. However, I was again mistaken because the tyrant God

---

[10]More latterly I found out that when Churchill was severely ill, after the Casablanca Conference in north Africa in 1943, that a specialist doctor was flown out from London to attend to him. That doctor was Evan Bedford.

would not leave me so easily. I gave Him a new home whose place of residence will soon become clear as the next chapter in my personal drama unfolds.

As I left the priesthood I shot a salvo of hatred at the Church. I left her not with love but with hatred. Could I have left with love? Had I faced my loss of faith I believe things would have been very different. I would then have told Uncle John and my cousins the simple truth that I had lost faith, that I no longer believed that the priest's words THIS IS MY BODY or HOC EST CORPUS MEUM changed that little sliver of unleavened bread into the body of Christ. I would have then presented myself as someone who had *lost* something. I also think had I really faced that, I would have become ill but in a different way. Rather than someone self-righteous and arrogant flailing and beating the air against the Church, I would have presented myself as someone who had lost a great treasure and there he was ill with the effect of it. I would have been free in a different way but also in a way which would have dismayed and troubled my family but also brought me into closer sympathy with them. Uncle John could not have attacked me for losing faith but only pray for me. Had I faced that, I could have gone out to Oporto and explained myself. It would have been very upsetting for them and for myself but would have brought me into relation with them as someone who was different but not to be attacked. It would have been a personal statement about myself but in it a loss would have been declared. What this explanation leaves out, however, is that underlying beliefs is the need in all human beings to belong to some human grouping; so, if I no longer belonged to the human grouping in which I had been reared, then where was I? Was I an isolate? Was there some new human grouping to which I could claim allegiance?

Is the tyrant God in substitution for the pain of a terrible loss? What did I lose when I made the shocking discovery of my mother's sexual infidelity? I lost, with indelible certainty, the belief that my mother and father were in a loving union with one another. Rather than face this loss, rather than hold it within myself, I rushed with passion into the Church. I totally gave myself to the Church. When I left I let Uncle John experience a terrible loss. He lost a sparkling jewel that had "caused wonders" and his disappointment was great while I was self-righteously striding forward brandishing a sword of upright defiance. Had I "come clean" and declared my loss of faith Uncle John's disappointment would have been as great, perhaps greater, but his loss and mine would have brought us as brothers into a loss which we shared. Of course the problem was not as simple as I am making it sound. I had not faced the fact that I had lost faith.

As this tyrant God was with me from so young an age—certainly the age of eight but I suspect much younger—and if it is a substitution for a loss, was it always a loss of the loving union between my mother and father? I have tried earlier in this inquiry to relate it to a loss of my mother at birth but was it a loss of love that I had longed to be present between my mother and father? It would explain my wanting not to disappoint my father on the occasion of my third Holy Communion; to compensate him for what was lacking. This way of looking at things puts the whole question of our going to Canada in a more questionable light. Aunty Aileen and her family went with Uncle John to England in 1940 but my mother and father parted. There were of course practical reasons for this. The British embassy in Lisbon had sent up a senior diplomat to Oporto and held a meeting with the English community. The Germans had now occupied the whole of France and were threatening the Spanish border. It was no longer safe for English subjects to be in Portugal in case of invasion. So the men were going to join up and mothers and children were advised to get away. Some mothers and children, like the Bull family, went to South Africa; my mother and we three children went to Canada, but other mothers stayed and some, like Aunty Aileen with her five children went to England. My father was going to join up so why did my mother with we three children go to Canada? Was it that there was already some abyss opening up within the marriage?

I feel sure that my mother's lesbian tendencies which seemed to erupt when she was about forty-three had most probably been active earlier, prior to her marriage to my father. She was twenty-five when she married my father. I do not know what her love life had been in South America and in London prior to her marriage but I think it likely that she had had some lesbian affairs. My only evidence for this comes from a woman called Jane Webster. She was a butch New Zealander and friend of my mother; when I was a priest she used to come and see me from time to time when I was in Bow and we used to have lunch together in a little Chinese restaurant in Bow Road. I asked her once whether she had ever been to Oporto and she told me that she had not and she further told me that when my mother had married my father my grandmother, my mother's mother, had asked Jane to promise her that she would never visit Oporto. Jane did not tell me the reason why but what I surmised was that there had been a sexual affair between her and my mother and that my grandmother had exacted this promise from Jane to protect the marriage.

If this is correct then it might be that from the start there was a problem in the marriage: on my father's side the trauma of his loss of his mother from which he had never recovered and on my mother's side a failure ever to detach herself from a natural sexual love for women.

Of one thing I feel sure: that I experienced both my father and my mother as two inwardly disappointed people and that this disappointment was somehow that each did not give the other the love that was yearned for. I found myself caught up with trying to compensate to each of them for what they lacked; I was trapped in this vortex. The question quite why I and not James was caught in this is what I don't know.

I think my mother had a deep-seated hatred of male power, of the erect phallus. In later life she could never stop herself attacking my father. She did so in harsh tones and fiercely. Her first child was my sister, Jill. That my mother had some unhealthy erotic love relation for Jill I am certain. She adored Jill and fawned over her in a way that was damaging to her well-being. Then James came along. So she had a girl and a boy. She tolerated this second baby as a boy but was resentful of him and often unfair to him. Then came a third child who was a boy again and this time she could not make that act of contemplative love that sets a child robustly on his journey. As with Jill I think she involved me in an erotic embrace but failed to give me a contemplative act of love which would have set me on my path.

* * *

I was so self-enclosed I had not really realised that this act of leaving the priesthood would alienate my family from me. I believed that I was enwrapped in a blanket of unconditional love and when, as I have said, I received no cards from the family at Christmas it was a terrible shock and I plunged into a state of self-pity. I was not aware at the time of this self-pity. It was only very much later, when I was about fifty-three or fifty-four, before I came to realise it. This disease, and that is the right word for it, held me in its grip for about twenty-five years and had some very deleterious effects. It made me a sitting duck for anyone who chose to sympathise with my plight. I was totally self-orientated. I had been unfairly treated and in this wounded state I looked with favour upon anyone who would come and sympathise with me and lick my wounds.

What is certain is that, at the time, I did not see the other. I did not truly see Uncle John's distress; I was preoccupied with defending myself against his criticism of me. There was I in a great deluge of enthusiasm dispensing God's love in the parishes but it was external; when examined against St Paul's criterion I failed the test. And it seemed that the place where I failed was in the two-person relationship. It was the relationship with Tony Beagle in Bow that broke open and revealed something rotten within: self-centredness and hatred.

The shock of not receiving Christmas cards from the family led not only to self-pity but also to paranoid fury. I was in an absolute rage with all my family and most especially my Uncle John and his wife, Aileen. Just as I had been in love with the Church so also I had been truly fond of all my family and believed that they were fond of me, and now they had cut me off and banished me from their sight. The only exception to this exclusion was my cousin, Ian, and his wife, Cynthia, who sent a Christmas card to my sister Jill and myself. His mother, Aileen, had I believe imposed this banishment upon me and directed her children to do likewise. Ian must have decided to break this directive. In the past he had sent a Christmas card to me alone so I think he must have slipped my name in along with the one to Jill. The card went to her address but inside it was for me also and I felt grateful to him for this. However, it was not only John and Aileen because I received the same silence from Uncle Maurice and his family. I am referring here to all my cousins who lived in Oporto. An exception to this command of banishment was my cousin Mary and her husband, Christopher. They befriended me through all this time of difficulty and I was and am very grateful to them for it; I know it cannot have been easy for them. Mary, who was born in the same year as me, married Christopher Campbell-Johnston and Christopher, although a devoted Catholic, has a fine principle which guides him: he stands by a friend through thick and thin. I admire and thank him for this admirable quality. I am particularly grateful to Mary who is the daughter of Uncle John. Despite the severe banishment from her father she, with her husband, stood as fast friends beside me. They did not agree with what I had done but the pledge of friendship was stronger for them than any ideological system of belief.

I responded to this decree of banishment with rage and righteous indignation. I became all the more certain that I was right. In fact there was never the slightest question in my mind but that I was right. I was right, I knew I was right. I was the most self-righteous person in existence and because of that when Uncle John thought he was right and showed signs of having the same traits as were in me I puffed up with righteous indignation. I was in a paranoid rage towards the Church, Cardinal Heenan, and my family. People then were either on my side, in my church, or in the enemy camp. I was still just as fanatical as I had been when I was pedalling as fast as I could go around the parish in Bow except that now it was clear that it was me who was being so passionately defended rather than the Church. The situation before was one where the "me" who was being so passionately defended had been projected into the Church. So I suppose the situation now was at least more honest—it was me and not the Church that was right; that it was the great me that I was so concerned to promote and defend. It took many years before I became aware of this self-righteousness and self-centredness in me. The paranoid fury was an offshoot of this condition of the soul. I believe that it had always been in me, right from the time I was a child. The tyrant God before whom I cringed at the time of that fateful third Holy Communion was ultimately a figure within me of whom I was in terror.

I did not feel this paranoid fury towards my father. I felt sympathy for him. When once he asked me why I had stopped going to church I tried to explain to him that I did not have the faith inside and he did not understand me. I felt sad rather than self-righteous. It must, I think, have been my love for him which pierced the self-righteous carapace and stretched my emotional hand to him and allowed me to touch him. I think also his human love for me as his son that led him to say that nothing I did would alter his affection for me touched my heart and got past the self-righteous tyrant God. I am sure it was a great effort for him to reach through to a human outgoing love.

When someone is in this self-righteous state there is only one solution. It is simply to be with them rather than to try to persuade them or be persuaded by them. Mary and Christopher carried this role very well towards me. They did not agree with what I had done or with my position but they remained friends. Standing by a friend, through thick and thin, was at the centre of their personal philosophy. I think this was particularly the position of Christopher and that Mary was imbued with this same spirit. When Cardinal Heenan gave me the short leave of absence letter I met Christopher for lunch and showed him the

256

letter; he said without reservation that he would stand by me and he did. This is all a friend can do when someone, as I was, is in such a self-righteous grip.

It must mean that underneath this swaggering self-righteousness I believed I was a rotten egg, an inferior being and worth nothing; there was a madness in me and it was this and the absence of love which it implied that filled me with inferiority. This arrogant self-righteousness is what my analyst had pointed out right at the beginning of my treatment and it was that which I hated. When I saw any sign of it in anyone else I was filled with a paranoid fury. "Paranoid" means a suspicious hatred of someone. The suspicion is due to the fact that I feel robbed by the person of something which is my own. The person has not in fact robbed me of it but that is how I feel. What has happened is that *I* have ejected it out of myself and disowned it into the other person. So what I did was to disown violently this self-righteous part of me into Uncle John, especially Uncle John, because now at this moment he was wielding the sword of righteousness. It was not that Uncle John was not self-righteous; he was but this violent action which I performed inflamed the passions in people—passions good and bad. What I did inflamed his self-righteousness and then I disowned my own into him. It could be that I left the Church in order to inflame self-righteousness into which I could then disown it in myself. I could remain the saintly innocent victim surrounded by self-righteous citizens. If this is right then the source of much of my difficulties in this regard was a violent hatred of this self-righteousness in me.

There is also another way of looking at this. That what I am calling self-righteousness is closely associated with a violent paranoia and that this has been in me from very early days and, at the same time, most violently disowned; but that in order to disown it and "justify" the paranoia I had to do a violent act that brought odium upon my head and then I could justifiably reproach Uncle John, Cardinal Heenan, and the Church for behaving in such an unloving way. I was squeaky clean and they were all dirty.

Yet this is too narrow and viewed too much in a self-condemning way. What was this self-righteousness and paranoia part of? Clearly another aspect of this was myself at a distance from others—that I was not emotionally close, that I was lonely. And yet I was clinging desperately. So there was a constellation of factors: there was God who directed me and whose commands I could not disobey[11] and then this self-righteousness. This can only mean that God was in me. I was right. After all it is only God who is always right. Then how does the paranoia come in? The paranoia is a hatred of the one who dares to be against me. I am God, you know. It is also towards someone who might be seeing my godliness. I am God but a hidden God. I must keep it hidden. So whenever there is a God installed outside then there is also one inside.

But then the question is: how did all that come about in me? I am sure that it was there from an early age. I think of that game in Canada where Sally would jump on me: a punishment turned into a pleasurable sexual game. There was also in this constellation a big dose of self-punishment and even in this account I am trying to avoid a self-condemning manner. So how is it that there was in me God, paranoia, self-punishment, and a very violent disowning of it all? I resort now to a more abstract level of reasoning.

Although I am God, a hidden God, yet I am enormously affected by all that happens to me. So it is really a tin God. Underneath I am a leaf blown by the wind. It makes me think of how, years later, when I was learning to fly, Richard used to say: "Fly the plane; you're letting the plane fly you." I was blown by the wind and in particular by some huge storm that had blown me over and from which I had never recovered. What was this storm? I must plough on to the next episode in my life to begin to try to unearth what it was.

* * *

So here I was now in the secular world.

It was only when I got to Brunel that I began to appreciate that I had received an education when I was in the Church and that I was not receiving one here at this new place of learning. This is, of course, not an accurate way to speak because all education is ultimately self-education so what I mean is that it was not an environment favouring education. There was no sense of psychology as a subject matter whose task it was to master it. It was all bits and pieces. A couple of photocopied pages of George Herbert Mead's book *Mind, Self and Society* would be handed

---

[11]This began to change on that first day when I arrived in the parish at Bow and had the subjective experience of me in relation to God and then when I made the decision not to say the whole office every day.

out or a recommendation that students read pages 112–116. There was no sense of trying to grasp and understand the deeper thinking of such a writer. Although my education in the Church had been within a narrow channel I now accepted that it had nevertheless been a true education. It is difficult, however, for me to sort out what the objective situation was. I was still longing for the Church and the educational atmosphere provided by such people as George Ekbery, Charles Davis, and Hubert Richards at St Edmund's. Part of the depression was on account of what I had lost and, through contrast, Brunel led me to feel it all the more deeply.

I had thrown my whole soul into the Church. I loved the Church. I had come to grasp her liturgy, her history, her theological tradition, her philosophical roots. I had grasped the unity behind diversity and I had thrown myself into my new priestly life down in Bow. And now here I was cast off, cast out, wandering, a lost soul blown like a bit of dust in the wind and not knowing where to settle. I was in a ripe state for exploitation and disaster, and it happened from an unexpected quarter.

* * *

CHAPTER EIGHT

Disaster and recovery

Sometime after Christmas 1968 when I had been banished from the family and was wallowing in self-pity I received a telegram out of the blue from Josephine Earth asking me to contact her and giving me her telephone number. I rang her and she invited me to visit her at Overstrand near Cromer in Norfolk. So I drove up one Friday, arriving in late afternoon. I spent the evening with her, the night with her, and by the next day had proposed marriage to her. Two months later in the Kensington Register Office we married. Fourteen months later we had parted. If I ever need evidence of my madness I have only to hold this episode up in front of me as a salutary reminder.

The madness lay in the fact that her violent and savage behaviour towards me was quite evident prior to marrying her. She had been married to a GP called Paul Earth and he had committed suicide. It was not difficult for me to see that being married to Josephine had been a contributory factor. She talked about Paul incessantly. I was still seeing Dr St Blaize-Molony for psychoanalytic psychotherapy and I mentioned this to him but I remember saying to him that this was alright because it satisfied the homosexual part of me. I don't believe that anyone could have stopped me. I was in the grip of a violent and inescapable force. A tyrant goddess had got hold of me and no rational process could release me from it.

She spoke about Paul incessantly, especially his exquisite manners. In the "courtship" time she once rang me at about ten in the evening and kept me on the telephone until four in the morning. I said goodbye and rang off at one point and she rang back. Had she detected some anger in me? "Oh no darling ..." I went most weekends up to her cottage in Norfolk. Often she would castigate me in the most ungovernable language. She would watch for the slightest hint of annoyance with her and should she detect it she would say how Paul was so much more a gentleman than me. On one occasion she came down to London and I met her at the station. All the people got out and there was no sign of her and then finally she emerged carrying a case. I took the case from her and I could tell that it was entirely empty. It later emerged that instead of putting clothes into the case she had thrown them all into a bath full of water. Her mother and father lived at King's Lynn in Norfolk but in no way would she let me meet them or any other member of her family. I was in the grip of this tyrant goddess and did nothing or could do nothing to extricate myself from it. I was in a hypnotic trance and totally governed from the magical strings which she pulled at will. She in no way hid her behaviour from me. I could not plead that it only began to go wrong once we were married. The very worst of her behaviour was there in front of me to see. What was this madness?

Why was I not able to act according to what I saw? Why did I succumb to this woman's viciousness? Why did I not just call off the planned marriage? Could it be that I had to keep the madness outside myself yet, at the same time, allow myself to know it? Mad though it was yet I think it was less mad than when I flew into the Church subsequent to the revelation of my mother's infidelity. On that occasion there was not the slightest hint that I was doing anything mad and it had the approbation of most of my family. Yet when I married Josephine it was obvious to everyone that something was severely wrong and finally after fourteen months of marriage I brought it to an end. At last I had acted. For some reason I had to finalise the union through marriage and only then could I act and detach myself from her. Similarly it was only when I had actually been ordained a priest and arrived in the parish that I said to myself I had made a terrible mistake and three and a half years later left. When I had been some three or four years in the seminary I sensed that the energy with which I had endowed the whole project was beginning to dwindle. I had filled the petrol tank but the petrol was now running out. So the heart of the madness with me seems to be acting with a great thrust of enthusiasm that overrode all doubt and questioning.

Surely the heart of madness lies in self-damage, self-destruction? But this is a generalisation and the particular form that it takes differs in different people. I have in subsequent years as a psychoanalyst been wary of these generalisations and prefer to listen to the particular form in which a pocket of madness operates in this person, and I have never known it to be exactly the same in another. The theme song of Uncle John's letter was the damage I was doing. The accent was more upon damage to others but also to myself because he speaks at one point of the happiness which I so much desire but am trying to reap in quite the wrong way so there is an implication of self-damage. In fact self-damage and damage to others are closely interlinked and in existential terms inseparable but only separable in abstract logic. Based on the principles of Vedanta philosophy or the *Philosophia Perennis*, I and the other both participate in being and therefore harm cannot be done to one and not the other. Thus madness and badness are two different angles on the same thing but sometimes the former rather than the latter comes into greater prominence. In this case the former was so clearly the dominant feature. When my brother first met Josephine, unfortunately subsequent to marriage, he saw straight away that some disaster had occurred.

In my case the madness was hidden and yet revealed. I married Josephine and a little over twelve months later I parted from her. There was a similar pattern to what occurred with the Church. I went into the Church and just under ten years later I left. The madness I believe consisted in the manner in which I went in—hounded into the Church by the tyrant God. When I married Josephine I was bonded to this tyrant God which had become embodied in her. I think the way I have put it just now is the right way. If I speak of her as a wicked tyrant goddess who captured me in her spider's web then I am in a paranoid mode. If I say that I was bonded to a tyrant God which has had different embodiments in my life then I can begin to get the lineaments of a structure that belong to me. Otherwise I go along as an unfortunate victim to whom all these disasters have occurred along life's journey.

This madness came out in its fullness in my relations with Josephine. It stands out absolutely clearly that I pledged myself to someone who castigated me in the most savage terms. The madness in me came out most clearly in the relationship between me and her—in a two-person

263

relationship and here with a woman. Sex has hardly been mentioned here except to say that when I left school and had an erection when dancing I was overcome with shame and guilt. I am not sure why but somehow I associate it in my mind with that guilt about the sacrilegious Holy Communion when I was eight years old. Enormous guilt is the common denominator. In this latter case it is consistent with the healthy theory of redemption that I had not harmed God but I certainly harmed myself. At the age of eight I administered to myself four years of inner torture. I submitted to a punishing tyrant God. I think I also submitted to a tyrant God who punished me for having an erection in adolescence, so what I was punished for was being potent. And there was something of this in my relations with Tony Beagle. My feeling about him was that his Christianity was wet, sentimental, and feeble. What I could not bear about it was its impotence. He was like a little child being cuddled by the Portuguese maids. "You will be loved and are loved as long as you are impotent. Become potent and you will be punished and castigated ..." I have referred to a belief I have that my mother "hypnotised" me. In the hypnotic trance she declared me a girl child. Emotional weakness is what I have always hated. It must be this element in me that I find unbearable. I believe I am a strange compound of opposites: extreme weakness and wetness, if you will, and, at the same time, an extraordinary determination and strength. Churchill's words, "We shall never surrender," have been a living icon for me, but it must be that I say these words to give strength to a weak child within being harassed by God's most savage attacks.

* * *

So we married in the month of May 1969 at the Kensington Register Office and we had a small reception back at my flat in Holland Park Avenue. Christopher made a little speech but he had tears in his eyes. He and Mary were the only members of the family there. I cannot remember whether my sister, Jill, was there but I imagine she was. My mother and father were in Portugal and we knew we would see them because we were going there for our honeymoon. My very good friend, Bill McSweeney, another ex-priest, was there and I think John Perry and his wife, Jo, must have been there too. Josephine's two children, Caroline and Richard, were at the time aged seven and four. Mary and Christopher Campbell-Johnston very kindly took care of them while

Josephine and I drove overland to Portugal. It is significant that I cannot remember anything of the journey except stopping at the town of Astorga in northern Spain to send a telegram to my parents at their house in Afife to tell them of the date and time of our arrival. I remember I signed the telegram "Nevojosa". We finally arrived and Clare and Charlie Carey were staying at the time. The stay is cloaked in a veil of fog. Josephine was ill much of the time and never stopped talking of Paul. I remember my mother looking at me and asking me if I couldn't get her to stop talking about Paul. Two or three times at night she entered a strange state. It was as if she were in a dream and yet she was wide awake and she was living one of the days when she had been married to Paul. She mentioned little details of events and people. Her eyes were wide open and she was looking at me but her eyes were living the particular events of a day back when she was married to Paul. It was very unnerving and I have never before or since encountered such a phenomenon and do not know quite what to call it. It happened two or three times. When in the morning I repeated to her some of the events, places, and people that she was talking about she verified that these were real from when she had been married to Paul. I came later to think that Paul was not psychically dead for her; that had she psychically registered that he was dead she would have been overwhelmed with guilt. I suppose that the severe castigation which she gave me daily was diverted from herself.

My brother, James, and his wife, Penny, came for one weekend while we were there. James was appalled and realised that something terrible had occurred. My mother had misgivings but kept them to herself. She told me later that she had done this because she feared that if she had voiced them I would have turned against her. I was in the grip of a shockingly violent punishing God that I was not going to be diverted from. When I was in that violent state administering to myself punishments that led me into the Church I was similarly in the grip of something stronger than me. I don't think anyone could have stopped me. Later, when I was in psychoanalysis with John Klauber, he believed that this was my mother colluding with my getting into a shocking mess. His evidence for this was that she did not reveal her misgivings to other members of the family. I think this was wrong. He did not realise the power of the force in whose grip I was firmly entrapped.

I have spoken about myself being hypnotised but I in turn hypnotised the whole group around me. Maybe only James was free of it.

265

They all somehow went along with this madness that I was in. The powerful madness in me "drew them in". I don't think members of the family ever said to themselves: heavens, Neville has gone mad; there is something severely wrong here. Throughout all this nightmare time of sheer madness I managed to convince myself that I was sane. Everything I did was right, just these unfortunate things were happening to me. This was despite the fact that she had castigated me with hatefulness and fury *before* I got married. I knew this but was still able to convince myself that I was perfectly sane; that these unfortunate things were happening to me. The reality of this must still be present to the extent to which I prefer to forget it. It has helped me to realise that people doing things which are clearly mad often cannot see it. And I know it is no use trying to make them see it. It may take years, if ever, to see it.

The only other thing I can remember is that we had intended to drive back through Spain and France to England but instead we returned by boat from Vigo and put the car on board with us. I have a vague memory of being in the cabin with Josephine and my not being able to have an erection and she getting furious. This was a rare event. The only other thing I remember of the whole event was driving along one day on the road from Afife to Viana do Castelo in a rage with my teeth grinding in fury. I was in a rage with Josephine.

The thing that strikes me most forcefully as I send my mind back to these events is how much I have blotted out. Not only is it all so horrific but I believe I must have been and probably still am deeply ashamed. Also, as I have suggested, it is a potent reminder of my madness. The violently self-destructive nature of this *damned thing*[1] in me is what I try to shut out and it must be that, to some extent, it is still in me and that I do not want to see it.

There is another element to this self-destructive virus in me. The whole cost of this disastrous marriage was enormous. I had been left some money by my grandfather in trust. The trust was broken and I was given my portion. The whole of it disappeared in the cost of the marriage and later, the marriage settlement. This particular viral stream of destruction has never left me and, whereas I should be a rich man had I been a good husbandman of my inheritance, instead I am poor and will have to work to the end of my days, whereas my

---

[1]Named after a short story by Ambrose Bierce.

266

brother, James, retired at sixty-two worth the golden storeroom at Fort Knox.

There is one saving grace: that I have *to some extent* been able to turn the consequences of this madness to good account. Later I became a psychoanalyst and, in due time, quite a famous one and I have written books on the subject and lectured in several countries worldwide. This has been due to a personal understanding of madness. I understand it from the inside and that, of course, is the only way to understand any human reality. Wilfred Bion made this point:

> While listening to the patient the analyst should dwell on those aspects of the patient's communication which come nearest to arousing feelings corresponding to persecution and depression. In my experience this gives as good a check on the soundness of one's interpretative validity as anything I know. On the whole I am more satisfied with my work if I feel that I have been through these emotional experiences than I do if the session has been more agreeable. I am fortified in this belief by the conviction that has been borne in on me by the analysis of psychotic or borderline patients. I do not think such a patient will ever accept an interpretation, however correct, unless he feels that the analyst has passed through his emotional crisis as a part of the act of giving the interpretation.[2]

The second feature has been that, because I have been poor, or at least had to earn my own living "by the sweat of my brow", rather than reap the benefit of huge investments, it has kept my mind alive as I have had to rely on it for an income.

So I settled down into married life or a make-belief married life. Here I was suddenly with a ready-made family. Caroline was seven and Richard was four. I bought a house in Crystal Palace. I was still only in my second year at Brunel University reading psychology. I did not manage to study at all. I was in a complete whirl. Josephine drank heavily and also overdosed and, on one occasion, I had to call an ambulance and she was carried off to hospital where she was pumped out. Who was this woman I had so impetuously married? I began to find out and, as I did so, more and more lies she had told me became evident. I was in a rage with her and, at the same time, she needed me day

---

[2]Bion, Wilfred (1992). *Cogitations* (p. 291). London: Karnac.

and night. Often I could not go to Brunel because she was collapsed in bed and I had the two children to look after.

She hated the house at Crystal Palace so we sold it and bought one in Dulwich instead and the whole operation of selling, buying, and moving took all my time. We had married in May 1969. By a year later things had reached a climax. I was still at Brunel but, as this was a "sandwich course", which means that in the summer students did something practical, I had a placement on one of the wards at Bethlem Royal Hospital.

* * *

In the midst of this cataclysm of disasters I had decided to apply for training at the Institute of Psychoanalysis in London. I received a reply from Enid Balint who was on the institute's admissions committee. I went to see her at her home and consulting rooms at Park Square West just off the southern side of Regent's Park. She clearly thought well of me and, in quite a short interview, led me to understand that she thought my application for training would be favourably received. However, shortly after, I had a letter saying they could not consider me for training until I had finished my degree in psychology at Brunel University. I decided to challenge this. The professor who was head of social sciences at Brunel was Elliott Jaques who was also a prominent psychoanalyst. I spoke to him and said, given my age, it would make a big difference if I could train at the Institute of Psychoanalysis concurrently with doing my degree in psychology at Brunel. He wholeheartedly agreed and told me to write to the Education Committee of the Institute of PsychoAnalysis quoting his support for this opinion and that, if they still did not listen, to contact him and he would write to the committee himself directly. So I wrote to the Education Committee and had a favourable reply: they sent me an application form to fill in and asked me for two referees. My academic referee was Charles Davis who, I gathered later, gave me a very favourable reference, saying that my academic level was much higher than that which would be represented by an undergraduate degree. I imagine that he indicated that I was more at the MPhil or PhD level. My other referee was Peter McNeale who was a probation officer I had known in the East End of London and continued to know after I left the priesthood. I think in his letter he referred more to my casework experience with alcoholics, delinquents, and others whom I had tried to help while a priest. My application form and these references were sufficient for the Institute of Psychoanalysis to arrange for me to have two formal interviews.

People who apply to the Institute of Psychoanalysis are always interviewed in depth by two different experienced psychoanalysts. My first interviewer was Dr Lothair Rubinstein who lived in Ferncroft Avenue in Hampstead. He was a warm, educated man whom the Portuguese would call *simpático*. I immediately felt relaxed in his presence and told him everything about myself. I told him about my mother's lesbian affairs and he said it was quite a common occurrence with menopausal women. I explained to him about my difficulties in the Church and told him about some of the violent feelings that were aroused when the liturgy went into English. He told me of a woman who was deeply troubled emotionally by this change and how he had been struck by the fact that she had been more distressed and angry about this than other things in her life which he thought would have worried her more. Because he gave of himself I gave of myself to him. I have always believed that the clinician needs to give of himself or herself if the patient is to give of himself. Rousseau said this: "It is a bad way of reading another man's heart to conceal one's own."[3]

I liked him and my only reservation about him was that he had a kindly, courteous nature not unlike my father. The suggestion was made that I go to him for analysis but I knew I would run into trouble with him; that I would feel too worried about hurting him. At the end of the interview he said to me that he thought it would be alright. I liked him but I never saw him again because a couple of years later he dropped dead unexpectedly of a heart attack while at the International Congress in Vienna.

My second interviewer was Isabel Menzies. She was more probing than Dr Rubinstein and consequently I was more reserved and did not give of myself as freely as I had to Rubinstein. It has taught me that someone will not give of their private self unless the clinician gives of him- or herself. The first thing she said to me was that she wanted to hear about this change of mine—leaving the Church. Whereas I felt that Rubinstein was interested in me as a person, interested in my life, I felt

---

[3]Rousseau, Jean-Jacques (1731–32). *The Confessions (Book Two)* (p. 84). London: Penguin, 1973.

she was probing for pathology. Paradoxically I think the former clinical attitude succeeds in getting closer to the pathology. Probably what I am saying is rather unfair because later in life I came to know her and liked her Scots down-to-earth or let's-get-down-to-brass-tacks manner. However, I think his approach was better than hers. But in neither interview did I speak about my disastrous marriage. I knew that it was a disaster and I hid it from my interviewers. I was *in* the disaster—so much in it that I did not speak about it. I was desperate to get a good analysis with a senior psychoanalyst but I do not offer this as an excuse. In those interviews I cheated and that is all that can be said about it. It is certainly something that St Peter would rightly mark down on the debit side of the balance sheet.

Some two or three weeks after these two interviews I received a letter from the Institute of Psychoanalysis saying that I had been accepted for training. Looking back on it now it seems to me fantastic that I could have been accepted when my life was in a shattering mess.

Now my job was to find a psychoanalyst to whom I could go. Students who are training to become psychoanalysts have to undergo an analysis themselves first, and because this is seen as particularly important only those psychoanalysts who have had considerable clinical experience and who have undergone a probing examination are allowed to conduct such analyses. They are known as training analysts. So I had to choose a training analyst but I had first another decision to make. The British Psychoanalytical Society was composed of three "schools"— the Anna Freud School as it was called then,[4] the Independent Group (sometimes known as the Middle Group), and the Kleinians. The history of this lay in a row that broke out between Melanie Klein with her followers versus Anna Freud and her disciples, and each group decided to have its own system of training; then there was a group which wanted to be independent of both of these and this was the Independent Group. I was drawn to the Independent Group. I sniffed some fanaticism in the other two groups and I thought I had had enough of that. I knew that there was something of this in me. I had also read and enjoyed some of the papers of Michael Balint who belonged to this group. So I decided that the Independent Group was the right place for me and now I had to find an analyst within that group. So I went back to see Enid Balint.

---

[4]Renamed the Classical Freudian School in about 1990.

Enid Balint was a lively, quick-witted woman. She said immediately that the best psychoanalyst for me would be John Klauber. I had no idea who he was and had never heard his name before but I trusted her intuition and a few days later I was walking down Elsworthy Road in Hampstead to reach his consulting room. He was warm, natural, and very polite, and I could see that he had a weakness for the sensual in life. He was dressed immaculately. I was terrified of him. I felt like a little urchin boy in the presence of this imposing and rather grand man. I could tell instantly that he was a well educated man of considerable refinement. I was not at ease with him as I had been with Dr Rubinstein. I sensed a shrewdness in him which unnerved me. After I had been speaking to him for some time he said,

"Do you mind if I be entirely frank with you ...?"
"No, please do," I said in terror.
"I think you are very ill, you know."

I almost cried with relief. He saw what no one else had seen. I had seen three very senior psychoanalysts: Enid Balint, Lothair Rubinstein, and Isabel Menzies, and none of them had seen what John Klauber saw. I felt immensely grateful to him, though I was also in terror. He asked me whether I wanted to come into analysis with him and I said I did. He then said that he thought it would be a long and difficult analysis but he thought it would be alright, adding that he would like to think about it for a couple of days before making up his mind. He also said that he thought I should be in analysis some time before starting the training. He said to me: "*Festina lente* is a good rule for psychoanalysis."

I thought he was a wise man, someone who would not be rushed, but also one who would speak the truth as he saw it. I had no doubt that he was the right analyst for me. Also he had not an iota of fanaticism. My sense that he was a sensual man, something which I perceived in that first interview, was of benefit to me because it was an antidote to the trait of puritanism that was in my character and that had led me into the Church. The fact that the patient makes an assessment of the analyst in the initial consultation is something which John Klauber himself emphasised:

When the patient visits the psychoanalyst for a consultation, it is not only the psychoanalyst who makes an assessment of the

271

patient—the patient also attempts to make an assessment of the analyst. Though the transference, which begins to be formed before the consultation, has an important share in the patient's subsequent reaction, the capacity of the patient's ego to evaluate is not paralyzed, as later analysis tends to reveal. Just as a psychoanalyst starts his report on a patient by describing what he looks like, how he moves and how he is dressed, so equally a fund of information about the psychoanalyst reaches the patient—about his capacity to respond, about his tastes and personal attitudes ...[5]

It was a great relief then when he rang two days later and confirmed that he would be prepared to take me into analysis.

I started my analysis with him about three months later: on 21st April 1970. Whereas before when I had been in analysis I was going just twice a week, now I was starting in full five-times-a-week analysis. He had given me a time for each day of the week. That was also a great relief.

I was at this time absolutely desperate. This analysis was my last hope. I knew at this time that candidates in training went to senior analysts and I think it was one of my motives in applying for training. I wanted a senior and experienced man. I knew that my previous psychoanalyst was seriously defective. Now at last I had arrived on the couch of a psychoanalyst whom I trusted, and I put all my hopes in him. My analysis now became the focal point of my life. It was also integral to my life; it became woven into the fabric of my aspirations. Everything else became secondary. But I must return now to my domestic life which was a disaster.

* * *

While still at the Crystal Palace house Josephine took an overdose. I had to ring for an ambulance and she was taken to a psychiatric hospital in south London. She was pumped out, stayed the night, and the next day was back home. She went to visit a psychiatrist at the hospital a bit later but only saw him for one visit. When driving in my car behind the ambulance taking her to the hospital a lightning flash of the horror I was

---

[5]Klauber, John (1981). The psychoanalyst as person. In: *Difficulties in the Analytic Encounter* (pp. 129–130). New York: Jason Aronson.

in struck me, a glimpse of the mad world in which I was living, but it soon closed over. I certainly never spoke to my family or friends about this incident.

The human scene is full of surprising events. There was one associated with this disaster that I have never forgotten. When Josephine had taken the overdose and was moaning in bed at our house in Crystal Palace I telephoned our GP who came around straight away. He saw immediately that Josephine was in an hysterical condition and he telephoned for the ambulance for her to be taken to hospital. When later I had started divorce proceedings my lawyer asked me to speak to this doctor and ask if he would give testimony as to Josephine's condition. This was about two years later. I went to see him. I have forgotten his name but it was a French name. I sat in his waiting room awaiting my turn amidst a bevy of patients also waiting. When my turn came I went in and I started by saying, "I don't know if you remember me ..." He stopped me and said he remembered me very well, told me my name, and quickly referred to the incident two years back. I told him that I was amazed that he should remember so well and especially that he should remember my name. He told me that he did not know why it was but he never forgot any patient who came before him in his consulting room. "I don't know how it is," he said, "but I have a mind like a computer and I never forget anyone." He went on to tell me that he remembered Josephine well, and he had come across several people like me in the course of his professional practice—observing that I was obviously an intelligent and educated man and yet had married so ineptly. He then went on to speak to me about the omnipotence of doctors. He said, "We are only technicians but we believe we are gods and take it upon ourselves to advise our patients on all sorts of matters that are way beyond our knowledge and competence ..."

Then he went on to tell me of a case of a woman with two children who fell into a depression and went to her GP, who advised her to have another child and that this would cure her of her depression. Shortly after the birth of this third child the woman committed suicide. We spoke briefly about my lawyer's request and he said if it was really crucial to my legal affairs he would consult his own lawyer first before making any statement. He wished me well and I went away. I decided there and then not to pursue my own lawyer's request any further. It was a brief encounter but I thought to myself, "What an amazing doctor"— obviously with a photographic memory, emotionally supportive, and professionally humble. I was sad when three or four years later I noticed in *The Times* deaths column that he had died. I suspect that the good he must have done in his small south London practice was incalculable.

Josephine's hatred of me was unceasing. She daily compared me to Paul. Paul, she repeatedly told me, was the quintessence of refinement. He was so well mannered. Also it became daily more evident that much of what she had told me about herself was a tissue of lies. When I think back to my own madness one of the supreme signs of it was that I never went to meet her parents who lived in King's Lynn in Norfolk. To think that I could have been so pulled over into her power as to agree to not meeting them is clear evidence of my madness, a madness where I was totally under the spell, the spider's web that Josephine had woven around me. I know now that I was mad but I did not know it then. When you are in the mad state you do not know it. Another thing is that you are in danger of knowing it if someone from outside can clearly see it so in the mad state you have to pull others into it to prevent the light falling upon the madness. This was why I was both terrified and at the same time relieved when John Klauber saw that I was very ill.

The question is: why was I so terrified of seeing my madness? To answer this question I must put forward my theory of madness. This is the only way I can explain it. My theory is my way of trying to answer that question. I think that madness is an auto-generated anaesthetic against pain. What was the pain that I was blotting out so effectively? It was multiple—a build-up like compound interest. Tracing it from the front backwards, the first thing was that leaving the Church was a punch in the stomach that winded me severely: all my inner being had been ripped out of me. I had thrust my whole being into the business of being a priest and I had the ideal of being holy. All this was now shattered; my life lay in ruins around me. My extended family had all banished me to outer darkness. But this is not quite right. I had not put my inner soul into the "Church venture". I know this because I used to try to hide my priestly status. I was embarrassed to wear the clerical collar. This was not with everyone but with those who either were hostile to the idea or whose commitment was to worldly values, who loved the human scene, who looked with favour upon sexual affairs with benign tolerance, who basked in the glory of this world. With such people I felt embarrassed and, deep down, I was not entirely happy with devout Catholics either—a sort of sense that I was an "actor-priest" and not the genuine article. This must have meant that the outer clothing I was wearing, the priest's garb, was not truly me. I had not discovered who I really was; the outer did not reflect the inner.

So my entry into the Church had been impelled by some painful fact that I was trying to escape. I posit this from a theory I have devised that pain is registered by the "me", the personal, so a phobic flight from the personal had been to insulate me from this pain. Hence what people were witnessing when they encountered this cassocked figure was a delusion. I had turned myself into a delusional object and somewhere in the depths there was a clamouring child, a child who was wounded and injured in his very being.

Now I can go back a stage further and say that this injury had occurred when I discovered that my mother was having a lesbian affair with Clay Wilson—that I felt a shocking betrayal but, now I come to think of it, I must have construed that my mother had not loved me *as I was*—a man, a boy child and not a female child. So then followed the shocking discovery that my mother was in love with another female and not me. Perhaps becoming a priest was an attempt on my part to both please my father who had such a devoted admiration for the Church and her priests and, in a contorted way, to please my mother and so become a woman-man. After all a Catholic priest is a eunuch and, when dressed in his flowing cassock, what could be more female than that? Additional evidence for this was that I was always trying to be "manly". I remember being struck by Scheeben, the German Catholic theologian, who said that Christians should not be just children of God but *mannliche Kinder gottes*. It was the word *mannliche* that appealed to me. There I was, a woman, a castrated man, fiercely trying to be manly. It took me many years to realise that to be gentle and tender is not only compatible with being a man but rather proves that manhood has truly been achieved within, that the fierce passions that assault one in the thoroughfares of life have been inwardly processed and that the so-called surly, aggressive, and assertive attitudes that are so often described as manly are in fact signs that the male has not been able to manage inner ignorance but instead has had to deflect it outwards in a display of assertiveness.

So I trace the pain, via the discovery of my mother's lesbian affair, right back to my childhood. I surmise that my birth was a great disappointment to my mother; that she had hoped for a girl and the sight of yet another boy collapsed her spirit so she withdrew emotionally and did not give to me what I most needed: an act of contemplative love that would have been a source of confidence in my inner being. And yet this cannot be completely true. I have certainly been mad for long periods in my life and emotionally the frailest of creatures, and yet there has been in me some resilience, some inner spirit of strength that has enabled me to push through some of these appalling fits of madness. "Fits" is not the right word—they have been long-lasting episodes, but there has been in me something of the Churchillian spirit that has said within me: *We shall never surrender*. So where did this come from? I have a feeling that something in my mother and father may have generated it. First let me give thought to the way a quality in one person can generate something equivalent in another. I only put this forward as a *possible* hypothesis. There is all the outer display of characteristics in someone. On the outer manifestation my father was emotionally frail; he could not manage any form of confrontation or criticism; in pain he withdrew into himself; he never shared with a living soul the enormous disappointment of his failed marriage and yet ... he had a determination, obstinacy if you like, that saw him through. My mother, without doubt, was the more courageous. When I left the priesthood she stood up for me with a powerful defiance, careless of what her friends and family thought of her. So let us say that between the two of them they had these two strengths: determination and courage. Now, I have had some portion of both of these and I think it likely that in some way it is right to attribute this to my parents. It was their gift to me, if you like, and yet I do not think that this was passed on to me as a cold or 'flu is passed on from one person to another. There were inner acts on my part that enabled me to generate in myself what I knew was in them. I did love my mother and I did love my father. I loved them enormously and still do. They both had in them a nobility of character, an inner strength, a resoluteness that I admired. That love, that admiration of mine was an inner act and I believe that it was this that laid for me a foundation that ultimately was stronger than all the madness and kerfuffle that blew like a great storm across the surface of my life. I think that I separated out the wheat from the chaff. My evidence for this is that right through my life I have never drunk in entirely the whole of a person's character. I have admired Churchill, I have admired Gandhi, I have admired Trotsky; I have admired Caryll Houselander, Solovyov, Tolstoy, Ruskin, George Eliot, Emily Brontë, G. K. Chesterton, Isaiah Berlin, John Macmurray, Sigmund Freud, Melanie Klein, Donald Winnicott, and Wilfred Bion; and within my own life I have admired greatly George Ekbery, Monsignor Sullivan, Bob Gosling, Wilfred Bion, Marion Milner, Frances Tustin, John Klauber,

276

Placid Spearritt, and Balvant Parekh, to mention just a few, but I have never swallowed any one of them whole. What I have admired in them has been inner strengths, nobility of character, and natural spontaneity, but in every one of them there have been certain outlooks and attitudes that I have disagreed with, deplored in fact. I have always made a separation in my mind between the inner strength and the outer inconsistencies and when I think about it I must have done this with my parents. I believe something like this must have happened: that I was "caught" by their madness, swept up in it but, at the same time, that in an act of love, an act of admiration, I took possession within myself of courage and determination.

There is another quality of character that I also possess: it is a generosity of spirit and I believe I admired this in my mother who enabled me to generate it in myself.

What enabled me to do this? If my mother turned from me in disappointment at my birth, how was I helped to be able to take in these qualities of the soul? I think of two possibilities: that my father had a burst of joy at the birth of another son and conceived for me an almost maternal love. The other strand takes me back to my time before birth. I believe that my mother, as I have suggested earlier, hated finding that she had an alien body struggling inside her, but this changed at my birth. I believe my mother conceived a love for me once I was born. Many years later, shortly before she died, I asked her about my birth, and as she spoke of it I could see clearly her memory of me as a tiny baby before her eyes. She told me how she had breastfed me and then given me to María do Carmo to feed me on the bottle but she watched and, as she told me this, I could sense her pleasure that accompanied that event. I know, from experience of working with young mothers who had become pregnant unintentionally, that what is hated in the womb often changes to a fond love once birth has occurred. I believe also that my father was full of joy at my birth and their joint love, together, laid for me a foundation that fills me with a gratitude so great that, even as I write this, I burst into tears.

So that is my theory, but there is something about it that is not right and it is this. In everyone there is some core that springs from within which can never be entirely explained by external circumstances and influences. There are character traits in the individual that cannot be explained by outer facts. Such an attitude is anathema to those devoted to a determinist perspective and is what all great religions have referred

277

to as "mystery". How something can be generated entirely from within I do not know, it confounds my mind but I believe it to be so. It is the mystery of life itself and I bow my head before it.

So back to my madness. I had been pulled into Josephine's crazy world and John Klauber was the first person to see it: "You are very ill, you know." What a relief! At last someone had seen through all the mess and chaos and made that simple statement. He had enormous prejudices, was easily seduced by a lot of absurd conventionality, but ... but he saw through to what was essential. I said to him several times that he must have had some particular gift that he had quite quickly seen what Enid Balint, Isabel Menzies, and Rubinstein had not. He agreed that it seemed to be so. He did acknowledge it but always with a hint of reluctance. I think he was fearful that I would idealise him. In this he was wrong. Clear acknowledgment of this gift would have helped me to separate again this particular quality of his from a lot of the rubbish and personal prejudices that flowed out of him. He was a wise man but also a foolish one. My gratitude to him is immense but he was also obtuse in ways which will emerge as we go on. It may sound that I am disparaging John Klauber but I don't think so. No one is consistent. No person on the planet has ever been entirely consistent and in this John Klauber was no exception.

* * *

Shortly after Josephine took her overdose we moved to a house in Dulwich which was more pleasant. Josephine promised me that if we moved house she would never again complain, that all her dreams would have been fulfilled, and I was swept up into this assurance while, deep in my heart, knowing that this would not occur. One of the catastrophes of my life has been the disparity between a madness where I am gullible and taken in by the words of assurance versus an emotional knowing that has been overridden by the words.

So here was my life situation on 21st April 1970, the day I started my analysis with John Klauber at his consulting room in Hampstead at 16 Elsworthy Road. I was in my second year of psychology at Brunel University and, as this was a sandwich course, I had already started my summer term spell as a nursing assistant at Bethlem Royal Hospital on Bob Hobson's ward at Tyson West Two. Bob Hobson was a well-known Jungian psychoanalyst and the ward was made up almost entirely of young university students who had had breakdowns. The job of the nurses was to speak to the patients, engage them in conversation, help them to communicate. So here I was working at Tyson West Two every day, going for my analysis five times a week, and trying desperately to manage a deteriorating situation at home in our new house in Dulwich.

Josephine's attitude went from bad to worse. Her hatred of me continued unabated. Every day she compared me to Paul: what a wonderful husband he had been, how marvellously he had attended to her; and the vitriol which she threw at me grew and grew. It was as if I had murdered Paul and she was throwing at me all the venom that belonged to the murderer of her husband. Paul had committed suicide and, in retrospect, I realise that, in some senses, she was the murderess and the hatred she was pouring upon me belonged in some degree to herself. Of course Paul himself had to take responsibility for killing himself.

Slowly, bit by bit, I began to realise that things Josephine had told me were not true. For instance, she had told me she had been a nurse at the London Hospital but I came to know that this was not true, and more and more lies began to be uncovered. My spirits had reached their lowest point. One morning when her violent hatred reached a climax I packed a small case and walked out of the house. I turned out of the gate and walked up Woodwarde Road, slowly, step by step, and in complete desolation. There I was, walking with my case, with a few belongings, with nowhere to go, no one to turn to. It must have been then that I realised I had to leave Josephine, that I would end up as Paul had done if I did not get out.

There were three people I spoke to. One day I took Bob Hobson into my confidence and as I told him briefly of my situation he said with his candid Lancashire accent that I had clearly made a mistake in marrying Josephine and that he did not think anything was to be gained by consolidating the mistake. I knew he was right. I also knew that Josephine was desperate to get herself pregnant and entangle me in an even worse situation so I avoided sexual relations with her. This made her suspect that I had another woman and so to her hatred was added a violent jealousy. She suspected that I must be having an affair with one of the nurses or doctors at Bethlem so, together with Caroline and Richard, she would frequently drive over to the ward and sit in the car outside to see if she could espy any liaison that was going on. When I told all this to John Klauber he said, "You have married a mad woman."

Another person I spoke to was Chris Farmer. He was the psychiatrist I had first met when I was in Bow; he was now living in Dulwich and had become seconded to Tyson West Two. He had come with his wife Ivy on one or two occasions to visit Josephine and me, first in Crystal Palace and then in Dulwich, and now, when I was working at Tyson West Two, he appeared as one of the psychiatric registrars on rotation. So I asked him if I could come and see him at his home in Dulwich one evening and he assented immediately. When I spoke to Chris it broke something. The spell that had bound me to Josephine, like Trilby to Svengali, was at last broken. It was the speaking of it to Chris that did it. I ask myself why speaking of it also to my analyst, John Klauber, had not broken the spell. This is an important question which is worth trying to dig into to understand.

It must somehow be that in analysis I was also in a trance. I certainly had John Klauber on a very high pedestal. He was a charming man, highly educated, and with a warm, hypnotic voice. Josephine's violent hatred of me must have been my unacknowledged hatred of perhaps not only John Klauber but the psychoanalytical process itself. The process entrapped me, lured me into its seductive web; there was a violent hatred of it in myself but a hatred so violent and so unacknowledged that it took up habitation within the persona of Josephine.

Yet this cannot be quite right because I left the Church and then became involved with Josephine when I was with my first psychoanalyst, Dr Ronald St Blaize-Molony. It must be that he was even more seductive than John Klauber. I have written of the vicious virus that took possession of me when I got involved with Josephine and yet what was it?

I am sure it was the same virus that impelled me with such force into the Church. When John Klauber said that I had married a mad woman I need to think of a mad presence within myself. When I talk of seductiveness then I think that either Molony was more seductive than John Klauber or that I was less susceptible. I think the former is the more likely. I did have a sense that Molony was trying to "prove himself" in a way which was not true of Klauber. I suspect that this need in someone to prove himself may have a very injurious effect on me. Josephine was desperately struggling against a huge sense of inferiority. She was a caricatured image of that first analyst of mine. It is what is probably best described as a "delusional identification". I did not dream of myself with a woman desperately needing to prove herself but I actually married such a woman. If I had dreamt it rather than done it then I would have been sane. There are "lived delusions" and this was one of them.

280

It seems that I have always had to go to the extremity in things. I shy away from what is domesticated and tame.

I think this must be true of me, of a part of me. I know I felt I was an unwanted baby. I remember saying to Klauber that by the time I came along my parents had become bored with me because there were photographs in the house of Jill as a baby and also James as a baby but none of me. There was some deep sense of being an unwanted child.

It was me who propelled myself onto the cold Yorkshire Moors. I was not going to be treated like some urchin child but I was going to be equal to the others. They were at school in England and I was not going to be treated as a "poor little thing", as "little Nevilinho", the one that had to be nursed at home. There was some violent protest in me against not being taken into the family lineage; that my mother had not really married my father; that she came from this South Sea colony; that she had scooped me up into a violent hatred of this patriarchal lineage. There was something about class, money, and position that Josephine hated in me and yet wanted: "I will get it through marriage," and yet hating the need to have to do it. She is not free thereby.

Is that sense of not being wanted the root of it? It could be that existence itself becomes rooted in the patriarchal lineage, in position, in status, and that I, this miserable worm, does not exist. I suspect that this is the heart of it. That the whole of my life has been a monumental effort to repudiate this powerful declaration that I do not exist; but that, instead of just asserting it to myself, in a quiet certainty I have instead screamed at the voice that makes the declaration that I do not exist. But if this is so does it answer the question as to why I am seduced by Molony and then Klauber? It must be that I get "pulled in" when I get onto intimate terms with someone who has the same problem. It is as if when I marry Josephine I am screaming at Molony: "Look what you are doing to me."

In other words I repudiate the deep belief that I do not exist by pulling in others against this awe-filled declaration. I will only be relieved of this appalling sense by joining together with another protester. It is as though there is a huge rally protesting violently against this archaic authority and I join in a contract of shared hatred. It is as if Josephine and Molony shared a hatred of being pronounced "non-existents" and they were not differentiated in my mind. That differentiation comes about through love whereas "merged amorphousness" comes about through hatred of a third party; that I merge with the other against the dictator's violent declaration.

The capacity to hypnotise therefore is based upon a merged together-ness against a third party which declares my non-existence. The ability to remove myself from the hypnotic trance is to switch my psychic attention away from the hated dictator to my own self and to reach a certainty that I do exist because I know it from observation and I will cease to believe in the dictator's declaration. I won't hate even the dec-laration but just know that it is absurd.

So this is how it ran. My mother had a hatred for my father because the declaration that she was a non-existent from a *terra nullius* had become located in him and his family lineage. As if she found him saying, "You do not exist," and so found in Jill and myself merged entities against this awe-filled declaration. And that this was the virus that continued on in me. I joined with an analyst against a declaration that he was a nothing, married him or Josephine in him against such declarations. So the virus was in my mother and passed on to me. The battle of my life has been a repudiation of this virus while at the same time I have been pulled in by it.

This excursion came about by examining why it was that when I spoke to Chris Farmer it broke the spell whereas when I was speaking to John Klauber, my analyst, it did not. I think it must be that I saw Klauber as, in some way, embodying that authority dictating that I did not exist whereas I saw Chris as a friend whom I turned to for help. He was a personal friend whereas Klauber was not. This was despite the fact that Klauber was personally and warmly responsive in a very striking way but he was, in my mind, still "an authority".

* * *

So the spell was broken. I told Josephine that I was going to leave. I took a room as a lodger in the flat of a bachelor living in Battersea and I moved there and lived there during the week and initially returned to Dulwich at weekends. Slowly I ceased to return at weekends. It was particularly at this time that Eila Renton was such a marvellous friend. She was the only person who came from the same social world as myself and yet who had had psychoanalysis and had considerable understanding of emotional matters. She was a marvellous support to me at this time and I went frequently and stayed with her and Ronnie at their house in the country near Thaxted in Essex. She was a friend in the very best sense in that she gave support but she also confided her own worries about me, and I remember one particular conversation where she said she worried whether I loved or knew how to love or what it was. She spoke in a firm but warm way and what she said made a deep impression. I have a great debt of gratitude to her.

She also said once that she saw me and Josephine like two lonely isolated children clinging desperately to one another. When I left Josephine it was a month before I was able to laugh. I was in the grimmest hell, what seemed an everlasting torment. I remember when I laughed again for the first time. I think I was with Richard Champion and I felt the first trickle of life returning to me.

At the same time I had a letter from Brunel University to say that I had done so badly in the second year of my studies that I would have to repeat the year. I was in a state of such wretchedness that I could not summon the resolve to repeat the year, so I wrote and asked for a leave of absence and postponement of my studies and this was agreed to. I had to find a job that I could do competently to start building my self-esteem. I found a job as a social worker in Wel-Care, the organisation that was once called Moral Welfare and was one of the social work arms of the Anglican Church. Its task was to offer assistance to young women who had become pregnant out of wedlock. It was in this job that I learned about these young mothers' attitude first to the foetus within them and then to the change that occurred once birth had happened. My task was to assist such mothers in arriving at a decision whether to keep their babies or give them away for adoption. Frequently they had decided to give the child for adoption before birth but the decision changed once the baby had been born.

Often these mothers came to me before they had told their families and usually they were in their late teens. Nearly always they imagined that their parents would cast them into outer darkness and never wish to see them again. When they told their parents the outcome was different. The parents were upset but I only came across one case out of many where the actual attitude of the parents harmonised with the young woman's fantasies. In all the others what the young women imagined far exceeded what occurred in reality. I found this experience was a symbol for many other instances in life where the fantasy is worse than the facts. Anticipation of death is frequently worse than the event itself. Shakespeare understood this well:

> By the apostle Paul, shadows tonight
> Have struck more terror to the soul of Richard

283

Than can the substance of ten thousand soldiers
Armèd in proof and led by shallow Richmond.[6]

I found this job difficult because I was the only male in a team of women social workers. I felt castrated; that I was not living up to my potential. After three months I was approached by the trustees of the Circle Trust and asked if I would consider taking up the position of administrator. The Circle Trust had been started by a probation officer called Douglas Gibson for the rehabilitation of prisoners. There was something about the masculinity of the job that appealed to me so I gave notice to Wel-Care and took the job as director of the Circle Trust. This organisation was located at 25 Camberwell Grove; a small flat at the top of the building went with the job and this felt a relief at the time.

So three important emotional processes were occurring at the same time. I was detaching myself from Josephine, I was developing an interest in prisoners, criminality, and psychopathy, and I was engaged in an analysis. I have to write about them separately but they were interrelated. I will write first of the analysis. John Klauber was a very different kind of man from Ronald St Blaize-Molony. He was aristocratic in his attitude to life. He was not in the least petty-minded, he had an inner generosity, and towards me a sense of shock at the disturbance which he found in me. He had very little understanding of the way in which outer figures were represented inwardly in the mind. If he spoke of my mother or my father it was as they were not as representing activities of my own mind. This was a serious lacuna in his understanding and outlook. His lack of understanding here was compensated for through his positive orientation to life. He had no negativism; he was not trying to sniff out jealousy and envy all the time. After I had finished my analysis I had a love affair with the Kleinians. I attended fortnightly supervisions with Herbert Rosenfeld and here I learned about the inner representation in the mind of outer people and events. But this group of analysts had a defect that Klauber did not have. For the Kleinians envy, for instance, was bad in itself and so was omnipotence. They did not seem to ask why these were present in the personality; they did not consider that these might be failed attempts to manage something of great difficulty. Although John Klauber did not formulate it yet his attitude was that the personality was trying to manage something.

---

[6]Richard III Act V Sc. 3 vv. 217–220.

There was a positive striving in the personality and he always backed this. So the Kleinians had lacunae, Klauber had lacunae. Every psychoanalyst has lacunae. Eventually each patient has to make his own personal synthesis.

All these reflections are the result of much thinking that has gone on years later. At this time when I was in analysis with John Klauber I was clinging desperately to him just like I had clung to God as a child. I felt so terrible that I frequently thought I would stop, that I could not go on any more, but something made me hold in there. The "*We shall never surrender*" chimed in my ears. John did know that I was very depressed but I don't think he realised how dreadful I felt inside, that I was near to collapse, that I wanted to give up.

He was shocked when I left Josephine, when I stopped my studies at Brunel. "Into the Church—out of the Church; into marriage—out of marriage," he said in agitated irritation. He said that my contract with the Institute of Psychoanalysis was that I would finish my degree in psychology at Brunel and here now I had given up. I reneged on my promises. He was annoyed when I referred to myself as "resigning" from the Church. I had "left" the Church, he said. He was critical of me but, at the same time, he recognised that I had been through "a massive crisis" and he used this phrase regularly. He saw that I did not realise what a crisis I had been through. So he was a mixture of two attitudes: condemnation and compassion for someone in crisis. He was entirely right to upbraid me for not keeping to the promises which I had made to the Institute of Psychoanalysis but I think in addition he condemned me for being mentally disturbed. I scooped him into the role of an omnipotent god, an archaic superego. Over time he slowly changed in his attitudes. I must attribute this change of attitude to the analysis and also some power in myself to change his outlook.

So this was a constant background. At the same time I was separating from Josephine. I now had my own little flat in Camberwell Grove. I had ceased to visit Josephine at weekends and the legal process of divorce had begun. But I blamed her while not asking why it was that I had married her. I was severely paranoid and this was never analysed. The focus of the paranoia altered but it remained untouched. To the extent that I have resolved this in myself it has been through my own life experiences and efforts at continued analysis over the years. The psychoanalytical process does tempt one into a passive submission which is itself a cornerstone of paranoia. I was incredibly paranoid and I think I married Josephine because I could disown this part of myself into her. "Look at her," I could say. "You can see she is a crazy paranoid woman," and it was true but the question remained unanswered, "Then why did you marry her, Neville?" One of the problems of paranoia is that you do not know it while you are in it. I can now say that I am a very paranoid person or that I have harboured a paranoid virus inside me for most of my life, but I can say it now because I am not in it or it does not have me in its grip in the way it once did. When Josephine was out of range, who then became the target of this paranoia? It passed to my brother, my cousins, my father, and my mother. And I always gathered allies on my side against whoever was the target at the time. The question though is, "Why was the analyst not the target?" I managed to pull him in as an ally against the target. I did not manage to do this entirely but only partly. In this way the analysis was partly successful but also partly a failure. Perhaps this is as life is. That a marriage is partly successful and partly a failure, that in any work role one is partly successful and partly a failure.

So the detachment from Josephine went slowly forward. Divorce proceedings were initiated and some two years later I became divorced from her and I never saw her or her two children again. I had to give her the house in Dulwich as part of the marriage settlement. I know that she sold it and I believe that she moved to become matron at a boys' school in Sussex. I did not know this at the time. The parting was in 1970 and the divorce was in 1972. In 1970 her elder child, Caroline, was aged seven and Richard was four. Years later, forty years later, I had information that Josephine had died. I was not sad but terribly sad to learn that Caroline had killed herself some five years before Josephine's death. Caroline had been such a beautiful child that her death in such circumstances was a tragedy. Richard, her brother, works and lives in China but I have not seen him. I would also like to express my regret to them that I did not fulfil a father's role to them. When one has lived and been intimate with children and their mother, however disastrous the relationship, there remains a bond of affection and I am so sad for Caroline that she had to end life in the way she did—throwing herself off a high building in a town in Sussex. Her life ended in suicide as had been the case with Paul, her father. So of that family only Richard remains and I wish him well with all my heart.

* * *

I want before taking leave of this grim episode to try to understand it more deeply. The way I see it is as follows. When at the age of fifteen, walking on a beach, I suddenly placed all my trust in God, I knew, but was not aware, that there was something wrong with me. What was it? I was a bag of broken bits. Someone had thrown all the pieces of a jigsaw up in the air and they had fallen in a scattered mess on the floor. That was the condition of my soul. The question as to why my soul was in this condition can only be a conjecture. My thinking is that when my mother registered that she was again pregnant, now for the third time, she cursed this invasion of her private body. That pregnancy and birth were a terror for her I am sure because I remember her telling a friend about my sister, Jill's, birth and the huge relief it was when the whole birth process took only five hours "and then it was over". I had a sense that the whole process of being penetrated by the penis, her body being taken over by a foreign invader, and the birth itself was a nightmare for her. I suspect that when she had had one girl and one boy she said to herself that that was enough. These are my conjectures but what is not a conjecture is that when I was born my mother was severely handicapped with a tubercular knee. My earliest memory is of her with her leg in a large white plaster placed upon a stool. My grandmother, my mother's mother, told me that my mother's tubercular knee came at the moment when I was born. To have all the bits inside together I would have needed the gaze of my mother's attention. This is my conjecture as to why I was in bits and why when I was fifteen I sensed that there was something wrong with me and so placed all my trust in God. What I did not know, though, is that it was not God I put my trust in but an idol. Religious mystics have differentiated between godhead and God. Meister Eckhart said that before humans appeared on the planet there was no God, that God was a human creation. Godhead refers to the mysterious fact of existence itself. But I knew nothing about godhead then—it was only later when listening to George Ekbery, which I have described in Chapter Five, when I was twenty-three years old, that I began to make the distinction between God and godhead.

When all is in bits inside then there is a desperate clinging to something outside. I think as a child I clung to Joan Smith, to Mecalina, to María do Carmo, but also to my mother, and when her infidelity was thrust in my face then I flew into the arms of Mother Church. But why did I then fling myself into the arms of Josephine when I knew of her hatred of me and her undisguised rage and fury towards me? I think there was a confluence of two things. There is shame when the psyche is an array of broken bits without any inner cohesion. Intense shame places one at the mercy of another. But Josephine had contempt for my fear-ridden surrender to her savagery. I think there was guilt also. In a primitive state I don't think shame and guilt are separated. They are a single sensation. There was guilt woven into the shame. The guilt was going ahead and letting myself be ordained and making vows of permanent celibacy when I knew that something was wrong. I was determined to be ordained. I was being ordained against ... who? Willi Hoffer, a psychoanalyst, when he heard of a couple getting married used to say, "Who are they marrying against?" So who was I being "ordained against"? I somehow sense that it was against the couple, the fertile couple, the sexual couple. I will leave it there.

* * *

So here I was at 25 Camberwell Grove in my little flat at the top of the building, with the role of guardian to men in prison and also men out of prison. On the ground floor of the building was a large club room and ex-prisoners came there four evenings a week. They had a meal, read the newspapers, and talked with people who offered their time to befriend these men. We had a very strict rule: that the place in which friendship was to be offered was on the club premises and we discouraged severely any social contacts outside. This was a harsh ruling but a necessary one. These men were extremely dependent, and a voluntary helper with good intentions who would invite a man to his home for a meal would then find the man on his doorstep again the following day, and in the end have to slam the door against him; then in vengeful fury the man would return and burgle the well-wisher's home, and this happened frequently. It was only much later that I came to understand better the problem of dependent clinging, and I know that to transform this into an autonomous form of relating is a long, slow, and painful business. Little did I know at this time that I was myself in a dependent clinging relationship and again I was able to disown this part of me into these men.

This work had similarities with my work as a priest. As soon as I was appointed to the job I put an advertisement in the personal column of *The Times* soliciting the services of people who wanted to offer voluntary help to prisoners. I had about fifty replies of which thirty became enrolled as "voluntary associates", and they all underwent a training which was organised by NACRO (National Association for the Care and Resettlement of Offenders). In addition to coming to the club where they offered friendship to these men they also would visit men in prison who were due to be released within a year. The idea behind this was to assist them in their transition into life outside prison. I did this job for two years and in that time developed a considerable interest in prisoners, prison reform, psychopathy, and the sociology of criminality. Apart from husbanding the club in Camberwell Grove I also visited many men in prison, so I became acquainted with many of the prisons in southern England, and I was frequently in court when men were being sentenced. I also had a close association with the Maudsley Hospital which was nearby. In particular I became friendly with John Gunn who later became professor of forensic psychiatry at the Maudsley. He remained a friend and continues so today.

A vivid memory is of one of our members, Frank Tamplin, who had spent about thirty years in prison since the age of sixteen. We had high hopes that this time he might stay out but again he committed a crime. On one of the occasions when he was out of prison he hit an old woman over the head as she was entering her ground floor flat in Pimlico. He was arrested. He was tried at the Old Bailey and he came before Judge Christmas Humphreys, the well-known Buddhist. Frank Tamplin was found guilty and Christmas Humphreys addressed Frank thus:

> I want you to know that I do not blame you for what you have done. I believe that you were in the power of forces stronger than you. I am going to send you to prison but not because I think you are culpable but because I must protect society from danger ...

I was much moved by the humanity of Christmas Humphreys and I wrote to him a few days later to tell him that I had been in court and how much I appreciated what he had said. I received a very gracious reply in which he said it made such a difference to him to know that someone had been in court who was in sympathy with his predicament.

However, as time went on I ran into trouble with my job at the Circle Trust. All went well until my own needs came to the fore. I was answerable to a management committee. When I put the advertisement into *The Times* at the very beginning of my appointment they were annoyed that I had not consulted them but they had the good grace to admit that it had produced an amazing result. Before the advertisement there were about four rather desiccated voluntary helpers. After the advertisement there were thirty voluntary associates and I deployed them to visit men due to be released from prison, to come to the club and help man the club evenings. So again I ran into a problem that has bugged me all my life—I found myself surrounded by pygmies. I have always thought and planned on a large canvas. The cautious attitude of mind, the one that says, "Well, we must be careful", "Look, we might upset people", "Look what people might think", and so on, has always sent a tremor of exasperation through me and, until very recently, a spitting contempt. So the members of this management committee were small people with small minds. Slowly I came to hate the chairman who was self-centred, seeking self-gratification, and, worst of all, had no concern for me, the great me. I was useful to him. I was expected to work enormously long hours, was underpaid, and was treated as the ignorant lackey of the management committee. In the end there was an explosion. My good friend, Guy Braithwaite, who was on the committee, walked out in fury at their antics. I was so furious at their lies and hypocritical behaviour that I gave notice and left.

The thought of returning to Brunel floated before my mind; I gripped the nettle and reapplied to Dan Miller who was the professor of psychology there; he nonchalantly accepted me and so I returned and studied there for a further four years. After I gave up my job with the Circle Trust I was taken on as a psychotherapist at Grendon Prison in Buckinghamshire. This was the only gaol in England that was run on therapeutic community lines and the governor, instead of being a lay-man, as in all other prisons, was a psychiatrist. So I combined doing my degree in psychology at Brunel, continuing my psychoanalysis, and working at Grendon Prison. I did this for about three years and, during this time, I became divorced from Josephine and also began my psycho-analytic training. In other words my analysis continued and I started the training programme at the Institute of Psychoanalysis.

I was inch by inch beginning to pull myself out of the mess I was in. I found myself a house in Clapham which I bought and I did it up. "Did it up" is shorthand for an important experience. While I was work-ing for Wel-Care at the St Giles Centre in Camberwell I one day met Percy. He walked into my office, large, bear-chested, and with an axe in his right hand. The blade of the axe had a small envelope of brown paper kept around it with an elastic band. Apparently this ridiculous small piece of brown paper allowed him legally to carry around what was a dangerous instrument. Percy was one of those rare characters who defies all classification. He was tall, extremely muscular, with a huge hairy chest which all could see because his shirt was always open. He stood there and in his inimitable cockney accent told me that he had come to collect a grant for his common law wife. Normally a cheque and so on had to be made out but I handed him the money in cash. I implicitly trusted him. He never forgot it. We became good friends and when I bought the house in Clapham it was he and I who modernised it. In the university of life he taught me a good deal.

* * *

Percy was one of those rare individuals who cut through all the normal observances of life. One day when he was teaching me how to panel my office with tongue and groove wooden slats I put on a kettle to make a cup of tea.

"Damn," I said, "I've run out of milk."
"I'll get some," he said.
"It's about a ten minute walk to the shop that sells milk," I said.
He beckoned me with his finger and said,
"Come with me."

We stepped out into the street and twenty yards up the road was a little hardware shop. I walked with him and in we both went. A middle-aged woman came forward to the counter.

"Look, luv," said Percy. "Could you let me and me mate 'ere 'ave a drop 'er milk."
"Yes, I can give you a bit."

And a couple of minutes later she reappeared with a small bottle of milk. I offered to pay but she said,

"No, no. That's alright, luv."

On the short walk back Percy said,

"Everything is in compartments these days. Milk from a milk shop. Wood from a hardware. I don't live in these compartments."

291

And he didn't. In the modernisation of that house in Clapham he did everything—the plumbing, the electrical work, the painting, the tiling of the roof. He was highly intelligent and full of practical wisdom. I have never been a handyman but those months with Percy taught me that I was *able* to do these things. I have chosen not to in order to devote my time to other pursuits.

We went often to different hardware shops to buy nails, screws, cement, and other things necessary to modernise the house. When we walked in he would say to the man serving,

> "Hey Bill, could you get me a bag of two inch nails."
> "Hey, my name's not Bill. I'm Sam."
> "Sorry Sam, I'm Percy, could you get me a bag of two inch nails."

In a moment he was on Christian name terms with the man behind the counter and there was something personal between them. He cut through all roles. It was Percy and Sam or Percy and Maureen. Most of us relate to people in roles. For him he lived in a community of friends. He was always getting into trouble for not paying his rates in time. He would be summonsed to court. No magistrate could ever fine him. His transparent openness and good nature defied punishment.

He judged people's characters by their movements and gestures. The way a man picked up his tankard of beer from the counter of the pub told him whether he was mean, generous, genuine, fake, happy, or sad. The same went for the way a man walked. When I was arranging the desk in my study in the Clapham house I was positioning the desk against the wall and my chair with its back to the room. "Don't hide away like that, don't hide away from the world. Face it with courage." He turned the desk around, put the chair behind it so that I would be sitting at the desk but facing out towards the room.

That way in which he cut past people's roles to the human person behind is something which I have always treasured. I believe that this is the way to be happy: for one's own person to be in relation to other persons and that this level of communication is what governs one's social way of being. Percy was limitlessly happy. You only had to see him striding down Camberwell Grove, shirt open, hairy chest, being waved at from every other house. There was no one who did not love Percy.

292

Perhaps there was one exception. He hated the blacks. But it was not just blacks but dole dodgers. I asked him one day why he disliked the West Indians so much. He said, "When I'm working on a building and sweat is pouring down me and I look out and see 'em West Indians lounging around the Social Security office I hate them."

He had no time for moaners, no time for self-pity. He strode into the world and met it with a confident air but one that was full of generosity and warmth. I loved him and had enormous fun in his company. He taught me a great deal and I gained a confidence in my own intuitions through my relationship with him. The idea that wisdom can only be obtained through a formal education is utter rot.[7] I doubt whether Percy had ever read a book on psychology but by observing life and himself he knew more about his fellow men and women than ninety per cent of psychologists, psychiatrists, or psychoanalysts.

I lost touch with him when the Clapham house was finished. I was every day at Brunel and at Grendon Prison and engaged in training at the Institute of Psychoanalysis. He took other jobs and our paths parted but I shall never forget him and he connected me to life in a way which has for ever remained with me. Yet, reluctantly, I have to admit that another reason why we drifted apart was not just that I and he were busy. The reason was that we belonged to different social classes. He was working class and I am upper middle class. I believe that class in Western society embraces a group in terms of their function. In fact sociologists classify individuals into classes according to occupation. It is therefore a group association according to function. Now a relationship which is personal such as I had with Percy cuts across those boundaries. It was more than functional. The class system demarcates a group of people and designates that leisure and social interaction of an intimate nature be chosen from within it, and it exerts a very strong pressure that permeates into the type of food that is preferred, the sort of furnishing in a house, the kind of restaurant enjoyed, and so on. The pressure against the possibility of developing a personal relationship outside the circumference of this class is enormous. This pressure on both of us caused us ultimately to drift apart and never see each other again.

---

[7] "... wisdom comes to all men, and not only to those who are learned. You can find quiet and often great wisdom among very simple people" (Tillich, Paul (1973), *The Boundaries of our Being* (pp. 136–137), London: Collins—Fontana).

At the moment of writing I do not know whether he is still alive or not but as a person he is very much alive, a living presence within me.

Percy was unique. You do not find him anywhere, in any defined section of society. Chesterton understood this:

> The truly great and gorgeous personality, he who talks as no one else could talk and feels with an elementary fire, you will never find this man on any cabinet bench, in any literary circle, at any society dinner. Least of all will you find him in artistic society; he is utterly unknown in Bohemia.[8]

But I did find him at the St Giles Social Service Centre in Camberwell.

* * *

So I was back at Brunel studying psychology, working at Grendon Prison out in Buckinghamshire, and doing my analytic training, and was still in psychoanalysis five days a week with John Klauber at 16 Elsworthy Road. The analysis was certainly the most significant of these activities, the next most significant was my job at Grendon Prison, and the least significant was my attendance at Brunel University. I just could not think of Brunel as an educational establishment. I came to value so much more the teachers and educational experience which I had had at St Edmund's.

Brunel was a cement jungle of building blocks out at Uxbridge. In fact it was used as the setting for the psychiatric prison in the film *Clockwork Orange* and the directors of that film chose their stage-set well. It was more like a factory than a place of learning.

But the focus of my life was on my analysis. John Klauber was a very humane man. He was broad-minded, widely educated, well-read, and contact with him as well as being therapeutic was also the most educative experience that I was undergoing at the time. As I have explained, during the early part I felt so depressed, so hopeless that some days I could hardly drag myself from the Tube station to his consulting room. What was it that slowly enabled me to get better? I often said to him that I thought he had a therapeutic personality. I do not know exactly what I meant by this but I must have sensed a healing quality coming from him to me.

---

[8]Chesterton, G. K. (1906). *Charles Dickens* (p. 256). London: Methuen.

There were certain qualities of character which were decisive for my recovery. I am going to try to enumerate them. He appreciated and put value upon good qualities. When I left Josephine and was feeling terrible both for myself and for leaving her he said to me: "Inwardly she will be relieved that she did not kill you as she had done with her first husband." That was a great comfort but I also think it was true. On another occasion when I was feeling that the bottom had fallen out of my world I said to him: "Things are so bad that I think things can only get better …" But he answered: "But they could get worse." I remember slumping forward inwardly but what he said helped me.

I have no doubt whatever that a generosity of character, a willingness to give in one person is capable to fertilising good qualities in another. He had a generosity which demonstrated itself on one occasion in a tangible form. When the Portuguese Revolution happened on 25th April 1974 all funds from Portugal were frozen and I had no money with which to pay for the analysis. I had been paying him a handsome fee for those times. I struggled to pay and I did so for several months. Once he had seen this he said one day that he would see me free of charge for three months. I mumbled a protest but he said, "No, have it on the house for the next three months …" and he said it with a generous tone that denoted something like *I am glad to do it*. Those words were not said but his tone carried such a message. There was also a certain good-humoured knowledge of the imperfection of life. There were one or two things he said in which he poked fun at some of his more solemn colleagues showing a bonhomous love and acceptance of the failings of men. He also pulled my leg unmercifully. He did not have an ounce of puritanism in him. He loved good food and wine.

His other great quality was his honesty. I once said in outrage when he referred to someone condescendingly: "My God, you are patronising …" and he laughed and said immediately, "Yes, I am aren't I."

So the question that interests me is, how does a quality in one person have an effect upon another? It is that loving qualities go out to those qualities that are inherent in the other. Saying this means that psychoanalysis is just one form in which that therapeutic "fertilisation of qualities" occurs. In fact I believe that an intimate human contact in which these qualities are present would be therapeutically more beneficial than a clinical psychoanalysis in which those qualities were absent.

I cannot say that I loved him but that I had great respect for him and was very fond of him; I was immensely grateful to him, I trusted him entirely and yet … I cannot say that I loved him. Why? It was some trace of cynicism that prevented me from loving him. Somehow he had too much regard for position, for success, for status, for reputation. I find it difficult to put my finger on it. As will appear later I came to know Bob Gosling and I loved him unreservedly. It was not that I could not see faults in Bob but he had some quality that George Ekbery had, that Percy had. I felt a similar love for Susan Marques. It is a quality that evokes in me a total giving. I have felt such love towards people I have never met but only known through reading their books. It is some human quality that stretches beyond the normal compartments in which much of human life is lived and constrained. Somehow John Klauber was too respectful of roles and position. I truly love someone unreservedly when the governing agency in his life is inner spontaneity, the very heart of life itself. Respectfulness of position, deference to status, or the elevation of role, if too great, throttles to a greater or lesser extent the spontaneous spring of life. He was certainly generous-hearted, a generosity from which I benefited and, as I have said, I am deeply grateful to him. He had the spontaneity that I love but that transcendent reality that surpasses and encompasses all within the human scene was not quite there.

There was something about the upper middle class English gentleman that he did not understand. He did not understand the English world in which I had been reared. It is somewhat complicated because he believed that he understood it but I don't think he did. With all his urbane manner and cosmopolitan culture yet … he did not really understand the type of English culture out of which my personality had been carved.

I had a distinct impression that my wild passions shocked him. I have in me some wild Irish recklessness. I say Irish because I suspect that it comes through my mother's influence. I had quite often the sense that he felt, "Who is this wild creature I have given birth to?" I had a sense that he wanted to tame me which is, of course, the very worst thing that someone can do to a person with a wild streak of temperament. But the puzzling thing is that I used also to have the same feeling about my parents, as if they looked at this child in the cradle and asked themselves, "How on earth did we give birth to this bizarre, idiosyncratic creature?"

I definitely have an addictive streak in me and this also shocked him. I would drink a whole bottle of wine, eat every one of a dozen apples I had just bought, stay up all night, read solidly for six hours without a stop, drive for twenty-four hours only stopping for the odd short nap. The sort of soft counsel, "You need to look after yourself", "You must be kind to your body", "We all need a good night's sleep"—all these good, sound, common sense admonitions, although I can see their good advice, are wasted breath on me. I have always flung myself with passionate intensity into what I do and keep going and going at it until I flop to the ground exhausted.

Another way of describing this is to say that I have in me a streak, and more than a streak, of madness. Anyone reading the account of my marriage to Josephine could not doubt it. Klauber was shocked by my madness. He retreated from it. To be able to analyse the sort of madness that I have described it is necessary to enter into relation with it. To stand with shocked horror on the sidelines is no good. I think it was this good-humoured distance of his that prevented me from loving him wholeheartedly. Yet, despite these deficits he had one quality that was so important that it pushed into the shade all the deficits. He made a personal relationship with me and it is the personal bond which undoes psychosis. This is something not emphasised in the psychoanalytic textbooks. I came to know him and he me. Psychosis is the embodiment within the individual of the amorphous group. It is reigned over by a fearsome superego. The "personal" gets under the firing range of the superego. Klauber knew this in his bones and he wrote about it in several of his papers. So I quote just one example:

> The most neglected feature of the psychoanalytical relationship still seems to me to be that it is a relationship: a very peculiar relationship, but a definite one. Patient and analyst need one another. The patient comes to the analyst because of internal conflicts that prevent him from enjoying life, and he begins to use the analyst not only to resolve them, but increasingly as a receptacle for his pent-up feelings. But the analyst also needs the patient in order to crystallize and communicate his own thoughts, including some of his inmost thoughts on intimate human problems which can only grow organically in the context of this relationship. They cannot be shared and experienced in the same immediate way with a colleague, or even with a husband or wife.[9]

---

[9]Klauber, John (1981). *Difficulties in the Analytic Encounter* [*Elements of the Psychoanalytic Relationship and Their Therapeutic Implications*—1976] (p. 46). New York: Jason Aronson.

He knew that no understanding can come about unless first a relationship has been made and this he was able to do. I can imagine a reader saying to him or herself, "But everyone can make a relationship." Nothing could be more untrue. Many, many people are defective in this area. Often psychoanalysts who have this kind of autistic difficulty are not aware of it; some such autistic professionals become psychoanalysts in order to legitimate this inability under the false belief that the analyst is supposed not to make a relationship. One essential component in making a relationship is that the person has to give of himself. John Klauber knew this and gave of himself and this enabled me to give of myself. This was so great a treasure that all his deficits dissolve away in the face of it. And when I say he gave of himself it was not that he said to himself, "I am a psychoanalyst and psychoanalysts should give of themselves so I will give of myself"; nothing could be further from the truth. This giving of himself was a natural endowment. He would have given of himself if he had been an engineer or an architect. He would have favoured Rousseau who said: "It is a bad way of reading another man's heart to conceal one's own."[10]

So I did get much better but the process of recovery continued on long after I had finished my formal analysis with Klauber. It was only later that I became aware first of my narcissism and then of my madness which was derived from it. It was ten years after my analysis was finished, while spending a sabbatical in the south of France, that I became aware of my narcissism. Then slowly my own madness began to swim before my eyes. I had been able to screen myself from my madness by attaching myself to a madness which I was able to define outside myself. I had clearly done this with Josephine, but who became my victim once she was out of the picture? The target then was my mother, my poor mother. I was not going to let her forget her sin and I quote the following lines from a long poem that I wrote:

> A poison viper dwelt inside
> Within my breast a hatred lay
> Filled with venom and foul sludge
> Hidden from the world around
> It bred there like a parasite.

---

[10]Rousseau, Jean-Jacques (1782). *The Confessions, Book Two: 1728–1731* (p. 84). London: Penguin, 1973.

298

But own it in myself did I?
Not a thought of holy me
Harbouring such viciousness.
Envy, greed and jealousy
Belonged to others not to me.

And hated I these vices now
And there they were in her I say
Her very presence did I loathe
And wished her from my hideous sight
Obliterated from my view.

A loathsome sight she was to me
All blame was heaped upon her now
All the vicious things in me
I hated in her character
Loathing even kind affection.

Never was a son so bad
He hated his maternal flesh,
Lest we turn to oldest classics
Of Ancient Greece and find it there
In Agamemnon's fateful breast.

Today I do not blame my mother; that poem which is very long ends with a strong expression of my gratitude to her. I had also blamed John Klauber for not seeing the inner figures of my psyche but, as I have stressed above, I do so no longer because he had and used a far more potent tool to demolish the psychotic structure. He often said that the important emotional development occurred after the analysand had left the consulting room for the last time. He knew this and acted accordingly. He had a faith in the developing inner process. Certainly in my case he was right. The emotional development has never stopped and I thank him with all my heart.

Klauber was shocked by my wildness, my disturbance. Now one reason why he may have been shocked was that I had come to him as a candidate who had been accepted to train as an analyst and he may have thought, as I am sure he did think, that I was too disturbed to be an analyst. Had I come to him just as a patient and not as a candidate in training he may have been less reproachful towards me. Yet I am not really sure that I believe that. There was something about me that shocked him. I call it my wildness. He was alarmed by me. In his urbane, humorous way he glanced down at this reckless creature and believed he could tame me through his gentle wisdom slowly winning me over, but I think what happened was that I became the pseudo-wise one and saw disturbance in others. I *became* him. But in fact Klauber loved spontaneity, a spot of adventure so, although he was alarmed by my wildness, yet there was something about it that he was in sympathy with. In fact colleagues used to comment that I spoke and acted like him. I can still hear myself talking to some of my early patients through him. I can think of one particular young woman who was a bit tempestuous and would sometimes go out slamming the door, and I can still hear myself speaking to her today just as Klauber spoke to me and I know that what I said to her was a gentle rebuke.

So how exactly did that happen? And how did I *become* him? And why was it that I turned with such hatred upon my mother? I put this in because I think it is connected. I think that what I became was the wise one, the sane one, and the mad me was projected outwards but, of course, not having embraced my own madness I had to discharge it. There is no middle way here. Either one embraces what is in one or discharges it—into others, into the body, into sexual activity, into drinking, into addictive behaviour.

Klauber did analyse me but he also hypnotised me. My hatred of my mother was that she had hypnotised me but I think Klauber did also. How did it happen that he hypnotized me? I believe that I installed him as God. What he said was true but because it came to me as a pronouncement from on high the words rang externally in my ears but there was no internal possession of the sentiments that he was giving expression to. The very essence of hypnotism is that you make someone different to what he is. The patient is diagnosed as ... manic, schizoid, phobic, and these are bad states so the hypnotist will make the patient sane but it will be and is an external state of affairs. Klauber used to speak to me of having had a "massive disappointment"— *massive* was a favourite word of his—but this did not give me any subjective experience of such a disappointment; rather, here was a sympathetic father being kind to this little boy. I heard him pronouncing but did not experience it subjectively. I was really a clockwork toy. There was no subjective self. I don't think Klauber realised this, but that is not quite right. He knew in his heart that there was something

300

much more important—to make a relationship with me and that this was the healing factor. In his writings this is muddled with a deification of interpretation. There was a mixture in him therefore, on the one hand, of the analytic tradition in which he had been raised which made interpretation *the* agent of change and, on the other, his own instinctive knowledge that the healing factor lay in the making of a relationship and that this was the foundation out of which understanding and hence interpretations came. This personal relationship which he fashioned between himself and me took on the harsh tyrant God inside me, but—and this is the vital point—it had not gone when the formal analysis came to an end but it did dissolve, bit by bit, later on. And for this I am forever thankful to him. He believed in me; believed that the important work would occur after the formal analysis had finished. Another deficit for me was something which was not only true of him but of most psychoanalysts. I don't believe he ever was on friendly terms with a "Percy". The time of being among Cockneys in East London was such a formative experience for me. That unapproachable something that soars high above all the divisions of class, race, or education was something that was barred off from him. There was a reverence for status that blotted it out.

It was only years later that I began to glimpse the child, the disappointed child in me. And paradoxically I came to realise that the child in the other, first in my father, was also the tyrant God. That is because it becomes the receptacle for this hated part, the disappointed child, within myself. So it is a raging child, a tyrant child and, when I really think about it, the great tyrants of history are all raging children. They throw themselves on the ground and have temper tantrums when they do not get their way—Hitler, Stalin, Napoleon, Saddam Hussein, and … numerous others and, as we all know, they wield enormous power. This power must come from the adult's adoration of the child.

So I got better, or so I believed, and generally I was in a more composed state, so where are we now? I was studying at Brunel, working at Grendon Prison, and having my analysis. I will take each one of these in turn.

I have already mentioned that concrete jungle known as Brunel University. It was only when I was at Brunel that I began to realise what a good education I had had in the Church. I did not feel that what was provided at Brunel constituted an education. The degree was made up of the different components that can be seen in any psychology textbook: perception, motivation, learning theory, cognition, and social psychology. The thing that I found most lacking was an historical or developmental perspective and an absence of underlying principles. There was no sense of the discipline as a whole and what it was out to achieve, how it had come about, how it broke off from philosophy in the late nineteenth century; and no study of the founding fathers of psychology: William James, Wundt, and so on. We were not encouraged to read the works of a great mind but to read pages 19–25 of George Herbert Mead's *Mind, Self and Society* or four pages from Freud's *Psychopathology of Everyday Life*. We were handed out four photocopied pages of Tinbergen's book on instincts or Hull's exposition of stimulus response theory. The only lectures that stand out in my memory were those of Elliott Jaques and John Vaizey. Elliott was the professor of social science at Brunel; he gave some lectures on his theory of work and I found those illuminating. John Vaizey, later Lord Vaizey, was professor of economics, and although economics was not one of my subjects, I nevertheless went to some of his lectures which were excellent. Neither of these lecturers did I need to go to as their subject matter was not part of what I was required to learn for my degree.

The absence of education so depressed me that I decided to go and do some serious reading. The library was not well equipped enough for what I wanted so I managed to get a reading ticket to the British Museum and I went there all day three days a week where I read and read, taking copious notes. I read sociology more than psychology. I read nearly all the works of Max Weber and Emile Durkheim and also of Karl Marx. I read Talcott Parsons. Max Weber's *The Protestant Ethic and Spirit of Capitalism* has always stayed with me as a deeply influential book. But I also read Durkheim's *Rules of the Sociological Method, Suicide,* and *The Elementary Forms of the Religious Life,* all of which were very influential. I came, through reading these works, to grasp the moving principles in society. I did also read some of the in-people who were capturing attention in the late 1960s like Erving Goffman's *Asylums* and *Stigma,* but nearly all my time was spent on the classics of the social sciences. I also read Franz Brentano's *Psychology from the Empirical Standpoint* and Rancurello's biography of Brentano. He had been a Catholic priest but then left the Church. In the 1870s he became professor of philosophy at Vienna University and I was fascinated to discover that Freud had attended his lectures for two years. I later wrote a paper entitled *Was Freud influenced by Brentano?*[11] I was sure that Freud had been influenced by Brentano but was interested to know why he hardly referred to him, and came to the conclusion that he did not want to be thought a disciple of "that old-fashioned Aristotelian" as Brentano was dubbed at the University; but Brentano's notion of a intentional relation to inner and outer events seemed to me to be the foundation stone of psychology and, as I later came to realise, was the same as that espoused by Melanie Klein. Brentano had been Husserl's mentor and while I only have a passing acquaintance with Husserl I believe his insistence that even receptivity is an active process probably owes its origins to Brentano. This sense that I actively enter into relation with the formative events of my life is what characterises the religious philosophical outlook as opposed to one that is deterministic. At Brunel I had been plunged into stimulus-response theory where we are all like wax tablets upon which are impressed the events surrounding us. I came more and more to distrust this outlook and I believe that Freud himself moved slowly from the determinist model of the mind to one that I call philosphico-religious.

I regret not having read Auguste Comte and Herbert Spencer, or William James or Wündt, but I read a lot and I came to understand the principles behind sociology which has always remained for me a natural perspective. The British Museum opened at nine in the morning; I would arrive by car about ten minutes before nine and line up in a little queue of other readers and, when the gates opened, would drive in and park free of charge in the forecourt. I would stay there all day reading and taking notes. I would go out for a quick lunch in a small café in Russell Street and then back into the reading room. It was a very good atmosphere for study. When I arrived I would fill out application slips for the books I wanted to read with my seat number on them and then go and sit as slowly the attendants would bring me the books. It was a wonderful service and absolutely free of charge. I am sure today it would not be so easy to obtain a reader's ticket and I am certain that free parking in the courtyard would not be possible. I am not sure whether knowing that many famous scholars, like Karl Marx, had studied there in that same room encouraged an atmosphere of scholarship, but perhaps it did. I used to see the same people around me each time I went there and I imagined scholarly works coming to life in some of the seats nearby.

---

[11]Published as a chapter in my book *The Blind Man Sees* in 2004 by Karnac.

When I am writing this I begin to think that I am quite well read but I never thought that was the case at the time. I always considered that I was very poorly educated. I said this once to John Klauber in one of my sessions and he said he thought this was not true but, just as when he said pejorative things about me, his statement did not change my view. Today I think I am quite well read and probably better read than most of my psychoanalyst colleagues but I am not a scholar. If I am anything I am a thinker rather than a scholar. Whenever I read something I find myself asking questions and when I have found the answer then another question opens up and I try to follow the trail but its pathway is often to be answered in another discipline of thinking. Compartmentalisation sets the boundary to the scholar's territory and this has never been my interest. For me one of the great joys of reading Karl Marx, Freud, Darwin, Nietzsche, Tolstoy, and other giants of the nineteenth century is that they were thinkers and you cannot really define them by a discipline. Darwin was a biologist, Marx an economist, Freud a neurologist but they all stood outside these disciplines of thought. They traced deeper principles that ran through biology, psychology, sociology, economics, or philosophy.

* * *

At the same time as being at Brunel I was working part-time at Grendon Prison. When working at the Circle Trust I had come to know Margaret Miller-Smith who was the psychiatric social worker at Grendon Prison and also ran an outpost, a sort of halfway house, for men who had just come out of prison. She suggested that I come to Grendon and work there as a psychotherapist on one of the wings. At that time the governor was Dr Bill Gray who was a psychiatrist. He was a dour Scotsman who ran the prison on very liberal lines. When the Mountbatten Report came out after the famous escape from Wormwood Scrubs of George Blake in 1966, all prisons containing men requiring high security had to have closed circuit television cameras and much greater security arrangements, but Bill Gray refused to install any such measures in his prison, and because he was an under-secretary of state and had become something of a law unto himself the Home Office allowed his liberal principles to continue. Under his guardianship no man ever escaped or even tried to escape. They respected what Bill Gray did on their behalf and refused to compromise him with the Home Office. Some may think this a somewhat romantic view but the fact that he knew that there was a lot of scapegoating of prisoners and that he treated them with respect, although firmly, created among the criminals a response of support for him.

In those days one of my pleasures was to read *The Times* in the morning. One day a week I stayed the night at the hostel in the grounds of the prison but could not obtain *The Times* in the morning. I mentioned this casually once to one of the prisoners and he said, "I'll make sure you get it in future ..." and, sure enough, from then on *The Times* was delivered for me on the morning I was there. I have no idea how this prisoner achieved this for me. He certainly managed what no other functionary outside the prison walls had been able to do.

So I was assigned to A Wing, which was run by a psychiatrist, Dr Phil Scott. He was a quiet but rather unhappy man. On the Wednesday night when I was at Grendon he and I would go into Oxford and have dinner together. We mostly discussed psychotherapy: what it could achieve and what it couldn't, but he also discussed his private difficulties a good deal which were considerable.

Many of the men on the wing were serving long sentences and were in for serious crimes. I had already developed an interest in criminology and the sociology of deviance when I was at the Circle Trust. I now became more interested in the psychology of these men and, in particular, of the condition which has been described as *psychopathy*. I read the psychoanalytic literature on the subject: Freud's *Criminals from a Sense of Guilt*, Edward Glover's *The Roots of Crime*, and Melanie Klein's insights into the problem of criminality. I also read some of the papers of Dr Hyatt Williams. However, none of these works seemed quite to hit the mark for me. They somehow seemed to me to be written too much "from the outside". I did not have the sense that any of these authors had understood it from within. I have only ever truly been fired by writers who understand "from within". Tolstoy has described this perfectly when talking of Vronsky's attitude to art:

> He had a talent for understanding art and probably, with his gift for copying, he imagined he possessed the creative powers essential for an artist. After hesitating for some time which style of painting to take up—religious, historical, genre, or realistic—he set to work. He appreciated all the different styles and could find inspiration in any of them, but he could not conceive that it was possible to

be ignorant of the different schools of painting and to be inspired directly by what is within the soul.[12]

Then one day my nose led me to read *Wuthering Heights* by Emily Brontë, and within the pages of that fantastic novel I was sure that Emily had drawn with amazing accuracy and sympathy the inner contours of the psychopath's character. I thought that Heathcliff was a psychopath and that Emily had understood him "from the inside". My head was reeling when I finished the novel and I lingered lovingly over the beauty of the last two sentences of the novel:

> I sought, and soon discovered, the three head-stones on the slope next the moor—the middle one, grey, and half buried in heath— Edgar Linton's only harmonized by the turf and moss, creeping up its foot—Heathcliff's still bare.
>
> I lingered around them, under that benign sky; watched the moths fluttering among the heath and hare-bells; listened to the soft wind breathing through the grass; and wondered how anyone could ever imagine unquiet slumbers, for the sleepers in that quiet earth.

What beautiful writing. Apart from *Anna Karenin* and *War and Peace*, *A Child Possessed* by R. C. Hutchinson, and *The Hidden River* by Storm Jameson, no novel has had such a powerful impact upon me.

At that time I was moving towards finishing my analytic training. I was already treating my second training case when the Institute of Psychoanalysis asked me if I would give a paper at a day's symposium on *The Mind of the Criminal*. I gladly accepted and wrote a paper entitled *The Response Aroused by the Psychopath*, which was based partly on Emily Brontë's psychological understanding of psychopathy. The paper was well received and I later sent it to the editor of the *International Review of Psycho-Analysis*. The paper was accepted and published in 1980. It is a paper that over the years continued to attract attention and interest and it has been published recently in a book called *The Mark of Cain*.[13] I think that day's symposium must have been in 1976 or about

---

[12]Tolstoy, L. N. (1986). *Anna Karenin* (p. 491). London: Penguin.
[13]Reid Meloy, J. (2001). *The Mark of Cain—Psychoanalytic Insight and the Psychopath*. Hillsdale, NJ: Analytic Press.

that time. The other two speakers were Hyatt Williams and Mervin Glasser and the day was chaired by Red O'Shaughnessy. A week or two before the symposium Hyatt, Mervin, and I met at Red's house to discuss the day. I told Hyatt that I was basing my paper on Heathcliff and quoted that amazing statement of Catherine:

> It would degrade me to marry Heathcliff, now; so he shall never know how I love him; and that not because he's handsome, Nelly, but because he's more myself than I am. Whatever our souls are made of, his and mine are the same ...

And a few minutes later she says,

> I cannot express it; but surely you and everybody have a notion that there is, or should be an existence of yours beyond you. What were the use of my creation if I were entirely contained here? My great miseries in this world have been Heathcliff's miseries, and I watched and felt each from the beginning; my great thought in living is himself. If all else perished, and *he* remained, I should continue to be; and if all else remained, and he were annihilated, the universe would turn to a mighty stranger. I should not seem a part of it. My love for Linton is like the foliage in the woods. Time will change it, I'm well aware, as winter changes trees. My love for Heathcliff resembles the eternal rocks beneath—a source of little visible delight, but necessary. Nelly, I *am* Heathcliff—he's always in my mind—not as a pleasure any more than I am a pleasure to myself—but as my own being—so don't talk of our separation again—it is impracticable.

And later in the book when Catherine has just died, Heathcliff says of her: I *cannot* live without my life! I *cannot* live without my soul.

When I quoted those words of Catherine, "I *am* Heathcliff," Hyatt's eyes gleamed with excitement. He knew the passage well and was excited by my discovery of them.

So I spent about three or four years at Grendon Prison. I learned a great deal and the time there was recuperative for me. I was not under any pressure and Phil Scott's kind companionship at lunchtime down in The Fox pub nearby and on Wednesday evenings at dinner in Oxford endowed the whole experience with a healing atmosphere.

There is one incident that stands out in my mind. One prisoner had failed to comply with his duty to clean the corridors of the wing, and the staff had decided that he should be returned to a normal prison. In the staff meeting there was a general belief that this prisoner was slacking. With these intentions in mind the staff went into a big therapeutic meeting where all the staff and all the prisoners met together in one big room. The prisoner was challenged for not having done his duty. He started in a rather shambling way to make excuses which no one believed but there was one very down to earth prison officer who spoke up in his defence. This prevented his removal to another prison. In the staff meeting afterwards his fellow officers turned upon this officer and he firmly but quietly went through the excuses that the prisoner had made and showed that he quite likely had good reasons for not being able to fulfil his task. I admired this prison officer enormously. The temptation to "go with the crowd" must have been enormous. I am full of admiration for the courage of someone who defies the pressure of the crowd. The conscience of that officer invited him to do what was right and not what would be comfortable for him.

So finally I finished my degree at Brunel and I got an Upper Second. This was in 1975. A year later, having done my infant observation and seen my two analytic cases, I finished all the requirements for an analytic candidate and in February 1977 I was elected an associate member of the British Psychoanalytic Society. Three years later I presented a clinical case before fifteen senior analysts and, having passed that hurdle, I was elected to full membership of the society. So this apprenticeship in psychology phase of my life was now completed and a new era began.

* * *

I had left the Church in 1968 at the age of thirty. I drove away from the presbytery in Tollington Park in north London, stripped inwardly and outwardly of all self-respect, on a date towards the end of February. Nine years later I was a qualified psychoanalyst. In that same year of 1977 I was appointed as senior psychologist in the Adult Department of the Tavistock Clinic. A year after that I was appointed chairman of the psychology discipline in the Adult and Adolescent Departments of the Tavistock Clinic. Again, in 1977 I finished my own personal analysis with Dr John Klauber.

An event occurred in 1974 which caused much turbulence in my family of origin: the Carnation Revolution in Portugal on 25th April. All my family's assets were in jeopardy while the almost weekly changes in government meant that any day the port trade might be nationalised and my mother, father, brother, sisters, and numerous cousins would lose everything. It did not happen but it caused a panic. This panic included me as I had financed the expensive training at the Institute of Psychoanalysis on money borrowed from an English bank but guaranteed by assets in Portugal. The day after the revolution I received a letter from the bank asking me to make good their loan to me immediately. All this caused some serious family rows and things were done and said that injured people considerably. I was guilty of acting under panic but so also were other members of the family. We all rushed to try to preserve our own little plot of land. Those members of the family, like myself, who had assets in the business but did not work in it felt that our position was ignored by those in the business. Those in the business felt that the threat to their livelihood and work was ignored by those of us who had professional lives outside the business. Both positions were right. In crisis we did not pull together but rather panicked and let individual selfishness rule our behaviour. It was not something about which any of us can be proud. Regrettably I cannot think of one family member who in that crisis gave a lead towards solidarity. There was no single mature figure who was able to "hold" things, think, stand back a bit, rather than act under impulse. As individuals we were all emotionally frail and driven by an attitude that was isolationist and paranoid. I have all my life looked desperately for emotional strength, for a strong father. I neither had this in my father nor in any other member of the family.

I did not find it in John Klauber either. Ultimately I have had to find it in myself. There is no doubt that after long years, as a consequence of the emotional crises that I have passed through, combined with an attempt to assimilate them, I have acquired some of the emotional strength I was looking for in others. I had to look within and find it there. On the walls of a monastery at Puebla de Sanabria in Asturias in Spain is a notice with these words: *"Let us occupy ourselves not with envying others but with finding in ourselves that which we envy."*

So I had to find it in myself. My conscience has always reproached me when I have acted in a cowardly way. I have not felt satisfied with myself when I have shirked difficult confrontations. My conscience has not only reproached me but also invited me to take up the challenge, however difficult it is. Today I can give myself a reasonably good mark in this sphere. I do have some moral courage. I started off on life's journey very deficient in this regard but have struggled and struggled to do better. With each act of moral courage I gained strength. Today I am proud of what I have managed.

I started off in my adult life as a timid little shrimp but today I am more robust. Acts of courage and acts of true inner generosity are what strengthens an individual's character.

This account is not a record of all my life but rather it is an emotional autobiography. So I will select those events that have slowly enabled me to build my character into something that I can view with respect.

* * *

One day in July 1976 Jane Temperley rang me:

> "Neville, could you give our social workers a year's lecture course on psychoanalytic theory?"
> "When do they start?"
> "The third week in September."
> "How many lectures would it entail?"
> "Well, there are three terms: ten lectures each term."
> "So a course of thirty lectures?"
> "Yes, that's right."
> "Yes, I'll do it."

So there it was. I was committed to giving thirty lectures to social workers who came one day a week to the Tavistock to be instructed in the mysteries of psychoanalysis. Two months later I found myself in one of the soulless classrooms on the ground floor of the Tavistock with thirty expectant faces looking me in the eye. Week after week I gave my lecture which would last three quarters of an hour to an hour and then there was discussion for three quarters of an hour or half an hour. In the week prior to the lecture I studied until at least three in the morning preparing the next lecture. I gave three introductory lectures followed by seven on Freud. The following term I gave lectures on Freud's early followers: Jung, Jones, Abraham, and Ferenczi. In the last term I gave nine lectures on Melanie Klein, Wilfred Bion, Donald Winnicott, and Michael Balint, and ended with a lecture summing up my own personal position. The lectures in that first year were extremely poor. I was just one step in front of my audience and sometimes one step behind. I was regurgitating the theories as I had read them during the previous week. The linkage between the theory and clinical practice was tenuous in the extreme. There was one bright social worker who criticised my lectures unmercifully and I felt small and humiliated. After this first year I continued to give a series of thirty lectures under different auspices and each year they improved. Slowly I digested the theories so they became personal possessions instead of robotic repetitions. When I started these lectures I had every word of what I intended to say typed out in front of me. In the last year I had in front of me just a blank table with a book. If I were lecturing on Freud I would have a volume of his in front of me, if on Melanie Klein a volume of hers, and so on. I never opened the book but the presence of the book which I would touch from time to time served as a magic talisman against some primaeval fear that I would suddenly find myself empty-handed or empty-minded.

These lectures in that first year had been to social workers alone and came under the social work discipline, but the following year the Tavistock asked me if I would undertake to give a series of thirty lectures to the mental health professionals generally. These were made up of social workers, psychologists, psychiatrists, and academics. These lectures had been given by John Padel for a number of years but he was retiring and had recommended me as his replacement. As the lectures yearly improved I became aware of the fact that they were being appreciated and the discussions after each lecture demonstrated this to me. These lectures had one virtue: I spoke always in simple language. This was not because I spoke down to my audience but I spoke only in the language that I understood. I did not understand these strange terms: ego, superego, projective identification, identification, cathexis, transitional object, idealisation, and a whole panoply of weird jargon. A six-year-old child spoke inside me clamouring that the adult explain these terms to him. The adult, who seemed to understand what the child needed, read the terms again and again in the writings of the authors who had invented them until the child began to understand. I spoke to my audience in language which the child within me was able to understand. Something of my father's unsophisticated simplicity spoke from inside me and this was appreciated just as I had appreciated my father teaching me about nature when I was a child. I always have in mind "a six-year-old child". Why six? It was when I was six that I returned from Canada and fell into the arms of my father's loving tuition. My father loved teaching his young son about butterflies, about birds, about *bichos* of all kinds. I love teaching and I believe my father passed on to me this treasure.

At the time I was thanked again and again for speaking in language which was jargon-free, and in the thirty-five years since that time I have been praised in similar terms with striking regularity. This convinces me that people must be hungry for someone to explain psychological terms in ordinary language; that they do not any more than me understand the arcane terms which are used with such fluency by so many mental health professionals. So there is the six-year-old child, yet there is an intelligent adult who is able to decipher these weird terms and explain them to the child. This ability comes neither from my father nor from my mother. Where does it come from? It is clearly part of that spirit of inquiry that I mentioned earlier but I think another quality informs it. Professional jargon fashions an isolated world. There is in me a deep desire to see the parts as sections of a whole and this desire is only achieved in the language of the common man and the common woman and the common child.

I also became convinced that it was possible to convey something of the analytic process by the *way* I spoke about the subject matter. Many analysts—for instance Wilfred Bion—stated, almost dogmatically, that psychoanalysis can only be experienced in the consulting room. I think the full experience can only be undergone there but glimpses of the experience can also be had in the lecture hall and also in many other social situations. I became convinced that if I lectured from my own personal experience and conviction, the audience also gained a personal experience and insight which is the goal of psychoanalysis. What they gained was less concentrated than in the consulting room but nevertheless quite definite and it was the same experience although in more diluted form.

There are two aspects to human experience: the events themselves which we pass through, and our assimilation of them into ourselves so that we possess the experiences rather than be possessed by them. The giving of these lectures was the beginning for me of taking inner possession of the experience of being analysed. Later I was to develop a theory that encompassed something wider and deeper than the analytical experience itself: a theory that encompassed both the whole of my

312

life and of the whole of mankind's evolutionary and historical development on the planet. Two things have been enormously important to me:
to make contact with my own experience and observation and to think
for myself a conceptual framework that represents it. So the yearly giving of these lectures at the Tavistock afforded me the opportunity to
conceptualise some of the tumults that I had passed through in the previous twenty years.

* * *

I was respected now in my profession. The lectures I was giving yearly
at the Tavistock were praised. Later these were turned into a book, *The
Analytic Experience* and this received the highest praise and got a wonderful review in the *British Journal of Psychiatry*:

> If this *Journal* invited reviewers to nominate their Books of the Year,
> *The Analytic Experience* would head my list. A new book always
> holds promise of treasures in store, but sometimes the gold is
> sparse, or the reader has to struggle with turgid prose and impen-
> etrable jargon to discover the buried bounty. Cause for celebration
> indeed that psychoanalysis is so lovingly and lucidly exposed by
> Symington in a work that is a joy to read from beginning to end,
> which clarifies areas shrouded in mystique and confusion that have
> been alien territory to many who spend their professional life con-
> cerned with the minds of men.
>
> For many years Symington was on the staff of the Tavistock
> Clinic, and his lectures to mental health professionals attending
> training courses there influenced the development of many young
> psychiatrists. This book is the result of these lectures, and should
> ensure that his influence will continue to reach a wide audience,
> although it must be a cause for regret that he has now emigrated to
> Sydney. A former Director of the Camden Psychotherapy Unit and
> a member of the London Institute of Psychoanalysis, Symington's
> extensive experience informs his exposition of psychoanalysis as
> it affects both patient and analyst, and many clinical examples
> are used to illuminate the nature of the psychoanalytic process.
> Humanity and humour shine through this book, which amply
> demonstrates the author's rare gift for communication, rendering
> the complex simple without ever being simplistic.

313

The student looking for a basic introduction to Freud's theory and the later developments of psychoanalysis could not do better, but experienced therapists too can benefit from this simple restatement of the familiar and the obvious. Free Association Books deserve an accolade for producing this text, and at the modest paperback price it is a bargain not to be missed. A must for the library, for psychotherapy reading lists, and for every clinician who is interested in the function of the mind and the potent therapeutic promise of the doctor/patient relationship.

I could not have asked for a more praiseworthy review than that.

So all was well—or was it? All looked well externally. When things look well externally they can be worn as a sort of cloak that makes one feel alright inside also—like donning an overcoat on a cold day. It makes you feel warm. I felt alright and yet I was mad. For instance I have related the madness in whose grip I was firmly entrenched in my marriage to Josephine, yet at this time, ten to a dozen years later, I did not know of that madness. For instance, John Klauber had said to me: "You have married a mad woman."

Yet that was just his external statement. I neither knew it nor felt it. This could only mean that I was still possessed by the madness rather than having taken possession of it. I am now writing this more than thirty-five years later when I know the madness. The rest of this account then is the story of how I came to realise this and how my life unfurled to allow that realisation to occur. But before I do that I want to select out those elements that might have been visible to a perceptive outsider.

* * *

I have already mentioned the first element: I hated my mother. Before asking why, I want to ask the wider question: is hatred of someone always a sign of madness? I believe it is. I want to try to examine this from my own behaviour in relation to my mother. I first want to be kind to myself and ask whether there was any understandable reason for my violent hatred of my mother. I think there was. I have described the shock to my system when my mother's lesbian affairs were suddenly fired uninvited into my soul. I believed that this had driven me into the Church and I attributed all my ills to it. But there is more to it than that.

An incident that stands out in my mind is something that occurred in about 1962 between my mother and my sister, Jill. I was still at St Edmund's at that time. Jill had translated from the Italian a book for the Faith and Fact Series. It was a book on some Christian theme but I have forgotten the title of it. My mother had done some of the typing for her. By this time Jill was divorced from her husband, Dick Dean, but she still carried his surname and was known by it so the manuscript went to press with the author's name and then the translator's name: Jill Dean. My mother bullied Jill with all her power to make her change the designation to Jill Symington. At the time Jill felt very pressured by my mother and she wrote to me about it. I encouraged her to put her name as she wanted it to be, which she did. The book appeared with translator, Jill Dean. The factor I want to emphasise is my mother's determination to make Jill do something against her own will.

So that was one incident. The other is this. I was ordained a priest on 23rd May 1964 in Westminster Cathedral. The following day I offered my First Mass at the Convent of the Sacred Heart in Brighton. Then I drove with my mother through France and Spain back to Portugal where I then offered a Missa Nova at the little baroque church at Nevogilde in Oporto. We must have taken four or five days on that journey back to Portugal. After the initial flurry of conversation a total emptiness opened up between us. I had nothing to say to her. There was no bond of communication between us. There was something elemental lacking. It was this empty presence that I hated and the extreme control that was demonstrated in that incident with Jill is the manifestation and outcome of that emptiness. It was the hollow drum that I hated. Yet that is not the right way to put it. The hatred is the emptiness in action. It is totally meaningless. Emptiness, hatred, and no meaning are different vertices of the same thing. Hatred, I believe, is the manifestation of inner emptiness. This is why people devote so much energy to controlling others: to fill up the emptiness inside.

When there is emptiness there is no relationship and then a substitute for a relationship develops. The question here is, why? The answer to this is that the passion to survive kicks in. So all the contract theories are right in one way and yet profoundly wrong in another. They are based on the idea that people enter into relations with one another for the sake of survival. This, though, is external relating: I need this other human being for my own survival and he or she are bent to serve my own needs. These needs become more and more intensified the greater the emptiness.

Now my hatred for my mother was based upon this emptiness. Somehow, in that encounter with my mother on that journey the emptiness came out and stared me in the face. It was the same emptiness that confronted me for two and a half years in the forced association with Tony Beagle. And yet ... it was me doing the hating. Is it that when the emptiness in the other stares me in the face it reveals the emptiness within myself? And in the hatred is the emptiness, the meaninglessness of an existence based purely upon survival? And that on the contrary, love is the manifestation of shared being. A mother and father have not only the biological task of generating new life but also of communicating being to the newborn infant. Communicating being is a synonym for contemplation. I think my mother's controlling behaviour was the fruit of this emptiness.

I have within me communicative life but also emptiness, hatred, meaninglessness, and isolation. How to convert the negatives into the positive? It is to realise this black hole. Such a realisation transforms it.

It is clear from the account of my marriage to Josephine that I was mad. What I need now to relate is how I began in slow steps to realise it and to transform it into something fruitful.

* * *

I remember once when I was walking stolidly along the corridor on the fourth floor of the Tavistock I passed Monica Lanman who was one of the trainees. As she heard my solid plodding she said, "You walk with such a reliable step. I would trust you with any patient ..."

I also received numerous compliments from fellow members of the Independent Group. I was becoming their darling boy. I was on the executive committee which was responsible for running the Tavistock and yet ... somehow I did not really feel part of it. I had shamefully hidden my priesthood away and yet it was so important to me. It had been the driving force in my young life. It had been my vocation, my life— but where was it? For the most part my colleagues conspired to solidify that repression. There was only one colleague who acted differently, Bob Gosling. He was chairman of the Tavistock when I first arrived.

I had started lecturing at the Tavistock in 1976. The following year a post came up for a senior psychologist in the Adult Department and

Harwant Gill pressed me to apply for it. I was at this time already director of the Personal Consultation Centre at the Camden Council for Social Service which was confusingly in Tavistock Place just near Russell Square. I decided I would apply but I was in an ambivalent state. I was not panting to get the job. If I got it then that would be good but if I did not it would be no disaster. This was a different state of mind for me. When I first left the priesthood and was disinherited of any acceptable social position I was desperate to get into jobs of some status and, for the most part, did not get the ones I applied for. My interviewers were right not to appoint me. I have since always thought it a mistake to appoint someone to a job who is desperate to get it. Someone in that position convinces himself that he will be able to do the job whereas in fact he cannot. So I went for my interview in a room that was to become familiar to me, on the left hand side at the end of the corridor on the fourth floor of the Clinic. I found myself in a room with about fifteen psychologists and one psychiatrist. The psychiatrist was David Malan, the expert on brief psychotherapy. Among the psychologists were Peter Hildebrand, John Boreham, Fred Balfour, Harwant Gill, and others whom I was to come to know quite will over the next eight years.

I had been told that I would be asked to present some clinical work with a patient. At the Personal Consultation Centre I had treated for two years a man aged thirty-three who was mentally handicapped. He had an IQ of 59, or so it was alleged. The assumption among most psychoanalysts and therapists basing themselves on a psychoanalytic understanding was that it was not possible to treat someone of low intelligence. It was generally thought that someone could not be treated by this method unless they had the sort of intelligence that would enable him to pass creditably through a university course. When I came across this man I felt sure that he could respond to psychoanalytical interpretations so I took him on and treated him once weekly for two years.

I am not sure what it is but I have always distrusted *dogmatisms* of this nature. I think they buttress *comfort*. It is as if the underlying statement is: *make comfort your first priority* and so don't take on someone of low intelligence. It will take more effort. It will disrupt your comfort zone. I also had to stretch down to simple imagery in order to talk meaningfully to him.

When I went for my interview I decided to present this patient. I spoke in an impassioned way for an hour or so as I described the adventure.

As I left the room Peter Hildebrand led me back down the corridor and said, "Very impressive." I got the job and so I went for my interview with Bob Gosling who was chairman of the whole Clinic.

I expected to be with him for ten minutes or a quarter of an hour at the most. He sat back comfortably and talked. I soon realised it was not going to be a ten minute formality. He was going to come to know this new recruit. He asked me about my time in the Church, what it was like coming out of it, how I found life within the psychoanalytical world, and we had a discussion about the modern generation's hatred of inequality.

He said: "We cannot talk of supervision groups any more. Now they are clinical 'workshops' ..." and he smiled. He had a deep throaty voice, like my old gardener José, and he stood up as I was leaving and said, "It's good to have a few oddballs around the place." Bob never flattered. I had not been in my new role for long before he asked if I could join him in running a lecture series entitled *Human Growth and Development*. The first term was devoted to childhood, the second to adolescence, and the third to adulthood. It was the section on adulthood that we worked together on. He said to me, "All these fellows here are stuck with their mouths on the nipple. I want to drag them out into the adult world."

Then he asked me to give at least two lectures on the place of religion in cultural and individual life. Even then I eschewed anything that touched too closely on my personal journey through Catholicism and the priesthood. I remember I gave one of my lectures on why Protestantism had given rise to capitalism. It was a resumé of Max Weber's *The Protestant Ethic and the Spirit of Capitalism*.[14] That was one of the books I had read in the reading room of the British Museum. It interested me a lot because his thesis in essence was that the state of not knowing whether you were one of those predestined for salvation or damnation was too great a burden on the human spirit for the average person, but whereas within Catholicism the signs of being saved were in the sacramental signs, within Protestantism which had dispensed with these an alternative sign was needed. Accumulation of wealth became the sign that the individual relied upon to believe he had found favour with God. This had only come about indirectly. Protestantism, especially

---

[14]Weber, Max (1971). *The Protestant Ethic and the Spirit of Capitalism*. Translated by Talcott Parsons. London: Unwin University Books.

in the Calvinist variety, condemned pleasure, so the devout Christian worked hard and did not spend his money but saved it and so a healthy bank account meant you would, at death, be in the bosom of God.

* * *

I have left out, however, the most momentous event of all. In September 1973 when I started my academic seminars at the Institute of Psychoanalysis I met at a seminar on dreams taken by Charlotte Balkanyi another trainee, Dr Joan Cornwell. We soon established a close friendship and liaison and in December of the following year we married at The Mint in Melbourne, Australia, which was her home town. We married on 21st December and we conceived we believe our first baby four days later on Christmas night. I have said little or nothing about this new love affair. Joan has been my companion for forty years. A whole new chapter in my life opened out and it requires a new book and a new outlook to describe it. A little over nine months later our dear son, Andrew, was born at Queen Charlotte's Hospital in London. As I saw the little slimy child being wiped and swaddled after an emergency Caesarian operation I slipped out to a café for a snack and while there wrote this poem:

THE FIRST BORN

The quiet voice that tells
Of birth by Caesar's section.
There is no time to fear it
Or manage comprehension.

The mother lay there silent,
Cheated of her labour,
But how could she resent it
When it comes as infant's saviour?

For labour to a woman
Is proof of womanhood.
The surgeon's rustling haste
Forgets what no mother could.

The father sits alone,
Imagining blood and hustle,

319

And knowing that his dear one
Lies oblivious of all the bustle.

The nurse appears and says
"Do you want to see your son?"
He looks at the screwed-up face
And barely believes it's come.

The mother comes around
And the little baby sees
The expression on her face
No lines on earth could seize.

He's growing tough and strong,
No need to fear he's weak.
It's Mum and Dad who will be frail
When he is at his peak.

In the year 1980 I had been married for six years. I was now the proud father of two boys, Andrew and David. We lived the first five years of our married life in a lovely Georgian house in Hackney. Joan was a consultant child psychiatrist at the Royal Free Hospital and I had eight sessions at the Tavistock Clinic. I was in a different space to where I had been ten years earlier, at the point where I was leaving Josephine and starting my analysis with John Klauber.

Our younger son, David, was born at the end of 1979 while we were still in our home in Hackney. In the middle of the following year we moved to a large house in Hampstead, a three minute walk from the Tavistock. Judging by externals nothing could have been better. We had two lovely young boys, we lived in a large and beautiful house in Hampstead with a large garden that had in it a huge black poplar tree that jangled as the wind passed through its leaves, leaving a musical note as distant from other trees' leaves as the violin is from the piano. I had a very agreeable job at the Tavistock. I was working in the Adult Department and was for a time chairman of the psychology discipline in both the Adult and Adolescent Departments, seeing patients, supervising trainees, and giving my lectures I had my private practice in a lovely room at the front of the house. Andrew was in a primary school and I could walk him up to it in Fitzjohn's Avenue in under ten minutes and return to my consulting room. If a patient cancelled I just had time to walk down to the swimming pool at Swiss Cottage, propel my body along my chosen lane, finish twenty laps, have a shower, dry myself, and walk back to the house in time for my next patient.

Joan also had her private patients whom she saw in another lovely room and had her job as consultant child psychiatrist at the Royal Free Hospital which was only a five minute drive away.

We were both respected and I think in general well liked. I could see the next thirty years stretching ahead of us like a narrowing path across a near and distant landscape but some spirit of discontent began to worry away at me. Things were too comfortable. It all seemed too good. Somehow I sensed that everything was not right. Cardinal Newman said, "I have never sinned against the Light." I could certainly not say that but I have never been able to blot out the Light when it starts glimmering. I think I have built my life around it. It is its emotional centre.

So Bob Gosling encouraged me to welcome into my conscious mind and into my conduct my past vocational life in the Church. Yet I still hid it from the wider community in which I now lived. Joan had trained within the Kleinian school and this had a definite anti-religious ethos; I was anxious to be acceptable to those in this group, partly because of being married to Joan but also because I believed at that time that these were probably the best clinicians. This was another source of unease.

I have always had in me something of the adventurer. I was very sympathetic to the remark made by Wilfred Bion that the greatest tragedy is when someone *settles* into middle age. There I was just about to settle. This had to be resisted at all costs. I needed a challenge. The very thought of stable suburban life suffocates me. So something was stirring. We would transport ourselves to Australia and set up practice there, and off we went in 1983 on a prospective visit. We spent time in the three cities of Perth, Brisbane, and Sydney. We already knew Melbourne. Joan came from there and we had married there and spent time there. I am not sure why we discounted Adelaide. I think I had the idea that it was a sleepy, placid town, something like Tunbridge Wells planted on the other side of the globe. In each city we visited we gave lectures and seminars. Perth was keen to have us. It did not seem to us that we would be very welcome in Brisbane. In Sydney the psychoanalysts told us that we would be very welcome. We returned to London in early January. Our decision had been made. We would emigrate to Australia and take up residence and practice in Sydney.

321

There would be an opportunity, though, to take a sabbatical in the period between leaving London and arriving in Australia. So we rented a house just outside the village of Seillans, west of Grasse in Provence, and there we stayed for eight months. It was here that the first big turbulence came upon me.

* * *

That there was a madness in me must be clear to anyone who reads this account but there was one individual to whom this was not clear—myself. What follows is the path through which that realisation came about.

The uncovering of my madness began during that sojourn in France. What I am trying to do in writing this is to understand how the realisation began to dawn. It began in France during those eight months of respite between leaving England and arriving in Australia. But it only began then. It continued for years after.

In the same way as I had flung myself into the Church so also I had impetuously rushed into marriage soon after I had left it. The disastrous consequences of that I have already tried to describe.

We arrived at our lovely little cottage outside Seillans a few days before Christmas 1985. Our two boys were then aged ten and six. We had a small, intimate Christmas and then we went on a trip to Venice and returned just in time for Andrew and David to start the Easter term at the little village school. I would drive them down to the school in time for half-past eight and pick them up in the afternoon at half-past four. After dropping them at school I went to the village café and had a coffee sitting at a table by the village pump under the protection of a plane tree. I sipped it quietly and in no hurry and then drove back to our little cottage. One morning in mid-January I went back and flung myself on the bed and Joan came in and … I cannot remember what she said but it was certainly something disapproving and I screamed. That was the beginning—but of what? Why did I scream?

What is this force? It is the force of the group devoid of integration. It seems that there are two forces operating in the human throng: the personal and the group devoid of the personal. The personal unifies: the group dissipates. The question is why does the group attempt to persuade? It seems that there is a knowledge that unification is the human calling and that the group parodies it: "We are all united—look, we all believe the same thing." It looks like a unity but it is not. In this group force the unity is in the outer sign. In true unity the cohesion lies in an act of inner creation whereas in the group it lies in an external similarity based upon sensation.

I don't think the "group" is quite the right word. Perhaps it should be called the "dissipating force". So then we have these two forces in the human throng: a dissipating force and a unifying power. But the dissipating force always masquerades as though it were the unifying power.

A new inner journey of discovery had started but this later chapter of my life is for another book.

* * *

My deepest regret is that I did not love my parents more. My mother and father suffered greatly on my behalf. They were always faithful and loyal to me. My father, in that letter I have quoted, said that whatever I did it would not change his affection for me and when I had some deep conversations with my mother before she died and I said how sorry I was for the unkind way in which I treated her she replied, "I do not remember any unkindness from you." She had forgiven me. My mother especially did not deserve the hatred I piled upon her. Both my father and my mother had their difficulties but their love for me was never in doubt. Yet I did not repay them with the gratitude they deserved. I was a difficult, turbulent son who disturbed their life and calm greatly. I did not give them the devotion and love which they deserved.